INSIDE SALAFI-JIHADIST GOVERNANCE

COLUMBIA STUDIES IN TERRORISM
AND IRREGULAR WARFARE

COLUMBIA STUDIES IN TERRORISM
AND IRREGULAR WARFARE

Bruce Hoffman, Series Editor

This series seeks to fill a conspicuous gap in the burgeoning literature on terrorism, guerrilla warfare, and insurgency. The series adheres to the highest standards of scholarship and discourse and publishes books that elucidate the strategy, operations, means, motivations, and effects posed by terrorist, guerrilla, and insurgent organizations and movements. It thereby provides a solid and increasingly expanding foundation of knowledge on these subjects for students, established scholars, and informed reading audiences alike.

Alexandra Rachel Phelan, *The Combination of All Forms of Struggle: Insurgent Legitimation and State Response to FARC*

Erica L. Gaston, *Illusions of Control: Dilemmas in Managing U.S. Proxy Forces in Afghanistan, Iraq, and Syria*

Andreas E. Feldmann, *Repertoires of Terrorism: Organizational Identity and Violence in Colombia's Civil War*

John Horgan, *Terrorist Minds: The Psychology of Violent Extremism from Al-Qaeda to the Far Right*

Harrison Akins, *The Terrorism Trap: The War on Terror Inside America's Partner States*

Rita Katz, *Saints and Soldiers: Inside Internet-Age Terrorism, From Syria to the Capitol Siege*

Tricia L. Bacon and Elizabeth Grimm, *Terror in Transition: Leadership and Succession in Terrorist Organizations*

Daveed Gartenstein-Ross and Thomas Joscelyn, *Enemies Near and Far: How Jihadist Groups Strategize, Plot, and Learn*

Boaz Ganor, *Israel's Counterterrorism Strategy: Origins to the Present*

Joseph M. Brown, *Force of Words: The Logic of Terrorist Threats*

Arie Perliger, *American Zealots: Inside Right-Wing Domestic Terrorism*

Erin M. Kearns and Joseph K. Young, *Tortured Logic: Why Some Americans Support the Use of Torture in Counterterrorism*

Lorenzo Vidino, *The Closed Circle: Joining and Leaving the Muslim Brotherhood in the West*

Aaron Y. Zelin, *Your Sons Are at Your Service: Tunisia's Missionaries of Jihad*

Mariya Y. Omelicheva and Lawrence P. Markowitz, *Webs of Corruption: Trafficking and Terrorism in Central Asia*

For a complete list of books in the series, please see the Columbia University Press website.

INSIDE SALAFI-JIHADIST GOVERNANCE

THE STRATEGIES AND CHARACTERISTICS OF ISLAMIST INSURGENT RULE

MARTA FURLAN

Columbia University Press
New York

Columbia University Press
Publishers Since 1893
New York   Chichester, West Sussex

Library of Congress Cataloging-in-Publication Data
Names: Furlan, Marta author
Title: Inside Salafi-Jihadist governance : the strategies and characteristics
of Islamist insurgent rule / Marta Furlan.
Description: New York City : Columbia University Press, [2025] |
Includes bibliographical references and index.
Identifiers: LCCN 2025001693 (print) | LCCN 2025001694 (ebook) |
ISBN 9780231562942 ebook | ISBN 9780231219860 hardback |
ISBN 9780231219877 trade paperback
Subjects: LCSH: Islam and state—Middle East | Islamic
fundamentalism—Political aspects—Middle East |
Salafàiyah—Philosophy—Middle East | Jihad—Political aspects—
Middle East | Civil disobedience—Middle East | Insurgency—Middle East
Classification: LCC JC49 (ebook) | LCC JC49 .F87 2025 (print) |
DDC 320.55/723/eng/20250—dc16

Cover design: Noah Arlow
Cover image: Shutterstock

GPSR Authorized Representative: Easy Access System Europe, Mustamäe tee 50,
10621 Tallinn, Estonia, gpsr.requests@easproject.com

TO MY PARENTS.

CONTENTS

TABLES

ACKNOWLEDGMENTS

As my research into Salafi-jihadist governance gradually turned into this book, I received support and assistance from various people and institutions whom I would like to thank.

First, I would like to express my sincere gratitude to Dr. Henning Tamm and Prof. Bruce Hoffman, whose detailed comments on subsequent drafts of this manuscript were fundamental in helping me to produce a more solid work. I am also indebted to Prof. Hoffman for introducing me to the editorial team at Columbia University Press. My gratitude also goes to Prof. Raymond Hinnebusch and Prof. Brynjar Lia, who provided me with excellent observations on specific sections of this work.

The publication of this book would not have been possible without Columbia University Press. I am grateful to the press's Faculty Publication Committee for supporting the publication of this book and to the editorial team for its constant and invaluable assistance throughout the processes of production and publication. A special expression of gratitude is owed to Caelyn Cobb, Emily Elizabeth Simon, Marisa Lastres, and Ryan Perks.

Above all, however, I am especially grateful to Gabriella and Gianni, whose constant love, support, and encouragement throughout the years has given me the confidence to pursue my aspirations. You taught me that for a mountain girl there is no peak that cannot be reached with patience, perseverance, and determination. I have made your teaching a treasure and have set on the journey with enthusiasm. I will never be able to thank you enough for being such amazing parents.

I cannot but remember and thank my grandparents. Armando, who taught me to love our mountains, to explore the world around me, and to appreciate the freedom that only nature can offer, and Liliana, whose exceptional sense of humor and contagious laughter have left an indelible mark on me. They would have loved to hold this book in their hands, but I believe that in some way they are.

I also want to thank Martina for her true friendship, for her constant encouragement over the years, and for always being there for me. Growing up with you has been one of the best gifts I could receive, and I know that growing older together will be just as amazing.

Finally, I want to thank Doron, my dear husband, whose love and care kept me company as I was writing these pages. You are the best person, friend, and husband. I thank you from the bottom of my heart for always supporting me as I pursue my goals, for listening to my needs, and for putting us first, every day. You have my deepest love, loyalty, and respect.

ABBREVIATIONS

AANES	Autonomous Administration of North and East Syria
AQAP	al-Qaeda in the Arabian Peninsula
AQI	al-Qaeda in Iraq
AQIM	al-Qaeda in the Islamic Maghreb
ASC	Aleppo Sharia Commission
CAS	Civil Administration for Services
CPI	Communist Party of India
DFNS	Democratic Federation of Northern Syria
FARC	Fuerzas Armadas Revolucionarias de Colombia (Revolutionary Armed Forces of Colombia)
FSP	Free Syrian Police
GAS	General Administration for Services
GSS	General Security Service
HNC	Hadramawt National Council
HTS	Hay'at Tahrir al-Sham
IS	Islamic State
ISI	Islamic State of Iraq
ISIS	Islamic State of Iraq and al-Sham
JaN	Jabhat al-Nusra
JFS	Jabhat Fatah al-Sham
LTTE	Liberation Tigers of Tamil Eelam
MSC	Mujahidin Shura Council

NATO	North Atlantic Treaty Organization
NGO	nongovernmental organization
PYD	Partiya Yekîtiya Demokrat (Democratic Union Party)
SDF	Syrian Democratic Forces
SSG	Syrian Salvation Government
UP	Unión Patriótica (Patriotic Union)
YPG	Yekîneyên Parastina Gel (People's Defense Units)

NOTE ON TRANSLITERATION

The transliteration of Arabic in this book follows the rules of the American Library Association and the Library of Congress, as detailed in the 2011 edition of the ALA-LC Arabic Romanization Table. However, for ease of reading, I have refrained from including the diacritics. Also, Arabic proper nouns and names that have entered common use in English are used in their most widely accepted form. Any quotation from secondary literature maintains the original spelling of the author.

INSIDE SALAFI-JIHADIST GOVERNANCE

INTRODUCTION

Why Salafi-Jihadist Governance?

In the spring of 2020, as the coronavirus pandemic was beginning to spread throughout the Middle East, civilians in a provincial capital of the region were provided by the local Ministry of Health with guidance on how to behave to prevent the transmission of the virus. Shortly thereafter, medical checks were introduced on residents crossing the border from abroad, places of public gathering (e.g., schools, markets, and mosques) were temporarily closed, quarantine centers were instituted to isolate symptomatic individuals, emergency teams were sent to monitor people's and businesses' compliance with the norms of hygiene imposed by the minister of the interior, and cooperation with the World Health Organization for the distribution of vaccines was pursued.[1]

Perhaps surprisingly to most, this effort at effective governance took place not in some well-functioning nation-state, but in the northwestern Syrian governorate of Idlib under the rule of the Salafi-jihadist group Hay'at Tahrir al-Sham (HTS). As early as 2012, in fact, HTS (which was then known as Jabhat al-Nusra, or JaN) had engaged in an insurgency with the aim of conquering territory, overthrowing the existing sociopolitical order, and establishing a new system of rule. As it progressively brought under its control swaths of territories throughout Syria, JaN implemented a system of governance to administer the daily life of the local population.

Far from being an isolated instance, many other Salafi-jihadist armed groups have engaged (or have attempted to engage) in similar activities of civilian administration, to the point that over the last decade the Middle East and North Africa region has become a real laboratory of Salafi-jihadist rebel governance experiments.[2] In this book, I will take readers on a journey into Salafi-jihadist territories to understand how Salafi-jihadist armed groups behave as rulers.[3] By "Salafi-jihadist armed groups," I mean those organizations that seek to overthrow the contemporary "apostate" regimes governing over Muslim territories, that aim to establish an Islamist polity based on sharia (Islamic law) for the entire *ummah* (world Islamic community), and that identify in jihad, meant as armed struggle, the preferred (yet not the only) way to achieve those goals.[4]

However, it is noteworthy that the transition from warfare to governance is not a phenomenon limited to Salafi-jihadist armed groups. Rather, it has been observed among many different armed groups worldwide: the Revolutionary Armed Forces of Colombia (Fuerzas Armadas Revolucionarias de Colombia, or FARC), Sendero Luminoso in Peru, the Liberation Tigers of Tamil Eelam (LTTE) in Sri Lanka, the Taliban in Afghanistan, Hezbollah in Lebanon—to mention some of the most renowned cases.[5]

While in political science the discourse on governance has traditionally been a state-centric one that regards the nation-state as the exclusive provider of governance,[6] the reality is often more complex. In many contexts worldwide, states are too weak to exercise their authority and (violent and nonviolent) nonstate actors emerge as alternative, or additional, providers of governance.[7] Recognizing that in areas of state weakness governance can be delivered to the people by a wide array of nonstate actors, in this book I focus on the specific case in which governance is provided by armed nonstate actors engaged in an insurgency against the incumbent government. In other words, I focus on armed groups that wage a struggle for power against the state.[8]

When insurgent armed groups manage to conquer some portions of the state territory, they often proceed to provide governance to the population residing there.[9] The purpose of those governance activities is for the armed group to acquire credibility as ruler, cultivate popular support, and present itself as a more efficient—and therefore more desirable—authority than the incumbent government.[10] However, armed groups may also engage in governance to capture the state and extract resources in a regular and sustainable way,[11] to implement a certain civilian-oriented ideology,[12] to outbid rival organizations,[13] to strengthen the group's organizational capacity,[14] to monitor civilians and punish defections,[15] to access political and social networks,[16] to secure international legitimacy and support,[17] and to strengthen their negotiation position ahead of peace talks.[18]

Once armed groups decide to engage in governance, they can perform a variety of tasks, the scope and sophistication of which depend on each group's opportunity, willingness, and capacity. Nonetheless, certain governance tasks are commonly observed among most armed groups. The provision of security, for instance, is a primary governance function in which ruling armed groups tend to engage because it allows them to claim monopoly over the use of force, obtain popular support among civilians prostrated by war, and engage in further governance tasks that require a minimum of security to be performed.[19] Similarly, the provision of justice is another governance priority for most armed groups because it allows them to obtain legitimacy among the civilian population, penetrate local communities, and impose a specific vision of society.[20] Public goods and services other than security and justice (e.g., electricity, health care, education) are also provided by many armed groups to erode the legitimacy of the state, attract recruits and sympathizers, and ultimately win the people's loyalty.[21] For its part, taxation is performed by most rebels to extract financial resources, consolidate control over society, and even emphasize the group's ideological commitments.[22] Finally, the regulation of behavior is often implemented by ideologically motivated groups that aspire to impose a specific system of values on society.[23]

GOVERNANCE BY SALAFI-JIHADIST ARMED GROUPS: A GROWING EXAMPLE OF REBEL RULE

To understand the importance of governance by armed groups, it is sufficient to consider that today approximately 150 million people worldwide live under the direct control of armed groups or in contested areas.[24] While the phenomenon is observed all over the world, it has particularly grown in frequency and intensity over the past decade in the Middle East and North Africa.

Between late 2010 and early 2011, many countries throughout the Arab world witnessed a series of mass uprisings that came to be known as the Arab Spring.[25] People took to the streets demanding the end of decades-long authoritarian rule, the end of abuses by police and security services, the end of corruption and nepotism, and the end of economic mismanagement, which was leaving too many educated and motivated young people unemployed. In other words, people took to the streets demanding economic opportunities, dignity, good governance, and rule of law.[26] As noted by Roberts, one of the characteristics common to the various movements that comprised the Arab Spring was the protesters' use of civil resistance—that is, political and social action relying on nonviolent methods such as demonstrations, industrial strikes, and noncooperation.[27]

However, protestors' initial tendency to refrain from violence was not mirrored by the regimes, which often opted for a heavy-handed response. In those cases, the ultimate, inevitable result was a militarization of the anti-regime opposition and the emergence of anti-regime armed forces.[28] As governments resorted to the use of force and violence escalated, a dangerous combination of civil war, power vacuum, and ungoverned spaces emerged in countries such as Libya, Syria, Egypt, and Yemen. With the collapse of the state and the emergence of ungoverned areas, nonstate entities found themselves in a position to exploit the situation and benefit from the widespread disorder.[29] In the specific case of the Arab Spring turmoil, it was Salafi-jihadist armed groups that stood to make the biggest gains.

To be sure, the Arab Spring movements and their reliance on nonviolent civil resistance was initially problematic for Salafi-jihadist armed groups, whose modus operandi had traditionally rested on the use of violence. The early success of the Arab Spring, in fact, undermined the Salafi-jihadist contention that autocratic regimes could be overthrown only by violence and raised many questions concerning the appropriateness and effectiveness of the Salafi-jihadist method. Moreover, the Arab Spring's demand for political and economic reforms within the existing state structures conflicted with the Salafi-jihadists' political vision and, more specifically, their rejection of modern nation-states and democratic political systems. Thus, in the early stages of the Arab Spring, Salafi-jihadists appeared to be "out of touch" and their reactions to events little more than attempts to steer the protest movements in an Islamist direction and show that they still had relevance.

For instance, in January 2011 al-Qaeda in the Islamic Maghreb (AQIM) issued a video that called on demonstrators to extend their movements in Tunisia and Algeria to overthrow the governments there, to institute sharia law, and "to send us your sons so that they receive military training."[30] Al-Qaeda's leader, Ayman al-Zawahiri, also delivered a "Message of Hope and Glad Tidings to Our People in Egypt." In the third part of the message, he responded to the Arab Spring by showing respect for it, but he tried to steer it in a fundamentalist direction. In the fourth part of the message, he emphasized that it was easier to get rid of one ruler than to establish a new system, assuming that he knew exactly what the people wanted—sharia and the establishment of a caliphate.[31]

However, as violence spread in most Arab Spring countries, the tide turned in favor of the Salafi-jihadists.[32] It was in that context, in fact, that an unprecedented number of Salafi-jihadist armed groups managed to exploit the situation of disorder and unrest to insert themselves into ongoing insurgencies, conquer territories, and eventually introduce their own practices and structures of governance.[33] In other words, many Salafi-jihadist armed groups took advantage of the situations of armed conflict and government collapse not only to obtain safe havens where they could hide, recruit, train, and prepare attacks (as they had done until then), but also to create their own alternative systems of rule and to transition from (exclusively) making war to (also) providing governance.

Contrary to the initial expectation that the Arab Spring, with its demands for democracy and freedom, would bring about the death knell of the Salafi-jihadist movement,[34] Salafi-jihadists eventually turned the uprisings into an unprecedented opportunity to replace "un-Islamic," "apostate" governments and establish their own sharia-based polities.[35] Thus, while instances of territorial conquest and civilian rule by Salafi-jihadist groups had been observed prior to 2011 in places such as Iraq and Somalia,[36] following the Arab Spring the phenomenon of Salafi-jihadist governance grew in both quantitative and qualitative terms. As argued by Lia, "although attempts to form proto-states have been a constant feature of contemporary jihadism over the past 25 years, in the post-2011

Middle East such attempts have multiplied and succeeded to a greater extent than in the past."[37]

WHAT WE KNOW ABOUT SALAFI-JIHADIST GOVERNANCE

Scholars in political science have increasingly come to recognize that building stable institutions in the aftermath of civil wars requires studying the institutions that regulate political life during conflict, including those institutions that are established by armed groups in areas under their control.[38] An increasing amount of scholarly research has thus come to focus on the phenomenon of governance by armed groups, which is better known in the literature as "rebel governance."

Thus far, the scholarship on rebel governance has focused mostly on communist, Maoist, ethno-nationalist, reformist, and predatory groups that are—or were—active in Latin America, sub-Saharan Africa, Europe, and Asia.[39] Conversely, it has devoted comparatively little attention to the growing instances of governance by Salafi-jihadist groups that have been observed throughout the Middle East and North Africa over the past decade. In fact, while several authors have studied the phenomenon of governance by Islamist non-Salafi-jihadist organizations—especially in the case of well-known and well-established groups with a long history of social service provision such as the Afghan Taliban, the Lebanese Hezbollah, and the Palestinian Hamas[40]—the more recent instances of governance by Salafi-jihadist groups have not received (at least not yet) the same degree of attention.

To be sure, there are scholars who have researched Salafi-jihadist governance. Lia, for instance, was among the first to devote his attention to the phenomenon. In an article that has become a must-read for anyone interested in governance by jihadist organizations, Lia studies past and contemporary cases of jihadist proto-states, such as Jund al-Islam in Iraq, al-Qaeda in Yemen, and Boko Haram in Nigeria.[41] He finds that those proto-states are most often ideological, territorially expansive, internationalist, irridentist, and committed to "effective, if harsh," governance.[42] According to Lia, those features are to be ascribed to the jihadists' rivalry with other Islamist armed groups and the jihadists' dependency on external constituencies.

Building on Lia but departing somewhat from his conclusions, Skretting offers a more nuanced picture of jihadist armed groups' governance.[43] Specifically, he advances a useful distinction between "pragmatist" jihadist proto-states that make ideological compromises to secure long-term outcomes and "purist" jihadist proto-states that refrain from any such compromise and prioritize ideological imperatives. Studying the Salafi-jihadist groups that in 2012 established the Islamic Emirate of Azawad in northern Mali, Skretting argues that the Emirate of Azawad opted to strike a balance between purist and pragmatist approaches, as its leaders recognized the opportunities that the situation presented as well as the precariousness of their position.

Other authors who have studied Salafi-jihadist governance since its earliest days, and whose contributions have been invaluable to advancing our knowledge of the topic, are al-Tamimi and Zelin. Focusing on the case of the Islamic State (IS) in Syria and Iraq, al-Tamimi shows that IS progressively transitioned from garnering support, to asserting its military presence, to establishing a governance structure.[44] Discussing the latter aspect, al-Tamimi emphasizes that IS's administration became increasingly sophisticated, professional, and complex over time and suggests that this evolution can be helpful in assessing the performance of its affiliates. The unprecedented systematization, bureaucratization, and formalization of IS governance is also discussed by Zelin, as he analyzes the group's transition from warfare to governance in the Levant, Yemen, and Libya.[45] Specifically, he focuses on IS's "territorial methodology" and how the group "attempted to expand, take over new territory, and then consolidate its control."[46] He distinguishes between a pre-territorial control stage and a post-territorial control stage and identifies five linear phases of establishing control—intelligence, military, missionary activities, morality police, and governance.

Most recently, Becker Aarseth has shed further light on the complex system of governance established by the Islamic State, offering a detailed account of the group's governance practices in the Iraqi city of Mosul with respect to policing, education, and health care.[47] Useful insights on IS have been offered also by Revkin. In one of her most influential articles, Revkin studies IS's policies of tax collection in Syria and finds that the group also opted to collect taxes in resource-rich districts (contrary to greed-based theories).[48] To solve the puzzle, she explains taxation policies by means of reference to ideology and the costs of war, showing that IS's preferences in matters of taxation were driven by both pragmatism and ideology.

Building on some of this earlier work on Salafi-jihadist governance but expanding the analytical time frame, Bamber adopts a historical approach whereby he studies IS's three governance cycles (2001–2004, 2004–2010, and 2010–2018) and accurately describes the evolution of its approach to governance over time.[49] Looking at IS's experiences in three distinct moments, Bamber highlights how the group's governance cycles comprised phases of insurgency, gaining territory, establishing institutions, and losing territory. After losing territory, IS typically engaged in a process of critical self-reflection aimed at improving its governance strategy.

Interestingly, the propensity to learn from past experiences to improve future performance can also be seen in accounts of other Salafi-jihadist groups. For instance, in her study of al-Qaeda in the Arabian Peninsula (AQAP), Cook reviews the group's governance experiences in Yemen and argues that after a first failed experiment AQAP learned from its mistakes and adjusted its governance system accordingly, providing public services that would win "hearts and minds," reducing corporal punishments, and establishing some cooperative relations with other actors.[50] This Salafi-jihadist capacity to establish opportunistic relationships with powerful local actors has also been emphasized by Skjelderup. In his article on al-Shabaab's relationship with traditional authorities in southern Somalia, Skjelderup discusses how the group opted for the co-optation of local clan elders to better secure its control over the population.[51]

However, scholars of Salafi-jihadist governance also note that cooperative relationships with other local actors are not necessarily static and that ruling Salafi-jihadist armed groups can always (and often do) reconsider their preferences. This, for instance, is what emerges from Berti's study of the patterns of cooperation and competition between Jabhat al-Nusra, the Assad regime, and other armed groups.[52] In her article, Berti convincingly argues that while JaN initially pursued cooperation with other armed groups, as conflict dynamics changed it increasingly pursued a hegemonic, unilateral, and competitive form of governance. Importantly, the reconsideration of previous practices can extend to the entire spectrum of governance activities. In their study on Boko Haram in Nigeria, Ladbury and colleagues argue that following a change in leadership in 2010 the group ceased to invest in administration.[53] This was true to the point that its governance became limited to a set of rules, a questionable police system, and mechanisms for punishment.

While most works on Salafi-jihadist governance focus on one single group, some scholars have broken with this predominant approach and have engaged in the comparison of different Salafi-jihadist organizations. An example in this regard is an article by Cook, Haid, and Trauthig in which the authors conduct a comparative analysis of how justice was provided by three Salafi-jihadist groups—AQAP in Yemen, HTS in Syria, and IS in Libya.[54] They find that, while each group established legal systems that dealt with internal issues and public matters as a mechanism to attract legitimacy, differences were observed with respect to the interpretation of sharia, the cooperation with other local actors, the enforcement of punishments, and the publicization of those punishments.

Differences between Salafi-jihadist groups in the use of jurisprudence are also identified by Bouhlel and Guichaoua, who compared Ansar ad-Din and the Movement for the Unity of Jihad in West Africa in northern Mali.[55] They find that the two groups differed in their use of violence and jurisprudence, and suggest that the greater restraint displayed by Ansar ad-Din was a deliberate choice to mobilize a jurisprudence minimizing violence and a decision to defer the use of violence following episodes of social contestation.

Adopting a similar comparative approach, Svensson and Finnbogason looked at al-Qaeda in Iraq (AQI), AQIM, and AQAP to explain civilian resistance to Salafi-jihadist governance.[56] They suggest that civil resistance is more likely to occur when Salafi-jihadists impose a type of rule perceived as alien by the local population and when civil society organizations capable of collective nonviolent mobilization are activated. In another work on the topic, Bamber and Svensson look at HTS, IS, and Ahrar al-Sham in Syria.[57] They argue that midrange opportunity structures of rebel governance with respect to rebel collaboration, civilian inclusion, alliance structure, and repression provide the strongest incentives to civil resistance, as they give enough space for civilian mobilization but little alternatives for expressing discontent.

WHAT WE DO NOT KNOW ABOUT
SALAFI-JIHADIST GOVERNANCE

The studies discussed above have made crucial contributions to our understanding of Salafi-jihadist governance. However, our knowledge of the phenomenon is still hampered by a series of lacunae. Firstly, most works are limited in either scope or depth. Some investigate in great detail a single aspect of Salafi-jihadist governance, such as Revkin's study on the taxation practices of IS or Berti's study on the relations that JaN built with other local actors in the context of the Syrian war. However, they offer little to no information on how Salafi-jihadists behave with respect to the (many) other aspects of governance in which they engage. Other works, on the contrary, adopt a comprehensive perspective and investigate multiple aspects of Salafi-jihadist civilian administration, as Cook did in her study of AQAP and as Skretting did in his study of the Islamic Emirate of Azawad. However, they do so at the expense of depth and detail, producing accounts that offer only a cursory picture of how Salafi-jihadists behave in the many areas of governance in which they intervene.

A notable exception in this regard is Becker Aarseth's work on the Islamic State's governance practices in Mosul. In her book, Becker Aarseth explores in great depth three aspects of IS's civilian administration in the Iraqi city—policing, education, and health care. However, while offering an empirical account of IS's governance experience that hardly has parallels, she devotes less space and effort to explaining the observed governance patterns. In fact, a limitation shared by many studies of Salafi-jihadist governance is that they do not engage in explanations of why Salafi-jihadists govern as they do. In this regard, it is also noticeable that while scholars such as Revkin and Skjelderup have offered some of the most valuable and telling explanations of Salafi-jihadist governance patterns, they have restricted their investigations to a single dimension of governance, thus leaving unaddressed the question of whether the identified explanations extend to other aspects of Salafi-jihadist civilian administration. Additionally, these and other studies, such as Skretting's work on Salafi-jihadist rule in northern Mali, have focused their attention on one single group. It remains to be understood whether the factors that explain Salafi-jihadist governance in one specific context and moment in time hold true across different groups.

Finally, existing works investigate Salafi-jihadist governance in isolation, without building any systematic comparison with non-Salafi-jihadist groups as far as patterns of governance are concerned. As such, they offer interesting studies on civilian administration as developed and implemented by Salafi-jihadist armed groups, but they fail to tell whether, and to what extent, Salafi-jihadist rebel rule is an unprecedented and unparalleled instance of insurgent governance, or whether it is, rather, an important yet unexceptional phenomenon. In fact, while authors such as Cook, Haid and Trauthig, Svensson and Finnbogason, and Bember and Svensson have adopted a comparative approach to the study of Salafi-jihadist governance, their comparisons do not extend to non-Salafi-jihadist groups. Recently, Boyraz offered an interesting comparison between the political projects of IS and the Kurdish Democratic Union Party (Partiya Yekîtiya Demokrat, PYD) in Syria.[58] However, while representing an undoubtedly important contribution, Boyraz's comparative analysis focuses on the two groups' notions of state, territoriality, and sovereignty rather than on their structures and practices of governance.

Considering the extent to which Salafi-jihadist groups have been increasingly exploiting governance vacuums to create their own alternative systems of rule, these are lacunae that need to be addressed to expand our knowledge of both rebel governance and Salafi-jihadist behavior. It is the aim of this book to advance our understanding of Salafi-jihadist rebel governance by means of studying the phenomenon in depth, across several dimensions of rebel rule, and from a comparative perspective. The specific research questions that this book aims to address can be grouped into three main themes, each devoted to a specific aspect of governance by Salafi-jihadist armed groups: the *characteristics* of Salafi-jihadist rebel governance; the *determinants* of Salafi-jihadist rebel governance; and the *uniqueness* of Salafi-jihadist rebel governance.

(1) How do Salafi-jihadist insurgents govern? Which similarities and differences can be identified across Salafi-jihadist groups? Is there a single model of Salafi-jihadist governance?

(2) What is the relationship between ideology and Salafi-jihadist governance? How do Salafi-jihadist governance experiments reflect the ideas inherent in the Salafi-jihadist ideology? To what extent do

ideological factors explain the features displayed by Salafi-jihadist governance?

(3) How does rebel governance vary across Salafi-jihadist and non-Salafi-jihadist rebel rulers? To what extent is Salafi-jihadist governance similar to, or different from, non-Salafi-jihadist governance? Is there a distinctive model of Salafi-jihadist governance?

Exploring how Salafi-jihadist armed groups govern is important because it allows us to understand the behavior of Salafi-jihadist insurgents beyond their engagement in warfare, shed light on the complex relations between Salafi-jihadist and other local actors in the territories where the former establish governance systems, and understand the experiences that local communities in the territories under Salafi-jihadist rulers go through. These are crucial elements to devise the most appropriate strategies to deal with Salafi-jihadist rebel rulers, appreciate the challenges, risks, and opportunities of countering Salafi-jihadist proto-states, and reflect on the introduction of effective alternative systems of rule in the post-conflict stage.

Investigating the relationship between Salafi-jihadist ideology and governance is also important because Salafi-jihadist groups typically claim to be committed to ideological purity.[59] Therefore, it is interesting to explore whether those groups truly behave according to their ideology even when embarking on the complex task of governing territories, when many other factors emerge that may influence a rebel group's calculations and preferences. Moreover, the study of the relationship between Salafi-jihadist ideology and Salafi-jihadist governance can contribute to illuminating the relationship between rebel ideology and rebel governance, which is a much-debated issue within the literature.[60] At the same time, understanding whether and to what extent ideology influences the patterns of governance developed by Salafi-jihadist armed groups can be helpful to inform appropriate approaches to deal with Salafi-jihadist proto-states.

Finally, Arjona, Kasfir, and Mampilly have noted that "rebel leaders who establish relations with civilians demonstrate significant political creativity in developing vastly different approaches to governance,"[61] which leads to a multiplicity of governance styles and opens a new category of government to comparative analysis. Therefore, determining whether Salafi-jihadist armed groups have given rise to a new sui generis style of rebel governance or are mostly replicating (more or less consciously) what other groups have done before them in other parts of the world promises to be of particular academic relevance and interest. Besides, it will also bear important implications for how to deal with these groups and their sociopolitical systems, especially with respect to the replicability of approaches that proved successful in dealing with other rebel rulers.

THE METHODOLOGY FOR STUDYING SALAFI-JIHADIST GOVERNANCE

To answer the proposed research questions, I conduct a qualitative case study analysis.[62] The benefit of doing qualitative research is that it allows us to study real-world phenomena in depth;[63] to offer insights into existing or emerging concepts that may help to explain human behavior;[64] and to collect data from a variety of evidential sources.[65] Additionally, qualitative approaches have been recognized as especially useful when little is known about a subject and when the researcher aims to develop a new concept, uncover a new hypothesis, or illuminate unknown causal mechanisms.[66]

For its part, the benefit of doing research through case studies is that this method is particularly well suited "when 'how' or 'why' questions are being posed . . . and when the focus is on a contemporary phenomenon within some real-life context."[67] More specifically, the case study method has four advantages that make it particularly appropriate to test hypotheses and develop theories: It has "potential for achieving high conceptual validity," it relies on "strong procedures for fostering new hypotheses," it is a "useful means to closely examine the hypothesized role of causal mechanisms in the context of individual cases," and it has the "capacity for addressing causal complexity."[68] The utility of this approach is further confirmed by the fact that case study analysis is the preferred research method adopted by those scholars who have investigated ruling insurgent groups—Salafi-jihadist and non-Salafi-jihadist alike.[69]

When studying the phenomenon of Salafi-jihadist governance, the universe of possible case studies is constituted by all instances of Salafi-jihadist rebel rulers; that is, by all those armed groups that display the following three characteristics: They are driven by the Salafi-jihadist ideology, they participate in an insurgency, and they engage in governance after conquering populated territories by force. Aiming to conduct a detailed analysis that will allow me to assess the selected Salafi-jihadist rebel groups with respect to multiple dimensions of civilian administration, I have decided to opt for a small number of case studies. In social sciences, in fact, researchers face "a persistent trade-off between depth and breadth" whereby they need to "choose to gather a broad range of information about a narrow range of cases or a narrow range of information about a broad range of cases."[70] Faced with this dilemma, I believe that for the specific purpose of this book it is more appropriate to privilege depth over breadth in order to offer the most accurate picture possible of Salafi-jihadist governance.

Within the universe of possible case studies, I will investigate the Islamic State in western Iraq and eastern Syria, Hay'at Tahrir al-Sham in northwestern Syria, and al-Qaeda in the Arabian Peninsula in southern Yemen. The decision to focus on these three groups was informed by multiple reasons, summarized in table I.1. Firstly, IS, HTS, and AQAP represent three of the most prominent cases of Salafi-jihadist insurgent governors registered to date: They have engaged in governance for a significant amount of time, they have intervened in an extensive range of governance activities, and they have governed over entire governorates and major cities.

As will be seen in greater detail when discussing these case studies in their dedicated chapters, IS governed from 2014 to approximately 2017 over large portions of Iraq and Syria, including urban centers such as Mosul and Raqqa; HTS began to engage in governance activities around 2012 and ruled over parts of northwestern Syria until November 2024, when it launched an offensive that culminated in the downfall of the Assad regime and the establishment of an HTS-led transition government in Damascus; AQAP ruled over territories of southern Yemen including large areas of Hadramawt, Abyan, and Shabwah Governorates and the important port city of Mukalla from 2011 to 2012 and again from 2015 to 2016. In these conquered territories, the three groups engaged in extensive governance activities, including the administration of justice, the collection of taxes, the regulation of public morality, and the provision of complex services such as electricity, health care, and education. Therefore, I believe that IS, HTS, and AQAP are important cases to study in and of themselves.

Conversely, Salafi-jihadist groups such as AQIM, Boko Haram, and the various affiliates of IS have engaged in governance for shorter periods of time, have overseen a more limited range of governance activities, and have ruled over smaller territories.

Furthermore, HTS and AQAP are particularly interesting because they have received comparatively less attention vis-à-vis IS. Indeed, while some remarkable exceptions do exist,[71] the prevailing tendency has been to focus on the practices and structures of governance implemented by the Islamic State. This has been true to the point that no Salafi-jihadist proto-state has attracted the intense media attention and the close scholarly scrutiny that the Islamic State has.[72] Thus, studying HTS and AQAP promises to shed light on certain characteristics of Salafi-jihadist rebel governance that may not have emerged from the exclusive study of IS. In other words, looking closely at HTS and AQAP across multiple dimensions of rule might complicate the existing picture of Salafi-jihadist governance, thus challenging what (we think) we know on the topic.

Finally, IS, HTS, and AQAP represent three distinct models within the Salafi-jihadist universe, which makes them particularly well suited to an intra-Salafi-jihadist comparison. The Islamic State is a transnational jihadist group. Initially focused on Iraq, it progressively expanded its ambitions, as testified by the replacement of the name "Islamic State of Iraq" with "Islamic State of Iraq and al-Sham" (ISIS). In June 2014, the group declared a transnational caliphate, urged the *ummah* to join its project, and defiantly claimed leadership of the Salafi-jihadist global movement.[73] For its part, like all close al-Qaeda affiliates, AQAP traditionally harbored local short-term ambitions and global long-term ambitions,[74] aspiring to establish a local Islamic emirate in Yemen destined to be part of a global al-Qaeda caliphate.[75] Initially, HTS had similar ambitions as well. Over time, however, the group emerged as a "third paradigm,"[76] affiliated with neither IS nor al-Qaeda. As part of its distancing from the global Salafi-jihadist movement, HTS embarked on a process of localization, or "Syrianization,"[77] and reframed its goal as the establishment of a local Islamic state in Syria.[78]

To investigate in depth the governance experiences of IS, HTS, and AQAP, I relied on a combination of different data. First, I referred to the textual, audio, and video materials produced and disseminated by the

TABLE I.1 The Salafi-jihadist armed groups selected as case studies

	Islamic State	Hay'at Tahrir al-Sham	Al-Qaeda in the Arabian Peninsula
Location of rebel governance activities	Eastern Syria and western Iraq	Northwestern Syria	Southern Yemen
Duration of rebel governance activities	More than three years	More than ten years	Two years (not continuous)
Scope of rebel governance activities	Extensive	Extensive	Extensive
Prominence in the rebel governance literature	Significant	Limited	Very limited
Status in the Salafi-jihadist universe	Independent (Islamic State model)	Independent ("third paradigm")	Traditional al-Qaeda affiliate
Scope of ambitions	Transnational (global caliphate for the *ummah*)	Local (local Islamic state, with no global ambitions)	Local and transnational (from local emirate to global caliphate)

three selected groups. These primary sources are in Arabic and English. They include administrative documents (e.g., court rulings, tax receipts, and regulations for the public) produced by the groups' relevant ruling bodies (e.g., judges, tax officials, morality police), newsletters and pamphlets distributed to the local population or spread online for external consumption, speeches and audio messages from the groups' leaders and spokesmen, videos documenting the groups' governance efforts and accomplishments, and fatwas (opinions on sharia) justifying the groups' decisions in matters of governance. By relying on this kind of data, I followed that growing trend of scholarship on Salafi-jihadist armed groups that refers for its analysis to the documents produced by the organizations themselves (among other sources of data).[79]

Regarding the sources of those primary documents, I referred to the open-access database that has been meticulously built by Aymenn Jawad al-Tamimi and hosted on his eponymous website. The documents collected in this database are reported in their original Arabic form and are accompanied by al-Tamimi's translation and, when necessary, explanatory notes. While more than seventy documents in al-Tamimi's database refer to HTS, the majority of them (more than one thousand) refer to IS. To compensate for this overrepresentation of IS, I referred to additional sources to collect more material on HTS and AQAP. In this regard, a particularly valuable source is the Jihadology website, founded and managed by Aaron Y. Zelin. Here, thousands of documents produced by Salafi-jihadist groups are reported in Arabic and, in a number of instances, also in English. Further sources of primary data for the Islamic State are the website Jihadica and *The ISIS Reader*, an edited volume that is an extraordinary source of materials produced by IS throughout the years of its governance experience.[80] Similarly, *The Al Qaeda Reader* is an extremely helpful source of primary materials related to al-Qaeda.[81]

Besides referring to Salafi-jihadist primary sources, I also consulted existing interviews with people who lived under IS, HTS, and AQAP. In fact, as the materials produced by Salafi-jihadist groups may offer an exaggerated picture of what the groups were doing during their time as rulers, reference to the accounts of those who directly experienced the governance of IS, HTS, and AQAP is necessary to gain a more accurate understanding of the systems of rule implemented by those armed groups. Such accounts were further enriched by a series of key informant interviews that I conducted with journalists, scholars, civil society representatives, humanitarian workers, and human rights activists based in northwestern Syria, Turkey, Jordan, southern Yemen, Europe, and the United States with a direct knowledge of the armed groups and territories studied in this book.

Starting from a network of connections that I built during my doctoral studies and during my professional experience in the humanitarian sector, respondents were located by means of reliance on the expert sampling technique. As interview participants were asked to connect the researcher with other experts, the snowballing sampling technique was also employed. The interviews were conducted remotely between February and August 2023 with the aim of corroborating some of the book's findings. Considering the sensitivity of the topics discussed and the security risks for people who are—or have families—in areas controlled by Salafi-jihadist armed groups, or by the latter's rivals, informants were anonymized.

Finally, the picture of Salafi-jihadist governance is completed by reference to the textual material produced by international humanitarian organizations, academics, and journalists who documented the governance experience of the three selected groups. Those secondary sources are important in that they offer more objective accounts than the materials produced by Salafi-jihadist groups themselves, who are most likely eager to exaggerate their governance performance and eager to downplay their governance failures. At the same time, secondary sources offer possibly more objective accounts than those offered by individuals who lived under Salafi-jihadist rule, whose recollection of events is inevitably influenced by their personal experiences, ideological postures, psychological traumas, physical abuses, and subjective interpretations of the surrounding events.

MAIN FINDINGS ON SALAFI-JIHADIST GOVERNANCE

Drawing from the study of IS, HTS, and AQAP, in this book I advance three main arguments on Salafi-jihadist governance. First, I argue that there are important similarities in the approach to governance maintained by different Salafi-jihadist armed groups. For instance, Salafi-jihadists display a tendency to adopt highly discriminatory approaches toward civilians. On the one hand, they adopt a discriminatory approach based on religious identity, whereby only Sunni Muslims are considered legitimate members of their desired polity. On the other hand, they adopt a discriminatory approach based on gender, whereby women are subjected to much stricter regulations than men in every aspect of life. Additionally, Salafi-jihadists are similar in that they tend to exclude the broad civilian population from participation in governance. Civilians are never included in the elections of their representatives and are hardly ever given an opportunity to voice their preferences and demands. The reins of decision making are tightly and exclusively in the hands of the Salafi-jihadist rulers.

At the same time, however, I also argue that differences between Salafi-jihadist groups in matters of governance are as evident as they are relevant. For instance, IS preferred to govern mostly in isolation, rather than in cooperation (or partial cooperation) with other actors, as HTS and AQAP opted to do. IS also employed more extensive, extreme, and publicized forms of coercion than HTS and AQAP, which used financial fines and corporal punishments at the same time, and to the same extent, that they used written publications, religious symbols, and public events. For its part, AQAP differed from IS and HTS in that it maintained preexisting institutions and practices of governance, such as tribal customary law, to a considerably greater extent. Following these observations, I argue that a single model of Salafi-jihadist governance does not exist. Rather, each group develops its own peculiar model of governance, which might differ (slightly, partially, or even significantly) from the models of governance developed by other like-minded groups.

Second, I argue that the patterns of governance adopted by Salafi-jihadist armed groups are shaped in important ways by ideology. In fact, the ideological imperatives imposed by Salafi-jihadism are useful to explain some of the behaviors displayed by Salafi-jihadist rebel rulers, such as the tendency to discriminate toward non-Muslims, non-Sunnis, and women, the rejection of democracy and the denial of broad civilian participation, the use of extensive coercion, including in a widely publicized fashion, the exclusion of other non-Sunni and non-Salafi-jihadist actors regardless of their capacity and legitimacy, and the preference for extensive sociopolitical innovations inspired by the Prophetic model.

However, I also argue that there are limits to ideology's capacity to explain Salafi-jihadist governance. Doctrine, for instance, cannot explain the propensity of HTS and AQAP to cooperate with several non-Salafi-jihadist actors, as well as the openness of IS to a certain cooperation with the "apostate" Syrian regime. Doctrine is also poorly positioned to explain the tendency of HTS and AQAP to include a civilian elite in governance and to refrain from extensively coercive practices. Equally, doctrine cannot explain the tendency of AQAP to maintain preexisting institutions and practices to a quite considerable extent, even when distant from the tenets of Salafi-jihadism. Therefore, while ideology is useful to illuminate several of the governance decisions made by Salafi-jihadist ruling armed groups, a more comprehensive and more accurate understanding of Salafi-jihadist governance requires going beyond doctrine. Additionally—and in accordance with the previous argument that different Salafi-jihadist groups can develop somewhat different models of rebel governance—I also argue that the extent to which ideology shapes Salafi-jihadist governance is not uniform across cases but rather varies (even considerably so) from one group to the other.

Third, as I extend the comparative analysis to non-Salafi-jihadist ruling armed groups, I argue that governance by Salafi-jihadist armed groups may display a series of uniquely peculiar features vis-à-vis the models of governance adopted by non-Salafi-jihadist rebel rulers worldwide. Specifically, the former distinguish themselves for their tendency to discriminate against non-Muslims, non-Sunnis, and women. Regarding the approach to preexisting structures and practices, IS and HTS also distinguish themselves for their propensity to introduce extensive innovations, whose foundations are to be found in the sources of Islam and the sociopolitical model of the earliest caliphates. Besides, IS also distinguishes itself by its propensity to exclude most other actors from governance—especially those who do not submit to the Salafi-jihadist authority—and by its use of extensively and widely publicized coercive practices.

However, I note that while some unique patterns of Salafi-jihadist governance can be identified, there are also important similarities between Salafi-jihadist and non-Salafi-jihadist ruling armed groups in their approach to governance. For instance, cooperation with other actors and the use of persuasion alongside moderation are patterns that HTS and AQAP have in common with non-Salafi-jihadist rulers. HTS and AQAP also resemble other non-Salafi-jihadist groups in their tendency to combine coercion and persuasion to comparable extents. Similarly, the maintenance of preexisting structures and practices of rule is observed among both AQAP and non-Salafi-jihadist rulers. Building on these observations, I emphasize that just as Salafi-jihadist governance is not necessarily uniform across different groups, so the distinctiveness of Salafi-jihadist governance is not universal and thus should be assessed individually for each Salafi-jihadist governance experiment. In other words, while Salafi-jihadist governance may display some unique features, the extent of such uniqueness varies across groups.

In conclusion, I suggest that the term "Salafi-jihadist governance"—which I use in the title of this book and which is widely employed by scholars, policymakers, journalists, and humanitarian organizations—should not be taken to allude to a universal and unique model of Salafi-jihadist governance, the existence of which is contradicted by the analysis of multiple case studies offered in the following chapters. Rather, it should indicate the act of governance by Salafi-jihadist armed groups, which is a heterogenous phenomenon whereby Salafi-jihadist insurgents engage in civilian administration, developing patterns of governance that do not necessarily assume the same characteristics across different contexts and that do not necessarily reflect the tenets of Salafi-jihadism to the same extent.

OUTLINE OF CHAPTERS

This book is divided into six main chapters. In the first chapter, I introduce the notion of nonstate governance and discuss the circumstances under which governance by armed groups is observed. I then refer to the writings of the most influential insurgent leaders of the past century, as well as the relevant scholarly literature, to explain why armed groups have an interest in civilian administration. I observe that once insurgents manage to conquer territories, they often decide to engage in activities of governance for diverse (and possibly overlapping) reasons. Having understood why insurgents often turn into providers of governance, I proceed to discuss the phenomenon in greater depth by reviewing the functions that armed groups most commonly perform once they transition from warfare to governance.

However, while scholars pay greater attention to governance by (armed) nonstate actors, we still lack conceptual frameworks that might allow us to capture the multiple relevant dimensions of rebel governance. In the second chapter, I attempt to fill this lacuna by proposing a multidimensional typology of governance by armed groups. Referring to the theoretical and empirical contributions of the academic literature, I identify five core dimensions of rebel rule: *inclusivity, civilian engagement, generation of compliance, approach to outsiders,* and *propensity to change.*

My proposed typology serves two research purposes: It allows me to both investigate how rebels govern from a multidimensional perspective and build systematic comparisons across cases. In this chapter, I also apply the typology to the study of three cases of non-Salafi-jihadist rebel rulers that I selected by virtue of their diversity—the LTTE, the FARC, and the PYD.

From there, in the third chapter I proceed to discuss Salafi-jihadism and how it relates to civilian administration in times of conflict. I refer to the writings of the most influential Salafi-jihadist ideologues, strategists, and insurgent leaders. Following this discussion, I elaborate a series of expectations on the features that rebel governance is most likely to display across the five dimensions of my proposed typology if it is influenced by the Salafi-jihadist doctrine. The aim is to build a baseline against which to compare specific cases of Salafi-jihadist rebel rulers and assess the extent to which ideology has or has not been an influencing factor.

The fourth, fifth, and sixth chapters focus on IS, HTS, and AQAP, respectively. I start by reviewing the three groups' respective transitions from insurgency to civilian administration and by identifying the activities of rebel rule that each decided to perform over the territories brought under their control. Following this, I investigate the ruling strategies adopted by IS, HTS, and AQAP in order to assess the groups' models of governance. Here, I refer to the five dimensions of governance proposed in my typology.

Following the three case studies, in a final concluding chapter I present and discuss the book's findings. Firstly, I compare the observations derived from the application of my typology to IS, HTS, and AQAP to identify differences and similarities across the three groups. Secondly, I compare the models of rebel rule adopted by IS, HTS, and AQAP with my expectations on the influence of Salafi-jihadism on governance to assess whether—and to what extent—ideology shapes Salafi-jihadist practices of civilian administration. Thirdly, I compare the observations derived from the study of IS, HTS, and AQAP with the governance patterns employed by the LTTE, the FARC, and the PYD to identify differences and similarities between Salafi-jihadist and non-Salafi-jihadist rebel rulers. As I present the book's findings, I also discuss their implications. To conclude, I suggest avenues for future research that could further advance our knowledge of Salafi-jihadist rule.

1

GOVERNANCE BY INSURGENTS

Context, Rationale, and Manifestation

I n political science, governance has traditionally been studied from a state-centric perspective that understands the nation-state as the exclusive provider of governance and associates the absence of the state to a situation of disorder.[1] The reality, however, is much more complex. In fact, when states are too weak to exercise their authority, the outcome is not necessarily a situation of anarchy. Rather, violent and nonviolent nonstate actors can emerge as alternative providers of governance. Far from being a recent development, or one limited to certain geographic areas only, cases of governance by nonstate actors have been observed in numerous places throughout history.[2] Recognizing that in areas of state weakness, or state absence, governance can be provided by a wide array of nonstate actors, in this book I focus on specific cases in which governance is provided by (Salafi-jihadist) armed groups. This phenomenon, known as "rebel governance," can be succinctly defined as "the organization of civilians within rebel-held territory for a public purpose."[3] In this chapter, I will unpack the phenomenon of rebel governance by discussing the circumstances under which it emerges, the reasons why armed groups have an interest in civilian administration, and the functions that armed groups most commonly perform as rulers.

UNDERSTANDING THE CONTEXT OF
REBEL GOVERNANCE

The struggle against power is as old as the wielding of power itself. Throughout history, whoever has come to rule has oftentimes been called to confront the challenges posed by armed actors resorting to the use of force to overturn the sovereign authority, assert control over parts—or all—of the incumbent's territory, dismantle the existing order, and introduce a new sociopolitical system.[4] The use of violence against the constituted power by armed groups of individuals that aim "to overthrow a regime"[5] and create "a totally new and revolutionary social and political structure, with the armed people in power,"[6] is commonly referred to as "insurgency."[7]

Regardless of the specific goal that an insurgency may seek to achieve, insurgents are always the (at least initially) weaker party.[8] When the insurgency breaks out, the counterinsurgent force has on its side manpower, weapons, diplomatic recognition, legitimate power, control of the administration and the police, finances, industrial and agricultural resources, and transport and communications facilities.[9] Nonetheless, insurgents benefit from other advantages. They have highly movable light armed forces, they are free from rigid territorial commitments, they have a potentially bottomless pool of manpower from which to recruit, and they have time.[10] In the case of the latter, it is interesting to recall the famous statement addressed by the Taliban to North Atlantic Treaty Organization (NATO) forces in the context of the former's insurgency against the NATO-supported Afghan government after 2005: "You have all the watches, we have all the time."[11]

In the context of asymmetry outlined above, insurgents prefer to avoid conventional wars. As argued by one of the best-known contemporary experts on insurgency, John A. Nagl, "an insurgent force has comparatively few weapons and no army; [therefore] if it openly appears on the same battlefield as the counterinsurgency force, it will be swiftly defeated."[12] The truth of this assertion was evident in the Nepalese civil conflict between the Maoist rebels and the Kathmandu government, which lasted from 1996 to 2006. As noted by an experienced observer, "the Maoists had moved away from guerrilla warfare to a conventional war practice . . . but a crushing defeat at the hands of the RNA [Royal Nepal Army] showed that they were not in a position to wage and win a conventional battle."[13] Aware of the imbalance of power and resources, insurgents most often opt for an irregular strategy of warfare whereby they operate in small, highly mobile cells, conduct hit-and-run attacks, strike the enemy's strategic outposts and lines of logistical support, engage in terrorist activities, and perpetrate acts of sabotage.[14]

However, while engaging in unconventional military operations, insurgents also attempt to shape popular narratives by engaging in propaganda, psychological warfare, and sociopolitical activities aimed at disassociating the population from the government and obtaining the people's sympathy and support.[15] For insurgents, in fact, separating the people from the regime and mobilizing them on their side is of fundamental importance because "the exercise of political power [to which the insurgents aspire] depends on the tacit or explicit agreement of the population or, at worst, on its submissiveness."[16] In their struggle against the government, most insurgents "consider mass support the primary condition for their success."[17] They believe that "war hinges on the behavior of civilians,"[18] that popular support is "the *sine qua non* of victory,"[19] and that failure to achieve civilian support is a likely path to defeat.[20]

As argued by the Chinese insurgent leader Mao Tse-Tung, "because guerrilla warfare basically derives from the masses and is supported by them, it can neither exist nor flourish if it separates itself form their sympathies and cooperation."[21] On a similar note, Ernesto "Che" Guevara, the Argentinian doctor who contributed to leading the Cuban insurgency against the Batista regime, wrote that the rebels "must have the support of the masses" because the masses give recruitment, supplies, intelligence, and transport to the insurgents.[22] Similarly, Menachem Begin, the leader of the Zionist militant group Irgun, which fought against the British Mandate in Palestine, believed that it was necessary for an underground army to secure the "understanding" and "sympathy" of the people.[23] In Uganda, Yoweri Museveni, the leader of the eventually victorious National Resistance Army, wrote that "the population is the one which gives [an insurgent force] food, shelter, and intelligence information about the movement of enemy troops. . . . Without the support of the people it cannot carry out the struggle alone, and successfully."[24]

WHY ARMED GROUPS DECIDE TO GOVERN

As noted above, most insurgents consider popular support fundamental to their success. To acquire civilian support, rebels often attempt to create systems of governance that "may deploy existing ideological or cultural beliefs that increase identification with the insurgent cause," and they "may also provide goods and services that improve civilians' lives."[25] In fact, once they bring territories under their control rebels seem to recognize that they can challenge the authority of the state, increase their legitimacy vis-à-vis the existing regime, and ultimately win the crucial support of civilians only by replicating some of the functions of the state.[26] In other words, once territorial control has been achieved insurgents often recognize that new administrative, social, political, and economic structures need to be established to dismantle the old order, develop a new one, and consolidate popular legitimacy.[27]

When these dynamics are observed, insurgents enter into a competition with the incumbent authority in which they attempt to "out-govern" the state.[28] In other words, rebels seek to "out-administer" and "out-legitimize" the state, rather than merely "outfight" it.[29] As part of this competition, they establish "parallel hierarchies" that lay the foundations for the creation of a new insurgent-led state structure.[30] As those rebel-led "parallel hierarchies" are progressively established, rebels and civilians reach a social contract whereby rebels offer a series of benefits to the population in exchange for support, and civilians accept the rebels' offer.[31] Once a social contract is instituted, the relation between rebels and civilians becomes one between rulers and ruled.[32]

However, while rebels often opt to rule local communities to facilitate and consolidate civilian support, there is more to this. Indeed, even rebels exclusively focused on profit and disinterested in developing a relationship with the local population can nonetheless decide to provide governance, not for the benefit of civilians, but rather for their own gain—to capture the state, extract resources from civilians, and increase profits.[33] In fact, one of the reasons why rebels may provide some form of governance is that the latter is seen as instrumental to extract resources in a sustainable and regular way.[34] In addition to this, rebels may decide to govern because they are driven by a civilian-oriented ideology, and once they conquer territories they want to put that doctrine into practice.[35]

Insurgent groups that conquer some populated territories may also establish institutions and practices of governance to outbid rival organizations,[36] using governance in an attempt "to differentiate themselves from other groups operating on the same territory [and] to acquire a greater share of public support at the local level."[37] Finally, armed groups may decide to engage in governance to strengthen organizational capacity,[38] to facilitate the tasks of monitoring and punishing defection,[39] to access political and social networks,[40] to secure international legitimacy and support, including from states, international organizations, nongovernmental organizations, and the media,[41] and to strengthen their negotiating position ahead of peace talks.[42]

This tendency on the part of insurgents to engage in practices of civilian administration is best explained by the insurgent leaders themselves. According to Mao, for instance, insurgents must pay attention to popular support from the very onset: "The moment that this war of resistance dissociates itself from the masses of the people is the precise moment that it disassociates itself from hope of ultimate victory."[43] To do so, they must introduce structures and practices of shadow governance aimed at forming a de facto state.[44] In this regard, Mao wrote that the insurgency "must lead the peasants' struggle for land and distribute the land to them ... safeguard the interests of the workers ... develop trade with outside areas, and solve the problems facing the masses—food, shelter and clothing, fuel, rice, cooking-oil and salt, sickness and hygiene, and marriage."[45]

Following Mao, the Vietnamese insurgent leader Võ Nguyên Giáp described the Vietnamese war as a people's war, in which it is crucial to educate, mobilize, organize, and arm the people so that they can take part in the resistance.[46] In this context, the creation of positive and friendly relations between guerrillas and civilians is indispensable,[47] which the Vietnamese insurgents did by taking part in efforts to increase agricultural cooperation, combat famine, drought, and flood, and build construction sites and factories.[48] Not too distant from Mao and Giáp's understanding of insurgency is that of the insurgent leader of Guinea and Cape Verde, Amilcar Cabral. Referring to the war against the Portuguese occupation as a struggle aiming to destroy the existing order and create a new sociopolitical system, Cabral argued that the war could not be limited to an exclusive military effort. Rather, military actions must be coordinated with political work since only in this way is it possible to deal with the people's social, political, and economic needs in the liberated areas and engage in the latter's administration.[49]

While Mao and other like-minded insurgent leaders advocated for the "subordination of the military struggle to ... political aims,"[50] Guevara developed an alternative "military-focus" strategy in which precedence is given to the military struggle.[51] Nonetheless, Guevara also believed that once territories have been conquered, the insurgents must strive for the people's support by means of performing governance tasks such as the organization of production, the collection of taxes, the adoption of laws and the creation of courts, the building of schools, the provision of health care, the creation of farming organizations, and all those activities that ensure the people's welfare.[52]

Instructive observations on the relationship between insurgency and governance have been advanced in more recent times by other insurgent leaders and commanders. For instance, the leader of the short-lived Peruvian Ejército de Liberación Nacional, Héctor Béjar, maintained that guerrillas must devote effort to activities of governance on behalf of the people and explained his group's transition to civilian administration by arguing that "we became nurses, advisers, teachers, all sorts of things which helped us to win their [the civilians'] confidence."[53] On a similar note, the Afghan Taliban published in 2010 a new version of their *Layeha* (code of conduct), in which they stated the importance of creating a series of provincial commissions designed to ensure the interests of the local population in the territories under their control.[54] In India in the early 2000s, the leaders of the Communist Party of India (CPI) referred to practices of governance for the people as necessary to "enhance and expedite the revolutionary high tide throughout the country, and through this, a basis can be laid for the building up of new base areas, and the gradual consolidation and expansion of the people's army and base areas."[55]

However, while armed groups fighting an insurgency against the state seem to have multiple reasons to engage in governance, it is also noticeable that not all insurgents that conquer territories decide to become providers of governance. According to Kasfir, for rebel governance to be possible three conditions must exist: Rebels must control some territory; civilians must live in that area; and rebels must commit an initial act of violence to become rebels and either continue hostilities or credibly threaten them.[56] On this latter point, Huang similarly writes that "as a wartime phenomenon, [rebel governance] only exists in tandem with, or as part of, military strategy; rebel governance without fighting is simply peaceful organization."[57] Yet, the presence of those conditions is not enough in and by itself, and "not all rebel groups achieve wartime state building and not all may even attempt to do so."[58] It is therefore important to acknowledge the great heterogeneity of rebel approaches to matters of governance and "abandon the unfounded assumption that all rebel groups aim to build full alternative governments as they wage war."[59]

Cases in which insurgents might prefer not to invest in civil administration even if presented with the opportunity to do so include groups that regard civilians as targets for predation and sources of collective or personal enrichment, especially when looting civilians is a strategy that rebel commanders use to retain the commitment and motivation of their fighters or when a group is mostly composed of opportunistic rather than committed fighters;[60] groups that see civilians as targets for ethnic cleansing;[61] groups that are small in size and unknown or little-known to civilians;[62] groups that do not need civilians to acquire resources because they already benefit from external support or from the exploitation of natural resources;[63] groups that lack the assets required by governance, including sufficient financial means, adequate manpower, expertise in nonmilitary affairs;[64] and groups that have "short-term time horizons" and are focused on gaining and maximizing immediate benefits.[65]

Nevertheless, despite the existence of cases in which basic conditions are met but rebel governance practices and rebel governance structures are not observed, "a surprisingly large number of rebel groups engage in some sort of governance."[66] As discussed in more detail below, this may vary considerably in scope across groups, "ranging from creating minimal regulation and informal taxation to forming popular assemblies, elaborate bureaucracies, schools, courts, and health clinics."[67]

WHAT ARMED GROUPS DO WHEN THEY GOVERN

As noted above, many insurgent groups that conquer a populated territory proceed to engage in activities of governance. But what do rebels actually do when they decide to govern? The range of governance functions in which armed groups engage is not fixed; rather it varies depending on the combination of governance opportunity, governance willingness, and governance capacity specific to each group. Nonetheless, some common patterns can be observed.[68]

The provision of security and the provision of justice are the primary governance functions in which most ruling armed groups engage.[69] For instance, at the apex of its territorial control in Somalia in 2009–2010, al-Shabaab took over existing police stations and established a secret police force as well as a Ministry of Intelligence and Internal Security.[70] In India, the CPI also invested greatly in the provision of security and created a system composed of village defense squads at the lowest level, local guerrilla squads at a higher level, and the People's Liberation Guerrilla Army at the top.[71] At the time of their first Islamic Emirate (1996–2001) in Afghanistan, the Taliban created Islamic courts in almost every district and a Supreme Islamic Court in the city of Kandahar.[72] As they returned to insurgent governance after the emirate's overthrow, justice continued to be "a centerpiece of Taliban rule."[73] They introduced a two-tiered justice system, established a judicial authority at the provincial level, appointed judges to every district, and introduced mobile sharia courts as well as standing courts.[74] In Sudan, the Sudan People's Liberation Movement/ Army promulgated a penal and disciplinary code, established three tiers of military courts, and co-opted traditional courts.[75] Similarly, the Eritrean People's Liberation Front established judiciary committees to address legal problems.[76]

The reasons why rebel groups attach great importance to the provision of security and justice are multiple. First, the creation of a security system allows insurgents to claim a monopoly over the use of force, thus gaining credibility as the dominant authority.[77] In addition, the provision of security is the most effective way to obtain popular support. Indeed, as war-torn civilians likely regard security as the most valuable good, providing security enables insurgents to win the "hearts and minds" of the people and encourages civilians to sustain the group—be it passively (e.g., nonresistance) or actively (e.g., provision of recruits). Finally, insurgent groups recognize security as a necessary condition to engage in further governance tasks. Indeed, if within the conquered territory there are constant security threats, insurgents will have to devote their resources to warfare at the expense of governance.[78]

Similarly, the provision of justice is seen by insurgents as an optimal strategy to present themselves as preferable to the incumbent government. More specifically, rebel rulers intervene in judicial matters because they recognize that "the ability and the acceptance of the right to adjudicate in disputes is the ultimate expression of the right to rule—indeed of legitimacy."[79] As such, performing judicial functions is seen as central to obtaining legitimacy vis-à-vis the state.[80] Finally, the insurgents' involvement in the provision of justice acts as a foundation for broader rebel governance because it can allow the group to penetrate a community very effectively in relation to both important and mundane aspects of civilian life.[81] Here, it is important to emphasize that, for ideologically driven groups, a monopoly on justice is also an effective strategy by which to impose their own doctrine on society.[82]

Beyond security and justice, a considerable number of ruling armed groups also provide (or attempt to provide) other public goods and services. These include the provision of electricity; the construction of roads, buildings, and markets; the provision of health care and education; and the creation and maintenance of a telecommunications system. Among the groups that have done so is Hezbollah, which since its emergence in the context the Lebanese Civil War in 1982 has been active in repairing roads and houses, collecting garbage, providing electricity, offering health care and education, and providing water.[83] Similarly, the National Union for the Total Independence of Angola established secondary and primary schools as well as hospitals and clinics.[84] In Pakistan, Lashkar-e-Taiba has been the most active group in the provision of welfare, which has included natural disaster relief, health care, and education.[85]

As noted with respect to security and justice, rulers choose to provide those collective goods as a way to obtain the people's immediate consent to be governed.[86] Groups engage in social welfare activities to erode the legitimacy of the state, win the loyalty of the population, and trade social service provision for recruits and sympathy from the people, thus supplanting the state's social contract with their own.[87] However, providing these kinds of public goods and services is particularly challenging, in that it requires a great amount of financial resources, a large pool of experienced personnel, and a stable presence over the territory. Because of this, not all ruling insurgent groups are willing, or able, to engage in governance to this extent.

As argued above, the provision of security, justice, and public goods and services are functions of governance in which armed groups engage to cultivate popular support and strengthen their legitimacy as rulers, both in and of themselves and vis-à-vis the government. However, there is more to this in rebel governance. Most often, in fact, armed groups also require from civilians the payment of taxes,[88] an activity of governance that may appear to go in the opposite direction with respect to the provision of goods and services and the attraction of popular support.[89] In India the National Socialist Council of Nagaland imposed taxes on every imported and exported item, market transactions, households, and government employees.[90] In Somalia, al-Shabaab created a Ministry of Finance that implemented an "increasingly efficient taxation system" whereby the group imposed taxes on workers, businesses, aid organizations, land properties, livestock, ships, private cars, and commercial trucks.[91] In Afghanistan, the Panjshiri insurgent leader Ahmed Shah Massoud taxed the export of lapis lazuli and emeralds and collected taxes from the local population as well as from Panjshiris living and working in Kabul.[92]

Most commonly, armed groups engage in taxation to extract the financial resources needed to sustain their activities (both military operations and governance functions) and guarantee their survival.[93] However, economic considerations are not always the driver, or at least not the sole driver, of an armed group's decision to collect taxes.[94] In fact, it has been noted that armed groups might opt to collect taxes also for ideological reasons, implementing systems of taxation that reflect their commitment to a certain ideology and that serve to impose certain values and behaviors on society.[95] Furthermore, it is worth mentioning that taxation—when levied consistently and nonarbitrarily—attaches a fundamental dimension of predictability and accountability to a group's rule, thus reinforcing its credibility and legitimacy as ruler.[96] Similarly, taxation can reinforce armed groups' legitimacy by enabling them to engage in governance functions and build state-like institutions.[97] Besides this, taxation enables an armed group to collect information about the population, which ultimately enhances its capacity to control it.[98]

Finally, most insurgent groups—and especially those that are ideologically driven—have seemed prone to engage in the regulation of public behavior, so as to impose their specific values on society. Regulation of public behavior includes prohibitions on the consumption of certain products; the imposition or prohibition of certain religious practices; the regulation of sexual behavior and gender relations; and the regulation of dress codes. For instance, many ruling armed groups in Colombia were involved in the regulation of personal appearance and behavior, whereby long hair and earrings were usually forbidden among men, women were prohibited from wearing short skirts, and homosexuality and adultery were punished severely.[99]

Political science has traditionally understood governance as a function pertaining exclusively to the state. However, this state-centric understanding does not reflect reality: In many situations of state weakness, governance is performed by a series of alternative nonstate actors. Among those nonstate actors, insurgent groups are armed organizations that fight against the constituted power to overthrow the existing order and introduce a rebel-led sociopolitical system. Once insurgent armed groups conquer populated territories, they often (though not always) decide to engage in activities of governance for diverse (and possibly overlapping) reasons. While the specific governance activities in which armed groups engage depend on the combination of governance opportunity, governance willingness, and governance capacity that each group faces, some common patterns can be observed. Specifically, the governance functions in which rebels are most likely to engage are security, justice, the provision of other public goods and services, taxation, and the regulation of public behavior.

2

STUDYING GOVERNANCE BY ARMED GROUPS

A Multidimensional Typology

s I noted before, scholarly attention to governance by armed groups has grown significantly in recent years. However, a conceptual framework that adequately captures the multiple dimensions of rebel governance has yet to be constructed. In fact, scholars who have studied the phenomenon have mostly done so by addressing a few dimensions at a time. Yet, rebel governance is a multidimensional phenomenon characterized by a great diversity of forms, and as such it requires a more elaborate set of distinctions. In this chapter, I will synthesize the many recent developments that have been achieved in the study of governance by armed groups, and I will present a typology of five dimensions of rebel governance. Importantly, the typology that I propose aims to make two major contributions, beyond the study of the specific phenomenon of Salafi-jihadist rebel rule: to allow researchers to study rebel civilian administration in depth with attention to multiple dimensions of governance, and to allow researchers to conduct systematic comparisons across different case studies. Having built the typology, I will proceed to apply it to the study of three well-known cases of non-Salafi-jihadist rebel rulers: the Liberation Tigers of Tamil Eelam, the Revolutionary Armed Forces of Colombia, and the Democratic Union Party. I will refer to the observations recorded from the three case studies to identify common features of non-Salafi-jihadist rebel governance, which will serve as a baseline against which to compare cases of Salafi-jihadist rebel rulers.

STUDYING REBEL RULE FROM A MULTIDIMENSIONAL PERSPECTIVE: THE PROPOSED TYPOLOGY

Building on the theoretical and empirical contributions of the literature on rebel governance, I have selected five dimensions of rebel rule that seem the most relevant to gain a comprehensive understanding of an armed group's approach to civilian administration.[1] I have also decided to limit the typology to five dimensions in order to offer an analysis of rebel governance that is both comprehensive and broad, but also detailed and accurate. In the proposed typology, which is discussed below and illustrated in table 2.1, I distinguish two extreme possibilities for each dimension of rebel governance. These, however, are not mutually exclusive options, but rather the poles of a continuum along which intermediate possibilities exist.

Inclusivity

This dimension indicates whether an armed group performs governance functions, imposes rules, and provides services to the entire community living on its territory or only to a specific ethnic, religious, social, or gender section thereof. Under the rule of some armed groups, civilians are constrained by the same obligations and entitled to the same benefits regardless of their ethnicity, religion, social status, gender, and other facets of identity. Justice is universally accessible, law is enforced without discrimination, taxes are imposed on everyone, goods and services are provided to every civilian. If this is observed, there is a situation of *universality*. This is true regardless of the reasons that might encourage an armed group to refrain from discrimination, whether it is an honest commitment to inclusivity, or an opportunistic calculation aimed at appeasing potentially subversive sectors of the population. For instance, in Pakistan the Islamist Lashkar-e-Taiba has been providing welfare services beyond its coreligious communities, including the Hindu-majority region of the southern Sindh Province.[2]

Conversely, under the rule of some armed groups, only the members of a specific ethnic, religious, social, or gender group are regarded as legitimate partners of the social contract that is instituted through governance. Therefore, different laws and regulations apply to different sections of the population, taxes are imposed differently according to a person's belonging to, or exclusion from, the insurgents' constituency, and services and goods are provided exclusively to those who are considered entitled beneficiaries. If this is the situation observed, *discrimination* prevails. For instance, the National Socialist Council of Nagaland in India established a system whereby security was reserved exclusively for the Naga people. In other words, ethnicity was used by the group as a criterion by which to define who was eligible for protection and who was not.[3] In the Afghanistan of the 1990s, the Taliban systematically discriminated against women, forcing them to comply with an intrusive set of morality laws, excluding them from education, and prohibiting them from playing any role in society.[4]

As I argued above, however, intermediate possibilities also exist. *Partial discrimination* indicates a situation in which discriminatory practices are adopted toward the members of most ethnic, religious, social, or gender groups but exceptions are observed; *discrimination and universality* indicates a more balanced situation in which the members of some groups are regarded as equally legitimate subjects while the members of some other groups are not; *partial universality* indicates a situation in which inclusive practices are adopted toward the members of most ethnic, religious, social, or gender groups but limitations are observed. To give an example of partial universality, the Indonesian Free Aceh Movement was founded as an Acehnese ethno-nationalist organization. Nonetheless, it regarded most ethnic groups as legitimate members of its aspired polity with the sole exception of the Javanese, who were despised because they were considered neocolonial settlers.[5]

Civilian engagement

When rebels set out to rule a territory, their primary concern is how to interact with the civilian community residing there.[6] In some cases, armed groups introduce mechanisms of civilian consultation by means of which the civilian population can advance demands and have a say in governance. To use Weinstein's words, armed groups might introduce "a system of checks and balances that enables the civilian population to express its preferences and shape the behavior of the rebel army."[7] For their part, civilians may be taking part in the rebel governance system "for mixed motives—including prudence and self-interest as well as support for rebel goals."[8] When such a situation is observed, civilian engagement in rebel-controlled territories takes the form of *participation*. In Peru, for instance,

Sendero Luminoso used to share power with civilians through the creation of popular committees in charge of representing civilian interests.[9] In Guinea and Cape Verde, the African Party for the Independence of Guinea and Cape Verde held both national elections and elections for village committees that were encouraged to embrace some degree of autonomy in their decisions.[10] In Nepal, the Communist Party of Nepal-Maoist created democratically elected people's committees that offered civilian input in governance and included women, members of ethnic minorities, and members of lower castes.[11]

In the opposite case, civilians are prohibited from participating in governance. All decisions are taken by the group and its members without any formal or informal consultation with the civilian population or its representatives. If this is the reality of rebel-civilian relations, the situation is one of *subjection*. An example comes from Sri Lanka, where the LTTE refrained from creating structures and practices that would enable civilian participation in matters of governance, preferring instead to maintain civilians as politically inactive subjects.[12]

Besides the extreme cases of participation and subjection, civilians can find themselves in *partial participation* when they are mostly, yet not always or systematically, allowed to participate in governance; *partial subjection* when they are mostly prohibited from participating in governance; *participation and subjection* when these two realities coexist under different circumstances, for instance when civilians can participate in certain matters of governance while being excluded from others. The latter situation is observed in the case of the Islamic Resistance Movement (Hamas) in Gaza. Civilians living under Hamas can cast their votes in the Palestinian national elections (though the latter have not been held since 2006, and it is uncertain when they will be held next), but elections to Hamas's bodies are open only to the group's members.[13]

Generation of compliance

This dimension refers to the way in which an armed group seeks to obtain the compliance of the community with its rules. In some cases, groups opt to generate compliance through an exclusively coercive approach, meant as the use of force, or the threat thereof, that goes beyond ordinary functions of law enforcement and crime prevention. This leads to what Podder calls "coercive compliance," whereby "obedience is entirely coerced" and "the conviction of civilian subjects about the appropriateness of rule is inconsequential."[14] In other words, coercive approaches seek to create what Weigand defines as coercion-based "involuntary obedience," or a situation in which civilians comply with rebel rule because "they *have to* obey."[15] As also noted by Kasfir, force and threats form "the basis of a political order if civilians consistently obey rebel rules because they dread the consequences."[16] If this is observed, the situation existing in the rebel-controlled areas is one of *coercion*. For instance, throughout the period 1989–1992 the National Patriotic Front of Liberia was employing exclusively coercive measures, to the extent that "rule of the gun" appropriately describes the group's rule.[17] In Nepal, the Communist Party of Nepal-Maoist organized the villages under its control using what the local population characterized as *atyanta kras* or *atas*, meaning "intense fear" or "terror."[18] In the 1990s, the Taliban in Afghanistan seemingly took pride in the fact that "our rules are obeyed out of fear."[19]

In the opposite situation, groups rely on noncoercive practices, or what Terpstra and Frerks call "'softer' forms of persuasion."[20] These can include promoting rebel ideology, referring to a shared identity and shared values, mobilizing a symbolic repertoire (e.g., flags, parades, mottos), providing public services and publicizing those efforts, mobilizing a historic narrative, and/or presenting the rebels' project as a divinely mandated mission.[21] If this is observed, the situation is one of *persuasion*. For instance, the Tigray People's Liberation Front implemented important noncoercive practices to generate the willful obedience of civilians. It emphasized the shared Tigrayan culture of peasants and rebels, it presented itself as the protector of religion, and it used its successful land reform and rural administration to convince locals of the advantages offered by the rebels' proto-state.[22] As opposed to the use of coercive mechanisms, the use of noncoercive mechanisms encourages what Podder calls "voluntary compliance"[23] and Weigand defines as legitimacy-based "voluntary obedience," or a situation in which civilians comply with rebel rule because "they *want to* obey."[24] Interestingly, voluntary obedience or voluntary compliance can rest on different motivations. On the one hand, civilians may voluntarily obey because the armed group addresses the people's needs and provides material benefits (or promises to do so in the foreseeable future), or because there is no other viable alternative. On the other hand, civilians may voluntarily obey the armed group because they believe in the rightfulness of the rebels' rule due to shared values, interests, priorities, beliefs, and ideology.

However, intermediate situations in which the ruling rebels employ both persuasive and coercive mechanisms seem more common, and "civilian compliance during civil war is usually based on a mixture of coercion and persuasion, on fear and sympathy."[25] *Extensive coercion and limited persuasion* indicates a situation in which the ruling rebel group resorts predominantly to coercive practices and only to a limited extent to persuasive measures; *coercion and persuasion* indicates a situation in which the ruling rebel group resorts to coercive and persuasive strategies to a comparable extent; while *extensive persuasion and limited coercion* indicates a situation in which the ruling rebel group resorts predominantly to persuasive practices and only limitedly to coercive measures. For instance, a situation of coercion and persuasion was observed in the South Kivu region of the Democratic Republic of Congo under General Padiri's Mai Mai. On the one hand, the group engaged in pillaging, extortion, and forced recruitment that compelled the people to support the rebels at a high cost "in terms of human lives and resources"; on the other hand, it presented itself as the defender of the culture, land, and rights of local autochthonous communities, referred to local spiritual notions and beliefs, framed its struggle as a divine mission, presented itself as a repository of spiritual power and divine authority, and framed the relationship between the rebel leader and civilians as an intimate relation between a caring father/patron and his children/clients.[26]

Approach to outsiders

Upon conquering a territory, rebels must decide not only how to interact with the civilian community residing there but also how to interact with other actors external to the armed group, such as tribal, ethnic, and religious leaders, civil society organizations, international aid workers and NGOs, and other insurgent groups. Some rebel rulers might decide to include other (legitimate, resourceful, and experienced) actors in their governance experiment. Interestingly, some rebels even go as far as de facto outsourcing governance in their territories.[27] Under these circumstances, the situation observed is one of *cooperation*. For instance, the Sudan People's Liberation Movement/Army co-opted traditional courts headed by chiefs and elders who were seen as capable of resolving disputes within any ethnic community and who were given the task of delivering judgments based on a mixture of sharia, customary laws, and rebels' guidelines.[28] At the same time, it co-opted many international aid organizations in its education and health-care systems, which enabled the group to take some of the credit for service provision without needing to invest its own revenues.[29]

However, cooperation is not always the case, and armed groups might decide to engage in governance in isolation. When this is observed, there is a situation of *exclusion*. For instance, when AQI established its presence over some territories of western and northern Iraq in 2006 its preferred strategy was to act unilaterally. It demanded from local tribal groups (a core component of Iraq's social fabric) that they accept its authority over their territories.[30] In the same way, it let other insurgents know that they had no choice: join the insurgency, surrender their weapons, or succumb militarily.[31]

Finally, *partial exclusion* indicates a situation in which the ruling rebel group adopts an exclusionary approach, but exceptions are observed; *exclusion and cooperation* indicates a more intermediate situation in which the ruling rebel group cooperates with some actors while excluding others; *partial cooperation* indicates a situation in which the ruling rebel group adopts a generally inclusive approach, but limitations are observed. An example of simultaneous inclusion and exclusion is offered by the Afghan Taliban after 2009. They cooperated with the state's Ministry of Education in the management of schools and the appointment of teachers in Taliban areas; with the Ministry of Health and international NGOs in the provision of health care; and with national and international companies in the provision of phone coverage and electricity. Conversely, the group adopted a unilateral approach in the field of justice, operating exclusively through its own structures and personnel, and unilaterally imposed morality laws in the areas under its control.[32]

Propensity to change

This dimension refers to the attitude of the ruling armed group toward the governance structures and practices established by the former ruler as well as toward the personnel employed by the former regime. It indicates the extent to which a ruling armed group prefers to maintain or rather innovate preexisting structures, practices, and personnel. As has been noted in the rebel governance literature, in fact, rebels can assert their control over a preexisting civilian administrative apparatus or relate to civilians through new structures that they create.[33] If a ruling rebel group relies on already-existing institutions and maintains in their posts previously appointed workers, a situation of *maintenance* is observed. For instance, the Rally for Congolese Democracy-Goma refrained from introducing innovations: In all the areas of governance in which it intervened (or sought to intervene) it maintained previously appointed workers as well as the structures and practices of governance that were already in place prior to its arrival.[34]

If a group introduces innovations, it will create new institutions and practices *ex novo* and will dismiss all the workers who had been employed by the former authorities, appointing its own members or sympathizers to the vacated posts. In this case, the situation observed in the rebel areas is one of *innovation*. Here, an interesting example is that of al-Shabaab, which introduced important innovations in its system of governance, as evidenced by the taxation system: It imposed taxes on livestock sales and agricultural sales; on transiting vehicles and transported goods; on international aid agencies willing to work in Somalia; and the Islamic charity tax *zakat*.[35]

Once again, it is important to remember that innovation and maintenance are not necessarily mutually exclusive options and that a combination thereof can be the preferred strategy of an armed group. I refer to *extensive innovation and limited maintenance* when rebels predominantly introduce new practices and personnel and resort only limitedly to maintenance; *innovation and maintenance* when rebels innovate and maintain to comparable extents; *extensive maintenance and limited innovation* when rebels predominantly maintain preexisting practices and personnel and innovate only to a limited extent. In India, for instance, the CPI engaged in a combination of innovation and maintenance: It found it convenient to maintain the social services provided by the Indian state, but it preferred to introduce new forums for the settlement of disputes and to create a new taxation system.[36]

TABLE 2.1 A multidimensional typology of rebel governance

Inclusivity				
Universality	Partial universality	Universality and discrimination	Partial discrimination	Discrimination
Civilian engagement				
Participation	Partial participation	Participation and subjection	Partial subjection	Subjection
Generation of compliance				
Coercion	Extensive coercion and limited persuasion	Coercion and persuasion	Extensive persuasion and limited coercion	Persuasion
Approach to outsiders				
Cooperation	Partial cooperation	Cooperation and exclusion	Partial exclusion	Exclusion
Propensity to change				
Maintenance	Extensive maintenance and limited innovation	Maintenance and innovation	Extensive innovation and limited maintenance	Innovation

STUDYING NON-SALAFI-JIHADIST REBEL GOVERNANCE FROM A MULTIDIMENSIONAL PERSPECTIVE

Having presented my proposed typology of rebel governance, I will now apply it to the study of the LTTE in Sri Lanka, the FARC in Colombia, and the PYD in Syria. I selected these groups because they are prominent examples of non-Salafi-jihadist rebel rulers, as they have engaged in governance for a considerable number of years over large swaths of territory. The extent of the governance experience of these three groups enables us to study in depth and detail, as well as across multiple dimensions, how governance was—or is being—delivered in the areas under their control. At the same time, the choice of these groups was informed by the existence of a considerable secondary literature on them, including scholarly books and papers, journalistic articles, reports by humanitarian organizations, and interviews with civilians who lived (or are still living) in those rebel-ruled territories. The richness of the data available enables us to evaluate each group with respect to each dimension of my proposed typology—something that could not be done in the case of groups whose governance experience has been less documented. Finally, the selected groups offer a sufficiently representative picture of non-Salafi-jihadist governance. Each of them, in fact, embodies a distinct non-Salafi-jihadist doctrine. This diversity is particularly helpful to study the various ways in which governance can be delivered by armed groups that are ideologically different from the Salafi-jihadist organizations that are the object of analysis in this book.

THE LIBERATION TIGERS OF TAMIL EELAM

The roots of the LTTE lie in the ethnic diversity that characterizes Sri Lanka, where the two largest groups are the Sinhalese and the Tamils, representing approximately 74 and 18 percent of the population, respectively. After independence in 1948 tensions between the two communities emerged, and in the 1970s a younger generation of Tamils began to articulate a more aggressive form of Tamil nationalism in the face of what they perceived as Sinhala oppression. In this context, the LTTE emerged as a Tamil ethno-nationalist group waging an insurgency against the Sinhalese government to secede and establish an independent Tamil state in the northeastern part of the country.

Over time, the LTTE managed to assert its direct control over some areas, and starting in 1987 it began to engage in governance practices that lasted until the end of the conflict in 2009. While doing so, it appropriated and mobilized symbols in which the Tamil community would recognize itself, such as the Tamil Eelam national anthem, the national Tiger flag, the national tree, the national flower, the national bird, the national anthem, and national holidays.[37] In the words of a local resident, "during public events, Tiger flags were raised and symbols were worshipped."[38]

Additionally, the LTTE referred to a common descent and to the continuity of a collective memory; emphasized its ideology as rooted in Tamil tradition and culture; honored the martyrdom of its cadres; and emphasized the atrocities of the Sri Lankan Army against the Tamil community.[39]

At the same time, however, the LTTE was an authoritarian movement that encouraged the worshipping of its founder and leader, Velupillai Prabhakaran, and that relied on coercive measures such as the burning of houses, abductions for ransom, assassinations, and suicide bombings in order to force the civilian population into obedience.[40] As argued by a local resident, "they [the LTTE] forcibly recruited the youth into the movement. They kidnapped people and they imposed compulsory taxes. They collected funds forcefully, for example by abducting people and demanding ransom. They abducted or murdered people who were not in favor of the movement."[41] A girl from Batticaloa, eastern Sri Lanka, reported that after receiving a letter from the LTTE requesting one child from each family, her family decided to leave. In response, the LTTE burned the family's house, along with the houses of about fifteen other families who had left for similar reasons. When they returned months later, the LTTE forcibly recruited her.[42]

As far as participation in the LTTE's proto-state is concerned, civilians reported that "citizens were not able to influence much of the rebel rule, as it was no democracy. It was imposed from above by the sole leader and the military and intelligence commanders."[43] As a matter of fact, the LTTE never built a political party, never engaged in electoral processes, and never organized local elections in which the Tamil population could voice its preferences for the political arrangement of the Northeast. In other words, civilians were regarded exclusively as subjects and excluded from the LTTE's governance system.[44] As noted by Stokke, "the dominant form of governance in the LTTE-controlled areas [was] that of a strong and centralized state with few formal institutions for democratic representation."[45]

In terms of institutions and personnel, the LTTE created a police force that was in charge of preventing and detecting crime, regulating traffic, and educating civilians about crime prevention.[46] The LTTE also built police stations and established a police academy.[47] As far as the functioning of the police is concerned, it is interesting to recall the comments of a fisherman from Pudukuduyirippu, northern Sri Lanka, as they also connect with some of the observations made above regarding the LTTE's coercion: "the LTTE established regional police departments to maintain their law. The people adhered to the law of the LTTE out of fear."[48] In the judicial realm, the Tamil insurgents initially set up village mediation boards comprised of retired civil servants, teachers, and other local intellectuals. However, those proved unsatisfactory because there was no proper legal code and members lacked legal training. In 1994, the LTTE introduced the Tamil Eelam Penal Code and the Tamil Eelam Civil Code, based on preexisting laws that were nonetheless updated and adapted. It also established six district courts and two high courts as well as a court of appeal and a supreme court.[49]

Innovation also characterized the LTTE's taxation practices and regulation of behavior. Tamil public servants, manufacturers, and service providers were taxed a percentage of their salaries, while farmers and fishermen had to contribute a share of their output either in cash or in kind. Taxes were imposed also on those employees that continued to receive their salaries from the government. Additionally, the group imposed fees on all the goods that were imported into LTTE territory, vehicle registration taxes, and taxes on property transactions.[50] In regulating public behavior, the LTTE went against the conservatism of traditional Tamil society. It enacted reforms for women, attacked the caste system, sought to reduce the influence of religion, and changed the traditional interactions between elders and youngsters.[51] In the words of Pararajasingham, head of the LTTE's judicial division, "we made special laws for women regarding their property rights, rape, abortion etc. Under our laws women are totally free and on par with men in property transactions. As you know, this is not the case under Jaffna's traditional law, Thesawalamai."[52] At the same time, and as reported by a local respondent, the LTTE prohibited prostitution, adultery, and homosexuality as well as provocative clothes: "no prostitution, no homosexuals, it was not allowed to cheat on your man or wife. Movies were not allowed. . . . Also there were dress codes."[53]

Conversely, in the provision of other public services the LTTE proved more conservative and more prone to cooperation with other actors,[54] having to balance its aspiration to address the people's needs with the constraints imposed on its governance capacities by its limited finances and

TABLE 2.2 The model of governance of the Liberation Tigers of Tamil Eelam

Inclusivity	Discrimination (Sinhalese and Muslims)
Civilian engagement	Subjection (no political party, no electoral process)
Generation of compliance	Coercion and persuasion (e.g., abductions and mobilization of Tamil symbols)
Approach to outsiders	Partial cooperation (Sri Lankan government and NGOs)
Propensity to change	Innovation and maintenance (e.g., Tamil Eelam Education Council and Sri Lankan Department of Education)

expertise. Thus, health-care services were still provided by the Sri Lankan Ministry of Health and medical staff were paid by the government, even though it was the LTTE that made final decisions about implementation.[55] In the North, for instance, the largest town under rebel control had a government-run hospital.[56] As noted by a local civilian, "they [the LTTE] were controlling most of the basic public services. But the healthcare, so the medical staff, was paid by the government."[57] In the education sector as well the LTTE allowed NGOs to continue their management of existing schools. A local NGO worker argued that "education was OK in the uncleared areas. People tried to read and educate themselves. . . . That was one of the few things that went on very well. Also the LTTE would allow us to do education projects."[58] Similarly, school principals were maintained in their posts and continued to be appointed by the government. At the same time, the Sri Lankan Department of Education continued to function (or, rather, was allowed to function) even in the areas under LTTE control. Nonetheless, the LTTE also established the Tamil Eelam Education Council that functioned as a sort of ministry of education within the rebel civilian administration and coordinated the provision of education with the provincial representatives.[59] Finally, it is worth noting that as the LTTE engaged in the above administrative functions it developed a single governance system for both civilians and rebel cadres. However, discrimination was observed in that the LTTE governance system applied only to the Hindu and Christian Tamil community, since the Sinhalese and Tamil-speaking Muslims were excluded from the nascent LTTE state.

Specifically, the LTTE regarded the Sinhalese as not belonging to its desired future Tamil state, while it became increasingly suspicious toward Muslims because they lived in areas controlled by the Sri Lankan Army.[60] As noted by a civilian from Batticaloa, "in the early years there also were Muslim LTTE cadres. But what they did after a while was killing their own Muslim cadres."[61]

THE REVOLUTIONARY ARMED FORCES OF COLOMBIA

After a decade of conflict known as *La Violencia* (1948–1958), in the mid-1960s a group of leftist guerrillas inspired by the principles of Marxism-Leninism launched an armed movement known as the Revolutionary Armed Forces of Colombia (Fuerzas Armadas Revolucionarias de Colombia).[62] The group described itself as a popular liberation movement that aspired to overthrow the Colombian government and implement social justice and communism.[63] In the mid-seventies, the group underwent an accelerated expansion as it used illicit drugs, kidnapping, and extortion to finance its operations, develop military capacity, and expand to new territories. By the early 1980s, a vast territorial enclave in southeastern Colombia fell under its control, and in the 1990s the FARC became the strongest of all Colombian guerrilla groups.[64] Once the FARC established a remarkable degree of territorial control, it proceeded to adopt state-like functions and provide governance to local populations.[65] The situation lasted until 2016, when most of the FARC signed a peace agreement with the government.

Throughout its governance experience, the FARC seemed prone to accept some degree of civilian participation. In many localities under its control civilians "found [informal] ways to communicate their preferences" to the rebel commanders and "influence some of the ways in which things were done."[66] In the words of a local leader, "it was not easy to talk when the guerrilla had just executed someone, especially someone who hadn't done anything. But the [civilian] leaders always had their voice about topics that were important for the community and had the capacity to tell the commanders about those problems."[67] Furthermore, following the 1984 accords with the government, the FARC cofounded the Patriotic Union (Unión Patriótica, UP) political party and joined the national electoral process. In fact, the FARC "viewed elections as a way to enhance political participation among those traditionally excluded, particularly throughout areas of the countryside in their spheres of influence, and among networks of supporters in the cities. They also saw the UP acting as the vehicle to increase political representation."[68] Following the UP's electoral success, however, thousands of party leaders and members were assassinated by the government and the paramilitaries.[69] In 2000, the FARC established a new political party, the Bolivarian Movement for the New Colombia, which was maintained as a mostly clandestine political body.[70] Significantly, in July 2017, following the above-mentioned peace deals between the government and the insurgents, the FARC announced its reformation as a legal political party under the name Revolutionary Alternative Force of Colombia.[71]

As far as inclusivity is concerned, there is no evidence to suggest that the FARC was adopting a discriminatory approach. In fact, the group's communist Marxist-Leninist ideology is characterized by a universal perspective, which suggests that it was never intended to inspire a system of rule for a single ethnic, religious, social, or gender group, as much as a system of rule based on social justice and communism for the entire population of Colombia. Nonetheless, it is worth bearing in mind that the FARC's natural constituency—and the sector of the population over which the group came to govern—was Colombia's rural poor, as opposed to the rich landowning class.

In terms of governance activities, the group maintained the preexisting applicable law. In some cases, insurgents invoked local customs proper to peasant life; in other cases, the laws applied were the official laws of the Colombian state. Importantly, the FARC also co-opted existing community justice mechanisms.[72] In the field of taxation, the FARC introduced new taxes that allowed the group to extract needed financial resources: It taxed coca-related activities, cattle owners, merchants, landowners, and large companies.[73] As far as the management of taxes is concerned, it was usually a committee elected locally that was in charge of deciding on disbursement and allocation of the collected taxes within its specific locality.[74] Throughout the years, the FARC's taxation system became characterized by increasing formality.[75] As a matter of fact, in 2000 the FARC formalized its taxation practice through a new law demanding a 10 percent tax from all corporations and individuals with a net worth of at least $1 million.[76]

In terms of regulation of behavior, the FARC introduced new norms that concerned a wide variety of issues, such as domestic violence, personal appearance, sexual conduct, freedom of speech, working hours, liquor consumption, and prostitution.[77] Mostly, this was done through public statements by FARC commanders and word of mouth. Another channel through which norms of conduct were communicated was the display in public places of the *normas de convivencia ciudadana* (regulations of civilian coexistence).[78] Interestingly, people interviewed by Arjona reported that even when there was no formal rule, civilians knew what was allowed and what was not.[79]

Conversely, in the provision of sophisticated public goods and services the FARC opted for the maintenance of preexisting structures and for the inclusion of state officials and local authorities. Indeed, there is no evidence that the FARC directly engaged in the construction of schools or hospitals. Rather, it often pressured local authorities to introduce or improve health and education services in the areas under its control. This allowed the group to directly influence how local government officials provided those services, without having to provide them itself. In other words, the FARC opted not to dismantle the local government altogether. Rather, it preferred to maintain some of the government's structures, functions, and officials and to subordinate them to the FARC's guidelines and the supervision of its members.[80]

To ensure civilian compliance the FARC often used coercion (e.g., kidnapping of tax evaders) and the threat thereof.[81] Strict monitoring and harsh punishments were observed in several localities where rebels would rely on informants to know instances of disobedience and punish them.[82] As has been reported by a local resident, "thieves were usually warned twice and, if they reoffended, were expelled or killed. Rapists and assassins were killed directly."[83] Additionally, the FARC was involved in the forcible recruitment of children.[84] That said, the FARC also relied on noncoercive mechanisms. For instance, it sought to promote its ideology during public gatherings and emphasize the "positive" effects of its activities.[85] It presented itself to local communities as the only organization with the capacity to fill the existing gap of state authority, provide a voice for the

TABLE 2.3 The model of governance of the Revolutionary Armed
Forces of Colombia

Inclusivity	Universality (Colombian people)
Civilian engagement	Partial participation (Patriotic Union and electoral process)
Generation of compliance	Coercion and persuasion (e.g., harsh punishments and public gatherings to promote ideology)
Approach to outsiders	Partial cooperation (state officials and local authorities)
Propensity to change	Innovation and maintenance (e.g., new taxation system and maintenance of local customs and state laws)

peasants, and introduce a more legitimate structure of authority.[86] Later on, when the cultivation of illicit coca crops expanded throughout FARC-controlled areas, the group presented itself as the organization with the capacity to intercede on behalf of the peasants vis-à-vis drug traffickers.[87] Material benefits were also part of the FARC's strategy. As argued by a communist leader from Viotá, central Colombia, "for those who didn't have the money to buy groceries, there were the FARC: 'here you go, for the groceries'; and also to pay debts. They helped many people."[88] Another reported that "one day they paid for an orchestra to play for two days . . . they killed two cows to give meat to everyone at the party. Who wouldn't gain support in that way?"[89]

THE DEMOCRATIC UNION PARTY

The Democratic Union Party (or Partiya Yekîtiya Demokrat) was founded in 2003 as the Syrian branch of the Kurdistan Community Union, a coalition of Kurdish political movements aligned with the Turkish Kurdistan Workers' Party.[90] When protests against the regime of Bashar al-Assad erupted in Syria in March 2011, the PYD eventually joined.[91] Its aim was to change Syria into a secular, democratic, and pluralistic state with more autonomy for the Kurdish regions.[92] More generally, the PYD's political objectives were to promote a form of decentralization in which the Kurds would enjoy self-rule and implement grassroots democratic participation, self-governance, gender equality, and an ecological society.[93]

In late 2012, the PYD took over Kobane, 'Afrin, 'Amuda, Derik, and parts of Qamishli, across northern Syria. Subsequently, it extended its territorial control to mixed Arab and Kurdish and non-Kurdish territories.[94] In January 2014, the PYD established the cantons of Jazirah (northeastern Syria), Kobane (northern Syria), and 'Afrin (northwestern Syria)—which were referred to as Rojava, the name used historically to designate the Kurdish areas of Syria.[95] In 2016, the region was renamed the Democratic Federation of Northern Syria (DFNS) and in 2018 Autonomous Administration of North and East Syria (AANES).[96] In 2017, the SDF (Syrian Democratic Forces, the military arm of the AANES) conquered Raqqa and Tabqa, in northern Syria, from the Islamic State. (To date, the PYD and the SDF maintain control over large areas of northern and northeastern Syria. However, the observations recorded here on the PYD's governance refer specifically to the period between 2012 and 2022.)

When engaging in governance, the PYD attempted to present itself as privileging universality, including Arabs, Syriacs, Assyrians, Turkmen, Armenians, Chechens, Circassians, Muslims, Christians, Yezidis in its governance project. This is stated explicitly in the 2016 Charter of Social Contract, which promises "fair representation of all ethnic components."[97] In particular, following the creation of the DFNS each region came to include a Kurdish canton and an Arab canton and the Kurdish term "Rojava" was replaced by the more inclusive "Northern Syria."[98] To be sure, however, some observers have accused the PYD of tokenistic inclusiveness and have (not improperly) called the PYD governance system one of "unequal citizenship," given the preeminence of the Kurdish component within it.[99] Where greater agreement is observed is in the recognition that the PYD extended universality to women. Every administrative structure was cochaired by a woman; women parallel institutions were established; and administrative councils assigned a 50 percent quota to women.[100] In other words, throughout PYD-controlled territories women asserted themselves—and were recognized—as political subjects, fighting agents, and self-determining actors.[101]

With respect to civilians, the PYD's Charter of Social Contract seemed to encourage some degree of participation. In 2017, for instance, the population of what was then the DFNS elected the co-chairs of approximately 3,700 communes.[102] At the same time, however, it has been noted that the PYD did not always conform to its democratic ideals.[103] Specifically, local critics and activists have repeatedly accused the PYD's leadership of being authoritarian, illegitimate, and exclusively aimed at increasing its own power.[104] Others have emphasized that positions in the PYD's governance structure were available only to those who played strictly by the group's rules: "the PYD operates like a cult; you are either in or out, there is no place for everyone who thinks differently or who would challenge it or try to hold it accountable."[105]

In terms of generation of compliance, the PYD often relied on noncoercive measures: the promotion of Öcalan's ideology, the display of flags with the colors of the Kurds, and references to a shared Kurdish identity.[106] Furthermore, the PYD resorted to the public commemoration of Kurdish martyrs, the exaltation of the PYD's provision of security—mostly through the People's Defense Units (Yekîneyên Parastina Gel, or YPG)— and the use of the Kurdish national anthem.[107] The provision of benefits such as the participation in administration was also used by the PYD to obtain the allegiance of non-Kurdish communities.[108] Nonetheless, the PYD also opted for coercive methods: arbitrary arrests, attacks on anti-PYD demonstrators, extrajudicial practices of surveillance and control, abuses and threats, forced conscription, deportations, and home demolitions.[109] This was especially the case in Arab-majority areas.[110]

As mentioned above, the PYD included in governance Arab tribal leaders and prominent members of the Arab, Assyrian, and Syriac communities.[111] For instance, in Manbij and Tel Abiyad, northern Syria, tribal leaders were put in charge of administering their cities in return for their allegiance.[112] In the words of a member of the Syriac Military Council in al-Hasakah, northeastern Syria, "we are working under the YPG [People's Defense Units] in order to protect the Syriac community."[113] Following the conquest of Raqqa, the SDF held meetings with local tribal leaders, and when the Raqqa Civil Council was founded it assigned twenty of the council's seats to representatives of local Arab tribes.[114] The co-optation of tribes implemented by the PYD/SDF has been regarded as the most successful experience of this kind in the Syrian Civil War.[115] However, it has also been noted that the external members appointed by the PYD had little more than nominal authority.[116] In fact, a resident from Qamishli,

TABLE 2.4 The model of governance of the Democratic Union Party

Inclusivity	Partial discrimination (non-Kurds de facto relegated to "second-class" status)
Civilian engagement	Partial participation (elections, but accusations of authoritarian rule)
Generation of compliance	Coercion and persuasion (e.g., house demolitions and mobilization of Kurdish symbols)
Approach to outsiders	Partial cooperation (Arab tribal leaders, Syrian government)
Propensity to change	Extensive innovation and limited maintenance (e.g., new multilevel judicial system and maintenance of Syrian laws)

northeastern Syria, reported that the PYD maintained overall decision-making authority, consigning the councils that it established to a largely symbolic role.[117]

The PYD also reached a de facto alliance with the Syrian regime on some matters.[118] For instance, the PYD engaged in smuggling the oil extracted from the PYD-controlled Rumeilan oil fields through regime-controlled areas, and senior engineers and technicians at the Rumeilan power plant were employees of the Syrian state.[119] Furthermore, in al-Hasakah and Qamishli PYD institutions existed and functioned in parallel to those of the state—an arrangement that apparently enabled the PYD to gain significant popular support through effective service provision.[120] According to a businessman from Qamishli, "both the PYD and the regime people work in the same building, each with their own budget. . . . The division of labor implies that while both plan together, the regime pays in some ways and the PYD implements."[121] A resident from the Jazirah region reported that the government was still paying the salaries of civil servants and school teachers.[122]

Interestingly, the PYD also experimented with important innovations. In terms of justice, it introduced a multilevel system including general committees responsible for conflicts and crimes and women's committees responsible for cases of patriarchal violence, forced marriage, and polygamy; people's courts; appeal courts; a regional court; a constitutional court; and a justice parliament. New laws were combined with preexisting

Syrian laws, for those cases that the former could not cover.[123] In schools throughout the AANES education came to be provided in Kurmanji, as well as in Arabic and Syriac. The new curriculum displayed direct references to Öcalan's ideology and sought to reinforce and celebrate Kurdish ethnic identity. To provide services such as water, electricity, and garbage collection, the PYD introduced its own taxation system, whereby it collected fees from its citizens and taxes on construction permits, land, business revenue, cars, agricultural income, border trade, and passage through the AANES.[124]

———⊶∞⊶———

Within the literature on rebel governance, scholars have mostly focused on a few dimensions of governance at a time. Yet, rebel governance is a complex phenomenon characterized by multiple relevant dimensions, and to study it appropriately it is necessary to adopt a multidimensional perspective. To this end, I have proposed a typology of rebel governance that allows us to study and compare different cases of rebel rule with respect to five dimensions—*inclusivity, civilian engagement, generation of compliance, approach to outsiders*, and *propensity to change*. In the specific context of this book, the typology aims to provide a framework through which to study the characteristics of Salafi-jihadist insurgent rule and build systematic comparisons across Salafi-jihadist and non-Salafi-jihadist groups. In this latter regard, I have applied the proposed typology to three cases of rebel rule that I believe are rather representative of non-Salafi-jihadist rebel governance. From the comparison of those groups, I suggest that governance strategies that seem to be more commonly observed across non-Salafi-jihadist rebel rulers include a tendency to avoid utterly discriminatory approaches; a propensity to allow some degree of civilian participation; a preference for the combination of coercion and persuasion, rather than relying predominantly on one of the two alternatives; a tendency to include other actors in matters of governance, especially (though not exclusively) when it comes to the provision of sophisticated public services; and the propensity to combine the introduction of innovative structures and practices of governance with the maintenance of some preexisting ones.

3

SALAFI-JIHADISM AND GOVERNANCE

From Making Jihad to Enforcing Sharia

As I noted in the introduction, following the Arab Spring of 2011 an unprecedented number of Salafi-jihadist armed groups across the Middle East and North Africa exploited the combination of civil war and power vacuum to conquer territories and implement practices and structures of governance. Considering the extent to which Salafi-jihadist groups have been attempting to create their own systems of rule, this book aims to advance our understanding of Salafi-jihadist governance by studying the phenomenon in depth, across several dimensions, and from a comparative perspective. In this chapter, I will introduce Salafi-jihadism and the core notions on which the doctrine rests. I will also present the writings of the most influential Salafi-jihadist ideologues, strategists, and leaders to explain how and why Salafi-jihadism has increasingly developed an interest in territorial acquisition and civilian administration. I will then elaborate a series of expectations as regards the characteristics that Salafi-jihadist rebel governance seems most likely to display if influenced by the tenets of the Salafi-jihadist ideology. The aim is to build a baseline against which to compare specific cases of Salafi-jihadist governance and assess the extent to which ideology has (or has not) been influencing their choices.

SALAFI-JIHADIST IDEOLOGY: *TAWHID,*
AL-WALA' WA-L-BARA', *TAKFIR,* AND JIHAD

Salafism is an ideological movement within Sunni Islamic fundamentalism that promotes a return to the model of public and private life established by the Prophet Muhammad (ca. 570–632) and the *al-salaf al-salih*. Literally meaning "the pious forefathers," the latter term refers to the first three generations of Muslims—namely, the companions of the Prophet, those who followed the companions, and those after the followers of the companions. For this reason, Maher appropriately defines Salafism as an ideology "that believes in progression through regression."[1] Furthermore, Salafism encourages a strict adherence to a literal interpretation of the Quran, the Sunna (the practice of the Prophet), and the hadiths (the collected sayings and actions of the Prophet) as exclusive sources of authority. Conversely, it rejects any man-made law, opposes any *bid'ah* (innovation) of the prophetic model, and condemns *shirk* (idolatry).[2]

Salafism regards modern borders, territories, and countries as artificial creations imposed by non-Islamic powers, while it emphasizes the belonging of all Muslims to the *ummah* and the importance of reuniting the latter within a single Islamic caliphate comprising multiple Islamic emirates.[3] The caliphate is the embodiment of uniquely Islamic notions of territoriality and political order and is the highest political, military, and spiritual authority. It is placed under the rule of a caliph.[4] The emirate, for its part, is placed under the rule of an emir who commands the obedience of his deputies, local commanders, administrators, and all those living within the emirate. He himself, however, is subject to the authority of the caliph.[5]

However, while Salafism embraces a single *'aqidah* (religious creed), there is diversity in terms of *manhaj* (method). On the basis of method, Salafists can be distinguished as either "purists," "politicos," "jihadists"—to follow the typology advanced by Wicktorowicz.[6] Purists propose exclusively nonviolent methods such as *da'wah* (proselytization), *tazkiyah* (purification), and *tarbiyah* (cultivation) and argue that open opposition to the ruler endangers the *ummah*. Politicos believe that they have a moral responsibility to discuss politics and argue that protecting the purity of Islam requires engaging in political activism. Jihadists advocate the use of violence to promote the Salafi creed and believe in politics as warfare.[7]

As explained by Kassim, "the most distinct fissure that sets *jihadi-Salafism* apart from the wider *Salafi* community is the exclusive affirmation of *jihad* as a *manhaj* [methodology] to establish *al-dawlatuh al-Islamiyyah* [Islamic state] as opposed to the quietist Salafis' quintessential accentuation of *tarbiyah* [Islamic education], *tasfiyah* [purification], rejection of various forms of innovation and a return to the seminal texts of the faith as practiced in the Prophet's generation."[8]

Salafi-jihadism is thus a specific school of thought within that universe of Sunni Islamic fundamentalism known as Salafism. It rests on the Salafi creed introduced above, but distinguishes itself by virtue of the following notions: *tawhid, al-wala' wa-l-bara'* , *takfir,* and jihad.[9] While Maher presents *hakimiyah* (sovereignty) and *tawhid* separately, here I discuss the two concepts together, in consideration of the fact that Salafi-jihadists have increasingly connected the two, leading to the notion of *tawhid al-hakimiyah.*

Tawhid ("making one" or "asserting oneness") is traditionally understood as the oneness of God, as captured in the *shahadah* (profession of faith) formula, "there is no God but God and Muhammad is the Messenger of God." Reflecting on the complexity of *tawhid*, the eighteenth-century scholar Muhammad ibn 'Abd al-Wahhab proposed to unpack the notion as follows: *tawhid al-rububiyah,* which is the belief that there is only one God; *tawhid al-uluhiyah,* which is the belief that there is nothing to be worshipped except God; and *tawhid al-asma' was-sifat,* which is the belief in the oneness of God's names and attributes.[10] However, Salafi-jihadists recognize—and attach the greatest importance to—a further category, *tawhid al-hakimiyah.*[11] To be accurate, the notion of *hakimiyah* was not elaborated by contemporary Salafi-jihadists. Already in the tenth century, the Islamic jurist Abu al-Hasan al-Mawardi wrote that "when we say *hakimiyya,* we mean to protect the right of Allah . . . for legislation, judging, and executing the judgements."[12] In the early and mid-twentieth century the Egyptian author and political theorist Sayyid Qutb and the Pakistani scholar and ideologue Sayyid Abul A'la al-Mawdudi called for the establishment of the *hakimiyah* of God in the political system.[13] It was only in the late 1990s that Salafi-jihadists revived the concept, introduced the argument that "*hakimiyya* is directly associated with *tawhid,*" and developed the notion of *tawhid al-hakimiyah.*[14] The latter is the belief in the oneness of Allah's legislation and the belief in the obligation to rule only by what Allah has revealed.[15] In other words, establishing a system of governance that deviates from sharia is a sin. Therefore, rulers who implement man-made laws and civilians who follow man-made laws commit idolatry.[16]

Proceeding with the core notions on which Salafi-jihadism rests, one finds *al-wala' wa-l-bara'* (loyalty and disavowal). As reported by Maher, the concept first emerged as a notion of ritual whereby early Muslims used to distinguish themselves by means of ritual differences (e.g., celebrating different festivals).[17] It was not until the nineteenth century that *al-wala' wa-l-bara'* became a political concept, developed to encourage political mobilization against the enemies of the state.[18] In the words of Wagemakers, "*al-wala' wa-l-bara'* in Salafi discourse developed from a call to Muslims to show their loyalty to Islam by shunning Judeo-Christian influences in worship into a duty for all Muslims to disown everything considered even remotely 'un-Islamic.'"[19] Today, Salafi-jihadists believe that *al-wala' wa-l-bara'* encourages Muslims to build associations exclusively with other members of the (Sunni) Islamic community and to disassociate from non-Muslims, so as to protect the purity and authenticity of Islam. At the same time, they believe that it requires Muslims to resist Muslim rulers who deviate from Islam. In fact, those rulers who fail to live by the teachings derived from *al-wala' wa-l-bara'* are guilty of heresy, and as such must be excommunicated and fought against.[20] More specifically, *al-wala'* has five meanings: to love, support, honor, protect, and respect Allah, the Prophet, and the Muslim community. The notion of *al-bara'* also has five meanings: to hate, abandon, dishonor, renounce, and humiliate the *kuffar* (unbelievers). Importantly, those forms of disavowal can be expressed in different ways, such as staying away from the unbelievers or migrating from the *dar al-kufr* (the lands of non-Muslims) to the *dar al-Islam* (the lands of Islam).[21]

Connected to the exclusivism promoted by *al-wala' wa-l-bara'* is the notion of *takfir*, which denotes the declaration of someone as *kafir* (unbeliever) and the excommunication of that person from the *ummah*. The sharia-based definition of *kufr* (unbelief or disbelief) understands it as the belief in something other than Islam. However, while the use of *takfir* against someone who has openly rejected Islam is uncontroversial, the use of *takfir* against someone who professes Islam but nonetheless engages in sinful behaviors is highly problematic because of the impossibility of knowing the person's real faith.[22] Today, traditional Salafism uses the practice of *takfir* in a cautious way, reserving it exclusively for those who openly reject and insult Islam (e.g., someone who insults the Prophet or desecrates the Quran). Conversely, Salafi-jihadists engage in the practice frequently and loosely, declaring apostates all Muslims who believe in the admissibility of man-made laws, all Muslim rulers who apply laws other than shariatic laws, and all Muslims who do not follow the Salafi-jihadist doctrine.[23] In the classification advanced by Maher, Salafi-jihadists engage in *takfir* against three major categories of people: Muslim rulers who are tyrannical or "apostate" and all those working for their state; criminal transgressors and oppressors; and idolaters and Shia Muslims.[24] In other words, *takfir* is a practice that Salafi-jihadists apply broadly to all those who are considered as deserving *bara'* .[25] The only exceptions seem to be those who convert to Sunni Islam and those Sunni Muslims who undergo *tawbah* (repentance) for their "deviation" from the "righteous" path. In fact, an entire sura of the Quran (*surat al-tawbah*) is devoted to repentance, stating that Allah welcomes the repentance of the disbelievers. Also, according to a hadith "repentance cuts off what came before."[26]

The final key notion is jihad. The translation of jihad is "struggle for the sake of God," and it includes a plurality of meanings, including the struggle against one's carnal soul; the struggle to do Allah's will in everyday life; the struggle to do good in society; and just war. In traditional Islamic jurisprudence, there are two forms of jihad as just war: *jihad al-talab* (offensive jihad), which aims to spread Islam to non-Muslim lands and is a *fard al-kifaya* (communal duty); and *jihad al-dafaʿa* (defensive jihad), which is waged when outside forces invade Muslim lands and is a *fard al-ʿayn* (individual duty). However, contemporary Salafi-jihadists understand jihad exclusively in the latter sense. As such, Salafi-jihadists conceive jihad as a religious duty, an act of worship, and a pillar of Islam comparable to the profession of faith, the five daily prayers, the *zakat* charity tax, the fast of Ramadan, and the pilgrimage to Mecca. For the contemporary Salafi-jihadist movement, jihad in the path of Allah is the pinnacle of Islam because it is through jihad that Islam is protected and advanced.[27] Importantly, *takfir* and jihad often intersect in the Salafi-jihadist thought, in that the designation of someone as infidel justifies waging jihad against them. In the specific case of an infidel ruler, it justifies waging jihad against the regime in order to overthrow it.[28] This marks an important difference with traditional Salafists, who believe that it is possible to accuse of apostasy a ruler and overthrow him only if he purposefully applies non-Islamic laws and declares them superior to Islam.[29] Furthermore, since the 1990s Salafi-jihadists have expanded the targets of jihad to include also the Western regimes (the "far enemy") that allegedly support "apostate" Muslim rulers (the "near enemy").[30]

Following the above discussion, I define Salafi-jihadism as the set of ideas that identifies the *ummah* as its referent group, the defeat of the "apostate" regimes and the creation in their stead of a "pure" sharia-based polity as its desired objective, and jihad as the program of action to reach that objective.[31]

FROM JIHAD TO SHARIA-BASED POLITIES

Salafi-jihadism aims to overthrow the allegedly apostate rulers in Muslim countries and replace them with a sharia-based polity.[32] As noted in the introduction, this sharia-based polity can be diversely conceived as a global caliphate for the entire *ummah*, as a local Islamist state confined to a specific territory, or as a local emirate destined to be subsumed into a wider caliphate. Regardless of the scope of their aspired sharia-based polity, Salafi-jihadists embrace a unique understanding of territoriality whereby religion is the sole criterion to define borders,[33] separating *dar al-kufr* and *dar al-Islam*. It is upon the latter that a polity embodying Allah's spiritual sovereignty and political authority is to be established. Jihad is the instrument through which to abolish the national borders of the contemporary nation-states and realize this "new territorialization."[34]

Importantly, such jihad is meant as an insurgent type of warfare in which the mujahidin (the fighters of jihad) launch a confrontation that is at the same time military, political, and psychological. As argued by Kilcullen, jihad can be thought of as a sui generis form of "global insurgency" that aims to change the status quo through violence and subversion, transform the entire Islamic world, and reforge the relationship between the *ummah* and the rest of the world.[35] This is particularly evident in the works of Salafi-jihadist strategists, ideologues, and commanders such as Ayman al-Zawahiri, Abu Bakr Naji, Abu Mus'ab al-Suri, ʿAbdel ʿAziz al-Muqrin, and Abu ʿUbayd al-Qurashi, who depict jihad in a way that is more similar to the secular insurgencies of the past century than general Western knowledge would expect.[36]

In the late 1990s and early 2000s, al-Zawahiri believed that spectacular military actions, mass-casualty attacks, and suicide bombings served to inspire the *ummah* and recruit Muslim youngsters to the cause of jihad.[37] In his successive writings, however, he proceeded to argue that the most important strategic goal is to seize territorial control, because "without achieving this goal our actions will mean nothing."[38] To do so, jihad, meant as armed warfare, is the answer.[39] However, rather than being an exclusively military effort, jihad must also be accompanied by a process of education and mobilization directed at the mujahidin vanguard as well as the Muslim masses.[40] As al-Zawahiri wrote to the leader of al-Qaeda in Iraq, Abu Musʿab al-Zarqawi, the best weapon in the hands of the mujahidin is the support coming from the Muslim masses. Without such support, the mujahidin would be "crushed in the shadows."[41] Therefore, jihadists must fight for the "hearts and minds" of the *ummah*, and the best way to do so is by performing governance activities—a topic to which al-Zawahiri would return in later writings, as will be discussed below.[42]

Not dissimilarly from al-Zawahiri, and adopting an approach that is reminiscent of Mao's, Abu Bakr Naji argued that, when waging jihad, the support of the masses is fundamental.[43] In his book *Management of Savagery: The Most Critical Stage Through Which the Islamic Nation Will Pass*, he suggested that once the government collapses and a situation of chaos ("savagery," to be precise) emerges, the mujahidin must assert their physical presence and address the people's needs.[44] If the "management of savagery" is successful, the final "establishment of the Islamic state" can take place.[45] Specifically, the mujahidin must preserve internal security and justice; provide food, medical treatment, and education; guarantee security from outside threats; establish sharia as the source of law and justice; establish a fighting society; spread sharia science and worldly science; construct an intelligence agency; enforce sharia government to unite the people; deter hypocrites and force them to repress their hypocrisy, hide their opinions, and comply with the authority; attack the enemy; and establish coalitions "with those with whom coalitions are permitted."[46]

Importantly, in his work Naji referred on more than one occasion to the writings of al-Qurashi, al-Muqrin, and al-Suri, whom he considered fundamental authors.[47] In an article published in the late 1990s under the tile "Revolutionary Wars," al-Qurashi argued that jihad is a revolutionary war fought by the weak against the strong in order to establish a new political, social, and economic structure. Reflecting on this revolutionary war, he adopted a Maoist approach, emphasizing the priority of politics.[48] Al-Qurashi also argued that the primary goal of a revolutionary war is to win the support of the people to gain access to information, food, shelter, and other foundational elements on which to build a successful insurgency. As for the strategies through which support can be secured, he emphasizes the role of governance: "most revolutionary movements spend some time to set up not only the local administration but also parallel governmental institutions which act as pivot point in the struggle for the people's loyalty. These alternative institutions are required to give a degree of legitimacy to the revolutionary army at the same time breaking the government's monopoly on legitimacy."[49]

On a similar note, in his *A Practical Course for Guerrilla Warfare*, al-Muqrin proposed to understand jihad as a revolutionary war aimed at destroying the old system and replacing it with "a pure Islamic system free from defects and infidel elements, . . . based on the Book [Quran] and the Sunnah."[50] Subsequently, he presented jihad as divided in phases that go from hit-and-run attacks, to the establishment of bases and media centers in liberated areas, to definitive territorial control.[51] As the mujahidin bring territories under their control, they should encourage popular support, which is a crucial factor for success insofar as the people can provide money, shelter, intelligence, food, and recruits.[52] To get such support, the mujahidin should introduce a parallel government inclusive of hospitals, sharia courts, and broadcasting stations. By doing so, they will translate military success into political success and replace the regime as legitimate authority.[53]

While Mao exerted significant influence on al-Zawahiri, Naji, al-Qurashi, and al-Muqrin, al-Suri seems to have been more influenced by Guevara. In his most influential work as jihadist strategist, *Call to Global Islamic Resistance*, al-Suri recalled Guevara's notion of a fighting vanguard. From there, he moved on to envision jihadist cells that are neither linked to each other nor part of any broader organization waging operations of urban and rural guerrilla warfare to defeat the enemy.[54] Organized in this way, the ultimate objective of the jihadist resistance would be to conquer physical territory, eliminate the existing regimes, and build an Islamic caliphate (what he calls the "end stage" or "liberation stage").[55]

More recently, in the context of the Arab Spring and the ensuing political turmoil, Salafi-jihadist insurgent leaders have given even greater attention to the challenges and opportunities that arise from governance in times of warfare. As early as 2011, in a letter addressed to the leader of al-Qaeda in the Arabian Peninsula, Nasir al-Wuhayshi, Usama bin Laden, the leader of al-Qaeda at the time, wrote that it is important for the mujahidin to acquire popular support prior to the construction of the Islamic state, and that the masses will support the mujahidin only if the latter prove that they care about their needs, including physical security, financial well-being, food security, and health care.[56] At the same time, however, bin Laden remarked that governance may not always be desirable. Confirming some of the arguments that were advanced in chapter 1 to explain why some rebels may decide not to govern, bin Laden warned the Yemeni mujahidin against attempting to establish a sharia-based polity unless they have the resources and the capacity to maintain control over it.[57] Equally, in a letter addressed to the leader of al-Qaeda in the Islamic Maghreb, 'Abdulmalik Droukdel, bin Laden warned al-Qaeda's Malian affiliate against trying to bring down the Sahelian governments, as an Islamic state should not be declared until the mujahidin had sufficient popular support and resources to govern effectively and meet the demands of its subjects.[58]

Reemphasizing some of his earlier arguments, in 2013 al-Zawahiri argued that "the jihad movement must come closer to the masses . . . work with the masses, preach, [and] provide services for the Muslim people. . . . We must win the people's confidence, respect, and affection."[59] Through these words, al-Zawahiri attempted to encourage within the al-Qaeda network a new way of thinking that recognized the limits of a strategy exclusively centered on jihad as warfare and emphasized the importance of engaging the people in the mujahidin's project by means of political and social activities. On this same line, the leader of Jabhat al-Nusra, Abu Muhammad al-Julani, openly defended the importance of engaging in activities that aid civilians in their basic needs. Among those, al-Julani mentioned administration of ovens and bakeries, provision of health care, engagement in reconstruction activities, delivery of security and order, and provision of mechanisms of dispute resolution.[60] According to al-Julani, only by providing the people with the public services and goods that the government is unable (or unwilling) to provide is it possible to gain the popular support needed to establish an Islamic emirate.[61]

Learning from bin Laden's advice and from his own experience in Yemen, al-Wuhayshi eventually inserted himself in the shift that occurred within Salafi-jihadism as its leaders realized that if they want to hold territory, they must learn how to govern it. In this regard, he wrote to his counterpart in Mali to share his observations on why Salafi-jihadist governance is needed and what forms it should take. In the first of two letters that he wrote in mid-2012 to Droukdel, al-Wuhayshi emphasized that, by providing governance, jihadists can obtain the support that is needed to build and maintain an Islamic emirate.[62] He also went deeper, suggesting that the mujahidin "try to win them [the people] over through the conveniences of life and by taking care of their daily needs like food, electricity and water. Providing these necessities will have a great effect on people and will make them sympathize with us and feel that their fate is tied to ours."[63]

Following bin Laden and al-Wuhayshi's recommendations, Droukdel wrote in a letter most likely authored in early July 2012 that ruling territories is of primary importance to jihadists and that this needs to be done in a constructive way.[64] Specifically, he urged his addressees to "gradually introduce sharia laws, not hasten to punish people, provide security and services, and consult elders and leaders amongst the people."[65] He also recommended that they abandon rivalries with other movements, integrate the mujahidin into the local tribes and society, proselytize al-Qaeda's version of Islam to local populations, adopt moderate rhetoric, emphasize the local nature of al-Qaeda, and refrain from declaring *takfir*.[66]

Over the past two decades, Salafi-jihadists have thus been devoting increasing attention to the subject of governance, considering the establishment of practices and structures of civilian administration a central component of their broader insurgent effort.[67] Even though the attention devoted to matters of governance is still considerably inferior compared to that devoted to warfare, Salafi-jihadists recognize governance as an effective (albeit not the only) strategy to obtain the popular support that the mujahidin need to establish and maintain sharia-based sociopolitical systems and to gain credibility, trust, and legitimacy as rulers—both in themselves and vis-à-vis the "apostate" alternatives.

HOW SALAFI-JIHADIST IDEOLOGY IS EXPECTED TO SHAPE SALAFI-JIHADIST GOVERNANCE

Having discussed the tendency of Salafi-jihadists to recognize the provision of governance to the civilian population as a crucial component of their wider jihad against "apostate" regimes, in this section I will invoke the ideological tenets of Salafi-jihadism that were previously introduced to outline a series expectations on the features that a system of rebel rule would be most likely to display if it was shaped according to, and as an embodiment of, Salafi-jihadist ideology. While doing so, I will refer to the five dimensions of my proposed typology, as illustrated in table 3.1.

As presented above, one of the core notions on which the Salafi-jihadist school of thought rests is that of *tawhid al-hakimiyah*. Driven by this notion, the great majority of Salafi-jihadists interpret the caliphate as a model of governance in which civilians are not entitled to participate in politics, contribute to decision-making processes, influence how the polity is run, and dissent from authority (unless the latter deviates from the path indicated by Allah in the scriptures).[68] Elections, in particular, are seen as a heretical process of innovation inspired by secular political systems that de facto transfers authority from Allah to the people, thus contradicting the principle of absolute and exclusive divine sovereignty.[69] Scholarly attempts to link the Islamic notion of *shura* (consultation) with the Western notion of democracy are often condemned by the Salafi-jihadists as unfounded and misleading.[70] Therefore, I expect that a Salafi-jihadist armed group that conquers territories and establishes a system of governance inspired by Salafi-jihadist doctrine will treat civilians as subjects.

The notion of *tawhid al-hakimiyah* can also inform expectations with respect to the approach to preexisting institutions and personnel. Following *tawhid al-hakimiyah*, Salafi-jihadists aspire to enforce God's law on earth and recreate what they regard as the sublime model of public and private life developed by the Prophet and his immediate successors. Therefore, I expect that a Salafi-jihadist armed group aiming to recreate that model will refrain from maintenance when engaging in governance. In fact, maintaining the structures and practices of rule that used to be in place under the previous regime would imply the acceptance of the system implemented by "apostate" leaders, which in turn would amount to a betrayal of *tawhid al-hakimiyah*. In other words, I expect that Salafi-jihadist rebel rulers committed to applying their ideology will annihilate everything that existed prior to their surge to power and will introduce extensive innovations that will serve as the foundations of a new and "pure" sociopolitical system. The only exception might be represented by the personnel employed by the previous regime. In fact, considering the value attributed to *tawbah*, Salafi-jihadists might opt to maintain in their workplaces those individuals who repent and serve the new sharia-based regime. Thus, Salafi-jihadist insurgent rulers may either replace former employees with trusted members and loyalists, or they may maintain former employees on condition that they repent and pledge *bay'ah* (allegiance) to the new polity.

Having in mind those activities of governance that I discussed in the first chapter, I also advance the following expectations. As far as the provision of justice is concerned, Salafi-jihadists can be expected to abolish any secular legal system and replace it with one in which sharia is the sole source of legislation. As noted above, in the Salafi-jihadist doctrine, ruling by anything other than God's laws and replacing sharia law with secular laws is a major deviation, and *takfir* can be declared against a ruler following this path.[71] In the writings of Salafi-jihadist authors, in fact, the preeminence of sharia is a dominant theme,[72] revealing the extent to which, in their eyes, "legitimacy can be conferred only through the adoption of Islamic law."[73] According to al-Zawahiri, for instance, when the mujahidin succeed in establishing an emirate, no concession will have to be made "in the laws of the Sharia."[74] As part of the broader process of innovation, taxes would be introduced that are sanctioned by Islamic law. These would include taxes such as *zakat* (mentioned above as one of the five pillars of Islam), *jizyah* (poll tax for non-Muslims of monotheistic faiths), *khums* (in Sunni Islam, a tax on spoils of war), *kharaj* (a tax on land), and *'ushr* (a tax on harvest). Public behavior will also be regulated according to the Salafi-jihadists' literal interpretation of the Quran, the Sunna, and the hadiths, which informs their understanding of what an ideal, "pure" Islamic society looks like.

Another fundamental concept on which Salafi-jihadism rests is *al-wala' wa-l-bara'* . Referring to this notion, I expect that ruling Salafi-jihadist insurgents will exclude from their governance system all those who do not share the doctrine of Salafi-jihadism and who, as such, are regarded as deserving *bara'* .[75] In other words, I suggest here that

Salafi-jihadist groups would be more willing to engage in governance in isolation, rather than in cooperation with other actors (whether individuals or groups). The exception may be like-minded Salafi-jihadist groups as well as individuals and groups that pledge *bayʿah* to the Salafi-jihadist polity. Additionally, the notion of *al-walaʾ wa-l-baraʾ* as understood by Salafi-jihadists can help to formulate expectations with respect to the understanding of who is a legitimate subject of the desired Salafi-jihadist polity. In this regard, I expect that Salafi-jihadist rebel rulers will make of Islam the exclusive criterion by which to decide whom to include in (and exclude from) their desired polity, as evidenced also by the dichotomic distinction between *dar al-Islam* and *dar al-kufr*.[76] In other words, they will adopt a discriminatory approach that considers Muslims the only legitimate subjects of their desired polity, while excluding all non-Muslims. In this latter respect, it is also relevant to note that a basic distinction is made by Islamists between two categories of people. On the one hand, there are those who are considered "apostates," including Shia Muslims, and thus to be fought until they convert or until they are killed, enslaved, or expelled. On the other hand, there are the *ahl al-Kitab* ("the people of the Book," the communities that possess the holy books revealed by God prior to the Quran). These are *dhimmis* (protected persons), and as such they should be guaranteed life, property, freedom of movement, and freedom of religious practice.[77] Under no circumstance, however, are the "people of the Book" entitled to membership in the *ummah*.[78]

Furthermore, I expect that, given the Salafi-jihadist literal and decontextualized reference to the Quran, the Sunna, and the hadiths, Salafi-jihadist rebel rulers will discriminate among civilians also according to gender. In fact, while stories of influential women are not missing in Islam, the Salafi-jihadists' literal reading of Islam's foundational texts encourages an understanding of men and women as equal in terms of belief but different in terms of societal functions and moral obligations.[79] Driven by the aspiration to revive the ways of public life that prevailed at the time of the Prophet and the *al-salaf al-salih*, Salafi-jihadism attempts to replicate as closely as possible the roles that they believe the Quran and the hadiths define for women in a pure and perfect Islamic society.[80] For instance, the twentieth-century Palestinian ideologue ʿAbdallah ʿAzzam, whose thought influenced subsequent generations of Salafi-jihadists, including Usama bin Laden, argued that women should always be accompanied by a *mahram* (a male guardian) and that their role should be

TABLE 3.1 The expected model of Salafi-jihadist governance as shaped by Salafi-jihadist ideology

Inclusivity	Discrimination (non-Muslims, non-Sunnis, women)
Civilian engagement	Subjection (rejection of democratic process)
Generation of compliance	Extensive coercion and limited persuasion (e.g., full range of *hudud* punishments and some persuasive measures, such as fatwas and *da'wah*)
Approach to outsiders	Exclusion or partial exclusion (exclusion of non-Sunnis and non-Salafi-jihadists, but possible cooperation with other Salafi-jihadists and individuals or groups who pledge *bay'ah*)
Propensity to change	Extensive innovation and limited maintenance (e.g., new sharia-based judicial system and maintenance of employees who engage in *tawbah* and pledge *bay'ah*)

confined to cooking, nursing, and similar activities.[81] Prior to 'Azzam, Sayyid Qutb prescribed that women belong to the domestic sphere and that the education system should reflect those roles, so as not to remove women from the "the natural aim of . . . life" and not to sacrifice women "on the altar of knowledge and labour."[82]

Finally, a fundamental tenet of Salafi-jihadism that needs to be considered is *takfir*. Once someone is accused of apostasy, punishment is a religious duty according to the Salafi-jihadists. Following the Salafi-jihadists' literal interpretation of the Quran and the hadiths, legitimate punishments against the infidels and those who deviate from the "right" path and from "righteous" conduct include the *hudud* punishments such as lashing, hand amputation, crucifixion, and stoning to death.[83] Therefore, I expect that when a Salafi-jihadist insurgent group engages in governance to create a polity that embodies the tenets of Salafi-jihadism, it will not refrain from extensively coercive practices in order to generate compliance with its allegedly pure Salafi-jihadist system of rule and punish any deviation therefrom. More specifically, I expect coercion to be employed against all those civilians accused of apostasy for committing acts that the Salafi-jihadist rulers regard as sinful.

At the same time, however, the sociopolitical model that Salafi-jihadists aspire to recreate is one in which obedience was created also through some

institutions and practices—such as the fatwas (legal opinions) of authoritative and respected figures—aimed at offering guidance on correct religious and social practices and encouraging civilians to internalize certain norms of behavior. In this regard, it is also interesting to refer to Naji,
who argued that the civilians' acceptance of the Salafi-jihadists' rule needs
to be transformed into active and genuine support through activities such
as da'wah that aim to increase the people's faith in the Salafi-jihadist ruling group, its sociopolitical project, and its ideology.[84] Therefore, when a
Salafi-jihadist insurgent group engages in governance, I expect that it will
employ extensive coercive practices but also certain noncoercive measures
aimed at persuading civilians.

Salafi-jihadism is an ideology associated with Sunni Islam according to
which the ummah needs to be reunited in a polity governed by sharia and
inspired by the sociopolitical model established by the Prophet. To achieve
this goal, jihad is the preferred, yet not the only, way. Importantly, Salafi-
jihadist strategists derive inspiration from insurgent leaders of the past
century from a variety of contexts and understand jihad in a way that goes
beyond exclusive military activities and also includes activities of governance aimed at achieving popular support and legitimacy. As far as those
activities of governance are concerned, reference to the core notions of
Salafi-jihadism allows us to infer a series of expectations on the characteristics that Salafi-jihadist governance is likely to display if decisions are
shaped by ideology. Importantly, these expectations aim to offer a baseline against which I will compare specific cases of Salafi-jihadist governance to determine whether and to what extent they are influenced by
ideology. Different Salafi-jihadist groups, in fact, might follow ideology
to different (even considerably different) extents in their practice as rebel
rulers, as was noted by Revkin and Wood when they argued that "organizations vary in their effectiveness [and, I add, willingness] in implementing their ideological programs."[85]

4

RESTORING THE CALIPHATE IN SYRIA AND IRAQ

The Governance Project of the Islamic State

A mong the Salafi-jihadist armed groups to emerge in the past decade as providers (or aspiring providers) of governance, the Islamic State has achieved the greatest notoriety, with its governance project attracting attention—and arousing concern—well beyond scholarly and policymaking circles. Despite having been written off in 2010 as a relic organization following the elimination of its top leaders,[1] in 2014 the Islamic State of Iraq and al-Sham (ISIS, as the group was then called) became a household name worldwide, a fact that attests to the success of its new leadership's strategy. With the images and videos of its brutality broadcast all over the world, terms such as "sharia," "caliphate," and "apostate" became familiar to an unprecedented number of people. Considering the enormous impact that the Islamic State's governance experience has had on the Middle East and beyond, in this chapter I will investigate the group's behavior as ruler. I will start by reviewing IS's transition from insurgency to civilian administration. I will then investigate the specific governance strategies that IS adopted referring to the five dimensions of governance of my proposed typology. As the Islamic State's capacity to engage in governance decreased dramatically with the progressive loss of territory, I will apply my typology to the period between 2014 and 2017, when IS controlled vast areas of Syria and Iraq. It is in those years and in those territories, in fact, that one can identify the group's governance patterns. While the group also extended its influence to Libya,

Algeria, Tunisia, Sinai, Yemen, Nigeria, Afghanistan, the Caucasus, Bangladesh, and the Philippines, in this chapter I will limit my investigation to the areas of Syria and Iraq where IS declared its caliphate in June 2014. In fact, the various provinces that IS proclaimed outside of Syria and Iraq were administered by local groups that pledged allegiance to IS's leader, Abu Bakr al-Baghdadi, but that nonetheless displayed a certain degree of autonomy, which limits the contribution that the study of those provinces can make to understanding how IS governed.[2]

FROM INSURGENCY TO GOVERNANCE

The Islamic State has its origins in a group known as Jama'at al-Tawhid wal-Jihad that was founded in 1999 by the Jordanian Abu Mus'ab al-Zarqawi, a veteran of the mujahidin war against the Soviets in Afghanistan. When the United States invaded Iraq in March 2003 to overthrow Saddam Hussein, al-Zarqawi's group decided to focus its operations on Iraq. In October 2004, al-Zarqawi pledged allegiance to bin Laden's al-Qaeda and rebranded his group as al-Qaeda in the Land of the Two Rivers, or al-Qaeda in Iraq.[3] The alliance has been described as a marriage of convenience: al-Zarqawi's group needed bin Laden's blessing to enhance its stature within the Iraqi insurgency and gain legitimacy within the Salafi-jihadist universe, while al-Qaeda needed a charismatic and efficient leader on the ground in Iraq.[4]

Al-Qaeda in Iraq rapidly became one of the most active participants in the Sunni insurgency against the American occupation and one of the biggest magnets for foreign fighters.[5] Its influence grew further after it united with five other Sunni jihadist groups under an umbrella organization known as the Mujahidin Shura Council. As leader of that body, al-Zarqawi increased attacks against Iraqi Shias to escalate intercommunal tensions and encourage the Sunni community to support his insurgency.[6] Those attacks were taking place in the background of Iraq's new political context, characterized by the execution of Saddam, the purge from Iraqi state institutions of members of Saddam's Baath Party, and the instalment of a new Shia-led government under Nuri al-Maliki.[7]

In 2006, al-Zarqawi was killed. The group was placed under the leadership of Abu Ayyub al-Masri and Abu 'Umar al-Baghdadi and was rebranded the Islamic State of Iraq (ISI), a clearer reference to the group's ultimate goal. In that same year, ISI managed to assert its control over a large portion of territories in Anbar Governorate, in western Iraq.[8] In April 2007, ISI announced a new governance apparatus and appointed a series of ministers—minister of war, minister of public relations, minister of security, minister of information, minister of martyrs' affairs, minister of petroleum, minister of agriculture, and minister of health.[9] However, ISI's institutions amounted to little more than a "paper state,"[10] and the group had neither the willingness nor the capacity to provide for the population's needs.[11] Its disinterest in activities that would benefit the local population, coupled with its authoritarian attitude toward Iraqi Sunni tribes, its questionable methods of financial extraction (e.g., car theft, smuggling, looting), and its imposition of codes of conduct that were alien to local customs ultimately encouraged popular discontent.[12] With American support, local tribes rose up against the group and expelled it from the region.[13] As noted above, when al-Masri and al-Baghdadi were killed in 2010, ISI seemed doomed to dissolution.

However, a major turning point in the life of the group was to take place. Abu Bakr al-Baghdadi—a Sunni scholar and former inmate at Camp Bucca, the internment facility managed by American armed forces near Umm Qasr, in southern Iraq—became leader. Shortly after, he strengthened ISI's internal bonds, reintroduced a centralized leadership, and simplified the inefficient bureaucratic apparatus that had prevailed during the previous phase.[14] At the same time, al-Baghdadi instrumentalized Sunni exclusion from the government to present ISI as the only option available to Iraq's Sunni community to retrieve power, relevance, and influence in Iraqi affairs. He even co-opted into his group former members of the Baath Party who had been excluded and humiliated under al-Maliki and collaborated with nationalist Baathist groups that had strong support bases in the rural areas of northern and western Iraq.[15]

Furthermore, as Syria collapsed into civil war, al-Baghdadi progressively expanded the group's original ambitions and came to identify in the Sunni heartland encompassing western Iraq and eastern Syria the ideal location of his desired Islamic state—hence the adoption of the name of Islamic State of Iraq and al-Sham in April 2013.[16] At the military level, al-Baghdadi calibrated different strategies for Syria and Iraq. In Syria, he sent a small exploratory contingent of fighters under the command of Abu Muhammad al-Julani that was named Jabhat al-Nusra,[17] as I will discuss in more detail in the next chapter. In Iraq, in July 2012 ISI launched Operation "Destroying the Walls," which was aimed at releasing captured group members.[18] Moreover, between 2012 and 2013 the group engaged in various attacks employing vehicle-borne improvised explosive devices, suicide vests, and mortars and carried out prison breaks in Tikrit, Kirkuk, Taji, and Abu Ghraib.[19] In July 2013, ISIS launched another operation, "The Soldiers' Harvest," whereby it increased the volume and frequency of its attacks against critical infrastructure.[20]

In the context of this unexpected resurgence, al-Baghdadi's group succeeded in conquering territories in both Syria and Iraq.[21] In Syria, it brought under its control the governorate of Raqqa, northern Syria, in March 2013 and the governorate of Deir ez-Zor, eastern Syria, in May 2014. Importantly, this territory included over 80 percent of Syria's oil fields and much of its agricultural land. It also captured Palmyra, in central Syria, Dabiq, in northern Syria, and territories in Aleppo Governorate, in northwestern Syria.[22] In Iraq, ISIS conquered Mosul, the capital of the northwestern Nineveh Governorate, in June 2014. On June 29, al-Baghdadi proclaimed the Islamic State, or caliphate, as a new political entity to which the whole *ummah* should pledge allegiance.[23] Afterward, IS extended its control to Tikrit, Ramadi, and Hit, in central Iraq, parts of Kirkuk and Bayji, in northern Iraq, and Tel 'Afar, in northwestern Iraq.[24] In August, it also conquered the Kurdish- and Yezidi-majority areas of Sinjar, Zumar, Mosul Dam, and Makhmour, in northern Iraq.[25] By then, IS was controlling 95,000 square-kilometers of territory across eastern Syria and western Iraq.[26]

The group then proceeded to engage in governance, thus transforming into what has been called an "emerging state actor"[27] or a "pseudo state."[28] However, before moving to investigate how IS ruled, it should be emphasized that important differences in the effectiveness and extent of governance were observed throughout the group's territory: While in governorates such as Nineveh and Raqqa IS managed to establish the full array of governing institutions, in governorates such as Homs, Aleppo, and Kirkuk, its rule did not go beyond basic functions.[29]

THE MODEL OF GOVERNANCE OF
THE ISLAMIC STATE

Having reviewed the process whereby IS transited from being a traditional insurgent group to governing large areas in western Iraq and eastern Syria, I will investigate the group's governance strategies.

INCLUSIVITY

As ruler, IS adopted "a narrow definition of who was included in [the group's] social contract" and enforced a highly discriminatory approach toward civilians based on religious identity.[30] Specifically, IS embraced an exclusionary interpretation of the concept of *'asabiyah* (kinship within the context of political organization) that regards only Sunni Muslims as legitimate subjects of its caliphate.[31] As a matter of fact, article 4 of IS's *watiqat al-madinah* ("document of the city," issued in Hit, Raqqa, and Mosul) stated that "funds will be spent in the *maslahah* (public interest) of the *Muslims* [emphasis added],"[32] while no reference was made to the non-Muslim communities living in IS-controlled territories and their public interest.

With respect to non-Muslim civilians, IS distinguished between "original disbelievers"—that is, people born in a religion other than Islam—and "apostates"—people who were born Muslim but either left the faith or embraced creeds, ideologies, and behaviors that IS regarded as deviating from "true" Islam.[33] "Original disbelievers" who belonged to the "people of the Book" were considered second-class subjects, allowed to live in the caliphate while retaining their faith as long as they accepted special obligations and restrictions. In July 2014, for instance, IS issued an ultimatum to Christians in Mosul whereby they were given the choice to convert, pay *jizyah*, or die.[34] Similarly, in a document published in Raqqa, Christians were urged to pay *jizyah*, accept the morality laws imposed by IS, refrain from building new churches and repairing existing ones, abandon the display of crosses and public prayer, and cease trading in pork and alcohol.[35]

In October 2014, a picture was posted on Twitter in which an IS fighter was purportedly guarding a church, with a caption reading, "A church under the protection of soldiers of the Islamic State . . . After [Christians] paid the *jizya*."[36] While the reality was not as positive as this picture might suggest, Syrians living in Raqqa reported that Christians who accepted the terms of the *jizyah* contract could avoid physical harm.[37] However, even for those who agreed to stay in their towns according to IS's terms, life was extremely hard. In the words of a fifty-seven-year-old man who lived under IS in Tel Abiyad, in northern Syria, "[for Christians] it wasn't life. I was in my home, and it was like a grave. I left my grave every day in the morning, just to go to the supermarket, buy what I need, and go back to my grave."[38]

Greater persecution and violence was reserved for "original disbelievers" who did not belong to the "people of the Book," such as the Yezidis in Iraq, who became victims of genocide under IS.[39] As a religious minority with roots in ancient, pre-Zoroastrian Iranic religions, the Yezidis were considered by IS "a pagan minority [whose] continual existence to this day is a matter that Muslims should question as they will be asked about it on Judgement Day."[40] As such, they were forced to choose between conversion to Sunni Islam or death.[41] Yezidi men and boys were systematically killed, while children were sent to IS training camps. A girl who was sixteen at the time of the massacre in Iraq's Mount Sinjar recounted that IS forced all women and children to witness the beheading of Yezidi men.[42] A Yezidi boy reported being kidnapped, forced to witness violence, and indoctrinated into fighting against the "apostates."[43]

Yezidi women, for their part, were abducted and sold in *sabayah* (slave) markets throughout the caliphate.[44] IS even published a disturbing document listing the rules to be followed when selling and buying slaves and the prices to be applied: $500 for girls between 1 and 5 years of age, $1,000 for girls between 6 and 10, $1,500 for girls between 11 and 12.[45] Once enslaved, Yezidi girls were victims of sexual abuse, violence, and forced conversion to Islam.[46] As bravely recounted by a Yezidi woman who was enslaved and sold multiple times, the IS members in whose houses she was forced to live regularly beat her, raped her, and abused her.[47] Another Yezidi girl reported that "he [the IS member who claimed her as *sabayah*] told me that according to Islam he is allowed to rape an unbeliever. He said that by raping me, he is drawing closer to God."[48]

Discrimination was also acute against Shia Muslims, whom IS considered apostates. For instance, the late IS spokesman Abu Muhammad al-ʿAdnani incited Sunnis against Shias in the following terms: "O Sunnis of Iraq, the time has come for you to learn the lessons of the past and to learn that nothing will work with the *rafidah* ["rejectors," a pejorative term used by some Sunnis to designate the Shias] other than slicing their throats and striking their necks. . . . They plot and conspire against [the Sunnis], and they trick and deceive them."[49] The thirteenth issue of IS's *Dabiq* magazine also argued that Shias "must be killed wherever they are" because they worship graves, follow the twelve imams in an act amounting to polytheism, and reject the Prophet's companions.[50] Throughout Iraq, members of Shia communities were systematically executed or kidnapped.[51] In June 2014, for instance, IS executed between 1,095 and 1,700 Shia cadets from the Iraqi Army in the Camp Speicher massacre.[52] Likewise, a young Christian boy from Bartalla, in northern Iraq, reported that IS forced him to witness the execution of a Shia man who had refused to convert to Sunni Islam.[53]

Furthermore, non-Muslims and non-Sunnis were often expelled from their houses by means of force and had their properties and their belongings expropriated. To ease identification, IS marked the properties of Christians with the letter *nun* (ن) for the Arabic word *Nasrani* (Christian) and the properties of Shias with the letter *ra* (ر) for the Arabic word *Rafidah*.[54] IS would then confiscate those houses and plots of lands, place them under the jurisdiction of its Diwan al-ʿAqarat wa al-Kharaj (Department of Real Estate and Land Tax) and Diwan al-Ziraʿa (Department of Agriculture and Livestock), and rent them to IS members and Sunni civilians.[55] One Christian woman from Mosul reported that her house was confiscated by IS, marked, and her possessions thrown away.[56]

Additionally, churches, Shia mosques, and other non-Sunni centers of prayer were subjected to destruction and pillaging.[57] The second issue of *Dabiq* displays a chapter entirely devoted to this matter, with pictures of several non-Sunni buildings blown up across Nineveh Governorate.[58] In Raqqa in 2013, IS attacked three churches and converted another into an office for IS's proselytization.[59] In May 2014, the Uwais al-Qarni Shia mosque in Raqqa was destroyed and Shiite tombs were desecrated.[60] IS also systematically destroyed Yezidi shrines and heritage sites, in acts that were meant "to cleanse the region of the physical manifestations of the Yezidi community as a whole."[61]

An interesting example of IS's discriminatory practices was directed toward the Kurds.[62] According to IS's proclamations, no distinction is made between Muslims on the basis of ethnicity. In the words of IS's Media Office, "the Sunni Kurds are our brothers in God . . . we will not allow any one of them to be harmed so long as they remain on the principle of Islam."[63] This, however, was not always the case as the reality often differed from the rhetoric. As the Kurdish-dominated YPG emerged as the leading force in the fight against IS in northern Syria and established an alliance with the United States and the international coalition forces, IS's suspicion and discrimination extended also to Muslim Kurds living in its territories. In June 2015, IS urged Kurds in Raqqa Governorate to depart within seventy-two hours, as it believed that some of them had cooperated with its enemies. The group urged those departing to register their property with the Department of Real Estate and Land Tax to show that they were Muslim and prevent their properties from being confiscated.[64]

Finally, another line of discrimination observed within the caliphate was based on gender and was directed against women, from the earliest stages of life until late adulthood. Starting in school, everyone had to study a strictly religiously oriented curriculum, as will be discussed below. However, girls were also trained in domestic skills such as caring for the house, raising children, sewing, and cooking.[65] This was meant to prepare girls for their future roles as wives and mothers and for a life exclusively centered around the domestic space. Furthermore, girls at times were not allowed to study beyond the first grades or were excluded altogether from certain institutes. For instance, a college for sharia sciences that was opened by IS in Nineveh Governorate accepted applications exclusively from male students.[66]

The dress code was much stricter for women than for men. While the latter were mostly required to wear trousers above the ankle, refrain from Western clothes, and grow a beard, women from a very young age were required to cover themselves entirely with a black niqab and abaya,[67] cover their eyes with a thin cloth, and wear gloves and thick socks.[68] In the words of a married woman from Mosul, "IS is very strict about the dress code for women. Women have to be fully covered up in black head to toe," to the point that they are "concealed in a sea of blackness."[69] Another woman complained that as a result of IS's regulations women became "invisible."[70]

A woman who fled from IS-controlled Manbij, in northeastern Syria, described her clothing being scrutinized at multiple checkpoints as she moved about the town and reported that "you can hardly see your way. . . . I fell many times. It is hard to breathe. You are walking in the street but it feels like a prison cell."[71]

While gender segregation applied to women and men alike, women were increasingly prevented from leaving their house without a *mahram*.[72] As argued by a woman who lived under IS, "every time I went out into the streets, I feared for my life. . . . One day, talking to a male shopkeeper was okay; the next you had to ask your male escort, a family member, to do it for you."[73] Being prohibited from leaving their houses unless accompanied by a close male relative, women without husbands, brothers, or sons found themselves in an extremely vulnerable situation whereby the simple act of going out to buy food or medicines was a risk. Interestingly, even between women there were discriminations informed by age. For instance, women aged fifty and above were allowed to travel without a *mahram* and reportedly faced less pressure to wear the niqab.[74]

CIVILIAN ENGAGEMENT

At the beginning, in places such as Deir ez-Zor and Raqqa, IS reportedly established grievances offices to receive complaints from civilians about IS members and collect suggestions and feedback from the people regarding the group's governance.[75] In Tel Abyad in 2014, a notification invited the people to express their grievances toward members of IS and set Thursday as the day on which such grievances would be received.[76]

However, while initially there may have been complaints bodies where civilians in (at least some) IS-controlled territories could express their dissatisfaction with the group's performance, it is doubtful that people could truly refer to them without fear of repercussions. This concern seems to be especially relevant given the group's propensity toward the use of violence—a topic that will be discussed below. As has been noted, in fact, IS acted as an organization that left "no room for political, religious, or civil dissent."[77] Furthermore, IS did not establish any real apparatus for the inclusion of civilians in its overall decision-making process. The various departments of the Islamic State ruled unilaterally, with no possibility for civilians to take part in them or to influence them in any significant way. Rather, civilians were the passive addressees of IS's decisions and were placed "into a subordinate position."[78] As noted, "civilians were in no way free to make any decision in matters of governance, or any other matters actually."[79] A humanitarian worker with extensive experience working in Syria also reported that IS's governance decisions were never taken with the people's participation.[80]

During his inaugural speech from the Grand Mosque of Mosul, al-Baghdadi invited the people to advise him if wrong and to disobey him if deviant from God's path,[81] in accordance with the practice of the early Islamic caliphs. However, there was never a mechanism for civilians to select, oust, or rein in the supreme leader, his commanders, and his officials. The Islamic State, in fact, rejected democracy and popular rule as a Western political concept that assigns sovereignty to men rather than to God and that, as such, is in contradiction with Islam and with the Salafi-jihadi *ʿaqidah*.[82] As argued by al-ʿAdnani, democracy is a Western idea that contradicts the Islamic religion and creed: "If, by Allah, you do not believe in democracy, secularism, nationalism and all the other rubbish and ideas from the West and instead adhere to your religion and your creed, then by Allah you will own the earth, and the east and the west will submit to you."[83]

It is thus unsurprising that IS's *watiqat al-madinah* lists the rights of civilians as the right to justice and due process of law, the right to security, and the right to IS's public goods and services. Conversely, no mention is made of the right to participation in governance.[84] Excluded from governance, civilians had no right to voice their preferences and choose their representatives.[85] As a result, "the Islamic State's social contract"—meant as a relationship of reciprocal duties between a ruling authority and the population that it governs—was "authoritarian and asymmetric."[86]

GENERATION OF COMPLIANCE

At the very onset of its governance experience, IS seemed to be adopting a somewhat moderate approach. A woman who returned to Mosul with her family shortly after IS captured the city said that "they [IS's fighters] aren't harming people."[87] Another resident of Mosul expressed a similar view one week after IS took over the city, saying that the streets were calm and that "they are not making any problems with the local people. ISIS only came for the army."[88] The son of a prominent tribal leader from Kirkuk also commented in those early days that "Sunnis now feel more safe, much more than before."[89]

Over the months, however, IS's coercive practices became ever more repressive and strict,[90] and the group resorted to "extreme violence—terror—as a tool."[91] As argued by the UN Special Rapporteur on the promotion and protection of human rights and fundamental freedoms while countering terrorism, "the brutal nature and overall scale of abuses [perpetrated by IS] appears to be intended to reinforce the group's absolute monopoly on political and social life and to enforce compliance and conformity among communities under its control."[92] Throughout the territories under IS's control, people were being constantly intimidated through harsh corporal punishments, arbitrary arrests, and public executions, to the point that they "were frightened" and "afraid of doing anything for the risk of execution."[93] In Raqqa, for instance, coercion became a major component of the group's governance machine, creating a situation whereby popular compliance was obtained through fear. In Iraq's Makhmur District, in the governorate of Nineveh, IS ruled for twenty-one months by means of summary executions, torture, and collective punishment of villagers.[94] In Mosul, beheadings and floggings became routine.[95] As reported by a Mosuli man, people lived in fear of "breaking one of their [IS's] rules, even by accident."[96]

IS's coercive measures varied in severity according to the violation committed and included monetary fines, arrests, physical punishments, and executions. For instance, IS's fines included $30 for a woman not wearing socks or gloves, $10 for a woman who showed her eyes, $25 for a person caught smoking cigarettes, $50 for a person installing a satellite dish.[97] A man from Syria also reported that he had to pay a very high fine for being caught price gouging.[98] In the case of more serious violations, however, alleged transgressors had not only to pay fines but were also required to hand over their ID cards; they would then have to appear before religious officials and pledge not to commit the offense again.[99] Beyond fines, punishments of a nonmonetary nature were also common. Shops that were kept open during prayer time were closed and people selling or using prohibited devices and products had them confiscated.[100] A man in Deir ez-Zor Governorate was arrested and had his property and lands confiscated for a period of two years because he had not paid *zakat*.[101] A man who used to transport perishables from Jordan to an IS-controlled part of Iraq reported that if he refused or failed to pay the import tax required by IS, the group would burn his truck or even arrest him.[102]

Harsh physical punishments were also a widespread reality throughout the caliphate, with the full range of *hudud* punishments being implemented.[103] A young man from Mosul reported that his brother was punished with twenty lashes for failing to close his shop during prayer.[104] A woman who admitted having served in IS's female morality police (an institution that will be discussed further below) said that women found in violation of morality norms were arrested and brought to a police station where they were tortured.[105] Another woman who worked in the same police force reported witnessing the whipping of a woman and her daughter who had been caught wearing "tight" clothes and makeup.[106] In another case, a woman recounted that she was condemned to twenty-one lashes for lifting the *khimar* (the fabric covering a woman's face) in public to eat.[107] According to a young man from Mosul, when he was caught by IS smoking a cigarette in his own shop, he was whipped fifteen times and charged with a fine.[108] A young boy who was seen drinking during Ramadan was also severely punished. According to a witness, "an ISIS member approached a 14-year-old boy after seeing him drinking water, then dragged him to the middle of the crowd in the street, announced his 'crime' and lashed him seventy-nine times."[109]

Executions were carried out by IS against people accused of sodomy, smuggling alcohol, communication with the YPG and the "Crusader alliance," disapproval of the Islamic State, apostasy, attempted defection or escape, and cowardice.[110] The group also executed teachers who did not comply with the curriculum imposed by IS. A woman from Deir ez-Zor reported that a friend of hers who worked as a teacher was discovered not respecting IS's curriculum and subsequently had a confrontation with the IS official who had come to monitor her education institution. Following the episode, she was accused of adultery, taken from her house, and stoned to death.[111]

Throughout the caliphate, IS's morality police, the *hisba*, was the body in charge of ensuring that people would behave in conformity with IS's regulations, instantly punishing deviant behaviors, and reporting to the courts the cases of greatest violations.[112] Specifically, the *hisba*'s mandate was to "promote virtue and prevent vice to dry up sources of evil, prevent the manifestation of disobedience, and urge Muslims towards well-being."[113] According to pictures and accounts, *hisba* members used to patrol streets, markets, and other public spaces from vehicles equipped with loudspeakers to broadcast religious guidance and spread IS's regulations.[114] They would remind people to attend prayers, they would oversee the interruption of business activities during prayer time, and they would supervise the demolition of "apostate" symbols and buildings.[115] To verify women's compliance with IS rules and take measures in case of disobedience, IS also introduced all-women morality police forces, the al-Khansa Brigade and the Umm al-Rayan Brigade.[116]

To deter people from engaging in prohibited behavior, IS made no secret of its most violent and brutal punishments. Indeed, it carried them out in the public space. As has been noted in the case of other rebel groups, the execution of punishments in public has a strong symbolic power and aims to demonstrate to the population that there is no viable alternative to obedience.[117] It is also meant to project the group's power and ideological commitments.[118] In a central square in Raqqa, for instance, heads were posted on spikes with a sign above them indicating what transgression the person had committed. Significantly, the square used to be called Sahat al-Na'im (Paradise) but under IS it was renamed by the people Sahat al-Jahim (Hell).[119]

Besides the use of violence, IS's repertoire of coercive measures also included travel bans to prevent migration from the areas under its control. As early as late November 2014, IS issued a decree requiring residents to obtain official permission from an IS court for travel.[120] Less than one month later, IS issued a fatwa clarifying that travel to the "lands of *kufr*" was permissible only "for the purpose of a temporary undertaking out of need/necessity" and was conditional "on the ability to show disavowal of the disbelievers and hatred of idolatry . . . and the ability to display the rituals of Islam perfectly."[121] Afterward, IS also instituted a system whereby prior to traveling people had to register their property, which would be confiscated if they failed to return.[122] By March 2015, an IS official warned in a speech broadcast over loudspeakers that anyone who left Mosul would be considered an apostate (a crime punishable by death), and their property would be confiscated.[123]

While engaging extensively and publicly in coercive practices aimed at generating compliance through fear, IS also employed certain noncoercive practices aimed at generating compliance through persuasion. Specifically, IS engaged in a series of *da'wah* activities that included Quranic recitation competitions, sharia courses for both adults and teenagers, and media points where IS members distributed ideological pamphlets.[124] At the same time, IS engaged in a propaganda effort through posters, flyers, and loudspeaker announcements.[125] It also intervened in the formulation of the sermons to be delivered during Friday prayers.[126] Through these channels, IS publicized the group's ideology as well as its public goods and services, social activities, and contributions to social development, so as to portray its system of governance as a highly desirable one.

In this regard, IS propaganda attempted to emphasize the group's governance achievements vis-à-vis the former regimes, especially in terms of provision of security, order, and justice.[127] It also emphasized the group's rejection of corruption, in contrast to the abysmal record of the Syrian and Iraqi regimes.[128] A man from Mosul, for instance, stated that IS "is more honest and merciful than the Shia government in Baghdad and its militias."[129] With respect to corruption, IS also tried to publicize the punishment of its uncompliant members to demonstrate that everyone was required and expected to comply with its laws. While in reality the punishment of IS members seems to have been inconsistent and selective,[130] the group's claim to hold its own accountable was initially effective in enhancing the image of the caliphate in the eyes of some civilians.[131] As argued by a Syrian with direct experience of IS's governance, "in al-Bukamal [in eastern Syria], most of the people that ISIS have imprisoned are ISIS members themselves. The ISIS regime does not hesitate to punish its own members when they break the law."[132]

The Islamic State also resorted to the mobilization of symbols—such as its black flag with the *shahadah* or the use of the term "caliphate" itself—in which the local Muslim population could identify itself.[133] The use of the term "caliphate," in particular, was of great importance. For many Muslims, in fact, the caliphate constitutes a symbol of Islam itself, one that evokes the glory and righteousness of the *ummah*. Therefore, returning to the earliest caliphal models emphasized the potential of the Muslim community to live up to the best interpretations of the Prophet Muhammad's teachings and stand up as a model for the rest of humanity.[134] IS also presented its governance project as guided directly by Allah for the sake of the *ummah* and emphasized the caliphate as a perfect reincarnation of the first Islamic community established by the Prophet in Medina. In other words, IS was attempting to present its caliphate as an ideologically superior and pious society, emphasizing to its citizens its commitment to "pure" Islam vis-à-vis its "apostate" predecessors.[135] Proving the success of this strategy, a man living in Tel Abiyad argued that "the Islamic State is walking in the Prophet Muhammad's footsteps. . . . They are saving the Islamic community from vice and destruction."[136] Nonetheless, this was far from a widely held view, and, especially as time went by, more and more people came to despise the group deeply and to deny its embodiment of any Islamic ideal. In the words of someone who experienced IS's rule in Raqqa, "living under IS was like a big jail. From the perspective of IS's members they were implementing their ideal model of Islamic governance, but for us the people it was not. It was a jail."[137]

APPROACH TO OUTSIDERS

As a ruling armed group, IS distinguished itself for its lack of cooperation with other rebel groups.[138] As noted, IS "neither sought nor accepted offers of cooperation from other Sunni Arab insurgent groups,"[139] but sought instead "to dominate rather than collaborate whenever it could" and "prefer[red] to govern alone."[140] This exclusionary attitude toward other armed groups was perhaps most evident in the judicial sector. When IS expanded throughout Syria in 2013, it established courts that demanded exclusive jurisdiction, even in areas where other insurgents were already operating their own judicial systems. When the Islamic Front and Jabhat al-Nusra attempted to negotiate a truce with IS and proposed the creation of neutral Islamic courts with judges appointed by each faction, IS insisted on exclusive jurisdiction and refused the proposal.[141] The only option available to other insurgent groups—even those that were ideologically closest to IS—was to submit completely or fight against it. By January 2014, IS had achieved notoriety for the killing of other insurgent leaders and its unwillingness to work with other rebel groups.[142]

Similarly, IS excluded humanitarian and aid organizations, considering them foreign entities whose presence and activities undermined the doctrinal purity and physical security of the Islamic State.[143] In this regard, it is noticeable that among the first actions of the Diwan al-Sihah (Department of Health) was the closure of many foreign humanitarian organizations working in IS's territories and the arrest of their employees, under the pretext that they were spying for enemy entities and conducting missionary work.[144] Initially, in the earliest months after the establishment of the caliphate, IS seemed to exhibit some flexibility, allowing international aid organizations to continue delivering aid such as food, water, and hygiene kits through cooperation with local counterparts—albeit in small quantities. Specifically, it was reported that "major international aid agencies [were] using individuals who have good relations and can mediate with IS to facilitate assistance."[145] Over time, however, IS became increasingly repressive and expelled from its territories all humanitarian organizations with connections to foreign governments over concerns of espionage. It also acted with immense brutality toward humanitarian workers—taking them hostages for ransom and killing them in an attempt to gain international media coverage.[146]

A somewhat less exclusionary approach was adopted toward certain Sunni tribes across Syria and Iraq. In 2009, in fact, a document redacted by ISI leaders and entitled "Strategic Plan to Improve the Political Standing of the Islamic State of Iraq"—a study of the factors that had led to the group's defeat in Anbar—had recognized the devasting effect of the tribes' disillusionment with ISI.[147] The document recommended the establishment of "Awakening Jihadist Councils, similar to the ones the Prophet—peace be upon him—convened at the Medina delegations."[148] It also advocated enlisting "honorable" tribal leaders to form militias composed of tribal members.[149]

Since then, tribal outreach became part of the group's strategy, to the point that in the first issue of *Dabiq* it was argued that the Islamic State aimed to cooperate with the tribes living within its borders in the joint creation of the prophetic caliphate.[150] In fact, IS had "to consider and include tribal leaders because the latter were very powerful and authoritative, especially in an area such as Deir ez-Zor."[151] Following this shift in approach on the part of IS, a situation emerged whereby Sunni tribes

that pledged *bay'ah* to IS were included in the group's governance practices,[152] albeit to a limited extent and only in some areas of governance.
For instance, local tribal leaders were assigned the task of collecting
zakat and presenting it to the local offices, preparing lists with the
names of the needy entitled to receive charity, and solving small disputes.[153] They were also asked to cooperate in the maintenance of law
and order by means of urging those tribal members fighting against the
Islamic State to repent.[154]

To facilitate its tribal outreach, IS set up the Diwan al-'Asha'ir (the
Department of Tribal Affairs), which was tasked with "gathering information on the tribes and their daily activities."[155] Moreover, "the Tribal
Affairs department also organised traditional councils (*majalis*) and
ceremonies with tribal leaders in which they apparently made a point of
honouring tribal traditions and rituals, and paying respect to tribal
shaykhs."[156] The department was also started to address problems of security, property disputes, and distribution of resources in conjunction with
tribal elders.[157] The latter issue, in particular, had been a major source of
tribal hostility toward ISI in Anbar, so that under al-Baghdadi IS opted
to reach some agreement on the terms of resource extraction in tribal territories and to share resources with local tribes.[158]

It has also been noted that in areas where tribes pledged *bay'ah* to IS,
the group's governing arm tended to be somewhat softer, with the morality police often turning a blind eye to sharia violations. For instance, some
tribes with many members within IS could continue to use the Internet
after restrictions had been imposed on the rest of the population by the
group.[159] Also, while IS prohibited the consumption of tobacco throughout its caliphate, a tobacco retailer from Deir ez-Zor reported that the
group could not do so in the village of al-Khasham, which was a key center for the trade of tobacco. Members of the al-Khasham tribe, in fact,
had achieved influence within IS, which in turn reduced the group's
authority over them.[160]

Much more difficult was the position of those tribes that did not pledge
bay'ah to IS and rebelled against its authority. Those tribes, in fact, were
not only excluded from IS's governance, but were also subjected to IS's brutality. For instance, in 2014 the al-Shaitat tribe in Deir ez-Zor had initially reached a compromise with IS whereby the latter could enter their

areas, but local leaders would remain in control. Shortly afterward, however, the tribe rebelled against IS's strict regulations and brutal punishments. As a result, IS killed more than seven hundred members of the tribe.[161] Similarly, in Iraq, IS killed more than eight hundred members of the Albu Nimr pro-government Sunni tribe near Hit, in Anbar Governorate.[162] In an interview, one of the tribe's sheikhs argued that IS managed to win quickly because "90 percent of the tribes in Anbar collaborated with ISIS or joined them except for ourselves [the Albu Nimr tribesmen]."[163] Significantly, what was noted above in the case of IS's publicized coercion against civilians was true also in the case of violence against the tribes: "reports of killings of tribesmen came to the fore in news media or via ISIS propaganda channels from time to time," where they were meant to have an "exemplary and 'educational' effect."[164]

At the same time, and perhaps surprisingly to some, IS maintained some degree of coordination and cooperation with the regime of Bashar al-Assad.[165] As argued by a Syrian businessman close to the government, "the regime has always had dealings with IS, out of necessity."[166] After IS established its control over at least eight power plants, including Syria's largest gas plant (the Conoco gas field in eastern Syria once controlled by Jabhat al-Nusra) and three hydroelectric facilities, the group reached an agreement with the regime regarding their management. The regime, in fact, controlled the national companies—and had contracted the private companies—with the know-how required to manage those plants for the production of electricity. Interviews conducted with Syrian energy employees also revealed agreements between IS and the Assad regime "that are less about cash than about services."[167] According to those interviews, Syrian national and private gas companies paid their employees working in the gas and oil fields and supplied equipment to the facilities. Subsequently, IS and the regime divided the electricity produced from dry gas and IS also retained the fuel products made from liquid gas.[168] Thus, gas plants conquered by IS became the de facto joint ventures between the insurgent group and the Syrian regime.[169] Additionally, mobile phone services in IS-controlled Raqqa were provided thanks to the Syrian regime and national mobile phone operators, which sent engineers to IS areas to repair damaged cell towers.[170]

PROPENSITY TO CHANGE

In some cases, IS opted to maintain preexisting structures, practices, and personnel. In fact, according to an IS document known as "Principles in Administration of the Islamic State," it was important to "preserv[e] the capabilities that managed the production projects under the prior governments."[171] As far as former employees were concerned, IS was seemingly aware that it "could not rely exclusively on employees from among its foreign and local members, and therefore had to rely on civilian employees to provide the expertise and competencies that its membership could not provide."[172] Thus, IS opted to rely on local Iraqis and Syrians who could act as teachers, doctors, engineers, nurses, bureaucrats, and civil servants, benefiting from their established expertise.[173]

Residents of Mosul reported that hours after the fall of the city IS sent some of its members around with loudspeakers to encourage public workers to return to their jobs.[174] In Ramadi, the Diwan al-Rikaz (the Bureau of Precious Resources) ordered the employees of the local gas plant to register and undertake regular duties.[175] In Raqqa, IS appointed a regime employee to manage flour distribution and bakeries throughout the city,[176] employed former engineers to repair the city's power grid following damage from air strikes,[177] and maintained in their position employees at the local dam.[178] It called on workers of Raqqa's National Hospital to remain in their posts and comply with the timetables set by the hospital's administration.[179] In the gas fields that IS managed together with the Syrian regime, state employees were maintained in their posts. One of them, who was employed by the Syrian national gas company at the Tuweinan gas plant, in central Syria, and later found himself working under IS, argued that "it was frightening [to work for IS], but I didn't have a choice."[180]

Coercive methods were most often used to force professionals to remain in their posts.[181] In fact, one of the main problems that the Islamic State was facing in the areas under its control was "brain drain, especially in the realm of medicine and health."[182] A man who worked as paramedic under IS reported that "when ISIS entered Raqqa, the group started harassing all paramedics, medical workers, hospital staff and pharmacists because they wanted everyone to work with them and under their laws."[183] A woman from Raqqa who served as a nurse under IS reported that the group told all medical staff that they had to show up to work. To force people to comply, the group's officials reminded them that they were in possession of everyone's address.[184] In Nineveh Governorate, IS issued an ultimatum for medical professionals and academics who had fled the region, urging them to return to the caliphate if they did not want to have their properties confiscated.[185] A similar injunction was issued in Hasakah Governorate, in northeastern Syria.[186] In Aleppo, IS's Department of Health communicated to all doctors the obligation to serve the caliphate's population and informed them that those who did not comply would be punished as collaborators of the crusaders—that is, with death.[187] A government employee at Mosul High School reported that after ignoring IS's calls to return to work, he received a threatening message forcing him to return to school and teach.[188]

When employees were maintained in their posts, they had to undergo *tawbah*—that is, they had to repent for their previous association with the former government.[189] Teachers had to sign documents of repentance that read as follows: "I [name] repent to God for the apostasy into which I have fallen. I hereby repudiate my affiliation with the previous education system. . . . If I ever renounce or change my pledge, I accept the judgement of God upon myself."[190] In one issue of *Dabiq*, a group of teachers is shown repenting for having previously upheld Baathist principles and "apostasy."[191]

As part of the repentance process, workers who retained their posts also had to undertake courses in sharia, creed, and *fiqh* (Islamic jurisprudence).[192] A well-informed account notes that "Daesh tried to recruit civilians as employees because it needed them, but those civilians who were recruited were required to follow Daesh's ideology strictly."[193] An IS document stated that teachers without teaching qualifications had to train for ten months in an ad hoc institute, that teachers with teaching qualifications had to undergo a sharia training for two months and sign a statement of repentance, and that university students aspiring to teach had to follow a sharia course for two weeks and then join an institute for the preparation of teachers.[194] A pharmacist from Raqqa reported that he was forced to follow an eight-days course focused on Islamic obligations, praying, and jihad in order to remain in the business.[195] Following *tawbah*, professionals were issued a paper testifying that they had repented, and they were required to carry such paper with them, as reported by a former policeman from northern Iraq.[196] While formal membership in IS was not a requirement to maintain or obtain an appointment, it is nonetheless noticeable that local civilians who were forced to work in IS's administration without becoming members of the group were known as *munasirin* and were given significantly inferior salaries and benefits and were subjected to worse treatment and conditions than those local and foreign workers who pledged allegiance to IS and were known as *muba'yain*.[197]

However, IS engaged to a larger extent in the introduction of innovations.[198] To guarantee security, it established two police services. One was al-Shurtah al-Islamiyah (the Islamic Police), which answered to the Diwan al-Qada' wa al-Madhalim (Department of Justice and Grievances) and was one of the first institutions introduced by IS in its conquered cities.[199] Members of the Islamic Police—who drove dedicated vehicles and wore specific uniforms—were responsible for ordinary law enforcement, for executing the courts' rulings, for maintaining internal security through the deployment of regular patrols and the establishment of checkpoints along the caliphate's major roads, and for monitoring public safety through such as conducting inspections, issuing fines, and resolving simple disputes.[200] The other police force, mentioned above in the context of the generation of compliance, was the *hisba* and its female counterparts, the al-Khansa and Umm al-Rayan Brigades. As noted, this police force was responsible for patrolling the streets of the caliphate to monitor and correct the people's behavior in accordance with IS's regulations.[201] Finally, the security sector was completed by the introduction of the Amniyat, which was responsible for collecting and processing intelligence information, performing clandestine security work, deploying spies, conducting constant surveillance, and eliminating dissidents, spies, and defectors.[202]

In the judicial sector, IS removed any secular system of law and adopted sharia as the exclusive source of legislation. At the same time, it introduced a three-layered system of courts. First were sharia courts that dealt with violations of Islamic law.[203] Second was the Diwan al-Hisba (Department of Hisba), which had to execute the provisions issued by the sharia courts and adjudicate the violations referred by the *hisba* police. And third was the above-mentioned Department of Justice and Grievances, which functioned as a complaints department dealing with grievances and disputes.[204] In terms of punishments, IS included *ta'zir* (discretionary punishments), *qisas* (retaliation punishments), and *hudud* (corporal punishments).[205]

An IS internal document from the governorate of Aleppo reports the following *hudud* punishments: death for blasphemy against God, Muhammad, and Islam; death for adultery if the adulterer was married or one hundred lashes if unmarried; death for homosexuality; amputation of the hand for theft; eighty lashes for drinking alcohol and for calumny; death for spying for the unbelievers; and death for apostasy.[206] Death sentences were also imposed on those who tried to leave the caliphate.[207] As horrifying confirmation of the actual implementation of these punishments, the second issue of *Dabiq* shows *hudud* carried out against eight individuals accused of colluding with the Syrian regime in Aleppo Governorate.[208] The seventh issue also discusses the punishments for those engaging in acts of "sexual deviance" (e.g., homosexuality) and shows pictures of these disturbing punishments being carried out.[209] According to testimonies released by people who lived under IS in Raqqa, people accused of sodomy were tied to a chair and pushed from the top of tall buildings.[210]

In the provision of goods and services, IS maintained some of the preexisting institutions, such as the University of Mosul (though not all departments were allowed to function).[211] At the same time, however, and to a larger extent, IS also opened its own schools. For instance, in the Deir ez-Zor countryside it opened elementary schools;[212] in Raqqa it opened a school specifically for the children of English-speaking IS fighters;[213] in Aleppo and Mosul it established sharia institutes.[214] In all major cities, IS opened schools of medicine, nursery, and engineering, reducing the traditional number of years of study needed to obtain the final degree in each discipline.[215] For instance, in Raqqa IS opened a free-of-charge medical college for both female and male students. There, students could graduate as doctors after only three years of study, during which they would follow theoretical courses in the first year and be introduced to practical work under tutelage in the second and third years.[216] For girls aged eighteen to twenty-five, IS opened a school for nurses, promising that graduates with top grades would be rewarded with a place in IS's medical school, where they could train to become doctors and surgeons.[217] Furthermore, IS introduced the Diwan al-Taʿlim (Department of Education) as the administrative body responsible for all schools, institutes, and colleges.[218]

Besides opening new schools, IS also introduced new regulations in terms of gender segregation and dress code and modified the school curriculum extensively.[219] It prohibited subjects such as music, national history, social studies, arts, sport, philosophy, and psychology while it imposed the study of the Quran, ʿaqidah, monotheism, Islamic jurisprudence, sirah (life of Muhammad), jihad training, Arabic, and mathematics.[220] Teaching on nationalism and patriotism was replaced with that emphasizing belonging to Islam and the ummah.[221] The group also produced its own textbooks in accordance with its revised curriculum.[222] According to excerpts from one IS textbooks, the following lessons were taught: purity, the quality of true ablution, wiping and purification with stones, removal of filth, ablutions, prayer, the Sunna traditions of prayer, and the consequences of abandoning prayer.[223]

Importantly, those textbooks were an instrument of radicalization not only through the subjects that they taught but also through the way in which they taught them. For instance, mathematics books explained arithmetic with reference to the number of guns and bullets and the number of infidels and mujahidin engaged in a battle.[224] In classes, teachers had to strictly follow this educational material and impart religious instruction as dictated by IS. As reported by a primary-school teacher who had to serve under IS, "[the Islamic State] wanted us to teach the verses of the Quran about jihad, war and murder."[225]

In the health-care sector, IS often maintained preexisting hospitals, medical centers, and pharmacies.[226] However, the group proceeded to impose its regulations on them, enforcing gender segregation between doctors, between doctors and nurses, and between doctors and patients, and introducing new medical tariffs—even for services that had traditionally been free of charge.[227] Female and male health-care workers were not allowed to stay together in the same room, and doctors could only visit patients of their own gender.[228] Across the towns under IS's control, the hisba was present on a daily basis in health-care facilities to ensure patients and workers were in compliance with the group's moral regulations.[229] Similarly, IS imposed new regulations on pharmacies, banning the import of all medical goods coming from Iran and imposing gender segregation.[230] For instance, a Syrian man reported entering a pharmacy and asking for medication from the pharmacist working there, who happened to be female. As an IS member had witnessed the scene, he was detained and threatened with death.[231] Another important innovation was the creation of the caliphate's Health Department, which was responsible for all health-related decisions and for managing hospitals and pharmacies in the caliphate.[232]

In terms of taxation, IS introduced the *jizyah* tax for those non-Muslims who were entitled to live within the caliphate under the *dhimmah* (protection) contract.[233] On its Muslim citizens, IS imposed *zakat*, the charity tax that is to be paid by every Muslim whose wealth reaches the minimum threshold known as *nisab*.[234] This tax could be paid in the form of cash but also in the form of livestock and agricultural produce.[235] To collect and distribute *zakat*, IS created its own Diwan al-Zakat (Department of Charity Tax).[236] In early 2015, for instance, in the town of al-Mayadin, in eastern Syria, IS informed civilians during the Friday sermon that it had established the Department of Charity Tax to collect and distribute charity funds.[237] An IS document from Salah ad-Din, northern Iraq, also reported that the local Department of Charity Tax would distribute food aid to the needy upon registration of their names with the relevant authority on a specific day and time and at a specific location.[238] In the second issue of *Dabiq*, people are shown sitting in a town hall where *zakat* is being distributed by the relevant department.[239]

A specific tax—*khums*—was also introduced for combatants. As combatants were the only category of people exempted from paying *zakat*, they had to pay 20 percent of their spoils of war to the Bayt al-Mal.[240] The latter was a public treasury "modeled after the financial institutions of the original seventh-century caliphate that it [IS] claim[ed] to be emulating."[241] Other taxes imposed by IS in its attempt to follow the model of the early caliphates were *'ushr*, a tax on agricultural production, and *kharaj*, a tax on land and real estate ownership.[242] Taxes were also imposed on trucks shipping goods to and from and the caliphate.[243] Furthermore, fees were introduced in exchange for IS's provision of services.[244] Shop owners had to pay taxes for cleaning services, electricity, water, and security;[245] and households had to pay monthly taxes for services like electricity, water, phone lines, street cleaning, and garbage collection.[246] Similarly, fees for students and for medical patients increased dramatically.[247]

Innovation was also observed in the imposition of new rules of behavior. Among those were the prohibition on gender mixing in all public places;[248] the prohibition on women leaving the house without a *mahram*;[249] the obligation for all businesses to close during prayer time (even in the case of non-Muslims);[250] the obligation for everyone to pray at the mosque five times a day;[251] the ban on smoking, drinking alcohol, playing pool, billiards, and listening to music;[252] the prohibition on traveling outside of the caliphate except with a permit and a guarantor;[253] the obligation to use the Internet only inside authorized cafés;[254] the obligation for women to show themselves in public only when fully covered;[255] and the obligation for men to wear trousers above their ankle and to grow a beard.[256]

Finally, IS introduced important innovations by filling vacated posts with new employees. In November and December 2014, IS issued a recruitment call for the newly created Department of Charity Tax and Department of Hisba in Raqqa.[257] In July 2016, IS issued a recruitment call for teachers in Nineveh open to all graduates and holders of sharia and scientific diplomas.[258] In this regard, it is particularly significant to emphasize IS's unprecedented capacity to attract not only fighters but also some professionals and supporters from abroad.[259] In fact, aware of the contribution that foreigners could make to the caliphate's advancement, in an audio message released in July 2014 al-Baghdadi proclaimed, "O Muslims everywhere, whoever is capable of performing hijrah [migration] to the Islamic State, then let him do so. . . .] We make a special call to the scholars, and callers, especially the judges, as well as people with military,

TABLE 4.1 The model of governance of the Islamic State

Inclusivity	Discrimination (Christians, Shias, Yezidis, women)
Civilian engagement	Subjection (rejection of democratic process)
Generation of compliance	Extensive coercion and limited persuasion (e.g., systematic *hudud* punishments in public display and some persuasive measures, such as *da'wah* events)
Approach to outsiders	Partial exclusion (exclusion of non-Sunnis and non-Salafists, but limited cooperation with Sunni tribes that pledged *bay'ah* and with the Syrian regime)
Propensity to change	Extensive innovation and limited maintenance (e.g., new sharia-based judicial system, new taxation system, new norms of conduct, and maintenance of professional workers upon engagement in *tawbah*)

administrative and service expertise, and medical doctors and engineers of all different specializations and fields."[260] By calling on Muslims worldwide to migrate to the caliphate, IS seemed to acknowledge "the need of administrative as well as other type of critical state positions and functions to establish their state."[261]

Following IS's call, many individuals from all over the world left to join the caliphate. Most were aspiring mujahidin willing to participate in battle, but some were indeed professionals and specialists willing to place their expertise at the service of the caliphate's sociopolitical project. Upon their arrival in the caliphate's territories, all new immigrants were required to fill in a form that included specific questions about their competences and experience.[262] Significantly, this shows the extent to which IS was attempting to exploit the talents of its members. For instance, IS appointed a Tunisian with a PhD in telecommunications to manage the telecommunications system in Raqqa, while an Australian doctor was recruited to work in that city's hospital.[263]

<hr />

In this chapter I have noted that the Islamic State adopted a discriminatory approach, whereby non-Sunnis and non-Muslims were considered either second-class subjects or nonsubjects. Furthermore, Sunni women were also subjected to discriminatory restrictions and regulations. In any case, even where male Sunnis were concerned, no system of civilian participation was developed. The group excluded most other actors, including those armed groups and factions that shared the Salafi-jihadist ideology. The only exceptions were cooperation with certain Sunni tribes that pledged bay'ah and cooperation with the Assad regime on certain matters of governance. With respect to preexisting institutions and personnel, in some cases IS opted for maintenance, especially with respect to professionals. To a greater extent, though, the group sought to establish its own system of governance ex novo. Finally, as far as the generation of compliance is concerned, IS combined extreme and widely publicized acts of coercion aimed at punishing and deterring noncompliance with more limited persuasive practices aimed at convincing its citizens to internalize the group's regulations and embrace its project.

5

BUILDING AN ISLAMIST POLITY IN NORTHWESTERN SYRIA

The Governance Project of Hay'at Tahrir al-Sham

As I argued in the introduction, most of the attention devoted by scholars to Salafi-jihadist governance has focused on the Islamic State. However, IS was not the only Salafi-jihadist group to attempt governance experiments in the post–Arab Spring period. In fact, other groups have similarly engaged in extensive governance efforts, some of which have been even more enduring than the Islamic State's. One such case is that of Hay'at Tahrir al-Sham, which began to engage in rebel governance around 2012 and governed over parts of northwestern Syria until its victorious offensive against the Assad regime in November 2024. Unlike most armed groups, in fact, HTS proved itself capable of adapting to continuously changing circumstances, managing to ensure the survival of the organization. In this chapter, I will focus on HTS, starting with a review of the group's transition from insurgency to governance. I will then investigate its strategies of civilian administration with reference to the five dimensions of my proposed typology. Importantly, I will apply the typology to the group's first decade of rebel governance, from 2012 until the end of 2022. However, as some of HTS's governance strategies have evolved over time, when contradictions between earlier and later periods emerge, I will apply my typology to the group's most recent experience. Therefore, any observation offered in this chapter is to be considered valid as of the end of 2022. Future studies on HTS will need to assess whether, and to what extent, the observations recorded here have either evolved or remained unchanged, especially as the group transitions from being the rebel governor of Syria's Northwest to leading the national transition government in Damascus.

FROM INSURGENCY TO GOVERNANCE

As was seen briefly in the previous chapter, the origins of Jabhat al-Nusra lie in the group known as the Islamic State of Iraq. In 2011, ISI's leader, al-Baghdadi, created JaN as a cell to be sent to Syria under the guidance of Abu Muhammad al-Julani. The cell was assigned the task of inserting itself into the Syrian insurgency and seizing territory that the government had already lost but that other rebel groups had failed to bring under their stable control.[1] For al-Baghdadi, in fact, the turmoil that had erupted in Syria in the context of the Arab Spring uprising offered an attractive opportunity to expand the ambitions and the operations of his own, Iraq-based group.

In March 2011, demonstrations took place in Syria as people went out to the streets demanding long-awaited economic and political reforms. Initially, unlike in other Arab countries, protesters called not for the fall of the regime but rather for changes within the existing system.[2] However, the government of President Bashar al-Assad responded with the use of violence and the dissemination of conspiracy theories of foreign meddling in Syrian affairs.[3] As regime violence escalated, the protesters' demands came to include regime change, which called forth an even more violent response from the government's security forces.[4] It was in this context that the opposition militarized and the regime resorted to air strikes and artillery. The country soon collapsed into open civil war.[5] By its second year, the internecine conflict had assumed clear sectarian tones as the regime sought to rally its minority Alawite base and part of the opposition adopted a Sunni sectarian identity.[6]

This was the overall situation in Syria when JaN appeared on the scene. JaN initially introduced itself as a group of Syrian militants returning from foreign jihad battlefields to support the Syrian people in the face of bloody repression.[7] Quickly, it emerged as one of the most prominent groups of the anti-Assad insurgency.[8] As it consolidated its position over the course of 2012, JaN "increasingly did so not as some isolated, clandestine organization, but rather in open collaboration with other insurgents fighting against the Assad regime."[9] Furthermore, JaN became increasingly self-sufficient thanks to the attraction of new funders, the development of remarkable bomb-making capacities, and the arrival of many local and foreign fighters.[10]

Threatened by JaN's growing power and autonomy, Abu Bakr al-Baghdadi attempted to restrain the group and in April 2013 announced that JaN was an extension of IS, which would be rebranded the Islamic State of Iraq and al-Sham. At that announcement, however, al-Julani objected and reiterated his allegiance to al-Qaeda's leader, Ayman al-Zawahiri. The latter intervened in the dispute, assigning the management of activities in Syria to JaN and the management of activities in Iraq to ISI.[11] After ISIS rejected al-Zawahiri's disposition, the dispute between al-Julani and al-Zawahiri on one side and al-Baghdadi on the other escalated until al-Qaeda's disavowal of ISIS in February 2014.

As a result, JaN and ISIS became two separate entities within the broader Salafi-jihadist universe. The former confirmed itself as al-Qaeda's branch in Syria with the goal of overthrowing the Assad regime and establishing a Syrian Islamic emirate that one day would be part of a bigger al-Qaeda caliphate. The latter asserted itself as an independent Salafi-jihadist entity whose goal was to establish a transnational Islamic caliphate that expand from Syria and Iraq to the rest of the Muslim world.[12] As recalled by al-Julani during an interview, "there were many attempts by leaders of the Islamic State to push us to start a war against the other factions, for example. We rejected this. We stood against him [al-Baghdadi]. So he released the audio that everybody heard, announcing that Jabhat al-Nusra was affiliated with the Islamic State. I responded saying that was unacceptable. There was an agreement between us that, if there was any disagreement, it would be taken up by the al-Qaeda organization, to Dr. Ayman al-Zawahiri. So we raised the issue, and the separation between us started."[13]

By 2013, JaN had managed to assert some degree of control in many of Syria's governorates, including Aleppo and Idlib, in northwestern Syria, Raqqa and Deir ez-Zor, in northern Syria, and Dara'a, in southern Syria. In the following months and years, however, al-Julani's group suffered a series of military setbacks and was driven out of several territories. By 2017, it had withdrawn to Idlib Governorate and to parts of rural Aleppo.[14] In the background of these territorial conquests and losses, two important turning points in the history of the organization were observed in 2016 and 2017.

In late July 2016, al-Julani rebranded his group as Jabhat Fatah al-Sham (JFS), a move aimed at rescinding publicly the group's ties with al-Qaeda and presenting JFS as an autochthonous Syrian group willing to serve exclusively the people of Syria.[15] Julani's announcement of JFS, however, suggested that the move was approved and guided by al-Zawahiri, as he stated that the decision to rebrand Jabhat al-Nusra as Jabhat Fatah al-Sham, as a group with no ties to any "external entity," was taken on the basis of "general guidelines and directives" coming from the al-Qaeda leadership.[16] The testimonies of two other prominent JaN figures, Sami al-ʿUraydi and ʿAbd al-Rahim ʿAtun, also give credence to the argument that the rebranding was not meant to truly severe ties with al-Qaeda.[17] At the same time, though, it is noticeable that more recent testimonies confirm that al-Zawahiri rejected the rebranding in a letter addressed to the leadership of JaN/JFS that arrived in Syria only by early autumn 2016.[18]

The second, more dramatic and more decisive turning point was observed in January 2017, when the group led by al-Julani, the Movement of Nur al-Din al-Zinki, Liwa al-Haqq, Jabhat Ansar al-Din, and Jaysh al-Sunna formed HTS. Contrary to the formation of JFS, the formation of HTS is widely believed to have marked the definitive rupture of Julani's group from al-Qaeda and the global Salafi-jihadist movement.[19] From that moment onward, the objective of al-Julani's group shifted from the establishment of an Islamic emirate to be incorporated into a future al-Qaeda global caliphate to the creation of a local Islamic state exclusively confined to Syria. The implementation of that objective started in the governorate of Idlib, that HTS brought under its hegemonic control in early 2019.[20] As has been noted, at that point in time the imposition of HTS's hegemony had three goals: to impose military domination over the province by subjugating the mainstream opposition and al-Qaeda loyalists, to manage the areas under the group's control by means of territorial anchorage, and to position the group in the broader strategic game around Syria.[21]

In late 2017, HTS also created the Syrian Salvation Government (SSG).[22] The creation of the SSG followed an initiative known as the Civil Administration Initiative, launched in Idlib by an educated and conservative urban elite in August 2017.[23] As far as the SSG is concerned, some observers have questioned its independence from HTS,[24] suggesting that the SSG was "no more than a tool to provide the 'legal' and administrative frameworks for HTS's takeover of the region's economy and resources,"[25] and that "the Syrian Salvation Government's raison d'être [was] to confer a modicum of respectability on HTS's rule in the eye of foreign actors and local communities, [which explains why] the most controversial aspect of Islamist governance in Idlib [was] not carried out by the Syrian Salvation Government but by bodies . . . directly commanded by HTS."[26] Others, conversely, have maintained that the SSG was not the same as HTS and that the former participated in HTS's power strategy but could not "be considered an offshoot . . . or its civil branch."[27] The relationship between HTS and the SSG was indeed a complex one, as testified by the fact that some members of SSG's ministries also participated in HTS's structures, as well as by the fact that HTS retained tight control over security and economic affairs in Idlib.[28] As far as governance is concerned, it thus seems that HTS had been trying to strike a balance between its direct influence on governance bodies and their preservation of a "quasi-independent status."[29]

Once it brought under its control several territories across Syria, starting as early as 2012 JaN opted to establish some form of governance in order to establish an Islamist, sharia-based polity.[30] In fact, as reported by Hisham in his memoir of the Syrian war, and life in Raqqa in particular, while few rebel groups had a vision for what would come once Raqqa was liberated from regime forces, Jabhat al-Nusra did engage in some governance functions since its earliest days.[31]

THE MODEL OF GOVERNANCE OF HAY'AT TAHRIR AL-SHAM

Having reviewed the process whereby JaN transitioned from being a traditional insurgent group to governing parts of Syria, I will investigate the group's specific governance strategies by referring to the dimensions of governance identified in my proposed typology.

INCLUSIVITY

At the onset of JaN's intervention in the Syrian Civil War, Abu ʿAdnan, a religious scholar and sharia law official associated with the group's leadership in the Aleppo area, reported that minorities had nothing to fear under the rule of JaN and that "whoever has not oppressed, or participated in the harming of the people," would enjoy inalienable rights and equal duties. To give more credibility to his statement, he emphasized the fact that the Prophet Muhammad himself had a Jewish neighbor.[32] Nonetheless, the reality on the ground was never as inclusive as the group tried to suggest. Similar to what was observed under IS, discrimination was maintained toward religious groups belonging to monotheistic faiths other than Islam—which in the areas controlled by HTS mostly meant Christians of various denominations—and religious groups deemed "apostates"—which in the same areas meant Alawite Shias and Druze.[33] The two latter groups, in fact, had been especially targeted by Ibn Taymiyya (the thirteenth-century scholar and judge who is a preferred reference for Salafi-jihadists) in a series of fatwas in which he argued that Alawites and Druze are more heretical and more harmful to the *ummah* than Jews, Christians, and polytheists.[34]

As early as August 2013, dozens of Alawite civilians were executed or taken hostage by JaN and other opposition groups in the Latakia countryside, in western Syria.[35] People who witnessed those events reported disturbing stories of their family members and neighbors being brutally killed by JaN.[36] One of those survivors recalled that armed JaN members "took the bodies [of those killed] and were burning them and were saying 'God is great and there is no God but God.' They were wearing *galabiyehs* [traditional tunics], calf length pants, and had black vests on. . . . They had a Jabhat al-Nusra black flag with them."[37] In a speech delivered in June 2016, the group's religious chief and deputy leader at the time, Sami al-ʿUraydi, encouraged Syrians to behave toward Shias as they would behave toward apostates and to purge the country of their presence.[38] Thus, regardless of the fact that al-Julani had previously promised Alawites that they would be protected if they chose not to fight against the group and pledged to leave their religion and abandon Assad, reality on the ground too often contradicted that promise.[39]

As far as the Druze are concerned, in January 2015 in Jabal al-Summaq, northern Idlib, JaN forced the local Druze inhabitants to convert to Sunni Islam under the threat of death.[40] A Druze resident reported that "they [JaN] claimed they were fighting infidels, and that we had to decide our own fate and our identity, to either be with the Muslims or the infidels. . . . They forced us to accept their interpretation of Sunni Islam, or else we'd be punished."[41] He also added that "those Druze who have left our villages had their property seized and confiscated [by JaN]" and "can never return."[42] Following these forced conversions, representatives of the Druze community were forced to sign a document according to which they agreed to disavow their religion in favor of Sunni Islam, implement sharia, destroy tombs and shrines, teach the Quran, Islamic creed, and Islamic jurisprudence to their children, impose the head covering on women, and prohibit gender-mixing.[43]

In another infamous episode of JaN violence in mid-2015, more than twenty Druze villagers in Qalb Lawzah, northwestern Idlib, were massacred and their properties confiscated by JaN, who either redistributed these to its members or rented them to Sunni civilians for a profit. Those whose lives were spared were forced to convert to Sunni Islam.[44] A Druze sheikh from the village reported that "they [JaN] have been coming to our homes, and want to remove our sons, our boys from ten to fourteen years old, and put them in a training camp for two months. We don't know what they are going to teach them, and they're threatening us."[45] This latter episode of violence against the Druze was followed by an official letter of apology from JaN that included the promise that those responsible— who reportedly acted without the leadership's consent—would be prosecuted and punished. In the apology, JaN sought to argue that since the beginning of the Syrian Civil War the group had fought only against Assad, deviant Khawarij (members of the Islamic State),[46] and corrupt factions.[47]

While little more than self-serving propaganda, this public apology underscores a remarkable difference between HTS and the Islamic State, which always touted its sectarian violence as a reason for pride. In this regard, in fact, it is interesting (and relevant for the purpose of this book) to note the condemnation to which IS subjected JaN over the latter's "mild" treatment of minorities, and of the Druze in particular. In the tenth issue of *Dabiq*, IS accused JaN of allowing the Druze to live in Syria under the protection of al-Julani. In particular, IS condemned al-Julani for the apology that his group issued following the massacre in Qalb Lawzah.[48]

Acts of discriminatory violence were also performed by al-Julani's group against sites of worship and of religious importance for non-Sunni and non-Muslim communities. For instance, JaN was reportedly involved in the destruction of the tomb of the Druze Sheikh Jaber as well as other tombs and shrines throughout the Druze territories.[49] In the words of a resident of Jabal al-Summaq, JaN "forced us to comply with a number of orders and decrees, including the destruction of our shrines. They dug up the tombs of a number of our saints, however we didn't protest."[50] A similar fate befell Christians as their churches were also attacked by al-Julani's group.[51] Non-Sunni communities had their lands and properties confiscated as well. As reported by a Christian resident of Jisr al-Shughur, northwestern Idlib, in 2018 HTS fighters stole the land belonging to the local Christian community, claiming the people's livelihood as "rightfully" theirs.[52] The same expropriations were observed in Idlib city, where HTS brought the properties of Christians who had fled under its direct control, renting them to Sunni civilians.[53] According to reports, in cases where properties had been rented by Christian absentee landlords to local civilians, HTS annulled the rental contract, confiscated the property, and established a new contract with the renter.[54] A Sunni man from Idlib city reported that he used to rent a shop owned by Christians and send the rent to the owners in Damascus until HTS seized the property, annulled the rental contract, and forced him to pay HTS directly.[55]

For those Christians who decided—or were forced—to remain under HTS, Christian life was largely relegated to the shadows: Christian religious garments were forbidden in the streets, crosses were removed or destroyed, church bells were silenced, and rituals were prohibited.[56] As argued by a Christian priest from Idlib, it was forbidden for Christians to publicly display the symbols of their faith.[57] Early pictures from the village of al-Quniyah show the local church with its crosses on top, while later pictures indicate that the crosses were removed at some point.[58]

More recently, claims have emerged that HTS's approach to Christians was improving, that some of the previously imposed restrictions were being lifted, and that HTS was promising to restore Christians' (and other minorities') rights.[59] For instance, al-Julani, asked in a 2021 interview about the situation of Christians in HTS-controlled Idlib, responded that the kind of sharia his group aspired to apply is the one that says that "religious minorities should be protected and that they should have the freedom to worship God in the way they see fit and as stated in their Sharias, and [that] this has been put into practice here in Idlib. . . . We actually put it into action, as part of our belief."[60]

In July 2022, al-Julani held a meeting with a group of Christians from the villages of al-Quniyah, al-Ya'qubiyah, and al-Jadida during which they asked al-Julani to return the properties (shops, orchards, lands) that JaN took in 2015. Reportedly, al-Julani agreed to form a committee to review those requests.[61] At the time of this writing, it remained unclear whether a decision had been reached. What is known, however, is that a few months after that meeting HTS allowed the reopening of a Christian (Armenian Apostolic) church in the Idlib countryside. A Christian notable who attended the event reported that "[d]ozens of Christians, including clerics, . . . took part on [August] 28 in the opening ceremony of St. Anna's church in Yacoubia. . . . For the first time in 10 years, Christians held a festive mass on Saint Anna's Day in the village. . . . HTS' security forces cordoned off the premises during the opening ceremony, set up checkpoints in the vicinity of the village and prevented the entry of anyone from outside the village to protect the Christians during the celebration."[62] Significantly, HTS's decision to allow the reopening of the church outraged many al-Qaeda affiliates, who accused the group of making Idlib "less Muslim" in the hope of earning international approval.[63]

In June 2022, al-Julani also paid a visit to the Druze community in Jabal al-Summaq, where he attended the opening of a water well in Qalb Lawzah.[64] During the visit, the HTS leader listened to the locals' grievances and promised to improve conditions there. Also, al-Julani sought to reassure the Druze community about their safety and the restitution of their properties.[65] Specifically, he was reported to have said to the Druze community that "we [HTS] do not accept injustice against anyone. You will receive your rights at your doorsteps. You are the rightful inhabitants of this area, you have been here for thousands of years."[66] Some observers, however, have questioned the honesty of those public visits and pledges, arguing that HTS continued to discriminate against religious minorities. According to an Idlib-based activist, for instance, al-Julani's "visit to Jabal al-Summaq is a notorious ploy designed to make him seem very popular among the inhabitants in areas under his control. But only the fools would believe that."[67] Only time will tell whether HTS's actions corresponded to a true and significant change in HTS's approach to religious minorities, or whether they were nothing more than a publicity campaign addressed to an international audience.

Besides discrimination toward non-Sunnis and non-Muslims, another noticeable form of discrimination under HTS was that between men and women. As argued in a report by the Syrian Network for Human Rights, "Syrian women in the areas controlled by HTS suffer from negative discrimination against them in general, with the restriction of freedom of movement and clothing being only one aspect of this repression. The violations against women go far beyond that, and their suffering increases exponentially if they are working or wishing to work in public affairs, or in civil society organizations of whatever kind, whether media, relief-oriented or political."[68]

In HTS-controlled territories, women were forced to follow a strict dress code, as their clothing had to be black, had to cover their entire bodies, had to be loose and thick, and had to be deprived of any adornment or embellishment.[69] A married woman living in Idlib recalled being harassed by HTS's morality enforcers for wearing makeup, for laughing too loud with her friends, and for wearing a dress that was deemed inappropriate.[70] Another girl enrolled in Idlib University reported being warned because she was wearing makeup.[71] Nonetheless, while women continued to be victims of discrimination, in more recent years the focus on women's individual attire declined somewhat under HTS and the SSG. For instance, the head of a women's association reported that "the pressure to wear the full veil (niqab) has . . . diminished."[72]

Women were also prohibited from leaving the house unaccompanied by a *mahram*.[73] These restrictions were imposed by JaN since the earliest days of its territorial control in some parts of Syria. Recalling those early experiences, a woman reported that women's lives changed dramatically under JaN as the group prevented women from going outside alone: "it was like we were in jail. We couldn't even go outside near our house. If we went outside, Jabhat al-Nusra would tell us to go back in our houses."[74] As JaN retreated to Idlib Governorate, those kinds of restrictions on women continued to be implemented. The director of a woman's advocacy center in Maʿarat al-Nuʿman, southern Idlib, lamented that HTS's regulation regarding the need of a *mahram* placed widowed women with young children in an extremely vulnerable position.[75] Eventually, unmarried women were also obliged to live with a sharia-compliant male member of their family, who would serve as *mahram*. Upon announcing the decision, the SSG released a statement saying that the aim was the preservation of the reputation of single mothers and widows.[76]

Some restrictions were also imposed on female education. Sources from inside Idlib reported that HTS prohibited married women from attending public schools and universities, presumably on the grounds that the most appropriate place for them is the house, taking care of their families. In the words of a sixteen-year-old from Idlib who got married when she was just fourteen, "I am one of dozens of married students who were deprived of education in Syria because of the decisions of the Education Directorate of the Salvation Government to prevent married female students from pursuing their studies."[77] For those who could attend school, gender segregation became the norm. One Idlib woman, interviewed in mid-2018, complained that "while there were battles on the frontlines, HTS members were manning positions in front of schools to make sure girls and boys didn't mix."[78]

Finally, HTS excluded women from its leadership and political organs. However, women were still allowed to work in certain occupations, especially in the education and health care sectors.[79] Thus, there were women working as teachers in Idlib's schools and universities. Other women were working for local or international civil society organizations seeking to provide medical assistance, psychological support, or vocational training to Idlib's female population.[80] As reported in April 2018 by an Idlibi woman who cofounded a women's center, "little by little, the center developed . . . and we started offering a range of courses. . . . [Today, it] encompasses eight women's centers [in the area around Kafr Nubl], including childcare centers so that the women can leave their children while they take the courses. There are also two medical centers. We also have a magazine. . . . About a year ago [in 2017], we started teaching women to run their own courses. Today, [our center] employs 100 people."[81] Despite the challenges faced, she said that they "carried on reaching women with [their] training from nursing to hairdressing, non-violent activism and weaving as well as economics, photography and journalism."[82]

CIVILIAN ENGAGEMENT

As far as the inclusion of civilians in governance is concerned, it is notable that the leadership of HTS progressively established (or portrayed itself as establishing) direct interactions with the population living in the territories under its control. For instance, on multiple occasions throughout 2021 and 2022 al-Julani toured the internally displaced persons' camps in Idlib and was pictured discussing with camp officials the people's needs.[83] During Eid al-Fitr in May 2022 and during Eid al-Adha in August 2020, al-Julani also engaged with civilians in the streets and in a restaurant in Idlib city.[84] Furthermore, HTS established and maintained consultative relationships with local elders and local tribal leaders. For instance, in July 2022, al-Julani met with the notables from the city of Hama and the surrounding countryside as well as with notables and people of the Jisr al-Shughur area and the city of Idlib.[85] In March 2022, prior to the beginning of the holy month of Ramadan, al-Julani visited the town of Ariha, in Idlib's southwestern countryside, and met with local dignitaries. As the attendees advanced their demands, al-Julani promised to address them and fulfill their requests.[86]

In the various meetings publicized by HTS in its media channels, pictures and videos give an impression of spaces where participants were welcome to voice their complaints and criticism. For instance, in the video of the meeting between al-Julani and notables from Jisr al-Shughur in July 2022, two participants complain about the difficulty of accessing water and electricity in their area and the generally poor performance of responsible authorities in providing services. However, while HTS sought to portray an image of open and constructive discussions, this was true only to the extent that such discussions took place in the time, circumstances, and form allowed by the group.[87] In fact, as will be seen below when discussing compliance, civilians who attempted to express their criticism freely in the public space (e.g., by means of staging demonstrations) ran the risk of being persecuted and incarcerated, perhaps even killed, by HTS.

What is more telling in terms of civilian participation is HTS's creation in 2017 of the Syrian Salvation Government as a ruling body composed of prominent civilian figures—engineers, businessmen, and technocrats—initially assigned to eleven ministries: Interior, Justice, Endowments,

Higher Education, Education, Health, Agriculture, Economy, Social Affairs and Displaced People, Housing and Construction, and Local Administration.[88] Following the creation of the SSG, HTS shared with the new executive body control over the administration and assigned to it most governance functions, de facto delegating some of its authority to segments of the educated urban elite in Idlib.[89] As such, the SSG has been defined as "the product of an encounter between a revolutionary Islamist movement forced to engage in the field of governance while lacking expertise and a pious middle class which benefits from a partial delegation of authority to be involved in local governance."[90]

However, as noted above, some of the government's members were also HTS-linked figures, which detracts from the image of the SSG as an exclusively civilian structure fully independent from HTS.[91] For instance, the SSG's Ministry of Religious Endowments, Islamic Call, and Guidance was traditionally entrusted to figures loyal to HTS.[92] In any other ministry, prospective members of the SSG who were not close to HTS needed to be approved by the group prior to assuming their posts.[93] Finally, it is notable that participation in the SSG was reserved exclusively for a restricted educated urban elite, while the majority of the population remained excluded from decision making and deprived of access to any channel through which to systematically voice their demands. Indeed, the members of the SSG were not elected by the people as their representatives in the different spheres of governance. As reported by an Idlibi civilian, "HTS see themselves as rulers of the area they are based in, and they govern civilian affairs through a civil administration in quotation marks. They want a civilian body but one that is weak and completely under their control."[94]

In February 2019, the SSG created a Shura Council to act as a sort of parliament that would elect the SSG's prime minister and oversee governance. The move was seen as an attempt by the SSG to increase its legitimacy and popularity. However, HTS refrained from conducting public elections in favor of organizing a poll involving only a small number of representatives from local communities, who nominated and elected people to the Shura Council.[95] As has been accurately noted, "the process allowed HTS to participate in the selection of representatives and candidates, giving it influence over both the process and the results."[96] As a matter of fact, HTS—exactly like the Islamic State—constantly rejected democracy as an un-Islamic form of government that contradicts the principles of Islam by entrusting governance to someone other than God. The group also argued that the belief held by some Muslims that democracy is compatible with the Islamic notion of *shura* originates from misunderstanding and from inadequate knowledge, which need to be corrected through education.[97] In a commentary published by 'Atun, the group "does not consider democracy to be right, as it contravenes the sole reference of authority for HTS which is the Islamic Shari'a. . . . Democracy in the doctrinal sense contravenes Islam, as Islam arises on making rule belong to God, whereas democracy arises on making rule belong to one besides God. . . . The one who uses the word democracy from the Muslim masses . . . does not know the extent to which democracy contradicts Islam."[98]

Nonetheless, even though participation in the SSG was confined to a small group, the mere existence of this body composed of prominent civilians who were not necessarily members of HTS indicates that the group—unlike the Islamic State—did not govern in an exclusively unilateral fashion. Rather, civilians under the rule of HTS were treated as partial subjects who, while not allowed to participate directly in decision making, could nonetheless claim an elite that was involved in governing structures and assigned real governance functions by al-Julani's group. At the same time, they benefited from the consultations between HTS's leadership and local community representatives and from the more sporadic encounters between al-Julani and civilians, even if carefully orchestrated by HTS for propaganda purposes. A female humanitarian worker from al-Dana, northern Idlib, when asked about civilian participation under HTS, reported that she saw the situation as being somewhere in the middle with respect to the extremes of full participation and utter exclusion, "though probably still more leaning toward the latter."[99]

GENERATION OF COMPLIANCE

Especially in the earlier stages, when it was still known by the name of Jabhat al-Nusra, al-Julani's group often resorted to coercion to ensure that people complied with its regulations.[100] The coercive measures employed by the group included the closure of schools in which gender segregation was not respected;[101] the closure of shops that remained opened during prayer time;[102] fines for all sorts of violations;[103] the confiscation of prohibited products (e.g., cigarettes);[104] and the closure of prohibited businesses.[105] For instance, a man from Tel Abiyad reported that if a woman was seen by JaN dressing "unproperly," members of the group would visit the woman's house and threaten her male relatives.[106] Similarly, people who lived under JaN in Aleppo, Ra's al-'Ayn, Tel Abiyad, and Tel 'Aran, in northern Syria, reported that women mostly complied with the group's regulations out of fear of punishment against them and their families.[107]

More recently, coercion—or the threat thereof—was used by HTS against those who dared to challenge the group's rule, voice criticism of or opposition to the group's practices or policies, and disagree with its regulations.[108] In late 2019, when some of the residents of Kafr Takharim, northern Idlib, refused to pay zakat on their olive harvest after the latest tax increase, HTS mobilized its military forces, besieged the town, and bombed its buildings, killing and injuring many civilians.[109] As the protests spread from Kafr Takharim to other towns across Idlib, HTS sought to repress all demonstrations by force, until an agreement was eventually reached.[110] Other reports described how HTS arbitrarily arrested residents accused of protesting against the group's governance across areas under its control, to the point that "Hayat Tahrir al-Sham's crackdown on perceived opposition to their rule mirrors some of the same oppressive tactics used by the Syrian government."[111] Female activists taking a stance against HTS were also targeted by the group, with many of them being threatened and intimidated if not beaten outright. For instance, a female reporter who was covering demonstrations at the Bab al-Hawa border crossing with Turkey reported that "a number of Hayat Tahrir al-Sham's personnel attacked me verbally using obscene words, under the pretext that filming is forbidden, and they confiscated my personal phone and my media equipment and directed offensive words at me and my husband."[112]

According to a well-informed report, "through such practices HTS has been able to extend its dominance over the population in areas under its control and to put an end to most protests against the group, and even to enlist individuals in the community to work for HTS for fear of being subjected to its repressive practices in retaliation for any refusal to do so."[113] Interestingly, though, there were other instances in which HTS proved more cautious in its use of coercion, or at least resorted to repression "on more subtle levels."[114] In Maʿarat al-Nuʿman, for instance, the duration and the magnitude of the resistance campaigns in the city discouraged HTS from the use of violence, fearing that this would have negative repercussions.[115]

Not unlike IS, another coercive strategy employed by HTS to generate compliance through fear was the introduction of the *hisba*, which was assigned the task of patrolling the streets to monitor the conduct of citizens.[116] For instance, a woman from Idlib recounted that one day she was stopped by a *hisba* member who accused her of dressing in an un-Islamic way because she was wearing a coat.[117] As people grew to despise the *hisba*, HTS rebranded it the Sawaʿid al-Khair (Goodwill Corps), a body composed of male and female civilians devoted to the enforcement of sharia. Through daily patrols in streets, markets, schools, and other public spaces, they imposed on the people strict norms of behavior and ensured that everyone complied with those norms. When violations were identified, the corps conducted investigations, arrested people, and imposed punishments. Verbal abuse, monetary fines, and corporal punishment thus became a reality of life under HTS and its Sawaʿid al-Khair.[118] It is worth noticing here that, unlike IS, HTS mostly refrained from carrying out its punishments in the public sphere, and instead mainly inflicted its most severe punishments in the group's prisons and detention centers.[119]

In early May 2020, it was reported that the Sawaʿid al-Khair had been rebranded into the Markaz al-Falah (Bliss Center).[120] As noted, "HTS usually changes the name of the apparatus as a way of mollifying public anger, especially when violations by its personnel and clashes with members of the public escalate."[121] However, and as a confirmation that the new name was nothing more than a facade, a Syrian activist reported that the various morality bodies were even manned by the same people as before.[122] Like the bodies that came before it, the Markaz al-Falah operated by means of patrols through the province's streets and markets.[123] Most recently, the Markaz al-Falah was replaced by a new morality police with similar responsibilities, affiliated with the SSG's police apparatus.[124]

At the same time that it adopted coercive practices, HTS also engaged in noncoercive ones. Specifically, it promoted its ideology and political project through propaganda activities and encouraged the population to internalize its norms of conduct. Here, a major role was played by Ebaʾ, a media network affiliated with HTS. Eba' was active distributing hard copies of its weekly newspaper to the people. This usually occurred in the public spaces of the main urban centers, where Eba' personnel would travel by car and hand out their materials to all passers-by.[125] At the same time, Eba' was also engaged in the production of online propaganda material covering a wide variety of topics and targeting different audiences.[126]

In the main towns and cities of Idlib and rural Aleppo, HTS also created *da'wah* centers that engaged in various propaganda activities: hanging posters and billboards in public spaces, distributing pamphlets, conducting *da'wah* sessions, screening videos, and organizing public information campaigns.[127] Other channels on which the group traditionally relied to communicate its regulations and encourage people to comply with them include public announcements and sermons at mosques, especially during Friday prayers.[128] For instance, the prohibition against publicly breaking the fast of Ramadan was communicated through media, social media, announcements at the mosque, and *da'wah* offices.[129] As a result, religious leaders and preachers close to HTS became an important vehicle through which to promote the group's ideology among the population.[130]

The group also sought to generate compliance by means of amplifying its governance efforts. This, for instance, was the case with respect to the provision of public goods and services, the maintenance of law and order, the building of roads, the restoration of water access, and the provision of employment opportunities.[131] At the onset of its activities in Syria, for example, JaN's public messages portrayed the group "as a force that serves the Syrian people by fighting the regime, while touting its 'true' Islamic credentials."[132] More recently, it also emphasized its contribution to people's well-being through the distribution of *zakat* to the needy and through its response to the health emergency caused by the coronavirus.[133] More generally, HTS was active in releasing statements and reports that highlighted its governance accomplishments for the benefit of the people: the construction of new roads, the restoration of access to water, the provision of employment opportunities, the restoration of the rule of law, and the maintenance of security.[134] In its own words from the Eba' newsletter, HTS presented its governance effort as an "exemplary model" for contemporary revolutions and as the "best model" available among the anti-Assad rebels.[135]

Finally, HTS recently organized public gatherings in order to connect with the local population and convey its interpretation of Islam in a direct and immediate way. For instance, it organized fun days for children that included activities such as tugs-of-war, ice-cream-eating competitions, and Quran readings. Similarly, family fairs were organized as part of Eid celebrations, during which dolls and other toys were distributed to children.[136] In mid-2018, the *Ma'an ila al-Janah* (Together to Heaven) campaign was organized by HTS to instruct people on the importance of complying with sharia.[137] In mid-December 2020, HTS organized a public exhibition whose aim was to encourage the people of Idlib to better understand and familiarize themselves with the figure of the Prophet.[138] Interestingly, the emphasis placed on proselytization was consistent with the importance attached by al-Julani to popular socialization and religious education; according to the leader of HTS, in fact, Syrians could not be expected to act immediately as impeccable Muslims, but rather needed to be encouraged through *da'wah* to integrate Islam into their daily lives.[139]

APPROACH TO OUTSIDERS

In terms of its attitude toward other actors, JaN—much unlike the Islamic State—opted from the outset for a certain degree of coordination and cooperation with other opposition groups. As early as 2013, in fact, al-Julani (who back then was still bound by *bay'ah* to al-Qaeda's senior leadership) argued that "Dr Ayman [al-Zawahiri], may God protect him, always tells us to meet with other factions. We are committed to this and this is a basic part of the principles of jihadist work in general."[140] Interestingly, JaN initially cooperated in matters of governance not only with other Salafi-jihadist organizations with whom it had clear ideological affinities, but also with non-Salafi-jihadist and more nationally oriented Islamist groups. Rather than on merely ideological grounds, cooperation with armed groups from the anti-Assad opposition was built on a shared presence in the same territories and a shared aspiration to build governance structures opposed to those of the Syrian state. The exception was represented by groups considered hostile or aligned with Western countries, such as the Syrian Revolutionaries Front and the Hazm movement.[141]

JaN initially associated itself with other armed opposition groups in the establishment of joint sharia courts in charge of arbitrating disputes, conducting trials, and punishing captured prisoners, alleged collaborators, and criminals.[142] The aim was to rely on existing and consolidated rebel networks to provide legitimacy and credibility to shared structures for the application of sharia.[143] For instance, in Aleppo in 2012 JaN together with the Islamist groups Liwa al-Tawhid, Ahrar al-Sham, Liwa al-Fatah, Harakat Fajr al-Islam, and Suqur al-Sham established the Aleppo Sharia Commission (ASC).[144] As has been noted, "[t]he Committee [sic] was intended as a joint venture set up by a number of distinct armed factions to regulate both civilian and military affairs, but also meant to have its own law enforcement capability, along with its relief work branch."[145]

As far as the ASC's judicial function is concerned, a spokesperson reported that it applied sharia while excluding the strictest *hudud* punishments. Local activists, however, revealed that sometimes executions were carried out to punish specific crimes.[146] The ASC also had a police force that was formed by selected members of the different factions and was its de facto executive body.[147] Besides being involved in judicial matters, the ASC was also involved in the provision of education, health care, the management of mills and mosques, and the reparation of electricity and water infrastructure.[148] To engage in those activities the ASC was relying on a series of offices, such as the Education Office, the Ifta Office, the Mosque Affairs Office, the Service Office, the Medical Office, the Judicial Office, the Grain Office, the Mills Office.[149]

Another instance of JaN's collaboration with other groups was observed in December 2012, when al-Julani's group and nine other factions in Deir ez-Zor announced the formation of the Mujahidin Shura Council (MSC) as a local anti-Assad coalition. In March 2013, JaN and other groups from the MSC formed the Sharia Board in the Eastern Region as a local court. As has been noted, the MSC "formed the backbone of [JaN's] governing coalition in eastern Syria and represents a successful [JaN] rebel network."[150] Similar to the ASC, the MSC also had a Da'wah Office, a police service, as well as offices overseeing services and aid provision.[151] In eastern Ghouta, in June 2014, JaN and groups such as Jaysh al-Islam, Faylaq al-Rahman, Ahrar al-Sham, and al-Itihad al-Islami li-Ajnad al-Sham founded a Judiciary Council in order to unify the various private sharia courts.[152]

Thus, at the beginning of its governance experience JaN opted to insert itself into multigroup judicial systems. However, those earliest experiments in cooperation were abandoned relatively quickly. According to a recording released by al-Julani, the problem with the existing sharia commissions was that "some [groups] looked at the commissions as a way to implement the sharia, which was right, while others looked at the commissions as a political front from which they wished to gain."[153] However, while al-Julani's comments suggest that JaN was willing to take the distance from governance structures that had been instrumentalized by some factions to reach their own political interests, it has been accurately noted that JaN's distancing from the joint sharia structures was part of a broader effort by the group to gradually engage in more exclusionary forms of governance. This propensity for a greater monopoly over governance occurred as JaN's "role and influence grew substantially due to its strong discipline, effective military performance, shrewd strategy of tactical and operational alliances, and ability to take advantage of the opposition's infighting and divisions."[154]

In a leaked recording from July 2014, al-Julani is heard saying that "the time has come . . . for us to establish an Islamic emirate in al-Sham, to implement the limits [hudud] and punishments of Allah and his laws in every sense of the word, without compromise, complacency, equivocation, or circumvention."[155] In that same month, JaN withdrew from the joint arrangements to establish its own direct governance in previously ungoverned areas in Syria's northwestern governorates.[156] In place of those shared structures, JaN established the Dar al-Qada' as its own judicial body in different towns of Idlib Governorate. According to a former judge in Idlib not affiliated with JaN and its judicial structures, over the course of 2016 the "Dar al-Qadaa began to dominate more and more judicial institutions."[157]

To be certain, however, JaN's cooperative attitude toward other armed groups of the Syrian opposition did not completely end with the formation of the Dar al-Qada'. In 2015, for instance, JaN entered into the Jaysh al-Fatah alliance alongside Ahrar al-Sham. This alliance even led to a joint Jaysh al-Fatah civil administration of places like Idlib city and Ariha, in Idlib Governorate.[158] As noted, this was "the province's first real experiment in joint governance by Idlib's Islamist factions."[159] At the same time, though, true governance collaboration failed because al-Julani's group and Ahrar al-Sham competed in the provision of services and maintained their own areas of influence.[160] The alliance inevitably broke down as al-Julani's group sought to assert its military and administrative hegemony.

Following the creation of HTS and the imposition of the latter's hegemonic control over the governorate of Idlib at the expense of other armed groups, al-Julani's group progressively abandoned cooperation with other armed factions (Ahrar al-Sham, for instance, was defeated militarily by HTS in July 2017).[161] Nonetheless, HTS began to pursue some forms of cooperation with other local actors. In some instances, the group pursued cooperation with local councils.[162] The latter were civilian bodies offering local governance in opposition-controlled areas that were originally conceived and developed to offer an alternative to the institutions of the state and serve as a cornerstone for any state-building effort in the wake of the civil war.[163] For instance, the head of the local council in the village of Kukaniyah, in the northern Idlib countryside, reported that HTS and the SSG engaged in administration together with the council, which had offices for services, relief, relations, security, and education.[164] The same was reported from the town of Harim, also in the northern Idlib countryside, where the local council's media office described its association with HTS and the SSG and their cooperation on areas where the council had offices, such as cleaning, technical matters, relief, financial matters, public services, administrative affairs, police, and veterinary services.[165] In the town of Ma'ardabsa, eastern Idlib, the local council also entered into a cooperation with HTS, with the HTS-affiliated Saraqib power station, and with local owners of generators in order to provide electricity to the households of several towns in the Saraqib countryside.[166]

However, the relationship between HTS and local councils was a complex one and cooperation was not always pursued. On some occasions, in fact, HTS opted to infiltrate local councils, sideline them through its alternative administrative structures, and even dissolve them.[167] For instance, in August 2017 HTS instructed some local councils in Idlib to hand over their offices to HTS's specialized institutions, under the pretext of unifying governance efforts and building "a united civilian administration of central institutions."[168] According to the head of the local civilian council in Kaftin, "in the province of Idlib and the north of Aleppo, the commission [HTS] is currently forming a civil administration in the name of the General Services Administration, and is directing for the previous administration represented in the local councils to become affiliated with this General Administration. . . . The council that will not accept this affiliation to it will be dissolved and a replacement will be formed for it."[169] Between October and November 2017, in the town of Saraqib, in eastern Idlib, several local residents reported that HTS seized a series of institutions affiliated with the city's council. These included the finance service, the land and civil registry, the water unit, and the potato market.[170] Local observers suggested that the seizure was part of HTS's effort to weaken the local council, take its revenues, and assert its own administrative and military control over the city.[171]

While cooperation with civilian councils was subject to variation across localities, HTS's cooperation with local notables, such as businessmen and technocrats, was more consistent.[172] As noted above, HTS included prominent and experienced individuals in its governance project through the SSG, which was born as "a largely technocratic body run by individuals from the educated middle class, almost all of whom had little or no link to HTS or its predecessors."[173] Its leadership included academics, civil society figures, independent Islamists, and local businessmen. For instance, the first prime minister of the SSG, Muhammad al-Sheikh, was an academic, and the second prime minister of the SSG, Fawaz Hilal, was a local businessman.[174] 'Ali Keda, prime minister of the SSG from 2019 until 2024, was also a local electrical engineer.[175]

Other interesting forms of cooperation took place with tribal leaders. Following the formation of the SSG, HTS held meetings with tribal sheikhs to convince them to join its governance project.[176] In one of the conferences organized under the auspices of the SSG in January 2018, the foundations were laid for the establishment of the Council for Tribes and Clans, which was announced later in June. The council included 125 members from prominent local tribes.[177] In early March 2020, the council established a new body known as the General Reconciliation Council, which then created three committees that worked in collaboration with HTS's institutions.[178] In fact, the cooperative relationship between HTS and the tribes is perhaps best exemplified by the degree of autonomy that HTS and the SSG accorded to Idlib's tribes to manage their own internal affairs.[179] As was noted by someone with direct knowledge of the daily reality in

Idlib, "HTS's attempts to associate the tribes to some authority is most evident in that the group has been allowing the application of certain tribal regulations, such as in terms of murder."[180] Regulations covering marriage were also reportedly left to the tribes' own jurisdiction and customs.[181]

Other indications of the importance that HTS attached to the inclusion of the tribes are the direct contacts between al-Julani and Idlib's tribal leaders, some of which were noted above. In May 2021, for instance, a video emerged on social media showing the leader of HTS in a tent meeting with a number of tribal elders during a visit on the occasion of Eid el-Fitr. At the meeting, al-Julani stated that HTS wanted to solidify ties with the tribes because it depended on them to restore what the Syrian government has destroyed.[182] This was not the first time that HTS's leader met with tribal leaders. Over the course of 2020, al-Julani met on multiple occasions with tribal elders in various areas of Idlib Governorate, such as Jabal al-Zawiyah, central Idlib, to discuss the situation in their territories, collect their comments, and address their demands.[183] Prior to that, in early August 2018 al-Julani met with the clan elders of Taftanaz, eastern Idlib, and other residents of the area.[184]

Besides local actors such as technocrats and tribal leaders, HTS and the SSG increasingly adopted a quite welcoming attitude toward international NGOs and aid organizations, on which Idlib was largely dependent—especially in the areas of health care and education.[185] As argued by al-Julani during an interview with the International Crisis Group in January 2020, "our policy towards NGOs has changed. We are willing to facilitate the work of any organization that would like to return to work in Idlib, and we pledge non-interference. We will reconcile with any organization we've had problems with in the past if they are prepared to help the people here."[186] In the context of the COVID-19 pandemic, the then head of the SSG, 'Ali Keda, even called "on humanitarian organizations and the World Health Organization to share its responsibility in the liberated north [the areas of Syria under HTS]."[187] Thanks to this greater cooperation with international organizations, in April 2021 HTS-controlled northwestern Syria received 53,800 doses of coronavirus vaccine through the global vaccine-sharing platform COVAX. Inoculations started one month later.[188] As of August 2021, 55,000 doses had been distributed in Idlib, with priority given to health-care workers, the elderly, and people with chronic diseases.[189] In September 2021, there was an additional delivery of 358,000 doses.[190]

Other cases of cooperation between HTS/SSG and foreign organizations were also observed. For instance, in December 2021 officials from HTS and the SSG attended the opening ceremony of a food market in Idlib—a project that was implemented by the 'Ata' humanitarian relief association with funds from the Qatar Charity Foundation.[191] In July 2022, the volunteer organization Syrian Civil Defense (also known as the White Helmets) reported that it was working alongside the SSG on a project aimed at pumping water into the irrigation canals that link the areas of 'Ain al-Zarqa and Sahl al-Ruj, in the western countryside of Idlib.[192] International NGOs working in or on Idlib also confirmed that the SSG was "relatively responsive to their demands, including by removing taxes on aid-carrying vehicles and lifting an insurance fee it once levied on projects."[193] In this regard, a senior SSG official said that "when we imposed a nominal tax on vehicles delivering aid across the border [in 2019], donors threatened to end their support, so we walked back our decision."[194]

At the same time, however, the relationship between HTS and NGOs was not always as positive as the group's official narrative tried to suggest. In fact, there are reports that HTS and the SSG sought to control the humanitarian aid that was being provided to Idlib and parts of the Aleppo countryside.[195] For instance, specific conditions were imposed on those NGOs willing to work in HTS territories, such as the obligation to provide HTS with pictures of all employees and a copy of their job contracts as well as the obligation to include HTS-affiliated individuals in the NGOs' projects. For projects that aimed to support women and youth, a special approval had to be obtained in advance.[196] Those NGOs that refused to comply with HTS's conditions risked seeing their workers arrested, their offices stormed, and their possessions confiscated.[197] HTS was also accused of illicitly acquiring part of the NGO-provided humanitarian aid.[198]

Finally, it is worth mentioning the forms of cooperation that took place over the past years between the SSG and Turkey, as the latter was increasingly attempting to deepen its position in Idlib. After the Syrian pound collapsed in early 2020, the SSG removed the currency from Idlib's market and replaced it with the Turkish lira.[199] Within hours of the announcement, truckloads of lira began arriving in Idlib from Turkey, via 'Afrin.[200]

Turkey also began to provide electricity to HTS-controlled territories,[201] where power outages used to be common, and admitted telecommunication towers into Idlib.[202] Interestingly, in each sector in which Turkish products were extended into Idlib, the SSG provided control to HTS fronts, such as the Sham Bank for the Turkish lira, Watad, Kaf Trading, and al-Shahba Petroleum for oil and gas, and Green Energy for electricity.[203]

PROPENSITY TO CHANGE

In some cases, HTS opted for maintenance. Similar to what was noted before in the case of the Islamic State, maintenance was observed in the case of professions requiring specific skills, such as jobs in oil plants and other infrastructure.[204] For instance, as soon as JaN established its control over the oil fields of eastern Syria in 2012–2013, employees in the local oil companies were allowed to remain in their posts. The condition for retaining one's job, however, was pledging *bay'ah* to al-Julani.[205] Similarly, in 2019 HTS disbanded the Free Syrian Police (FSP)—a network of police forces affiliated with the opposition's Syrian Interim Government—in western Aleppo and Idlib. It gave to the former members of the FSP the opportunity to join its own Islamic Police as long as they underwent "security examination" and training.[206] Police members interested in the opportunity were required to submit a formal application to the SSG's Interior Ministry in Idlib.[207] As reported by the chief of the FSP, "the SSG asked us either to work under its umbrella or hand over our stations and equipment. This is what eventually happened; we handed over everything, including all machinery, equipment and vehicles."[208] A police officer within the FSP also reported that "two members of the Syrian Salvation Government visited our station in Haritan . . . to conduct an inventory of the number of officers, individual weapons, cars and vehicles, and offered to [let us] join the Islamic Police."[209]

Other instances of maintenance were observed in the education sector, where HTS closed some preexisting schools and institutions for higher education and asserted its control over those left open, justifying the move as an effort to unify and better regulate education throughout its territories.[210] As far as curriculum is concerned, in the beginning there were some attempts to reform religious education. With the passing of time, however, these efforts were progressively abandoned. Even the curriculum taught in secular schools did not undergo substantial change.[211] According to a person from Idlib directly involved in the education sector, "Arabic language, mathematics, English language, sciences, religion and physical education are taught. With regards to the content of the curricula, it has remained as it was before the revolution with some simple changes."[212] Another person discussed those curricular changes as being mostly the elimination of any reference to the Baath Party and the insertion of more hours devoted to religious studies.[213]

However, while maintenance was observed in some respects, HTS engaged to a greater extent in the introduction of innovations. As noted, "HTS replaced almost all that existed before and replaced it with their new structures and practices for doing things."[214] In the security sector, JaN initially operated through a joint sharia police. Over time, however, it progressively abandoned those shared formations and proceeded to provide security and order through its own personnel and police stations. For instance, in an administrative document dating to January 2015 the group announced the closure of the police centers of 'Anadan, Hureitan, and Kafr Hamra, northwestern Syria, that were linked to the Free Police of Aleppo.[215] In a later document, JaN described the opening of its own police stations in the same towns. Interestingly, all equipment, ammunition, weapons, and vehicles that had been in possession of the previous police stations were transferred to JaN's new stations.[216]

As seen above, when in 2019 HTS established its hegemonic control over Idlib, it disbanded the FSP and imposed its own Islamic Police as the force in charge of law enforcement.[217] In the security realm, moreover, HTS also came to operate through the General Security Service (GSS), which functioned as an intelligence-gathering body. The GSS has been referred to as "HTS' version of the FBI, though existing in an authoritarian framework and with far less sophisticated means of forensic investigation."[218] Five key components of the GSS were its regional information office, the internal security division, the organized crime portfolio, the regime portfolio, and the extremists' portfolio (which was created to deal with the Islamic State's cells and members, with the al-Qaeda-linked Hurras ad-Din group, and with foreign fighters reunited in Jund Allah and Jund al-Sham).[219]

As seen above, in the judicial sector JaN initially participated into joint rebel courts.[220] In those joint judicial structures, a combination of sharia, some provisions of the Syrian civil code, and local customs was often observed, as was the case in Dara'a.[221] At a later stage, however, JaN created the Dar al-Qada' as its own exclusive judicial authority. According to a judge in rural Aleppo, the Dar al-Qada' included an office responsible for receiving and recording claims, scheduling judicial cases, transmitting notifications and warrants, and archiving cases; an office in charge of reaching reconciliation between the parties of a dispute; an office responsible for financial disputes and financial dealings; and an office responsible for criminal cases and punishments. In addition to those four offices, there were the prisons and the executive force.[222] In fact, the Dar al-Qada' was conceived as the only body with authority in matters of arrest and detention; indeed, all military factions were prohibited from arresting and detaining a person—even if caught committing a crime—and obliged to consult the Dar al-Qada' "to undertake the necessary judicial proceedings."[223]

Unlike previous formations, the Dar al-Qada' was in charge of enforcing JaN's version of sharia. The punishments for those who transgressed JaN's legal system included ta'zir and qisas.[224] Conversely, hudud seem to have been applied only in exceptional, specific, and serious circumstances. As was reportedly recognized by al-Julani, in fact, flexibility and moderation needed to be shown when applying sharia and Islamic practices of governance. For instance, in the province of Aleppo hudud punishments—specifically, stoning to death and execution by gunfire—were applied against people accused of fornication and homosexuality.[225] In another case in the province, five men were sentenced to death after being accused of having collaborated with the "apostate" Syrian regime.[226] Interesting innovations were also introduced in terms of personnel. Upon creating the Dar al-Qada', JaN issued a call for employees encouraging all those with an expertise in Islamic jurisprudence and who deemed themselves sufficiently qualified for a job in the judiciary to present themselves for an interview.[227]

Following the creation of the SSG, judicial affairs were entrusted to the Ministry of Justice, which presided over a network of sharia courts.[228] Reportedly, the judicial system in the areas under the SSG was structured into chambers for civil and commercial suits, which included a Court of

Cassation, a Court of Appeal, and a Court of First Instance; chambers for criminal suits, which included criminal courts, a First Criminal Court, and a Second Criminal Court; administrative judiciary, which comprised an Administrative Court; military judiciary, which included military courts, Third Military Court, Second Military Court, First Military Court.[229] As noted above, moreover, recent years witnessed a greater propensity on the part of HTS to allow tribes to continue the application of their traditional regulations for intra-tribal matters related to murders and marriages.

To provide other public goods and services, JaN initially created the General Administration for Services (GAS) (also known as the Public Administration for Services) as the responsible administrative body. First introduced in the city of Aleppo, it was later expanded to Idlib as well.[230] The GAS was itself divided into different directorates, each dealing with a specific aspect of service provision: Mills and Bakeries; Electricity; Water and Sanitation; Technical Services; Agriculture and Irrigation.[231] In 2017, the GAS was converted into the Civil Administration for Services (CAS), which, similar to the GAS, included a series of sub-bodies such as the Economic Office, the Office for Supervision of Organizations and Associations, and the Public Institution for Electricity.[232] The CAS was later brought under the SSG's Ministry of Services. The first head of the SSG, Muhammad al-Sheikh, reported that the government held a meeting with the CAS's directors after which it took over all the services that the body was running, including water, electricity, and transportation.[233] In the reports of Idlib's residents, the ministry was indeed described as engaged in the provision of water and electricity as well as the reparation of sewage lines and the paving of roads.[234] According to a video published by the ministry itself, reparation of sanitation facilities was also undertaken.[235]

In the education sector, institutions of learning were mostly maintained and no particular change was introduced to the curriculum, as noted above.[236] However, in the case of universities, HTS and the SSG redesigned some degrees: at the University of Idlib, for instance, the Department of Law and the Department of Islamic Studies were unified under a single department. There, students were required to study the legal and religious aspects of jihad and were examined on issues including the rights of prisoners, the treatment of spies, the spoils of war, the difference between suicide and martyrdom, as well as the status of Christians and Alawites and the applicability of *jizyah* to them.[237] As argued by a student from Idlib, "everywhere else the law and studies of Islam are two separate departments, but not at the University of Idlib. After all, Abu Fath al-Farghali [a prominent Egyptian-born radical religious figure within HTS] teaches there, so this is not surprising."[238]

Some innovations were also introduced with respect to the institutions responsible for educational affairs. Prior to the creation of the SSG, education was under the responsibility of the Higher Education Council, while following the creation of the SSG this was placed under the responsibility of the government's Ministry of Education.[239] Innovations were also observed with respect to morality laws. At the University of Idlib, for instance, gender mixing was prohibited, to the point that even mixed-gender education groups on social media were banned by the SSG.[240] Some exception to the ban on gender mixing was reported in smaller schools.[241] Prior to that, a dress code notice had been issued for female and male students, with the former required to "wear loose clothing that covers the entire body up to the ankles, and is free of any adornment."[242] Wearing high-heeled shoes, using perfumes, and applying cosmetics were also prohibited.[243] Medical facilities, which were also maintained to the extent possible, were also subjected to a series of innovations in terms of morality laws. Following the creation of the SSG, in fact, the Ministry of Health was charged with the task of managing Idlib's hospitals and medical centers and regulating the health-care sector.[244] Among the ministry's first measures was the imposition of a strict sharia dress code and gender segregation on all medical workers and patients in the hospitals under its control.[245]

In the field of taxation, JaN/HTS traditionally engaged in the collection of *zakat* and its distribution to the needy, which the group saw as a way to demonstrate its governance capabilities.[246] For instance, in June 2015 in the town of al-Dana, JaN released a statement urging all those in possession of some wealth to register with the group's tax authority in order to pay the corresponding *zakat*, in either cash or goods.[247] Several videos released by HTS show members of its General Authority of Zakat going from house to house to distribute *zakat* shares.[248] In other cases it is the people themselves who go to the authority's offices to collect envelopes containing their *zakat* money.[249] These videos show that in the case of business owners, such as the proprietors of jewelry shops, sweet shops, and clothing shops, *zakat* was collected in cash, while in the case of farmers it was collected in the form of produce.[250]

Besides *zakat*, HTS imposed fees for public services such as electricity and water.[251] As argued by a woman who lived under HTS, "al-Hei'a [HTS] imposed a lot of taxes—on water, electricity, transport."[252] HTS also imposed taxes on car registrations, shops, and street vendors.[253] At the same time, HTS intervened in the imposition of education fees, quadrupling the cost of studying at the university level. A student from Idlib, for example, said that while they used to pay a tuition fee of $300, they needed to pay $1,800 to study in the universities accredited by HTS.[254] A man displaced from the Aleppo countryside to Idlib reported that "you need a lot of money every month [to pay taxes]."[255] Some civilians, moreover, complained that the taxes raised by HTS in exchange for its services were not proportionate to what it actually offered. A man from Kafr Takharim expressed his feelings on the issue in the following terms: "HTS wanted to control everything, they wanted a share in everything. They imposed taxes on 'services' and 'hygiene.' Those two features were non-existent. As my friend keeps saying: is hygiene hiding from us? Because I can't find it."[256]

Furthermore, aid organizations that wanted to operate in HTS's territories were often required to pay, which became a source of friction between NGOs and HTS.[257] In the words of a field coordinator working on conflict resolution, HTS would often try to "impose *atawat* [royalties] on organizations distributing aid but the outcome of such attempts depends mostly on how much resistance the group faces. In some cases, the organizations will give in. . . . But in other cases, some organizations either reject to pay or refuse to increase HTS' percentage and threaten to terminate their services."[258] As far as NGOs are concerned, taxes could be collected in different ways, but the most common method seemed to be that of giving to HTS a percentage of the organization's aid. In other cases, the organization paid cash to HTS.[259]

Moreover, road taxes were levied on people and goods passing through territories controlled by HTS.[260] As noted by well-informed scholars, "crossings with the regime and with Turkey are considered the most important and foundational aspects of HTS's financial empire in NW Syria, in terms of both strategic significance and revenues."[261] In June 2017,

HTS took over the Bab al-Hawa border crossing—the most significant civilian, humanitarian, and commercial crossing with Turkey—and proceeded to administer it through its General Administration of Crossings.[262] As noted by a media activist who resides between the countryside of Aleppo and Idlib, the entry and exit fees at the Bab al-Hawa crossing on the Turkish-Syrian border were particularly important for HTS.[263] Similarly, an SSG employee reported that "most of the SSG's resources come from taxes and royalties on citizens and organizations, as well as entry and exit fees at the Bab al-Hawa crossing."[264] In fact, reports put the amount of monthly revenue from Bab al-Hawa at $10–$15 million.[265] However, taxes were also imposed on internal crossings connecting Idlib to the Aleppo countryside, such as al-'Ais, al-Mansurah, and al-Ghazawiyah.[266]

In terms of regulation of behavior, JaN/HTS introduced some new norms of conduct. These included a prohibition against gender mixing in schools in all grades above the fifth; the ban on smoking; the regulation of dress codes, especially for women; the closing of shops during prayer time; preventing women from accessing public space without a *mahram*; the banning of entertainment stores with billiards, table football, and computer games; rules against breaking the fast of Ramadan; and the ban on firing guns at weddings and funerals as expression of joy

TABLE 5.1. The model of governance of Hay'at Tahrir al-Sham

Inclusivity	Discrimination (Christians, Druze, Shias, women)
Civilian engagement	Partial subjection (rejection of democratic process, but creation of SSG)
Generation of compliance	Coercion and persuasion (e.g., punishment of dissenters and *da'wah* materials)
Approach to outsiders	Partial cooperation (cooperation with businessmen, technocrats, elders, tribal sheikhs, international aid organizations, Turkish government)
Propensity to change	Extensive innovation and limited maintenance (e.g., new sharia-based judicial system, new taxation system, new norms of conduct, and maintenance of employees upon engaging in *tawbah*)

or grief.[267] However, it is noticeable that some of those regulations were progressively moderated over the years, as HTS asserted its hegemony over Idlib. Finally, and as seen above when discussing the generation of compliance, HTS introduced monitoring bodies to ensure that people behave in conformity with its regulations.[268] While the names of those bodies were repeatedly changed over time, their responsibilities and functions remained mostly unchanged.

In this chapter, I have observed that HTS did not rule equally over everyone, distinguishing between Sunni Muslims, on the one hand, and Shias, Druze, and Christians, on the other. At the same time, different rules were applied to women. In any case, no system of broad civilian participation was developed. Nonetheless, a small elite was included in governance through the SSG, and elders and tribal sheikhs were engaged in consultation. On some occasions, HTS also engaged in functions of governance in cooperation with other actors. With respect to preexisting institutions and personnel, in some cases HTS opted to maintain trained and experienced professionals. In most cases, however, it introduced extensive innovations. Finally, it is to be noted that HTS resorted to both coercion and persuasion to generate compliance.

6

RAISING THE BLACK FLAG IN YEMEN

The Governance Project of al-Qaeda in the Arabian Peninsula

A mong the many Salafi-jihadist armed groups that have engaged in governance following the 2011 Arab Spring uprisings, al-Qaeda in the Arabian Peninsula (AQAP) has received perhaps the least attention, which is probably a consequence of the little consideration that the international community has traditionally devoted to Yemen. To be sure, some important and valuable exceptions do exist, as we saw in the introduction. However, the dominant tendency has been to focus the greatest attention on the Islamic State, while much less interest has been devoted to Yemen and AQAP. Believing that greater attention needs to be given to the Yemeni context if we want to develop a comprehensive understanding of Salafi-jihadist governance, in this chapter I will focus on al-Qaeda in the Arabian Peninsula. Following the same approach that I employed in the previous two chapters, I will start by reviewing AQAP's transition from insurgency to governance. I will then investigate the governance strategies that AQAP adopted throughout its experience as ruler, again referring to the five dimensions identified in my typology. As I mentioned in the introduction, AQAP engaged in governance twice—in 2011–2012, in the context of the Arab Spring uprisings, and again in 2015–2016, in the context of the civil war that erupted as the Houthis (Zaydi Shias from the northern governorate of Saʿda) launched an insurgency against the government. In this chapter, I will apply my typology to both periods of governance. However, when contradictions between the first and the second period are identified, I will refer exclusively to AQAP's most recent experience, during which the group did indeed reconsider some of its previous approaches to governance.

FROM INSURGENCY TO GOVERNANCE

The predecessor of al-Qaeda in the Arabian Peninsula was founded by Usama bin Laden shortly after al-Qaeda's attacks against the United States on September 11 with the goal of launching jihad inside Saudi Arabia, driving the Americans out of the kingdom, and overthrowing the "infidel" Saudi monarchy.[1] After a series of attacks against American and Saudi targets in 2003, that cell became the target of Riyadh's counterterrorism campaign. By 2006, several al-Qaeda-linked jihadists saw themselves forced to abandon Saudi Arabia and opted to seek refuge in Yemen.[2]

Yemen, in fact, had long retained a place of importance in al-Qaeda's strategic vision.[3] In 1996, bin Laden, whose own family hailed from Yemen's southern Hadramawt Governorate, stated that the country's mountainous geography and armed tribes offered ideal conditions to establish an al-Qaeda safe haven there.[4] Two years earlier, a letter authored by an al-Qaeda operative suggested that Yemen, characterized by ineffectual governance and internal conflict, was the "flank" of the Arabian Peninsula, a location from where it would be possible to threaten Western military forces and economic interests in the region.[5] In 2006, Abu Mus'ab al-Suri (whom we encountered in chapter 3 as one al-Qaeda's main strategists) concurred that Yemen's topography, demography, and history made the country "the most ready for jihad among countries in the Arab world" as well as a "fundamental pillar" of jihad.[6]

In February 2006, twenty-three al-Qaeda-affiliated jihadists (including prominent figures such as Nasir al-Wuhayshi and Qasim al-Raymi, who would become leaders of AQAP) staged a daring escape form the Sanaa Central Prison, in the Yemeni capital. Half a year later, a group calling itself al-Qaeda in the Land of Yemen launched vehicle-born suicide attacks against Western oil facilities in Ma'rib, northern Yemen, and Hadramawt.[7] In 2009, the Yemeni and the Saudi branches of al-Qaeda merged and adopted the name of al-Qaeda in the Arabian Peninsula.[8]

As far as the formation of AQAP is concerned, however, one must also consider the role played by the regime of 'Ali 'Abdullah Saleh. In fact, it is widely believed in Yemen that the government allowed AQAP to emerge and thrive as part of a strategy to secure American financial and military aid to ostensibly combat the group, while actually reaching a tacit nonaggression pact with it out of convenience.[9] In other words, it is a common understanding in the country that AQAP and the regime had been engaged from the outset in a relationship of both competition and collaboration.[10] Interestingly, this understanding of the AQAP-government relationship continued to prevail even after the Saleh regime collapsed in 2011 and a new government took power.[11]

In 2011, the Arab Spring uprisings that had already taken place in Tunisia and Egypt arrived in Yemen as well. There, people from different backgrounds—poor people, members of the lower middle class, intellectuals, rural inhabitants, urban men and women, people from strongly tribal areas, people from areas where tribalism is of little relevance—took to the street demanding the end of President Saleh's rule and the transformation of the country's social, political, and economic structures.[12] As has been noted, "the slogan that brought everyone together and kept the largest numbers out in the streets was 'irhal' (roughly translated as 'get out'), directed at President Saleh, but it implied not just getting rid of him personally but getting rid of the whole corrupt and nepotistic structures around him."[13]

A turning point occurred on March 18, 2011, when Saleh's forces responded to peaceful demonstrations by killing fifty-two protesters and injuring around three hundred more. Following that episode, General 'Ali Muhsin al-Ahmar, commander of the army's First Armored Brigade, abandoned the regime and sided with the protesters, taking half of the Yemeni Armed Forces with him. Weakened by the defection of a large part of the army, Saleh's political survival appeared increasingly at risk. He was eventually deposed in February 2012.

Taking advantage of the combination of instability, insecurity, and power vacuum, AQAP launched a military campaign aimed at conquering territories outside the state's control.[14] In fact, AQAP's leader, Nasir al-Wuhayshi (also known by his *kunya*, or nom de guerre, Abu Basir), saw in the unfolding disorder and spreading insecurity of 2011 an unmissable opportunity for his group to build an Islamic emirate in Yemen, which one day could be part of a larger al-Qaeda caliphate.[15] For AQAP, in fact, the ambition was to establish "the rule of Islamic sharia," "defeat the systems of *jahiliyya* [pre-Islamic ignorance], disbelief, secularism, socialism, Shia and others who have taken democracy as a religion," and "bring back the Islamic *khilafa* [caliphate] and . . . rule according to shar'iah."[16]

In this regard, al-Wuhayshi wrote to al-Qaeda's bin Laden that "our situation, thanks to Allah, is improving for the mujahidin," and "if you ever wanted Sanaa, today is the day."[17] As "the political conflict [in Yemen] [was] deteriorating" and "the situation of the country [was] about to fall apart," al-Wuhayshi's fear was that if the mujahidin did not take advantage of such an opportunity, someone else would—whether the Muslim Brotherhood–affiliated Islah Party, the "southern communists" (i.e., the southern secessionist forces that wanted the reestablishment of an independent South Yemen, as had been the case under the former People's Democratic Republic of Yemen), or the Houthis.[18] Yet, bin Laden had learned his lesson from the failure of the Islamic State of Iraq in Anbar Governorate and was in favor of a more cautious approach. As noted in chapter 3, in the context of the Salafi-jihadist approach to matters of governance in the aftermath of the Arab Spring, bin Laden warned al-Wuhayshi against establishing a state before being capable of maintaining it. In his words, "we [al-Qaeda Central] want to establish an Islamic State in Sanaa, but first, we want to make sure that we have the capability to gain control of it."[19]

Despite the reticence of al-Qaeda's senior leadership, al-Wuhayshi, Qasim al-Raymi (AQAP's military commander), and Sheikh Abu Zubair 'Adil al-'Abab (AQAP's sharia official) were determined to take advantage of the opportunities offered by the Arab Spring. As noted by Ibrahim Abu Salih, one of AQAP's founding members, the "scholars" of the past, including the medieval theologian Ibn Taymiyyah, "could not tarry while Muslim lands are being governed without the sharia of God."[20]

In 2011, AQAP created Ansar al-Sharia as its insurgent arm in order to separate its local component from the tainted al-Qaeda brand. As argued by al-'Abab, "the name Ansar al-Sharia is what we use to introduce ourselves in areas where we work to tell people about our work and goals."[21] However, people on the ground in Yemen did not take long to recognize that AQAP and Ansar al-Sharia were simply two names for the same entity.[22]

As the government and the various powerbrokers were focusing their attention on Sanaa and disregarding the rest of the country, AQAP/Ansar waged an insurgency and managed to conquer some territories. Specifically, the group gained control of the town of Ja'ar in the southern governorate of Abyan, renaming it as the Islamic Emirate of Waqar (which means "dignity" in Arabic).[23] From Ja'ar, the group attacked and conquered Abyan's provincial capital, Zinjibar, gaining control over the strategic road connecting Shabwah Governorate to the historic port city of 'Aden.[24] After conquering those territories, AQAP proceeded immediately to exercise some form of rebel rule.[25]

However, this early experiment in governance did not last long, as bin Laden had warned. Indeed, as a result of its uncompromising application of sharia, which did not always reflect the customs of the local Yemeni Sunni community, AQAP quickly lost the popular support—or at least acceptance—that it had initially gained.[26] Merely one year after the establishment of its emirate, local tribes built an alliance with the new government of President 'Abd Rabbuh Mansur Hadi against al-Wuhayshi's group in what came to be known as Popular Committees and expelled it from the conquered territories.[27] As lamented by al-Wuhayshi, "the whole world was against us."[28]

Nonetheless, despite losing its safe haven, AQAP was far from being defeated in any definitive way and managed to rise again in early 2015, after the Houthis, who had allied with Saleh's loyalists, launched a military campaign against the government.[29] Known officially as Ansar Allah, the Houthi movement is a group from northern Yemen whose members belong to the Zaydi sect of Shia Islam. For more than a millennium beginning in the ninth century, Zaydi imams ruled over northern Yemen. In 1962, the imamate was toppled in a military coup with Egyptian support, and the Yemen Arab Republic was established in its stead.[30] Since the abolition of the Zaydi state in 1962, successive Yemeni republican governments continued to feel nervous about Zaydis' traditional political activism and revolutionary ideology. To contain them, Saleh encouraged activities of proselytization by Saudi-backed Wahhabi institutions in the Zaydi strongholds and deliberately neglected the North. In the early 1990s, the Houthi movement was founded as an expression of Zaydi interests, and between 2004 and 2010 it engaged in six rounds of military confrontation with the government.[31]

When the Arab Spring uprisings arrived in Yemen in early 2011, the Houthis joined the opposition.[32] After Saleh was removed from power in February 2012 and replaced with his vice president, Hadi, a National Dialogue Conference was held between March 2013 and January 2014 to smooth the transition and ease negotiations between the different parties. As the conference ended, however, the Houthis' demands for power, territory, and resources remained unsatisfied.[33] It was in that context that they allied with Saleh and launched their insurgency, which saw them conquer Sanaa in September 2014.

The disorder ignited by the success of the Houthis' military campaign played into AQAP's hands. AQAP managed to insert itself into Yemen's chaos and assert its control over parts of the southern governorates of Shabwah, Abyan, Lahij, and Hadramawt.[34] Importantly, AQAP seized control of Mukalla, the capital of Hadramawt and one of Yemen's three major port cities, as well as the towns of Shuqrah, Ahwar, Zinjibar, Ja'ar, and al-Hawtah. This time, AQAP's territorial control lasted until April 2016, when Yemeni, Emirati, and American military forces launched an offensive against the group and forced it out of those areas.[35]

Upon reconquering large swaths of southern Yemen, AQAP refrained from officially proclaiming an emirate and invested its best efforts in governance to ensure the sustainability of its desired sharia-based polity. As in 2011–2012, AQAP once again sought to provide those public services that the government had long been unable (or unwilling) to provide, especially in the peripheral southern governorates that had traditionally been neglected because they were deemed less politically valuable than the capital and its surroundings.

THE MODEL OF GOVERNANCE OF AL-QAEDA IN THE ARABIAN PENINSULA

Having reviewed how AQAP evolved from being an internationally focused organization, to a locally oriented insurgent group, and ultimately to a nonstate governor, I will proceed to identify the specific governance strategies adopted by the group.

INCLUSIVITY

Like IS and HTS, AQAP adopted a discriminatory approach whereby belonging to its Salafi-jihadist proto-state was determined exclusively by religious and sectarian identity. In other words, AQAP "transcend[ed] class, tribe, and regional identity,"[36] but not religious identity. Specifically, AQAP understood Sunni Muslims to be the only legitimate subjects of its Islamic emirate, while it regarded Shia Muslims as enemies to be fought. In the eleventh issue of its magazine Sada al-Malahim (The echo of epic battles), in an article penned by Ibrahim al-Rubaysh (member of AQAP's Sharia Committee), AQAP presented the Shias as the enemies who "arm and prepare themselves [against the Sunnis] . . . infiltrate important positions in the army and positions of influence in other sectors . . . [and] seek to monopolize the economy and take control of it from Sunnis so that they have the upper hand over the markets anytime they wish."[37]

In a lengthy treatise entirely devoted to Shiism, AQAP's Sheikh Harith al-Nazari referred to the Shias as "rejectors" and criticized the Shia imamate. He argued that the imamate, which for the Shias is one of the pillars of Islam, is a false invention replete with inner contradictions that corrupts the true spirit of Islam and deviates from God's revelation as found in the Quran.[38] Similarly, in its English-language magazine, Inspire, AQAP depicted a triangle of enemies for the Sunnis that consists of the crusader-Zionist alliance, the "apostate" regimes in the Muslim world, and the Shias. It also referred to the Shias as a sect that is "alien to Yemen and that was only imported recently [to the country] from Iran."[39]

The Houthis, in particular, were condemned by AQAP as apostates against whom the mujahidin must fight. A number of issues of Sada al-Malahim contain articles in which the Houthis are referred to as apostates and are accused of colluding with Iran and with the United States against the Sunnis.[40] Similarly, in 2011 AQAP's Madad News Agency published a headline in its newsletter that read, "Shaykh Ibrahim al-Rubaysh: The Houthi Microbe is like cancer; it can only be treated by cutting it out. Other types of medication relieve temporarily and then this microbe turns against it."[41] In the early years of AQAP's ascent, al-Rubaysh and other AQAP senior leaders were calling on Sunnis everywhere to fight jihad against the Houthis, accused of "spreading their Shiite perversity, fables, and innovations among the Muslims."[42] In a 2012 fatwa issued by AQAP's

Sharia Committee, the Houthis were again declared a deviant sect responsible for a series of crimes against Islam and for imposing innovations that contradict the Quran and the Sunna. Jihad against the Houthis was sanctioned as defensive jihad and, therefore, as an individual duty for every Muslim.[43] In line with its bellicose and sectarian rhetoric, over the years AQAP launched a series of attacks against the Houthis.[44] Significantly, the group justified those operations in the following terms: "we launched those operations to defend the honor of Prophet Muhammad.... The Shi'a danger is coming [and] if the Sunnis do not face it properly the Rawafidh Shi'a will do to you what they did to the Sunnis in Iraqi and Afghanistan. The Saudi and Yemeni armies do not represent the Sunnis."[45]

AQAP's hostility toward non-Sunni Islam extended also to shrines. For instance, as early as May 2012, AQAP released a video in which some of its militants are shown demolishing tombs and Sufi shrines in the villages of al-Tareyyah, al-Darjaj, and Sayhan near Ja'ar. In the video, al-Rubayshi provided the following justification: "Here are the mujahideen ... carrying out what Allah commanded them to do ... they are destroying the domes which are being worshipped other than Allah, along with the graves and mausoleums, which people try to get close to other than Allah the Great and Almighty."[46] In January 2015 reports emerged that AQAP had destroyed the eight-hundred-year-old tomb of the Sufi scholar Sufyan bin 'Abdullah, with photos of the destroyed shrine appearing online.[47] A journalist from Mukalla also confirmed that AQAP became locally notorious for its acts of destruction directed against Sufi shrines.[48]

However, it is also important to note that the territories of southern Yemen over which AQAP came to establish its governance in 2011 and 2015 are mostly inhabited by Yemen's Shafi Sunni population, which made the identification of the group's envisioned community and the discrimination between them and the others somewhat less problematic and confrontational than it was under IS and HTS in Syria and Iraq. It is also interesting to note that Zaydi Shia and Shafi Sunni communities had historically shared positive relations in Yemen.[49]

Interestingly, the Islamic State criticized the group of al-Wuhayshi for what it condemned as a lenient approach toward the Shias. Similar to IS's condemnation of al-Nusra's apology to the Druze population of Syria, IS accused AQAP of giving the Houthis a free hand to expand in Yemen as well as being incapable—and perhaps even unwilling—of defending Sunni Muslims: "[as a result of AQAP's approach] the evil of the Houthis and the new taghut [idolatry] in Yemen became exacerbated! . . . They [AQAP] refrain from killing those whom they fear may be from the Muslims whether soldiers of the taghut or Rafidi Majus [Shia]! . . . [AQAP's leaders] used to argue to excuse the Houthis and would not decisively make takfir of them because they were 'Zaydi.' . . . This is the position of most of the organization's 'senior sharia leaders' in Yemen. For this reason, they would avoid targeting the Houthis except after their evil recently became exacerbated and they took control of the lands and shed the blood of Allah's slaves."[50] In other words, the Islamic State accused AQAP of treating the Zaydi Shias too mildly and claimed that such mild treatment was the ultimate proof that the group could not be considered a legitimate Salafi-jihadist organization.[51]

Besides discriminating against non-Sunnis, AQAP also adopted a discriminatory approach toward women. Like IS and HTS, the Yemeni al-Qaeda affiliate imposed stricter regulations on women than it did on men—especially during its first experience in governance. As will be seen in greater detail below, the imposition of a strict gender segregation implied that women were discouraged from leaving the house—unless it was strictly necessary and unless they were accompanied by a male relative—in order to prevent their mixing with unrelated men. As a result, women saw their access to work and education considerably restricted.[52] It was only when AQAP returned to governance in 2015, that some of those regulations were softened and women were allowed to walk in the streets.[53] Gender segregation, conversely, continued to be imposed throughout the two periods of AQAP's governance.[54]

Women and girls six or older were also subject to a strict dress code whereby they had to cover not only their heads—already the practice in Yemen's conservative society—but also their eyes.[55] In the words of a woman who lived under AQAP in Mukalla and was forced to leave her job at a local radio station and stay home, "women had the toughest time here under al-Qaeda. Armed brigades patrolled the city and ensured women stuck to religious dress code."[56] To remind women of their obligation to dress properly, an AQAP billboard in Mukalla read, "Faithful woman: protect your pure body from prying eyes."[57] A woman who lived under AQAP reported that she would only leave the house if and when necessary, in order to avoid hearing orders to wear a veil on her face. Another woman said that a member of Ansar would stay at her workplace every day to prevent men from entering her store: "He would say: 'Close the gate, you cannot keep it open because men outside can see you . . . men cannot enter this place at all . . . only women are allowed into your shop.' I would keep the door open, so he hung a curtain to make sure that no one could see me . . . he would just come and sit inside, and when men came in, he would say: 'Go to pray, go to pray . . .' and they would leave."[58] A woman working at a clinic reported that once, while walking in the street with her sister, a member of Ansar approached them telling them that they could not walk around showing their faces and that there would be consequences if they did not comply with AQAP's dress code regulations.[59]

CIVILIAN ENGAGEMENT

During the group's first governance experience, there is no indication that civilians were included in any way in governance. However, when the group returned in 2015–2016 it introduced certain power-sharing deals and established new administrative structures composed of local civilian figures with no formal affiliation to AQAP—though still responsive to AQAP's demands.[60] The most prominent example in this regard is the Hadramawt National Council (HNC), which was founded in Mukalla and was composed of prominent figures from the local Sunni (and largely Salafi) community—tribal leaders, religious scholars, dignitaries, and elders.[61] In the seventh issue of its newspaper al-Masra, Ansar wrote that upon conquering Mukalla they informed the scholars and the notables of the city that they had not come as conquerors and that the door was open for everyone to contribute to the management of the city and the provision of services to its population in accordance with sharia.[62] Other similar, yet smaller, examples were the civilian councils in the Hadrami towns of Ash-Shihr and Ghayl Bawazir.[63]

Leading the HNC were a tribal leader and a prominent Salafi figure.[64] According to the HNC's secretary general, the agreement reached between AQAP and the local dignitaries rested on three points: Government institutions would be handed over to a council formed by the people of

Hadramawt; the council would be in charge of security and police stations; and AQAP (which in those days in Mukalla was acting under the name of Sons of Hadramawt to emphasize its connection with the religious, tribal, and political milieu of Hadramawt)[65] would provide the council with financial assistance to help restore basic services.[66] According to reports, AQAP provided the HNC with a budget to offer services to the people.[67] Thus, the HNC was in charge of running the local government and administering the city, while AQAP mostly operated the religious police force in charge of monitoring people's behavior and carrying out punishments for violations.[68]

The HNC's secretary general also took care to emphasize that the council's members "[were] not Qaeda stooges" but rather local civilians who "formed the council to avoid the destruction of the city."[69] A resident from Mukalla's Khalaf District also reported that "when they [AQAP] set up their administrative council, it was headed by prominent tribal leaders who didn't ascribe to their ideology. So they weren't this group of power-hungry jihadists that the media portrays."[70]

Thus, in 2015–2016 AQAP revealed itself to be somewhat open to sharing a certain degree of power with the local civilian population. To be certain, however, participation in the HNC (and similar councils in other cities) was restricted to a civilian elite composed of local prominent individuals, while the majority of the population remained excluded from decision making and policymaking. Indeed, the members of those civilian bodies were not elected by the people as their representatives but were rather selected in conjunction by local dignitaries and AQAP. As noted by a local Yemeni expert, the council was "exclusively formed by AQAP's supporters or by Salafi figures ideologically close to the movement," which meant that it was not representative of the interests of the wider population.[71] The councils remained close to AQAP and responsive to AQAP's preferences and guidelines. In other words, even with the councils in place, the wider population was deprived of any direct and significant influence on governance and was excluded from the exercise of power.

Thus, even though in 2015–2016 AQAP opened some channels for power sharing, the majority of the people still could not intervene in governance. As a matter of fact, AQAP—exactly like the Islamic State and HTS—rejected democracy as an un-Islamic form of government. A fighter with Ansar reported in an interview that "democracy has failed in the

Arab world. It failed in Tunis and in Egypt and Libya. It failed in Yemen. . . . Democracy only brought injustice and ignorance and backwardness and a desire to follow the West."[72] AQAP's al-'Abab also delivered a lecture in which he argued that "our [AQAP's, but, more broadly, the Salafi-jihadists'] loyalty is for the believer, who has rejected the democracy that defies mankind and resists being ruled by Allah alone. So he who fought the democratic program which is contrary to the Quran and Sunna, we will befriend him."[73] Another document penned by al-'Abab promoted the view that democracy is a Western notion that equates apostasy and contradicts sharia, and fiercely criticized those who had argued that democracy and sharia could be compatible (a position very close to that of HTS on the matter).[74] According to al-'Abab's document, democracy was imposed on the Muslims by the West as an alternative to Islamic rule and was erroneously embraced by some Muslim scholars. However, al-'Abab takes pride in the fact that many of those scholars who had initially given their support to democracy later repented when Ansar took power, removed democracy, and began to rule exclusively according to its interpretation of sharia.[75]

In a similar vein, Shaykh Fahad al-Quso, a leader in AQAP, explained that "the democratic game is rejected by us on the basis of shariah, because it is based on the rulership of the people by the people and also based on majority votes. And this is a contention with Allah's exclusive right to rule His creation. Therefore, the sovereign authority should be for Allah alone, not for democracy which in reality has proved that it only legislates for injustice, corruption, tyranny and autocracy, especially in the Arab countries."[76] Another AQAP document dated February 2013 rejected claims that the group intended to form a political party that would join the country's multiparty system and participate in elections, and reiterated its condemnation of democracy as a system of government that "require[s] giving [to] humans the right to legislate that is with Allah."[77]

GENERATION OF COMPLIANCE

AQAP often employed coercive practices to ensure compliance with its system of rule. Especially during its first experience in governance, the group assaulted anyone who failed to attend mosque for the five daily prayers. Shopkeepers who were suspected of not attending mosque had their shops closed by the group for a certain period of time, which left the "sinner" temporarily deprived of income.[78] Women who were not dressed up according to the rules imposed by AQAP, along with those who were found in the company of men who were not close relatives, were also subjected to verbal harassment and physical punishments.[79]

During its first year in governance, AQAP also implemented the entire range of *hudud* to punish what it regarded as the most serious violations of sharia.[80] In 2012, al-ʿAbab reported that

> days ago, here in Jaar, the Ansar al-Sharia caught a thief stealing while drunk, and I met him the next day. I asked him whether he was drunk, and he said "yes." I said did you know that drinking alcohol is prohibited, and he also said "yes." I said did you know that your punishment would be whipping, and he said: "Yes but cleanse me please." May God reward him. We whipped him forty lashes and that was the first implementation of *hudud* here. . . . We apply *hudud* as much as we can whenever we have the ability.[81]

Flogging was also used against people accused of smoking. For instance, a man accused of smoking cannabis was given eighty lashes with a rod in Jaʿar's Nadi Khanfar Square.[82] The practice of cutting off the hands of thieves was initially widespread under AQAP. In the town of Jaʿar, three people accused of stealing had their hands cut off by AQAP.[83] In the horrifying account of a man who suffered directly from AQAP's *hudud* punishments after being accused of stealing, "they detained me in a room for five days. They kept beating me hard . . . and tortured me with electric shocks. . . . After five days they gave me an injection, and I slept. When I woke up, my hand was not there."[84]

For greater crimes, AQAP resorted to executions. According to a document produced by Ansar's sharia court in Abyan in February 2012, men accused of spying against AQAP were punished with death.[85] During those executions, which were most often carried out in public, placards on the ground described the person's crime and a voice from a loudspeaker read the court's sentence. Among those who suffered such a fate, a man from Jaʿar accused of working for the Yemeni security forces against Ansar al-Sharia was crucified and his body left exposed in a main road for several days.[86] Individuals suspected of sorcery and mischief were also executed. In June 2012, AQAP issued a message of admonition in which it invited everyone engaged in magic to abandon their witchcraft and to remember the death sentence that had been carried out against a man engaged in sorcery in Hadramawt. The group also called everyone who belonged to the people of Islam (*ahl al-Islam*) to inform AQAP of the whereabouts of every sorcerer that they knew of, so that they could be punished accordingly.[87]

Following those episodes, local inhabitants found themselves living in terror. As argued by a resident of Ja'ar, "now no one dares to raise his voice in Jaar, let alone steal. This town has gone quiet."[88] A resident from the same town said that "in the beginning when [Ansar] came here, they were simple people and weak. . . . We aligned with them in the beginning. We found out . . . that they are liars . . . they love blood, and they are terrorists."[89] Similarly, a woman from Zinjibar said that the "horrors" of Ansar al-Sharia were "unthinkable," and that she was "incredibly happy" at their forced departure from the town in mid-2012.[90]

However, while many locals resented AQAP and deeply despised its violent practices, others supported the group, arguing that "al-Qaeda members made us feel safe, they cut off the hands of thieves. This is part of sharia: those who steal should have their hands cut off."[91] Another interviewee said that "when al-Qa'ida was here it was good. There were no robberies. People treated each other in a decent way. No one would try to make problems."[92] A street vendor from Ja'ar also praised the group's methods, saying that "people felt secure and safe. People would leave their shops open when they went to pray and when we came back our goods were untouched."[93]

AQAP's use of coercion was somewhat moderated during its second experience in governance, when *hudud* punishments were applied less frequently than before—even though they continued to be implemented in certain circumstances. In an issue of *al-Masra*, AQAP discussed the introduction of *hudud* in Mukalla as a necessary means of deterring anyone from disturbing the city's security and curbing the spread of crimes such as prostitution, alcohol consumption, and drug abuse. It also discussed the imposition of *hudud* in public spaces as a means of sending a clear message to potential wrongdoers that "the present is not like the past."[94]

A local resident from Mukalla, for instance, reported that during the group's rule in 2015–2016 a man and a woman accused of adultery were

stoned to death and two men suspected of being Saudi spies were crucified, but that "such incidents were rare."[95] Other reports also confirmed
that women accused of extramarital intercourse by the group could be
sentenced to death.[96] People accused of sorcery also continued to be targeted. In March 2016, for instance, AQAP executed some people accused
of witchcraft in the towns of Ghayl Bawazir and ash-Shihr, in Hadramawt.[97] In June 2015, AQAP publicly executed two men accused of providing intelligence to the enemy, leading to the elimination of al-Wuhayshi,
and hung their bodies from a bridge.[98] At the end of July, the group also
publicly flogged individuals accused of using hashish.[99]

Besides *hudud* punishments, more general forms of coercion also continued to be a defining feature of AQAP's rule throughout the second
period of governance. For instance, people who were involved in demonstrations against al-Qaeda's rule were kidnapped and arrested. A woman
whose husband and brother, both reporters, covered a protest against al-
Qaeda's rule in Mukalla said that the two men were arrested and that she
was left without news of her husband: "from that day on I have not heard
my husband's voice or seen him at all. I've heard nothing for three years."[100]
Mukalla residents reported that markets where people sold *qat* were
burned by AQAP, and that people found selling *qat* were punished with
a fine and with the confiscation of the vehicle used to sell the narcotic.[101]
They also reported that as prayer time was approaching, AQAP officials
used wooden bats to intimidate shop owners to leave their businesses and
go to pray.[102]

The authority in charge of monitoring people's behavior and punishing cases of disobedience was AQAP's *hisba* police.[103] According to observers as well as to the group's own reports, *hisba* members patrolled the
streets of the cities in cars equipped with loudspeakers in order to intimidate people and make sure that they would behave as instructed by the
group.[104] A phone number was also written on the front of the car, so that
people could call and report violations.[105]

However, like HTS, AQAP not only employed coercion; it also resorted
to persuasive practices. Specifically, AQAP focused on winning hearts and
minds by claiming that it was the only group willing and able to provide
infrastructure, electricity, education, and justice—which Kendall referred
to as a "Robin Hood-like propaganda narrative that sought to position

AQAP as the saviour of local communities."[106] In other words, AQAP developed a narrative in which it presented itself as the sole organization that could solve problems caused by years of neglect and state corruption.[107] To achieve this result, AQAP's media agencies prioritized the dissemination of materials depicting the ways in which AQAP improved the lives of its subjects.

For instance, the "Eye on the Event" film series was used to show all the activities conducted by the group in the interest of the community: resolving disputes quickly, fairly, and satisfactorily, managing the distribution of foodstuffs (wheat, rice, oil, beans, lentils, and more), fixing utilities, and cleaning streets.[108] Other media material also exhibited AQAP's provision of food, security, water, electricity, education, and justice. A news report from June 2012, for instance, showed a street market in which people were conducting business thanks to the "security and order" provided by the mujahidin.[109] A similar news report from March 2012 reported that Ansar's members in Ja'ar were renewing the electricity network and connecting water pipelines inside the city, and that the costs of the projects would be sustained exclusively by Ansar.[110] The first news report by Madad News Agency pictured AQAP distributing food and clothing to hundreds of poor families during the month of Ramadan as well as repaving roads that were damaged by floods.[111]

This same strategy was pursued by AQAP during its second governance experience. In January 2016, a Twitter feed for AQAP's al-Athir News Agency began publishing photos and videos of Ansar's public works. The first photos showed food baskets that were handed out to the needy in Mukalla. Additional photos documented a project intended to improve residents' access to electricity, a crew of workers paving streets, and garbage trucks removing trash in Hadramawt.[112] In January 2016, AQAP launched a new newspaper, the above-mentioned *al-Masra* newspaper, in which—among the other things—the group celebrated and publicized the community development works undertaken, or facilitated, by the group.[113] In April 2016, for instance, *al-Masra* published an article devoted to AQAP's governance in Mukalla that praised the group's capacity to provide services, public projects, and security. According to the author, Ansar provided medical devices to hospitals, reopened the operations and emergency departments in the city's hospitals, and helped poor citizens to purchase medicines. At the same time, the article depicted the group as being active in the education sector, where it restored schools and equipped classrooms. It also engaged in the production and distribution of electricity, to the point that Mukalla no longer experienced power cuts.[114]

As AQAP promoted its provision of public services, it managed to obtain some degree of support from local residents; in the words of a resident of ʿAzzan, in Hadramawt, "they brought back peace and put an end to robbery and theft. Power and water services were available all the time."[115] Similarly, a fisherman from Mukalla interviewed after the liberation of the city argued that AQAP "paved roads, built hospitals. It was far from perfect, but they were better than the current [state] administration," to the point that "life was better under al-Qaʾida, compared with now."[116]

Another strategy employed by AQAP to influence people's behavior was education on the group's norms of conduct. In the towns controlled by AQAP, small offices known as Islamic Education Centers were in charge of distributing the group's newsletters and DVDs to every passerby.[117] Proselytization trucks were also driven around by AQAP members, with the side of the truck advertising CDs, *nashids* (chants typical of the Islamic tradition), films, lectures, books, and copies of the Quran.[118] Furthermore, the group was engaged in the organization of *daʿwah* events for adults and children, as well as community events and street festivals aimed at capturing people's interest and engaging the youth.[119] For instance, in the pages of a news report published in 2012 by the Madad News Agency, a short article was devoted to the *daʿwah* weeks organized by the group for purposes of proselytization in Jaʿar. In the article it was explained that during such weeks AQAP's preachers were informing people on a series of issues, such as the importance of arbitration according to sharia and the rejection of democracy and secularism.[120] In the sixth issue of *al-Masra*, it was reported that Ansar organized a festival in which different topics were discussed. During the three-day event, the mujahidin established a *daʿwah* point where they presented their message and organized a series of prize competitions for youngsters.[121] In March 2016, one month before suffering its definitive territorial losses, AQAP held in Hadramawt a "Festival of Martyrs of the American Bombing," in which schoolboys participated in a competition to design anti-U.S. posters. The aim of this event was to exploit local anger toward the U.S. drone strikes to present AQAP as the sole option for revenge and resistance.[122]

AQAP's choice to resort to these kinds of events is discussed at length by al-'Abab. In his words, "we hope to show people the principles of monotheism and simplify our message for the masses, offering Shariah as the solution to their problems. Thus, we organize presentations for them in the marketplace using projectors and other broadcasting tools."[123] Again, according to al-'Abab, AQAP/Ansar "sought to spread tawhid through giving lessons, speeches and sermons in mosques, and public and special social meetings, and through posters, videos, audios and presentation through modern means."[124] He also suggested that "spreading elim [knowledge] and dawah is considered a gain achieved by Ansar al-Sharia since with the guidance of Allah sessions were held for memorizing the Holy Quran, Sunnah and lessons of knowledge, and many of the ordinary Muslims learned how to recite the Quran correctly . . . and many of them have benefited much from the dawah and dawah weeks and cultural festivals [that] were held."[125]

Over time, AQAP also extended its influence over mosques to make sure that the sermons delivered by the imams were in accordance with the group's ideology. In this way, it turned mosques into a platform for the cultivation of popular support. One imam reported, "I would prepare my Friday sermon and as I would be getting ready at the mosque on Friday, Abu Mohajer [from Ansar al-Sharia] would come and tell me that there was another preacher who would replace me for this sermon. . . . I could not say no. . . . I would just go to any other mosque and pray there. . . . [Eventually] they were in control of all the mosques."[126]

AQAP's use of local cultural traditions, dominant among them poetry, was also an important component of the group's strategy to appeal to and connect with local populations.[127] Interestingly, while at the beginning poetry was mostly found in the pages of AQAP's magazine Sada al-Malahim, over time poetry came to be delivered mostly in a musical format, either through sung poetry sessions or through nashids.[128] At the same time, AQAP also mobilized symbols of Islam—such as the black flag with the shahadah on it. The aim of this symbolic mobilization was to confer religious legitimacy and credibility on the group's governance project as well as to promote the identification of the local Sunni Muslim population with its Islamic emirate.

APPROACH TO OUTSIDERS

In a way that is reminiscent of HTS, AQAP's approach to governance was partially inclusive, and some space for intervention in matters of governance was accorded to other actors. Among those, local Sunni tribes were given particular attention by the group.

Determined not to commit the sort of fatal mistakes that were made by ISI in 2006–2007,[129] AQAP tried to connect with local tribal leaders.[130] Among AQAP's leadership, in fact, there seemed to be a "pragmatic acknowledgment that [the group's] success depends on local tribes accepting its presence" and a belief that "tribal leaders still have a central role and influence which can serve to facilitate or obstruct the spread of AQAP."[131] In other words, there seemed to be a certain awareness among AQAP that the group's survival would depend on its ability to appeal to, root into, and connect with local tribes.[132] As early as 2009, AQAP released a video in which it appealed to the Yemeni tribes by means of presenting tribal honor, heroism, and jihadism as aligned in a common struggle against the government of Sanaa.[133] In fact, AQAP was trying to frame its operations in the language of *qabyalah* ("tribalness")—a conscious attempt to forge deep relations with the tribes.[134]

However, during the group's first experience in governance AQAP's inclusionary rhetoric was not always accompanied by an equally inclusionary practice. At the very least, the latter suffered from a series of important limitations. Most prominently, AQAP imposed a strict Salafi version of sharia that superseded and marginalized local tribal law. At the same time, the group neglected traditional Yemeni religious practices, "some of which have tribal, even pre-Islamic roots."[135] This undermined the authority of tribal leaders, who were not prepared to transfer their power and influence to men who were not from the area, were not members of local tribes, and in some cases were not even Yemeni (which was the case with AQAP's members from Somalia and Saudi Arabia).[136] As seen above, this tendency of AQAP to overcome the preexisting tribal structures and customs did cost the group dearly, as tribes allied with the newly installed government of Hadi and expelled the group from their territories.

As the opportunity to engage in governance presented itself again in 2015, AQAP was careful to learn from the past and rethink its approach.

Rather than asserting its exclusive authority over the conquered territories, it opted to work with local communities to establish a shared system of governance.[137] In the words of a southern Yemeni journalist and analyst, "AQAP understood that it depends on the support of tribal leaders, they cannot exist without them."[138] Thus, AQAP sought to deepen and enhance its ties with the tribes, including them in matters of governance. As was seen above, local tribal figures were included in power-sharing structures such as the HNC and given responsibilities over certain areas of governance. The available reports, as well as conversations with local experts, suggest that the inclusion of tribal leaders and prominent figures was not conditional on their having formally pledged *bay'ah*. However, and as noted above, the HNC's members were aligned with AQAP and were under the group's close scrutiny.

AQAP also capitalized on tribal grievances and tribal distrust toward the state and appealed to tribal honor and tribal religiosity in order to present itself as an ally of the tribes in the fight against an inimical regime.[139] The rise of the Houthis and their conquest of Sanaa in September 2014 allowed AQAP to use the pretext of a Sunni defense against a Shia offensive to make common cause with local tribes and blend with them.[140] According to well-informed reports, AQAP even managed to marry some of its members into local tribes and to initiate joint activities of smuggling and arms trafficking, which made relations with AQAP financially profitable for tribal leaders.[141] Significantly, AQAP also developed a narrative that sought to appeal to the tribes by means of emphasizing humiliation, underdevelopment, injustice, and destruction of properties in tribal areas at the hand of the Houthis and foreign interventions.[142]

A senior official within AQAP argued that "we [AQAP] are as one with the tribes like never before. We are not al-Qaeda now. Together we are the Sunni army."[143] In the words of an AQAP member, "we are [society's] sons and part of the social fabric of our tribal and popular environment. . . . We are rooted in the land. . . . We are not outsiders."[144] AQAP's penetration of, and integration with, local tribes was in fact successful to the point that a resident from Hadramawt similarly argued that "we don't support [AQAP]. But they are our kinsfolk. We let them go about their businesses and we go about ours."[145] As reported also by the HNC's leadership, most of AQAP's fighters who took control of the city in 2015 were "from famous Hadrami families."[146]

Besides the more cooperative relationship with the tribes, in 2015–2016 AQAP also pursued more cooperative relationships with other prominent members of society. Following the conquest of Mukalla, AQAP's local members took the name of Sons of Hadramawt, as mentioned above. After AQAP (re)took control of Zinjibar and Ja'ar in December 2015 and the remaining parts of Abyan Governorate in February 2016, the group's members there adopted the name of Sons of Abyan. The aim of this rebranding was to conceal once more the group's link with al-Qaeda (interestingly, the same logic that Jabhat al-Nusra would follow a few months later with its rebranding as Jabhat Fatah al-Sham).[147] After renaming itself Sons of Hadramawt, AQAP created the HNC and assigned most governance functions to it. As seen previously, the HNC was formed not only by tribal leaders, but also by local elders, dignitaries, and scholars.[148] Therefore, although AQAP still retained the reins of power in its hands, during its second experience in governance it also adjusted to power-sharing models.[149]

At the same time, it is noticeable that AQAP developed some cooperative (yet sporadic) relationships with international aid organizations—just as HTS began to do in recent years. In this regard, AQAP members held meetings with the organizations' representatives in order to coordinate relief and allowed some humanitarian operations to be conducted in its territories.[150] As a matter of fact, already in a news report dated May 2012, it was reported that Ansar had allowed a group of five workers (three doctors and two nurses) from the International Committee of the Red Cross to visit captured regime soldiers held in Abyan in order to evaluate their health.[151]

Conversely, with the other Salafi-jihadist group present in Yemen—notably, the Islamic State, which declared its presence in the country in November 2014—AQAP had a conflictual relationship that largely reflected the inimical relationships between IS and al-Qaeda affiliates elsewhere.[152] In the framework of this competition, AQAP condemned the brutal tactics of IS, such as its attacks against mosques attended by civilians.[153] For its part, IS criticized AQAP for its tendency to forge ties with local communities, accusing al-Wuhayshi's group of prioritizing "building ties with local groups and refraining from a strict application of sharia, the legal code of Islam."[154] The same article also contains an aerial view of Mukalla, with the caption "The city of al-Mukalla in Yemen, where al-Qaeda made no effort to implement the sharia after seizing control."[155] As noted above, moreover, IS was deeply critical of AQAP's approach toward Yemen's Shia population, accusing the group of being too mild and accommodating.

PROPENSITY TO CHANGE

AQAP introduced a series of important innovations from its earliest engagement in governance. As early as 2011, for instance, it began to impose a judicial system that referred to sharia as its exclusive source of law.[156] As argued by a member of Ansar, "we were aiming for this control from the start. Control under sharia is our basic goal. Nothing else."[157] Similarly, Ansar leader Jalal Muhsin Balidi al-Murqoshi stated that "we want to implement the Shari'a of Allah in [Abyan] and redress injustices."[158] In the words of AQAP leader al-Rubayshi, "our goal is to implement the sharia . . . we won't keep our arms down until we are ruled by the sharia of our Lord or perish before that. . . . Implementing the sharia isn't from the specificities of al-Qa'ida and rather it is an obligation imposed by Allah on every Muslim."[159] Upon introducing sharia as the exclusive source of law, AQAP opened and ran sharia courts.[160] In the town of 'Azzan, the city's former police station was converted into a sharia court. Inside the court, the judge sat in a room on whose wall hung the symbols of sharia justice as interpreted by AQAP—a black flag, an AK-47, and a stick used for corporal punishments.[161] Under AQAP, in fact, the punishments for violating the group's sharia were *qisas*, *ta'zir*, and *hudud*.[162]

Because of Yemen's governance weakness, many government courts had been traditionally absent or failed to function. In this context, AQAP's sharia courts emerged as a somewhat welcome and novel aspect of governance for many local inhabitants.[163] For instance, a resident of Rada'a, in al-Bayda Governorate, who had a land dispute resolved by AQAP noted that "I went to Al-Qaeda and they were able to resolve the dispute. Since then, I have gone to them as an alternative to court."[164] As far as dispute resolution is concerned, a judge for Ansar who was interviewed in April 2012 stated that AQAP's new court system had resolved forty-two cases in two weeks and that "people come to us from parts we don't control and ask us to solve their problems. The sharia justice system is swift and incorruptible. Most of the cases we solve within the day."[165]

This same argument was also advanced by al-ʿAbab, who wrote that "everyone knows that they were before the ruling of Allah and there is no difference between them, and it is not surprising that two opponents come to the Ansar al-Sharia court to resolve between them from outside our domain of control."[166] Articles published in a news report by Madad News Agency also claimed that Ansar's sharia courts had the capacity to quickly resolve even those cases that the state courts had failed to resolve in the course of years.[167] Indeed, AQAP was often praised by the locals for the speed of its judgments. As argued by a resident of Mukalla, "the AQAP judicial system is fair and swift and therefore preferred over the government's corrupt system. Many prominent cases that had lingered for years were resolved in a single day."[168]

Besides the judicial sector, AQAP introduced innovations in the security sector as well. As shown in a video shot after AQAP's defeat in 2012, there was a police force in charge of security and order in the towns controlled by the group.[169] According to a document penned by al-ʿAbab, to maintain order and security the police would establish checkpoints at the entry and exit routes of the main cities as well as along public roads connecting major towns, which allegedly allowed people and merchants to move and to transfer their goods in safety throughout Ansar-controlled territories.[170] The police, according to al-ʿAbab, was also the body that received the people's complaints and sought to reconcile the disputants. In cases where reconciliation could not be reached at the police station, disputes would be referred to the court of justice.[171] In terms of innovations in the provision of security, it is also noticeable that after being ousted from power in 2012, AQAP introduced a "Telephone for Help," which was meant as a service whereby Abyan citizens suffering from "looting and robbery" at the hands of government forces could report their problems and security concerns to Ansar.[172] Furthermore, and as mentioned above, there was also a *hisba* police force in charge of "promoting virtue and preventing vice."

In the other areas of governance, a committee was in charge of ensuring that education did not contradict the principles of sharia and respected the new AQAP-sanctioned curriculum. The school curriculum, in fact, had been revised by the group to remove national education and devote more hours to Quranic studies.[173] A school teacher reported that "from the beginning of the second semester, [AQAP's] demands increased. . . . They wanted us to use official documents papers with Ansar al-Sharia's letterhead . . . marked 'the governorate of Abyan, the emirate of Waqar [the name of Ansar's emirate], the Islamic Education Office' and with the logo of the black flag [of Ansar al-Sharia]. . . . They also added a subject called 'jihad' and wanted to make other changes in the curriculum. We were very uncomfortable and eventually we just closed the school."[174] A Yemeni young man with direct experience of life under AQAP also reported that "primary and secondary schooling existed in AQAP's territories but the group changed the curriculum, introduced Islamic extremism, and recruited teachers who supported AQAP, expelling all the others."[175] According to another person with deep knowledge on the matter, AQAP also segregated classes by gender in the schools under its control.[176]

A social committee was reportedly introduced to administer civic affairs (e.g., market regulation) and provide services free of charge (e.g., food aid). Other committees distributed water and electricity and delivered them to people's homes (in the document authored by al-'Abab, it is stated that these were "*Muslims*' homes [emphasis added]," in a further indication of the religion-based discrimination discussed above).[177] A propaganda video filmed in March 2012 and distributed through AQAP's Madad News Agency shows the group's members connecting electricity lines in Ja'ar and shows lights and electric fans inside private homes operating without interruption. A local resident interviewed in the video notes "how many times have we asked for it and demanded it, electricity and water, no one responded to our request. . . . [AQAP] didn't fail us."[178] Since the onset, AQAP was also involved in the distribution of rice, wheat, cooking oil, beans, lentils, salt, and other food products.[179] Similarly, the group was involved in the reconstruction of roads that had been destroyed by flooding.[180] Another component of AQAP's governance activities that attracted significant sympathy among local residents was its distribution of financial compensation to families who had lost their homes to drones and air strikes.[181]

Finally, AQAP innovated by means of imposing new norms of behavior. Among those new regulations, there was the ban on *qat*;[182] the prohibition against men wearing soccer shorts and the requirement to grow a beard;[183] and the requirement for women to cover their eyes and avoid public spaces as much as possible.[184] Listening to music, dancing, and engaging in any form of entertainment associated with Western culture was also prohibited.[185] For instance, a resident of Mukalla said that AQAP "banned songs and dancing at weddings."[186] Another Mukalla resident who used to sell CDs said that one day AQAP members arrived at his shop and ordered him to erase all recorded music and films, offering instead "videos of al-Qaeda operations in Afghanistan, Iraq, and Syria."[187] As mentioned, gender segregation was imposed in public spaces, in hospitals, and in schools—which, in a country where the majority of teachers are women, left most boys deprived of access to education.[188] The obligation to attend mosque for the five daily prayers was also imposed.[189] To make sure that people would comply, AQAP ensured that calls to prayer would take place at the exact same time in all mosques, so that no one could escape the obligation to pray by pretending that they had already done so or that they would soon be doing it.[190]

In terms of personnel, AQAP sought to appoint loyal and skilled workers. Already in 2009, the group called for skilled workers to help the mujahidin in their state-building project:

> The jihadi arena needs all powers, skills and abilities [such as] doctors, engineers and electricians. It also requires plumbers, builders, and contractors, just as it needs students, educators, door-to-door salesmen and farmers. It is searching for media specialists from writers and printers [to] photographers and directors. It also needs conscientious Muslim reporters and sportsmen, skilled in martial arts and close combat. It is searching for proficient, methodical, organized administrators, just as it is in need of strong, honest traders who spend their wealth for the sake of their religion without fear or greed. . . . It will accelerate the pace of achieving our great Islamic project: establishing an Islamic Caliphate.[191]

In the words of al-'Abab, also, "[t]oday we have a radio station in Jaar, but we do not have the media crew to run this radio station that broadcasts at a distance of 60 km. So that we need media professionals and media specialists, technicians and internet experts as well to help us in media work."[192]

Constrained by the lack of sufficiently experienced personnel, AQAP was also forced to maintain some of the former workers in their places.

TABLE 6.1 The model of governance of al-Qaeda in the Arabian Peninsula

Inclusivity	Discrimination (Shias/Houthis and women)
Civilian engagement	Partial subjection (rejection of democratic process, but creation of HNC and other similar councils)
Generation of compliance	Coercion and persuasion (e.g., occasional *hudud* punishments and *da'wah* activities)
Approach to outsiders	Partial cooperation (cooperation with Sunni tribes, prominent Salafi figures, and some international aid organizations)
Propensity to change	Innovation and maintenance (e.g., sharia-based judicial system and maintenance of traditional *'urf*)

Those who remained could approach Ansar through a "Telephone of Repentance" through which employees of the government could repent for their association with the "apostate" regime.[193] Teachers, in particular, were allowed to remain in their posts, but they had to refrain from teaching the old curriculum.[194] Upon conquering Mukalla in 2015, AQAP offered government soldiers the opportunity to remain and work for the group in exchange for a monthly salary, which was three times the sum paid by the government.[195] Workers employed in crucial companies, such as those devoted to the provision of water and electricity, were also maintained in their posts, but were placed under the supervision of al-Qaeda members.[196]

Beyond former employees and professionals, the greater propensity for maintenance became a feature of AQAP's governance once the group returned in 2015.[197] This was perhaps most evident in the decision not to uproot *'urf* (tribal customary law), which constituted the foundation of the local social order. Thus, during its second experiment at governance, AQAP waited some months before proceeding to apply sharia and allowed for customary law to be used instead. Later, when it proceeded to implement sharia as well, it opted to apply it gradually, to refrain from the strictest interpretations of the law, and to avoid full-scale enforcement.[198] For instance, the group conceded to women a greater freedom of movement than it had in the past, allowing them to be outside of their houses after sunset, and did not stop people from walking in the streets, watching football matches, or listening to music.[199] The ban on *qat* was reimposed, but somewhat more gradually, so that people could get used to the new regulation and internalize it. In the words of a Mukalla resident, when AQAP conquered the town, "the group's members were very reassuring towards the residents. They said that they had no intention of applying sharia law straight away, but favoured dialogue with the local population. But little by little, the group began imposing its laws."[200]

In fact, as al-Wuhayshi had written in his 2012 letter to Droukdel, "you have to take a gradual approach with them when it comes to their religious practices. You can't beat people for drinking alcohol when they don't even know the basics of how to pray. We have to first stop the great sins, and then move gradually to the lesser and lesser ones. When you find someone committing a sin, we have to address the issue by making the right call, and by giving lenient advice first, then by harsh rebuke, and then by force. We have to first make them heed monotheism and fight paganism and sorcery, and then move on to enforcing punishments of great sins."[201]

In this chapter, I have observed that AQAP adopted a discriminatory approach whereby it considered Sunni Muslims the only legitimate subjects of its desired emirate. A discriminatory approach was also adopted vis-à-vis women, who were subjected to stricter requirements as compared to men. Concerning Sunni Muslims, no system of broad civilian participation was developed. Nonetheless, a civilian elite selected by AQAP and composed of elders, tribal leaders, and dignitaries was entitled to intervene in matters of governance. On this same line, AQAP developed some cooperative relationships with local actors, especially at the time of its return to governance in 2015. With respect to preexisting institutions and personnel, AQAP introduced innovations in several areas of governance, while also maintaining some local customs, practices, and personnel. Finally, AQAP often resorted to coercion to ensure people's compliance with its governance and punish instances of noncompliance. At the same time, however, noncoercive practices were also employed.

CONCLUSION

Inside Salafi-Jihadist Governance

I started this book with the intention of bringing the reader on a journey through Iraq, Syria, and Yemen to understand how daily life unfolds in those territories controlled and governed by Salafi-jihadist armed groups. In this concluding chapter, I will return to the questions raised in the introduction and offer answers to them. First, I will compare the observations on the Islamic State, Hay'at Tahrir al-Sham, and al-Qaeda in the Arabian Peninsula to assess how Salafi-jihadists govern, what similarities and differences exist between different Salafi-jihadist groups, and to what extent it is possible to identify a single model of Salafi-jihadist governance. From there, I will focus on the relationship between ideology and Salafi-jihadist governance, comparing the models of governance adopted by IS, HTS, and AQAP with the expectations advanced in chapter 3. Finally, I will compare the observations on IS, HTS, and AQAP with the findings on non-Salafi-jihadist governance that I presented in chapter 2 as I studied the Liberation Tigers of Tamil Eelam, the Revolutionary Armed Forces of Colombia, and the Democratic Union Party. The aim is to assess how governance varies across Salafi-jihadist and non-Salafi-jihadist rebel rulers, the extent to which Salafi-jihadist governance is similar to, or different from, non-Salafi-jihadist governance, and whether there is a distinctive model of Salafi-jihadist governance. As I present the book's findings, I will also discuss their implications.

HOW DO SALAFI-JIHADIST ARMED GROUPS GOVERN?

Comparing the observations derived from the application of my proposed typology to the three case studies of IS, HTS, and AQAP, I argue that there are important similarities in the way in which different Salafi-jihadist armed groups approach governance. For once, Salafi-jihadists display a tendency to adopt highly discriminatory approaches toward civilians. On the one hand, they adopt a discriminatory approach based on religious identity, whereby only Sunni Muslims are considered legitimate members of their desired polity. Civilians belonging to other faiths (e.g., Christians, Druze, Yezidis) and to other Muslim sects (i.e., Shia Muslims) are subjected to very different treatment. Depending on their faith, they may be forced to comply with a series of strict, discriminatory, and humiliating conditions to continue to live in their towns, suddenly part of a Salafi-jihadist polity. In other cases, they are forced into exile, compelled to convert, or subjected to persecution, violence, and even genocide.

On the other hand, Salafi-jihadists adopt a discriminatory approach based on gender, whereby women are subjected to much stricter regulations than men in every aspect of life—dress code, employment, education, and public access and comportment. As such, they are considerably more affected than men by violations to their fundamental rights. To recall some of the most common violations observed in the Salafi-jihadist polities studied in this book, women are forced to follow strict dress codes, are prevented from moving in public without a *mahram*, are excluded from many job opportunities, and need to comply with gender segregation by reducing their appearances in the public space.

Additionally, Salafi-jihadists are similar in that they tend to exclude the broad civilian population from participation in governance. As noted, HTS and AQAP did include to some extent a civilian elite unaffiliated with either group to which it delegated some authority on specific matters. However, the members of those civilian structures were carefully selected and necessarily approved by the Salafi-jihadist leadership, while civilians were never included in the elections of their representatives and were hardly ever given an opportunity to voice their preferences and demands on matters of administration. Across the three cases studied, the reins of decision making remained firmly in the hands of the Salafi-jihadist rulers.

At the same time, however, I also argue that differences between Salafi-jihadists in matters of governance are as evident as they are relevant. For instance, with respect to preexisting institutions and personnel, IS and HTS introduced extensive innovations across all areas of governance. Most prominently, they reformed the judiciary, introduced new taxation systems, and changed—sometimes in dramatic ways—the norms of public behavior. Conversely, AQAP engaged in greater maintenance, as was especially evident in its decision to preserve local tribal customs that had long dominated local life and to implement sharia in a moderate and gradual fashion.

A further difference is observed in the relationship with other actors. As was noted, IS opted to govern mostly in isolation. The only limited exceptions were the collaboration with Sunni tribes that pledged *bay'ah* to the group and were subsequently assigned some governance tasks in tribal areas and the collaboration with the Assad regime with respect to oil and electricity. HTS and AQAP, for their part, included a much wider and more diverse range of local actors— tribal sheikhs, local elders, technocrats, businessmen, foreign aid organizations—even where these stakeholders had not formally pledged allegiance to either group. They also engaged in cooperative patterns to a much greater degree and in more areas of governance.

Finally, IS sought to generate compliance by relying on extensive, even extreme, coercion and limited persuasion. For their part, HTS and AQAP combined coercive measures and persuasive practices in similar ways, using financial fines and corporal punishments to the same extent that they used written publications, religious symbols, and public events. As far as *hudud* punishments are concerned, it was noted that in the areas controlled by HTS the implementation of *hudud* was a rare occurrence, while in the territories controlled by AQAP the implementation of *hudud* was deliberately decreased over time. This is an important point of difference with the Islamic State, which systematically implemented the full range of *hudud* punishments and did so in a widely publicized fashion.

From this comparison, I argue that a single model of Salafi-jihadist governance does not exist. Rather, each Salafi-jihadist group develops its own peculiar model of governance, which might differ (slightly, partially, or even significantly) from the models of governance developed by other Salafi-jihadist rebel rulers. This argument bears important implications. Recognizing that a single, universal model of Salafi-jihadist governance does not exist suggests that a one-size-fits-all approach cannot (and should not) be pursued when dealing with these groups. Rather, each Salafi-jihadist rebel ruler should be dealt with individually, considering its specific features and behaviors. In this regard, understanding the patterns of governance of each Salafi-jihadist rebel group, its interactions with the civilian population living in the areas under its control, and its relations with other local actors is a necessary step to devise the most appropriate strategies to deal with it.

For instance, and as suggested by the experience of the Islamic State of Iraq in Anbar Governorate in 2006–2007 and by the experience of AQAP in southern Yemen in 2011–2012, when powerful local actors such as tribal leaders are excluded from governance by the Salafi-jihadist rebel rulers, there is an opportunity to cooperate with them in counterinsurgency efforts—a course of action that would be much more difficult to pursue where a Salafi-jihadist group includes the tribes in its governance project.[1] However, it is noticeable that when cooperating in counterinsurgency efforts with local actors who have been excluded, alienated, or neglected by the Salafi-jihadist rebel rulers, attention must be paid to the structures of governance that the latter have been able to introduce, to avoid jeopardizing those that provide essential public services. Doing so, in fact, would ultimately harm the local population, delegitimize the intervention, and strengthen the Salafi-jihadists' ability to portray themselves as the only ones interested in the people's wellbeing.

WHAT IS THE RELATIONSHIP BETWEEN SALAFI-JIHADIST GOVERNANCE AND IDEOLOGY?

Having identified the characteristics of Salafi-jihadist governance, I proceed to assess whether, and if so to what extent, ideology influences the models of governance adopted by Salafi-jihadist ruling armed groups.

The religion-based discriminatory approach embraced by IS, HTS, and AQAP is consistent with the notion of *al-wala' wa-l-bara'* as interpreted in the Salafi-jihadist doctrine. The more detailed distinction made by IS and HTS between "apostates," "original disbelievers," and "people of the Book" is also noticeable. While every non-Sunni community has been subjected to marginalization, expropriation, and violence under the rule of Salafi-jihadist armed groups, communities regarded as "apostates" (e.g., the Druze community in northwestern Syria and the Yezidi community in northern Iraq) have been victims of immense persecution, violence, and suffering. Similarly, the gender-based discrimination prevalent in the territories controlled by IS, HTS, and AQAP is consistent with the literal and decontextualized reference that Salafi-jihadists make to the foundational texts of Islam and their prescriptions for a "pure" Islamic society.

The preference of IS, HTS, and AQAP for the exclusion of the civilian population from governance is also consistent with Salafi-jihadism, and more specifically with its condemnation of democracy as a heretical system, whereby the involvement of civilians in decision making opens the door to the adoption of man-made laws that deviate from the principle of absolute divine authority, *tawhid al-hakimiyah*. As was noted, in the case of HTS and AQAP, the only exception to this exclusionary approach was represented by a small group of carefully selected civilians, who were allowed some degree of participation in governance but were under the close supervision of the Salafi-jihadist authorities.

In the case of IS and HTS, the introduction of extensive innovations and the limited maintenance of some former institutions, practices, and employees is also consistent with Salafi-jihadism's understanding of *tawhid al-hakimiyah*. Importantly, the innovations introduced by IS and HTS touched on many areas of governance—from the formulation of sharia-based laws to the imposition of sharia-based public morality regulations, the revision of secular school curricula and the introduction of new Islamist courses of study, and the imposition of a Quranically inspired taxation system. Employees who were allowed to retain their positions had to undergo a process of repentance and indoctrination.

Finally, IS's preference for ruling largely in isolation and excluding most other actors from governance is consistent with the ideological imperatives of *al-wala' wa-l-bara'* as understood in Salafi-jihadist thought. Here, the only remarkable exception to this principle was represented by some form of cooperation with the "apostate" Syrian regime. IS's reliance on extensive coercion and limited persuasion also reflects Salafi-jihadism's propensity to sanction the use of extensive violence to punish and correct deviations from its ideal model of societal and individual conduct.

I thus argue that many patterns of governance adopted by Salafi-jihadist armed groups are influenced in important ways by ideology. However, it needs to be assessed whether factors other than ideology may also offer valid alternative explanations. Regarding inclusivity, it is widely understood that religious, ethno-linguistic, and sectarian groups typically provide governance exclusively to civilians who share their same identity.[2] An alternative argument that goes beyond ideology and identity emphasizes the role of end goals and suggests that groups that seek to replace the central government are typically discriminatory, providing governance to active supporters only.[3] However, this does not explain the patterns of discrimination implemented by IS, HTS, and AQAP, which aspired to replace the government but used gender identity and sectarian identity, rather than active support, to determine and define inclusion.

With respect to the exclusion of civilians, groups with economic resources—external patronage, exploitation of natural resources, or criminal activities—lack incentives to share power with the people.[4] However, this cannot explain why IS, HTS, and AQAP opted to exclude civilians from governance altogether, as none of them could rely exclusively, consistently, and significantly on economic resources independent from the civilian population.[5] Even IS, which benefited from expropriation, looting, and smuggling, still depended on civilians to sustain the costs of war and governance. For instance, it needed civilians for the collection of taxes, for the extraction of resources, and for the continuation of economically productive activities throughout the caliphate.[6] Besides, endowments have been invoked to suggest that groups with access to revenue-generating resources are more likely to employ extensively coercive measures.[7] However, this does not explain why IS, which was not entirely independent of civilians in generating revenues, mobilized extensively coercive practices. It has also been noted that rebel governance becomes more coercive as territories and resources contract.[8] While this may hold true with IS, extensive coercion was always a feature of the Islamic State's rule, including during its period of greatest expansion.[9] Finally, foreign fighters tend to be associated with greater violence against civilians.[10] However, while the role of foreign fighters in the Islamic State is not negligible, coercive practices were devised and enforced by the group's leadership. They were not violent acts arbitrarily carried out by foreign fighters.

Regarding preexisting structures and practices, innovation seems more common when the ruling armed group has significant resources and relevant experience or when the preexisting system of governance is poorly functioning and deeply resented.[11] However, this does not satisfactorily account for the innovation displayed by IS and HTS. While IS had governance experience from its time in Anbar, that was quite limited—especially relative to the experience required to run the vast territory of the caliphate.[12] HTS was even more inexperienced when it came to administering territory. Moreover, resentment toward governance (or the lack thereof) in places such as Mosul and Raqqa may have encouraged IS to introduce innovations.[13] However, this was not true everywhere, as illustrated by the civilian councils that won respect among many Syrians and the traditional tribal structures that enjoyed legitimacy in eastern Syria and western Iraq.[14]

Finally, reflecting on the exclusion of other actors from governance, it has been suggested that rebel rulers are prone to cooperation when other actors are more capable, more legitimate, or more resourceful.[15] Turning this argument around, rebel rulers would be more likely to govern in isolation when other actors are less capable, less legitimate, or less resourceful. However, this does not explain IS's approach. Even in areas where tribal leaders had greater legitimacy, al-Baghdadi's group did not go beyond a mere facade of cooperation. Similarly, even though international NGOs had more experience in many aspects of governance as well as more resources, IS banned them from operating on its territories.

Based on this discussion, it seems that ideology offers a more convincing explanation for certain patterns of Salafi-jihadist rule displayed by IS, HTS, and AQAP, such as gender- and religious-based discrimination, the rejection of democracy and the denial of broad civilian participation, the use of extensive coercion, the exclusion of other non-Sunni and non-Salafi-jihadist actors regardless of their capacity and legitimacy, and the preference for extensive innovations inspired to the Prophetic model. However, there are also clear limits to ideology's capacity to explain Salafi-jihadist governance. Specifically, doctrine is poorly positioned to explain the tendency of HTS and AQAP to include a civilian elite in governance and to refrain from extensively coercive practices. Ideology is also not helpful in explaining the propensity of HTS and AQAP to cooperate with several non-Salafi-jihadist actors, as well as IS's openness to cooperation with the "apostate" Syrian regime. Similarly, ideology cannot make sense of AQAP's preference for maintaining preexisting customs and practices, even when distant from Salafi-jihadism.

The explanatory limitations of ideology suggest that other factors need to be considered. While a detailed discussion of those lies beyond the scope of this book, some preliminary thoughts will be offered here. As noted in the rebel governance literature, pragmatic considerations often encourage maintenance, especially if an armed group has limited resources (finances, manpower, experience) or if previous governance systems are widely accepted.[16] In these circumstances, maintenance may allow a group to save resources, enhance its credibility, and secure greater support. Considering that traditional tribal structures and practices of governance enjoyed immense legitimacy in southern Yemen, it is understandable that AQAP opted for some degree of pragmatic maintenance during its second experiment in governance, which allowed the group to enhance its position among local communities. In addition to this, the fact that AQAP's experience in governance—both in 2011 and in 2015—was short-lived is probably another factor that negatively affected the group's capacity to introduce extensive innovations.

Pragmatism and opportunism may also encourage rebel rulers to cooperate with more capable, more legitimate, or more resourceful actors. Even when such cooperation would seem counterintuitive due to the military hostility or the ideological distance between the parties,[17] it may still be pursued if it allows rebel rulers to address the people's needs, strengthen their governance structures, and obtain legitimacy.[18] This helps to illuminate how HTS and AQAP sought to benefit from cooperation with better-resourced international NGOs, with more experienced technocrats, and with more legitimate tribal leaders. Even IS, which privileged an overall exclusionary approach consistent with its ideology, opted to cooperate with the "apostate" Syrian government for purely opportunistic reasons on the extraction of oil and the production of electricity—areas of governance that were seemingly more important to IS's leadership than the areas of health care and education into which international NGOs could have channeled their know-how and resources.[19]

Finally, pragmatic considerations may discourage armed groups from excessive coercion. Indeed, most rebel rulers recognize that a predominantly coercive approach can be detrimental to their cause.[20] This is especially, yet not exclusively, the case for armed groups with no, or limited, economic resources.[21] These considerations are helpful in understanding the behavior of HTS and AQAP. In the case of AQAP, the realization that popular support was crucial to avoid an uprising such as that of 2012 encouraged the adoption of a more moderate approach, aimed at inspiring sympathy rather than instilling fear. In the case of HTS, the concern that popular opposition may compromise its proto-state, reinforced by the scarcity of economic resources, encouraged the group to improve its public image by avoiding unnecessary coercion.[22] Besides, the pursuit of international recognition seems to have also played a role in encouraging HTS's moderation with respect to the use of coercion.[23] Similar considerations of the perceived importance of civilian support to ensure the sustainability of their Salafi-jihadist polities may also help to understand why HTS and AQAP progressively decided to include a small group of civilians in governance.[24]

Therefore, while ideology is useful to illuminate many of the governance patterns employed by Salafi-jihadist ruling armed groups, a more comprehensive and more accurate understanding of Salafi-jihadist governance requires going beyond doctrine. In other words, while Salafi-jihadist groups engage in some patterns of governance that are consistent with their belief systems, they also operate in complex environments where the literal application of their ideological tenets may not always serve their best interests. Additionally, and in line with my previous argument that different Salafi-jihadist groups can develop different models of rebel governance, the extent to which ideology shapes Salafi-jihadist governance is not uniform but rather varies across groups. Therefore, instead of seeking a universal answer to the question of the relationship between ideology and rebel governance, it seems that different answers may exist for different rebel rulers, even those who belong to the same ideological (in the context of this book, Salafi-jihadist) universe.

Finally, the identification of the relationship between doctrine and governance in the case of Salafi-jihadist rebel rulers bears important implications. It suggests that policy responses that take into due consideration the role of Salafi-jihadism should be recognized as valuable instruments. For instance, once violence toward non-Sunni communities and discrimination toward women are recognized as governance patterns informed by Salafi-jihadism, influential Sunni religious leaders and respected Sunni scholars can play a fundamental role in questioning and undermining the foundations of this policy. This approach, for instance, was followed by a group of Muslim scholars who wrote a letter to Abu Bakr al-Baghdadi in which they condemned his group's most brutal practices and discredited their presumed foundations in Islamic law and Islamic theology.[25] While it is hard to assess whether the letter had any impact on IS's leaders and members, it nonetheless represented a symbolic defeat for the Islamic State.

HOW DOES REBEL GOVERNANCE VARY ACROSS SALAFI-JIHADIST AND NON-SALAFI-JIHADIST ARMED GROUPS?

To conclude this study of Salafi-jihadist governance, I compare the models of governance put forth by IS, HTS, and AQAP with the observations on non-Salafi-jihadist governance collected in chapter 2. The aim is to determine whether, and to what extent, Salafi-jihadist governance is different from non-Salafi-jihadist models of rebel civilian administration.

As I extend the comparative analysis to non-Salafi-jihadist ruling armed groups, I argue that the Salafi-jihadist models of rebel governance may display some unique patterns vis-à-vis the models of governance more commonly adopted by non-Salafi-jihadist rebel rulers worldwide. Specifically, Salafi-jihadist rulers distinguish themselves by their tendency to discriminate in a systematic and institutionalized fashion against other religious (non-Sunni and non-Muslim) communities, as well as against women. IS and HTS have also distinguished themselves by their propensity to combine the limited maintenance of preexisting structures and pre-appointed workers with the introduction of extensive innovations whose foundations are to be found in the sources of Islam and the sociopolitical model of the earliest caliphates. Finally, IS distinguishes itself by its use of extensively coercive practices and limited persuasive measures as well as by its tendency to exclude most other actors and to engage in governance largely in isolation. At the same time, however, Salafi-jihadist and non-Salafi-jihadist rebel rulers also display certain important similarities—perhaps surprisingly so. For instance, HTS and AQAP resemble other non-Salafi-jihadist groups in their tendency to combine coercion and persuasion to comparable extents. Besides, they also share with non-Salafi-jihadist rulers their tendency to establish wide-ranging patterns of cooperation with other actors. Finally, AQAP also has in common with most non-Salafi-jihadist rebel rulers the maintenance of pre-existing practices of governance to a considerable extent.

Building on these considerations, I argue that just as Salafi-jihadist governance is not necessarily uniform across different Salafi-jihadist groups, so the distinctiveness of Salafi-jihadist governance is not universal and should be assessed instead on a case-by-case basis for each Salafi-jihadist rebel ruler. In other words, while Salafi-jihadist governance does display some unique features, the extent of such uniqueness varies across groups.

The argument that Salafi-jihadist governance is not in itself unique but may nonetheless display some distinctive features is of great interest, as it suggests that approaches that have worked in the past to deal with certain rebel rulers may not always be replicated successfully in the case of Salafi-jihadists, and that new approaches may need to be devised instead. For instance, it has been noted that the 2016 peace agreement between the Colombian government and the FARC included mechanisms that supported the armed group's transition from insurgency to political participation.[26] By impacting positively on the FARC's political participation and by incentivizing the group to pursue its political goals democratically, the agreement had "the potential to enhance democratic, political, and societal participation."[27] However, it would be unrealistic and undesirable to pursue a similar strategy with armed groups—such as the Salafi-jihadist groups studied in this book—that are not interested in transitioning to participation in legitimate political systems and that reject democracy altogether as an "apostate" system.

In conclusion, I suggest that the term "Salafi-jihadist governance"— which I use in the title of this book, and which is widely employed by scholars, policymakers, journalists, and humanitarian organizations— should not be taken to allude to a universal and unique model of Salafi-jihadist governance, the existence of which is contradicted by the

TABLE C.1 Salafi-jihadist governance assessed and compared

	IS	HTS	AQAP	Salafi-jihadist expected model of governance	LTTE	FARC	PYD
Inclusivity	Discrimination (Christians, Shias, Yezidis, women)	Discrimination (Christians, Druze, Shias, women)	Discrimination (Shias/Houthis and women)	Discrimination (non-Muslims, non-Sunnis, women)	Discrimination (Sinhalese and Muslims)	Universality (Colombian people)	Partial discrimination (non-Kurds de facto relegated to "second-class" status)
Civilian engagement	Subjection (rejection of democratic process)	Partial subjection (rejection of democratic process, but creation of SSG)	Partial subjection (rejection of democratic process, but creation of HNC and other similar councils)	Subjection (rejection of democratic process)	Subjection (no political party, no electoral process)	Partial participation (Patriotic Union and electoral process)	Partial participation (elections, but accusations of authoritarian rule)
Generation of compliance	Extensive coercion and limited persuasion (e.g., systematic *hudud* punishments in publicly display and some persuasive measures, such as *da'wah* events)	Coercion and persuasion (e.g., punishment of dissenters and *da'wah* materials)	Coercion and persuasion (e.g., occasional *hudud* punishments and *da'wah* activities)	Extensive coercion and limited persuasion (e.g., full range of *hudud* punishments and some persuasive measures, such as fatwas and *da'wah*)	Coercion and persuasion (e.g., abductions and mobilization of Tamil symbols)	Coercion and persuasion (e.g., harsh punishments and public gatherings to promote ideology)	Coercion and persuasion (e.g., house demolitions and mobilization of Kurdish symbols)

Approach to outsiders	Partial exclusion (exclusion of non-Sunnis and non-Salafists, but limited cooperation with Sunni tribes that pledged *bay'ah* and with the Syrian regime)	Partial cooperation (cooperation with elders, tribal sheikhs, international aid organizations, and Turkish government)	Partial cooperation (cooperation with Sunni tribes, prominent Salafi figures, and some international aid organizations)	Exclusion or partial exclusion (exclusion of non-Sunnis and non-Salafi-Jihadists, but possible cooperation with other Salafi-jihadists and individuals or groups who pledge *bay'ah*)	Partial cooperation (Sri Lankan government and NGOs)	Partial cooperation (state officials and local authorities)	Partial cooperation (Arab tribal leaders, Syrian government)
Propensity to change	Extensive innovation and limited maintenance (e.g., new sharia-based judicial system, new taxation system, new norms of conduct, and maintenance of professional workers upon engagement in *tawbah*)	Extensive innovation and limited maintenance (e.g., new sharia-based judicial system, new taxation system, new norms of conduct, and maintenance of employees upon engaging in *tawbah*)	Innovation and maintenance (e.g., sharia-based judicial systems and maintenance of traditional *'urf*)	Extensive innovation and limited maintenance (e.g., new sharia-based judicial system and maintenance of employees who engage in *tawbah* and pledge *bay'ah*)	Innovation and maintenance (e.g., Tamil Eelam Education Council and Sri Lankan Department of Education)	Innovation and maintenance (e.g., new taxation system and maintenance of local customs and state laws)	Extensive innovation and limited maintenance (e.g., new multilevel judicial system and maintenance of Syrian laws)

analysis of multiple case studies offered in this book. Rather, it should indicate the act of governance by Salafi-jihadist armed groups, which is a heterogenous phenomenon whereby Salafi-jihadist insurgents engage in civilian administration, developing patterns of governance that do not necessarily assume the same characteristics across different contexts and that do not necessarily reflect the tenets of Salafi-jihadism to the same extent.

This book has laid the foundations for a more solid understanding of Salafi-jihadist rebel governance. Proposing an original typology of insurgent governance and applying it to three cases of Salafi-jihadist ruling armed groups, I have studied Salafi-jihadist governance in depth, from a multidimensional perspective and through a comparative approach. I have identified similarities and differences between different Salafi-jihadist groups and argued that a single model of Salafi-jihadist governance does not exist. I have found that ideology is an important factor to explain many (yet certainly not all) features of Salafi-jihadist governance, even though its influence varies across groups. I have also extended the comparison to non-Salafi-jihadist rebel rulers, finding that Salafi-jihadist governance may display certain specific governance patterns as well as certain similarities with non-Salafi-jihadist rebel governance, which contradicts the notion of Salafi-jihadist governance as a unique, sui generis phenomenon.

Of the three Salafi-jihadist armed groups studied in this book, two have been defeated militarily and forced out of their conquered territories—AQAP in 2016 and IS in 2019. Beyond those two, many of the Salafi-jihadist proto-states that were established in the last decade have been defeated militarily and either erased from the map altogether or reduced to some small pockets of contested territory. However, the phenomenon of Salafi-jihadist governance is not going to disappear. As situations of state weakness, conflict, and power vacuum continue to characterize many of the countries in which Salafi-jihadist armed groups are present, the possibility that those groups will launch insurgencies, recruit supporters, conquer territories, and establish some (even rudimentary) forms of governance cannot be excluded. As such, Salafi-jihadist governance will continue to be a source of concern for scholars, politicians, humanitarians, journalists, and the larger public in the foreseeable future.

Faced with this reality, scholars should continue to look inside Salafi-jihadist governance to further our understanding of the phenomenon, and with it our capacity to address it appropriately.[28] First, future studies could explore and compare Salafi-jihadist governance across additional dimensions of rebel rule, other than those studied here. In fact, looking into alternative dimensions of rebel governance can illuminate features of Salafi-jihadist rule that remained unexplored and unexplained in this book. This might offer an even more comprehensive and detailed picture of Salafi-jihadist governance. Additionally, comparing Salafi-jihadist and non-Salafi-jihadist groups with respect to new dimensions of rebel rule might unveil new similarities and/or differences between Salafi-jihadist and non-Salafi-jihadist governance.

In this regard, I believe that a dimension of rebel governance that would be interesting to investigate with respect to Salafi-jihadist groups is rebel diplomacy, meaning a rebel group's conduct of foreign affairs during civil war for the purpose of advancing its military and political objectives.[29] Thus far, diplomacy has been quite neglected in the rebel governance literature. Yet, it is an important element to consider, since "to fully understand the phenomenon of rebel governance, we ought to examine not only how rebels govern those under their control, but also how they pursue what we might call the externally oriented face of governance, procuring goods and legitimacy through foreign engagement and the strategic use of talk."[30] While this book focused exclusively on how Salafi-jihadist rebel rulers provide governance to the people living under their control, future studies could investigate why, when, and how Salafi-jihadist ruling armed groups engage in—or refrain from—rebel diplomacy as a wartime tactic. It would also be relevant to interrogate the political implications of Salafi-jihadists' engagement in diplomacy, including how external actors may use the offer of diplomatic engagement to influence the behavior of those groups.

Second, a further avenue for future research would be to study Salafi-jihadist governance with greater attention to variation across time and space. Specifically, future studies might opt to study how Salafi-jihadist governance evolves over time. Having in mind that the process of rebel rule is iterative and that armed groups' behaviors and relationships change over time,[31] it becomes relevant to adopt a longitudinal approach and study whether, how, and why the governance patterns employed by a Salafi-jihadist group change with the passage of time. In this way, greater emphasis would be placed on in-group rather than cross-group variation and a more accurate picture of each group's evolving approach to governance could be offered. While some important studies have been produced on this,[32] there is certainly more left to unveil and explain.

This line of research would also be useful to understand the conditions under which Salafi-jihadist rebel governance may become more pragmatic over time and, therefore, to identify leverages that could be used with Salafi-jihadist groups to encourage their transition toward less ideological and less uncompromising patterns of behavior. This would be especially relevant with respect to those patterns of Salafi-jihadist rebel governance that most negatively affect the human rights of people living in Salafi-jihadist-controlled territories, such as religious-based discrimination, gender-based marginalization and violence, the use of extensive coercion, and the imposition of strict and repressive regulations concerning public life. Along this same line, it would also be interesting to explore how the governance experiences of certain Salafi-jihadist rebel rulers differed from one locality to another, especially for groups that controlled large swaths of territory, such as the Islamic State, or groups that control geographically discontinued territories, such as al-Shabaab.

Third, it would be interesting to study Salafi-jihadist groups, such as Boko Haram, that did not engage in extensive practices of governance even when in control of some territories. Exploring why Salafi-jihadist groups may not develop an interest in governance, even when the minimal conditions for a governance experiment seem to be present, would help to better understand Salafi-jihadist behavior. While this book purposefully selected three Salafi-jihadist groups that engaged in governance for a considerable period of time and to a significant extent in order to meaningfully analyze and compare their governance practices, focusing on Salafi-jihadist groups who decided not to turn into rebel rulers would advance our knowledge. In other words, if this book contributed to our understanding of why and how Salafi-jihadist armed groups may want to govern, it remains to be understood why Salafi-jihadist armed groups may prefer to refrain from governance. Relatedly, explaining under what circumstances Salafi-jihadist armed groups may be unable to establish a system of governance, even if interested in doing so, would help us to unpack some of the challenges that stand in the way of Salafi-jihadist governance, which may be similar to the challenges experienced by other, ideologically distinct armed groups, or may be specific to Salafi-jihadist non-state actors.

As I recalled above, two of the three cases of Salafi-jihadist rebel governance studied in this book were ultimately defeated militarily, each group losing control over the territories they had previously held. Far from being exceptional cases, most Salafi-jihadist groups that held territory at some point in time and attempted to engage in some form of governance over those territories suffered a similar fate. Moving from this consideration, future research could study the implications of Salafi-jihadist governance for individuals, communities, and societies. While this book set out to build an unprecedented picture of civilian life under systems of Salafi-jihadist rebel governance in Syria, Iraq, and Yemen, a valuable next step would be to understand the consequences of those systems of rebel rule in the medium and long term. For instance, recalling the observation that Salafi-jihadist rebel rulers enforce a deeply discriminatory system of governance based on religious identity, it seems important to investigate the potential consequences of this for relations between different sects after the Salafi-jihadist rulers cease governing.

Finally, this book studied Salafi-jihadist governance by exploring and explaining the behavior of Salafi-jihadist armed groups in control of populated territories. However, it seems important to investigate not only what Salafi-jihadist rebel rulers do, but also how the civilian population living in those territories respond. Here, an interesting body of literature has been developing that looks into civilian resistance to Salafi-jihadist governance, exploring the circumstances under which civilians resist Salafi-jihadist rule and the consequences that such resistance may have on Salafi-jihadist governance patterns. While valuable studies have been published on civilian resistance to Salafi-jihadist rulers,[33] this area of research can benefit from more detailed and systematic investigations. Relatedly, more work needs to be done on civilians' demand for rebel governance and the Salafi-jihadists' responses to it. This would allow us to explain how Salafi-jihadist rebel rulers address the demands advanced by local populations and how those demands help to shape an armed group's choices as ruler.

NOTES

INTRODUCTION

1. Marta Furlan, "Rebel Governance at the Time of Covid-19: Emergencies as Opportunities for Rebel Rulers," *Studies in Conflict & Terrorism* 46, no. 8 (September 2020): 1446–1451, https://doi.org/10.1080/1057610X.2020.1816681.

2. For a discussion of rebel governance in the Middle East over the last decade, see Ibrahim Fraihat and Abdilhadi Alijla, eds., *Rebel Governance in the Middle East* (Palgrave Macmillan, 2023).

3. In the book, I use the terms "armed groups," "rebel groups," "insurgents," and "rebels" interchangeably.

4. Shiraz Maher, *Salafi-Jihadism: The History of an Idea* (Oxford University Press, 2016).

5. Carolyn E. Fick, "The Haitian Revolution and the Limits of Freedom: Defining Citizenship in the Revolutionary Era," *Social History* 32, no. 4 (May 2008): 409, https://doi.org/10.1080/03071020701616696; Nazih Richani, *Systems of Violence: The Political Economy of War and Peace in Colombia* (State University of New York Press, 2002), 89; Kasper Hoffmann, "Myths Set in Motion: The Moral Economy of Mai Mai Governance," in *Rebel Governance in Civil War*, ed. Ana Arjona et al. (Cambridge University Press, 2015), 158–179.

6. Robert I. Rotberg, "The Failure and Collapse of Nation States: Breakdown, Prevention and Repair," in *When States Fail: Causes and Consequences*, ed. Robert I. Rotberg (Princeton University Press, 2004), 1–45; Francis Fukuyama, *State Building: Governance and World Order in the XXI Century* (Cornell University Press, 2004), 43–91.

7. Kevin P. Clements et al., "State Building Reconsidered: The Role of Hybridity in the Formation of Political Order," *Political Science* 59, no. 1 (June 2007): 45–56, https://doi.org/10.1177/003231870705900106; Volker Boege et al., "Hybrid Political Orders, Not Fragile States," *Peace Review* 21, no. 1 (February 2009): 13–21, https://doi.org/10.1080

/10402650802689997; Thomas Risse, "Limited Statehood: A Critical Perspective," in *The Oxford Handbook of Transformations of the State*, ed. Stephan Leibfired et al. (Oxford University Press, 2015), 152–168.

8. Bard E. O'Neill, *Insurgency and Terrorism: From Revolution to Apocalypse* (Manas 2006), 15, 32–37.

9. Ana Arjona et al., "Introduction," in Arjona et al., *Rebel Governance in Civil War*, 1.

10. Jeremy Weinstein, *Inside Rebellion: The Politics of Insurgent Violence* (Cambridge University Press 2007), 163–170; Didier Péclard and Delphine Mechoulan, "Rebel Governance and the Politics of Civil War," Working Paper 1/2015 (Swisspeace, July 2015), 17, https://www.swisspeace.ch/assets/publications/downloads/Working-Papers/3b4a3ca a24/Rebel-Governance-and-the-Politics-of-Civil-War-Working-Paper-15-swisspeace -didier_peclard.pdf; Antonio Giustozzi, *Empires of Mud: Wars and Warlords in Afghanistan* (Hurst 2012), 193–194; Gérard Chaliand, *Guerrilla Strategies: An Historical Anthology from the Long March to Afghanistan* (University of California Press, 1982), 15; Eqbal Ahmad, "Revolutionary War and Counterinsurgency," *Journal of International Affairs* 25, no. 1 (1971): 1–15, https://www.jstor.org/stable/24356753; Victor Asal et al., "Doing Good While Killing: Why Some Insurgent Groups Provide Community Services," *Terrorism & Political Violence* 34, no. 4 (May 2020): 837–843, https:// doi.org/10.1080/09546553.2020.1745775.

11. William Reno, "Predatory Rebellions and Governance: The National Patriotic Front of Liberia, 1989–1992," in Arjona et al., *Rebel Governance in Civil War*, 265–266.

12. Nelson Kasfir, "Rebel Governance—Constructing a Field of Inquiry: Definitions, Scope, Patterns, Order, Causes," in Arjona et al., *Rebel Governance in Civil War*, 40; Mara Revkin, "What Explains Taxation by Resource-Rich Rebels? Evidence from the Islamic State in Syria," *Journal of Politics* 82, no. 2 (January 2019): 761, https://doi.org /10.1086/706597; Ana Arjona, "Civilian Cooperation and Non-Cooperation with Non-State Armed Groups: The Centrality of Obedience and Resistance," *Small Wars & Insurgencies* 28, nos. 4–5 (July 2017): 760, https://doi.org/10.1080/09592318.2017.1322328.

13. Romain Malejacq, "From Rebel to Quasi-State: Governance, Diplomacy and Legitimacy in the Midst of Afghanistan's Wars (1979–2001)," *Small Wars & Insurgencies* 28, nos. 4–5 (July 2017): 873, https://doi.org/10.1080/09592318.2017.1322332.

14. Ana Arjona, *Rebelocracy: Social Order in the Colombian Civil War* (Cambridge University Press, 2016), 7.

15. Arjona, "Civilian Cooperation," 760.

16. Arjona, 760.

17. Megan A. Stewart, "Civil War as State-Making: Strategic Governance in Civil War," *International Organization* 72, no. 1 (Winter 2018): 206, https://www.jstor.org/stable /26569466.

18. Victor Asal et al., "It Comes with the Territory: Why States Negotiate with Ethno-Political Organizations," *Studies in Conflict & Terrorism* 42, no. 4 (October 2017): 364, https://doi.org/10.1080/1057610X.2017.1373428.

19. Zachariah Mampilly, *Rebel Rulers: Insurgent Governance and Civilian Life During War* (Cornell University Press, 2011), 63; Ana Arjona, "Wartime Institutions: A Research

Agenda," *Journal of Conflict Resolution* 58, no. 8 (September 2014): 1361, https://doi.org /10.1177/0022002714547904; Mathilde Becker Aarseth, *Mosul Under ISIS: Eyewitness Accounts of Life in the Caliphate* (I. B. Tauris, 2021), 47.

20.   Benedetta Berti, "Violent and Criminal Non-State Actors," in *The Oxford Handbook of Governance and Limited Statehood*, ed. Thomas Risse et al. (Oxford University Press, 2018), 280; Mampilly, *Rebel Rulers*, 64; Timothy Wickham-Crowley, "The Rise (and Sometimes Fall) of Guerrilla Governments in Latin America," *Sociological Forum* 2, no. 3 (June 1987): 473–499, https://doi.org/10.1007/BF01106622; Frank Ledwidge, *Rebel Law: Insurgents, Courts and Justice in Modern Conflict* (Hurst & Co., 2017), 16–32; René Provost, *Rebel Courts: The Administration of Justice by Armed Insurgents* (Oxford University Press, 2021), 10.

21.   Weinstein, *Inside Rebellion*, 38; Alexus G, Grynkewich, "Welfare as Warfare: How Violent Non-State Groups Use Social Services to Attack the State," *Studies in Conflict & Terrorism* 31, no. 4 (April 2008): 353–355, https://doi.org/10.1080/10576100801931321.

22.   Revkin, "What Explains Taxation," 761–763; Bert Suykens, "Comparing Rebel Rule Through Revolution and Naturalization: Ideologies of Governance in Naxalite and Naga India," in Arjona et al., *Rebel Governance in Civil War*, 150; Tanya Bandula-Irwin et al., "Beyond Greed: Why Armed Groups Tax," *Studies in Conflict & Terrorism* (February 2022): 4–14, https://doi.org/10.1080/1057610X.2022.2038409.

23.   Arjona, *Rebelocracy*, 185.

24.   Irénée Herber and Jerome Drevon, "Engaging Armed Groups at the International Committee of the Red Cross: Challenges, Opportunities and Covid-19," *International Review of the Red Cross*, no. 915 (January 2022): 1026, https://international-review.icrc .org/articles/engaging-armed-groups-at-icrc-challenges-opportunities-covid-19-915.

25.   For more on the Arab Spring, see Mark L. Haas and David W. Lesch, *The Arab Spring: The Hope and Reality of the Uprisings* (Avalon Publishing, 2016); Larbi Sadiki, ed., *Routledge Handbook of the Arab Spring: Rethinking Democratization* (Routledge, 2015).

26.   Adam Roberts, "Civil Resistance and the Fate of the Arab Spring," in *Civil Resistance in the Arab Spring: Triumphs and Disasters*, ed. Adam Roberts et al. (Oxford University Press, 2016), 270–275.

27.   Adam Roberts, "The Fate of the Arab Spring: Ten Propositions," *Asian Journal of Middle Eastern and Islamic Studies* 12, no. 3 (January 2019): 276–280, https://doi.org/10.1080 /25765949.2018.1546977. See also Chibli Mallat and Edward Mortimer, "The Background to Civil Resistance in the Middle East," in Roberts et al., *Civil Resistance in the Arab Spring*, 1–29.

28.   Roberts, "The Fate of the Arab Spring," 280.

29.   Roberts, 284.

30.   Roberts, "Civil Resistance," 321.

31.   Roberts, 321.

32.   Aisha Ahmad, *Jihad & Co.: Black Markets and Islamist Power* (Oxford University Press, 2017), 161.

33.   Brynjar Lia, "Understanding Jihadi Proto-States," *Perspectives on Terrorism* 9, no. 4 (August 2015): 35, https://pt.icct.nl/article/understanding-jihadi-proto-states.

34. Fawaz Gerges, "The Rise and Fall of Al-Qaeda: Debunking the Terrorist Narrative," *Huffington Post*, January 3, 2012, https://www.huffpost.com/entry/the-rise-and-fall-of-alqa_b_1182003?ref=tw.

35. Daveed Gartenstein-Ross and Tara Vassefi, "Perceptions of the 'Arab Spring' Within the *Salafi-Jihadi* Movement," *Studies in Conflict and Terrorism* 35, no. 2 (November 2012): 838–841, https://doi.org/10.1080/1057610X.2012.720241.

36. Matthew Bamber-Zyrd, "Cyclical Jihadist Governance: The Islamic State Governance Cycle in Iraq and Syria," *Small Wars & Insurgencies* 33, no. 8 (September 2022): 1320–1325, https://doi.org/10.1080/09592318.2022.2116182; Stig Jarle Hansen, *Al-Shabaab in Somalia: The History and Ideology of a Militant Islamist Group, 2005–2012* (Oxford University Press, 2013), 49–103.

37. Lia, "Understanding Jihadi Proto-States," 31.

38. Didier Péclard et al., "Civil Wars and State Formation: Violence and the Politics of Legitimacy in Angola, Cote d'Ivoire and South Sudan," Working Paper (Swiss Network of International Studies, July 2019), 2, https://snis.ch/wp-content/uploads/2020/01/2016_Pe%CC%81clard_Working-Paper.pdf.

39. Arjona et al., *Rebel Governance in Civil War*; Mampilly, *Rebel Rulers*; Arjona, *Rebelocracy*; Weinstein, *Inside Rebellion*.

40. Ahmad, *Jihad & Co.*; Antonio Giustozzi, *The Taliban at War: 2001–2018* (Oxford University Press, 2019); Benedetta Berti, "Non-State Actors as Providers of Governance: The Hamas Government in Gaza Between Effective Sovereignty, Centralized Authority and Resistance," *Middle East Journal* 69, no. 1 (2015): 15–29, https://www.jstor.org/stable/43698207; Judith Harik, *The Public and Social Services of the Lebanese Militias* (Centre for Lebanese Studies, 1994), 22–31.

41. Lia, "Understanding Jihadi Proto-States," 33–38.

42. Lia, 31.

43. Vidar B. Skretting, "Pragmatism and Purism in Jihadist Governance: The Islamic Emirate of Azawad Revisited," *Studies in Conflict & Terrorism* 47, no. 7 (January 2022): 731–743, https://doi.org/10.1080/1057610X.2021.2007562.

44. Aymenn Jawad al-Tamimi, "The Evolution in Islamic State Administration: The Documentary Evidence," *Perspectives on Terrorism* 9, no. 4 (August 2015): 119–125, https://pt.icct.nl/article/evolution-islamic-state-administration-documentary-evidence.

45. Aaron Y. Zelin, "The Islamic State's Territorial Methodology," Research Notes No. 29 (Washington Institute for Near East Policy, January 2016), 1–5, https://www.washingtoninstitute.org/sites/default/files/pdf/ResearchNote29-Zelin.pdf.

46. Zelin, 1.

47. Becker Aarseth, *Mosul*, 45–120.

48. Revkin, "What Explains Taxation," 761–3.

49. Bamber-Zyrd, "Cyclical Jihadist Governance," 1320–1336.

50. Joana Cook, *"Their Fate Is Tied to Ours": Assessing AQAP Governance and Implications for Security in Yemen* (International Centre for the Study of Radicalization, October 2019), 17–19, https://icsr.info/wp-content/uploads/2019/10/ICSR-Report-Their-Fate

-is-Tied-to-Ours-Assessing-AQAP-Governance-and-Implications-for-Security-in-Ye men.pdf.

51. Michael Weddegjerde Skjelderup, "Jihadi Governance and Traditional Authority Structures: Al-Shabaab and Clan Elders in Southern Somalia, 2008–2012," *Small Wars & Insurgencies* 31, no. 6 (August 2020): 1179–1186, https://doi.org/10.1080/09592318.2020 .1780686.

52. Benedetta Berti, "From Cooperation to Competition: Localization, Militarization and Rebel Co-Governance Arrangements in Syria," *Studies in Conflict & Terrorism* 46, no. 2 (June 2020): 215–219, https://doi.org/10.1080/1057610X.2020.1776964.

53. S. Ladbury et al., "Jihadi Groups and State-Building: The Case of Boko Haram in Nigeria," *Stability: International Journal of Security and Development* 5, no. 1 (November 2016): 4–12, https://stabilityjournal.org/articles/10.5334/sta.427.

54. Joana Cook et al., "Jurisprudence Beyond the State: An Analysis of Jihadist 'Justice' in Yemen, Syria and Libya," *Studies in Conflict and Terrorism* 46, no. 5 (June 2020): 562–573, https://doi.org/10.1080/1057610X.2020.1776958.

55. Ferdaous Bouhlel and Yvan Guichaoua, "Norms, Non-Combatants' Agency and Restraint in Jihadi Violence in Northern Mali," *International Interactions* 47, no. 5 (March 2021): 864–870, https://doi.org/10.1080/03050629.2021.1898954.

56. Isak Svensson and Daniel Finnbogason, "Confronting the Caliphate: Explaining Civil Resistance in Jihadist Proto-States," *European Journal of International Relations* 27, no. 2 (2021): 580–587, https://www.diva-portal.org/smash/get/diva2:1585191/FULLTEXT01.pdf.

57. Matthew Bember and Isak Svensson, "Resisting Radical Rebels: Variations in Islamist Rebel Governance and the Occurrence of Civil Resistance," *Terrorism & Political Violence* 35, no. 5 (February 2022): 1133–1139, https://doi.org/10.1080/09546553.2021.2019023.

58. Cemil Boyraz, "Alternative Political Projects of Territoriality and Governance During the Syrian War: The Caliphate vs Democratic Confederalism," *Geopolitics* 26, no. 4 (December 2020): 1099–1104, https://doi.org/10.1080/14650045.2020.1855580.

59. Maher, *Salafi-Jihadism*, 145.

60. Francisco Gutiérrez-Sanín and Elisabeth Jean Wood, "Ideology in Civil War: Instrumental Adoption and Beyond," *Journal of Peace Research* 51, no. 2 (March 2014): 213–226, https://doi.org/10.1177/0022343313514073.

61. Arjona et al., "Introduction," 4, 18.

62. John Gerring, "What Is a Case Study and What Is It Good for?," *American Political Science Review* 98, no. 2 (May 2004): 341–354, https://doi.org/10.1017/S0003055404001182.

63. Robert Yin, *Qualitative Research from Start to Finish* (Guilford Press 2011), 6.

64. Yin, 8.

65. Yin, 9.

66. John Gerring, "Qualitative Methods," *Annual Review of Political Science* 20, no. 1, (2017): 20, https://doi.org/10.1146/annurev-polisci-092415-024158.

67. Robert Yin, *Case Study Research: Design and Methods* (Sage Publications, 2003), 1.

68. Alexander L. George and Andrew Bennett, *Case Studies and Theory Development in the Social Sciences* (MIT Press 2005), 19–22.

69. See Revkin, "What Explains Taxation"; Berti, "From Cooperation to Competition"; Cook et al., "Jurisprudence Beyond the State"; Svensson and Finnbogason, "Confronting the Caliphate."

70. John Gerring, *Case Study Research: Principles and Practice* (Cambridge University Press, 2007), 245.

71. Cook et al., "Jurisprudence Beyond the State"; Svensson and Finnbogason, "Confronting the Caliphate"; Jerome Devron and Patrick Haenni, "The Consolidation of a (Post-Jihadi) Technocratic State-Let in Idlib," Project on Middle East Political Science, 2020, https://pomeps.org/the-consolidation-of-a-post-jihadi-technocratic-state-let-in-idlib; Regine Schwab, "Insurgent Courts in Civil Wars: The Three Pathways of (Trans)Formation in Today's Syria (2012–17)," *Small Wars & Insurgencies* 29, no. 4 (August 2018): 801–826, https://doi.org/10.1080/09592318.2018.1497290.

72. Brynjar Lia, "The *Jihādī* Movement and Rebel Governance: A Reassertion of a Patriarchal Order?," *Die Welt des Islam* 57, nos. 3–4 (2017): 459, https://www.jstor.org/stable/26568534.

73. Aaron Zelin, "Introducing the Islamic State Select Worldwide Activity Map," Washington Institute for Near East Policy, March 21, 2023, https://www.washingtoninstitute.org/policy-analysis/introducing-islamic-state-select-worldwide-activity-map.

74. "Striving for Hegemony: The HTS Crackdown on al-Qaida and Friends in Northwest Syria," Al-Muraqib, Jihadica, September 15, 2020, https://www.jihadica.com/striving-for-hegemony-the-hts-crackdown-on-al-qaida-and-friends-in-northwest-syria/; Aaron Zelin, "Living Long Enough to See Yourself Become the Villain: The Case of Abu Muhammad al-Maqdisi," Jihadica, September 9, 2020, https://www.jihadica.com/living-long-enough/; Bryce Loidolt, "Managing the Global and Local: The Dual Agenda of Al Qaeda in the Arabian Peninsula," *Studies in Conflict & Terrorism* 34, no. 2 (January 2011): 107–114, https://doi.org/10.1080/1057610X.2011.538831; Gregory Johnsen, "The End of AQAP as a Global Threat," Sana'a Center for Strategic Studies, March 5, 2020, https://sanaacenter.org/publications/analysis/9164; Thomas Joscelyn, "Fifteen Years After the 9/11 Attacks, al Qaeda fights on," *Long War Journal*, September 11, 2016, https://www.longwarjournal.org/archives/2016/09/fifteen-years-after-the-911-attacks-al-qaeda-fights-on.php.

75. International Crisis Group, *Exploiting Disorder: Al-Qaeda and the Islamic State*, Special Report No. 1 (International Crisis Group, March 2016), 15–33, https://www.crisisgroup.org/global/exploiting-disorder-al-qaeda-and-islamic-state; Ulf Brüggeman, "Al-Qaeda and the Islamic State: Objectives, Threat, Countermeasures," Security Policy Working Paper No. 9 (Federal Academy for Security Policy, 2016, https://www.baks.bund.de/sites/baks010/files/working_paper_2016_09.pdf; Sarah Phillips, "Al-Qaeda and the Struggle for Yemen," *Survival* 53, no. 1 (2011): 106, https://www.tandfonline.com/doi/epdf/10.1080/00396338.2011.555605?needAccess=true.

76. Silvia Carenzi, "A Downward Scale Shift? The Case of Hayat Tahrir al-Sham," *Perspectives on Terrorism* 14, no. 6 (December 2020): 92, https://www.jstor.org/stable/26964728.

77. Mackenzie Holtz, "Examining Extremism: Hayat Tahrir al-Sham," Center for Strategic and International Studies, August 3, 2023, https://www.csis.org/blogs/examining-extremism/examining-extremism-hayat-tahrir-al-sham-hts.

78. Dareen Khalifa "The Jihadist Factor in Syria's Idlib: A Conversation With Abu Muhammad al-Julani," International Crisis Group, February 20, 2020, https://www.crisisgroup.org/middle-east-north-africa/east-mediterranean-mena/syria/jihadist-factor-syrias-idlib-conversation-abu-muhammad-al-jolani; Ines Khalifa Barnard and Charlie Winter, "Reframing Jihadism: Deciphering the Identity, Politics, Agenda of Hayat Tahrir al-Sham in Northwest Syria," in *The Handbook of Media and Culture in the Middle East*, ed. Joe F. Khalil et al. (John Wiley & Sons, 2023), 396–413.

79. Skretting, "Pragmatism and Purism," 727.

80. Haroro J. Ingram et al., *The ISIS Reader: Milestone Texts of the Islamic State Movement* (Oxford University Press, 2020).

81. Raymond Ibrahim, ed. and trans., *The Al Qaeda Reader* (Doubleday, 2007).

1. GOVERNANCE BY INSURGENTS

1. Francis Fukuyama, *State Building: Governance and World Order in the XXI Century* (Cornell University Press, 2004), 43–91; Robert I. Rotberg, "The Failure and Collapse of Nation States: Breakdown, Prevention and Repair," in *When States Fail: Causes and Consequences*, ed. Robert I. Rotberg (Princeton University Press, 2004), 1–45.

2. Ann Mason, "Colombia's Conflicts and the Theories of World Politics," *Items & Issues* 4, nos. 2–3 (2003):7–11, https://issuu.com/ssrcitemsissues/docs/i_i_vol_4_no_2-3_2003; Thomas Risse, *Governance Without a State? Policies and Politics in Areas of Limited Statehood* (Columbia University Press, 2011), 9; Thomas Risse, "Limited Statehood. A Critical Perspective," in *The Oxford Handbook of Transformations of the State*, ed. Stephan Leibfried et al. (Oxford University Press, 2015), 152–168; Kevin P. Clements et al., "State Building Reconsidered: The Role of Hybridity in the Formation of Political Order," *Political Science* 59, no. 1 (June 2007): 45–56, https://doi.org/10.1177/0032318707059000106; Volker Boege et al., "Hybrid Political Orders, Not Fragile States," *Peace Review* 21, no. 1 (February 2009): 13–21, https://doi.org/10.1080/10402650802689997.

3. Nelson Kasfir, "Rebel Governance: Constructing a Field of Inquiry: Definitions, Scope, Patterns, Order, Causes," in *Rebel Governance in Civil War*, ed. Ana Arjona et al. (Cambridge University Press, 2015), 24.

4. David Galula, *Counterinsurgency Warfare: Theory and Practice* (Praeger Security International, 2006), 1–2; Steven Metz, *Rethinking Insurgency* (U.S. Army War College, 2007), 1–49; Robert J. Bunker, "Changing Forms of Insurgency: Pirates, Narco Gangs and Failed States," in *The Routledge Handbook of Insurgency and Counterinsurgency*, ed. Paul B. Rich and Isabelle Duyvesteyn (Routledge, 2012), 45; David Kilcullen, "Countering Global Insurgency," *Journal of Strategic Studies* 28, no. 4 (January 2007): 604–607, https://doi.org/10.1080/01402390500300956; Bard E. O'Neill, *Insurgency and*

Terrorism: From Revolution to Apocalypse (Manas 2006), 20–8; Bruce Hoffman, *Inside Terrorism* (Columbia University Press, 2006), 35.

5. Menachem Begin, *The Revolt* (Steimatzky, 1977), 59.

6. Carlos Marighella, *Mini-Manual of the Urban Guerrilla* (Abraham Guillen Press, 2002), 4.

7. O'Neill, *Insurgency and Terrorism*, 15, 32–37. For more on insurgencies, see Anthony James Joes, *Modern Guerrilla Insurgency* (Greenwood Publishing Group, 1992); David Kilcullen, *Out of the Mountains: The Coming Age of the Urban Guerrilla* (Oxford University Press, 2013); Ian Beckett, *Modern Insurgencies and Counter-Insurgencies: Guerrillas and their Opponents Since 1750* (Routledge, 2011); John A. Nagl, *Learning to Eat Soup with a Knife* (Chicago University Press, 2005).

8. Galula, *Counterinsurgency Warfare*, 3–4.

9. Galula, 3–4.

10. Robert Taber, *The War of the Flea: The Classic Study of Guerrilla Warfare* (Brassey's, 2002), 20.

11. James Shinn, "'NATO Has the Watches, We Have the Time,'" *Wall Street Journal*, October 26, 2009, https://www.wsj.com/articles/SB10001424052748704335904574497120548934550.

12. John A. Nagl, foreword to Galula, *Counterinsurgency Warfare*.

13. Prashant Jha, *Battles of the Republic: A Contemporary History of Nepal* (Hurst & Co, 2014), 60.

14. Gérard Chaliand, *Guerrilla Strategies: An Historical Anthology from the Long March to Afghanistan* (University of California Press, 1982), 1; Marighella, *Mini-Manual*, 21; Thomas H. Johnson, "Taliban Adaptations and Innovations," *Small Wars & Insurgencies* 24, no. 1 (February 2013): 9–21, https://doi.org/10.1080/09592318.2013.740228.

15. Galula, *Counterinsurgency Warfare*, 4; Thomas H. Johnson, *Taliban Narratives: The Use and Power of Stories in the Afghanistan Conflict* (Oxford University Press, 2017), 266.

16. Galula, *Counterinsurgency Warfare*, 4.

17. Eqbal Ahmad, "Revolutionary War and Counterinsurgency," *Journal of International Affairs* 25, no. 1 (1971): 14, https://www.jstor.org/stable/24356753.

18. Stathis N. Kalyvas, *The Logic of Violence in Civil War* (Cambridge University Press, 2006), 91.

19. Roger Trinquier, *Modern Warfare: A French View of Counterinsurgency* (Praeger, 1964), 8.

20. Peter G. Thompson, *Armed Groups: The 21st Century Threat* (Rowman & Littlefield, 2014), 141; Timothy Wickham-Crowley, *Guerrillas and Revolutions in Latin America: A Comparative Study of Insurgents and Regime Since 1956* (Princeton University Press, 1992), 8; O'Neill, *Insurgency and Terrorism*, 70–89; Taber, *War of the Flea*, 11–12; José Ciro Martínez and Brent Eng, "Stifling Stateness: The Assad Regime's Campaign against Rebel Governance," *Security Dialogue* 49, no. 4 (2018): 235–253, https://doi.org/10.1177/0967010618768622; Begin, *The Revolt*, 80–81, 109.

21. Mao Tse-Tung, *On Guerrilla Warfare*, translated Samuel B. Griffith III (University of Illinois Press, 2000), 4.

22. Walter Laqueur, *Guerrilla Warfare: A Historical and Critical Study* (Routledge, 1976), 47–49.

23. Begin, *The Revolt*, 80–81, 109.

24. Bakulumpagi Wamala et al., *Mission to Freedom: Uganda Resistance News, 1981–1985* (Directorate of Information and Mass Mobilisation, NRM Secretariat, 1990), 151.

25. Ana Arjona et al., "Introduction," in Arjona et al., *Rebel Governance in Civil War*, 3.

26. Jeremy Weinstein, *Inside Rebellion: The Politics of Insurgent Violence* (Cambridge University Press 2007), 163–170; Didier Péclard and Delphine Mechoulan, "Rebel Governance and the Politics of Civil War," Working Paper 1/2015 (Swisspeace, July 2015), 17, https://www.swisspeace.ch/assets/publications/downloads/Working-Papers /3b4a3caa24/Rebel-Governance-and-the-Politics-of-Civil-War-Working-Paper-15 -swisspeace-didier_peclard.pdf; Ora Szekely, "Doing Well by Doing Good: Understanding Hamas' Social Services as Political Advertising," *Studies in Conflict & Terrorism* 38, no. 4 (February 2015): 284–287, https://doi.org/10.1080/1057610X.2014.995565; Victor Asal et al., "Doing Good While Killing: Why Some Insurgent Groups Provide Community Services," *Terrorism & Political Violence* 34, no. 4 (May 2020): 837–843, https://doi.org/10.1080/09546553.2020.1745775.

27. Chaliand, *Guerrilla Strategies*, 15.

28. David Kilcullen, *Counterinsurgency* (Oxford University Press, 2010), 149.

29. Ahmad, "Revolutionary War," 34.

30. Ahmad, 27.

31. Mara Revkin and Ariel Ahram, "Perspectives on the Rebel Social Contract: Exit, Voice and Loyalty in the Islamic State in Iraq and Syria," *World Development*, no. 132 (August 2020): 2–4, https://doi.org/10.1016/j.worlddev.2020.104981.

32. Ana Arjona, "Civilian Cooperation and Non-Cooperation with Non-State Armed Groups: The Centrality of Obedience and Resistance," *Small Wars & Insurgencies* 28, nos. 4–5 (July 2017): 760, https://doi.org/10.1080/09592318.2017.1322328.

33. William Reno, "Predatory Rebellions and Governance: The National Patriotic Front of Liberia, 1989–1992," in Arjona et al., *Rebel Governance in Civil War*, 265–266.

34. Ana Arjona, *Rebelocracy: Social Order in the Colombian Civil War* (Cambridge University Press, 2016), 7; Arjona, "Civilian Cooperation," 760; Reyko Huang, *The Wartime Origins of Democratization: Civil War, Rebel Governance and Political Regimes* (Cambridge University Press, 2016), 10.

35. Kasfir, "Rebel Governance," 40; Mara Revkin, "What Explains Taxation by Resource-Rich Rebels? Evidence from the Islamic State in Syria," *Journal of Politics* 82, no. 2 (January 2019): 761, https://doi.org/10.1086/706597; Arjona, "Civilian Cooperation," 760.

36. Romain Malejacq, "From Rebel to Quasi-State: Governance, Diplomacy and Legitimacy in the Midst of Afghanistan's Wars (1979–2001)," *Small Wars & Insurgencies* 28, nos. 4–5 (July2017): 873, https://doi.org/10.1080/09592318.2017.1322332.

37. Adrian Florea and Romain Malejacq, "The Supply and Demand of Rebel Governance," *International Studies Review* 26, no. 1 (March 2024): 8, https://doi.org/10.1093/isr /viae004.

38. Arjona, *Rebelocracy*, 7.

39. Arjona, "Civilian Cooperation," 760.

40. Arjona, 760.

41. Megan A. Stewart, "Civil War as State-Making: Strategic Governance in Civil War," *International Organization* 72, no. 1 (Winter 2018): 206, https://www.jstor.org/stable /26569466.

42. Victor Asal et al., "It Comes with the Territory: Why States Negotiate with Ethno-Political Organizations," *Studies in Conflict & Terrorism* 42, no. 4 (October 2017): 364, https://doi.org/10.1080/1057610X.2017.1373428.

43. Tse-Tung, *On Guerrilla Warfare*, 44.

44. Tse-Tung, 140–145.

45. Tse-Tung, 147.

46. Vo Nguyen Giap, *People's War, People's Army* (University Press of the Pacific, 2001), 27.

47. Giap, 79.

48. Giap, 125.

49. Amilcar Cabral, *Resistance and Decolonization* (Rowman & Littlefield, 2016), 78; Ronald Chilcote, "The Political Thought of Amilcar Cabral," *Journal of Modern African Studies* 6, no. 3 (1968): 378–386, https://doi.org/10.1017/S0022278X0001747X.

50. Laqueur, *Guerrilla Warfare*, 239.

51. Laqueur, 334–335; Ernesto Guevara, *Guerrilla Warfare* (Ocean Press, 2006), 13; Kenneth Payne, "Building the Base: Al Qaeda's Focoist Strategy," *Studies in Conflict & Terrorism* 34, no. 2 (2011): 125–126, https://doi.org/10.1080/1057610X.2011.538832.

52. Régis Debray, *Revolution in the Revolution?* (Grove Press, 1967), 55–56; Guevara, *Guerrilla Warfare*, 89.

53. Héctor Béjar, *Peru 1965: Notes on a Guerrilla Experience*, trans. William Rose (Monthly Review Press, 1970), 51; Richard Gott, *Rural Guerrillas in Latin America* (Penguin, 1973), 460–461.

54. Thomas H. Johnson and Matthew C. DuPee, "Analysing the New Taliban Code of Conduct (Layeha): An Assessment of Changing Perspectives and Strategies of the Afghan Taliban," *Central Asian Survey* 31, no. 1 (March 2012): 80–85, https://core.ac.uk /download/pdf/45464654.pdf.

55. Bert Suykens, "Comparing Rebel Rule Through Revolution and Naturalization: Ideologies of Governance in Naxalite and Naga India," in Arjona et al., *Rebel Governance in Civil War*, 144.

56. Kasfir, "Rebel Governance," 26.

57. Huang, *Wartime Origins*, 52.

58. Huang, 82.

59. Huang, 82.

60. Kasfir, "Rebel Governance," 26–27; Weinstein, *Inside Rebellion*, 173.

61. Kasfir, "Rebel Governance," 26.

62. Kasfir, 26.

63. Weinstein, *Inside Rebellion*, 173.

64. Kasfir, "Rebel Governance," 26.

65. Arjona, *Rebelocracy*, 50–55.

66. Arjona et al., "Introduction," 1.

67. Arjona et al., 1.

68. Adrian Florea, "Rebel Governance in De Facto States," *European Journal of International Relations* 24, no. 4 (May 2020): 1007–1014, https://doi.org/10.1177/1354066120919481; Huang, *Wartime Origins*, 60.

69. Zachariah Mampilly, *Rebel Rulers* (Cornell University Press, 2011), 63; Benedetta Berti, "Violent and Criminal Non-State Actors," in *The Oxford Handbook of Governance and Limited Statehood*, ed. Thomas Risse et al. (Oxford University Press, 2018), 279; Ana Arjona, "Wartime Institutions: A Research Agenda," *Journal of Conflict Resolution* 58, no. 8 (September 2014): 1361, https://doi.org/10.1177/00220027145 47904.

70. Stig Jarle Hansen, *Al-Shabaab in Somalia: The History and Ideology of a Militant Islamist Group, 2005–2012* (Oxford University Press, 2013), 74–75, 83–84.

71. Suykens, "Comparing Rebel Rule," 147.

72. Carter Malkasian, *The American War in Afghanistan: A History* (Oxford University Press, 2021), 35–52.

73. Malkasian, 103–128.

74. Antonio Giustozzi, "Hearts, Minds and the Barrell of a Gun," *PRISM* 3, no. 2 (2012): 74–75, https://apps.dtic.mil/sti/pdfs/AD1042581.pdf; Ashley Jackson, *Life Under the Taliban Shadow Government* (Overseas Development Institute, June 2018), 18–21, https://odi.org/en/publications/life-under-the-taliban-shadow-government/; Frank Ledwidge, *Rebel Law: Insurgents, Courts and Justice in Modern Conflict* (Hurst & Co., 2017), 68; Malkasian, *American War in Afghanistan*, 103–128.

75. Mampilly, *Rebel Rulers*, 155–156.

76. David Pool, *From Guerrillas to Government: The Eritrean People's Liberation Front* (Ohio University Press, 2001), 122.

77. Mampilly, *Rebel Rulers*, 63.

78. Arjona, "Wartime Institutions," 1361.

79. Ledwidge, *Rebel Law*, 16, 32.

80. Regine Schwab, "Insurgent Courts in Civil Wars: The Three Pathways of (Trans)Formation in Today's Syria (2012–17)," *Small Wars & Insurgencies* 29, no. 4 (August 2018): 801–805, https://doi.org/10.1080/09592318.2018.1497290.

81. René Provost, *Rebel Courts: The Administration of Justice by Armed Insurgents* (Oxford University Press, 2021), 10; Arjona, *Rebelocracy*, 73.

82. Joana Cook et al., "Jurisprudence Beyond the State: An Analysis of Jihadist 'Justice' in Yemen, Syria and Libya," *Studies in Conflict and Terrorism* 46, no. 5 (June 2020): 561–562, https://doi.org/10.1080/1057610X.2020.1776958.

83. Judith Harik, *The Public and Social Services of the Lebanese Militias* (Centre for Lebanese Studies, 1994), 22–31.

84. Jakkie Potgieter, "'Taking Aid from the Devil Himself': UNITA's Support Structures," in *Angola's War Economy: The Role of Oil and Diamonds*, ed. Jakkie Cilliers and Christian Dietrich (Institute for Security Studies, 2000), 262.

85. Yelena Biberman and Megan Turnbull, "When Militias Provide Welfare: Lessons from Pakistan and Nigeria," *Political Science Quarterly* 133, no. 4 (December 2018): 713, https://doi.org/10.1002/polq.12832.

86. Weinstein, *Inside Rebellion*, 38.

87. Alexus G. Grynkewich, "Welfare as Warfare: How Violent Non-State Groups Use Social Services to Attack the State," *Studies in Conflict & Terrorism* 31, no. 4 (April 2008): 351–355, https://doi.org/10.1080/10576100801931321.

88. Kasfir, "Rebel Governance," 36; Rachel Sabates-Wheeler and Philip Verwimp, "Extortion with Protection: Understanding the Effect of Rebel Taxation on Civilian Welfare in Burundi," *Journal of Conflict Resolution* 58, no. 8 (September 2014): 1474–1499, https://doi.org/10.1177/0022002714547885; Tanya Bandula-Irwin et al., "Beyond Greed: Why Armed Groups Tax," *Studies in Conflict & Terrorism* 47, no. 12 (February 2022): 3–14, https://doi.org/10.1080/1057610X.2022.2038409.

89. Jori Breslawski and Colin Tucker, "Ideological Motives and Taxation by Armed Groups," *Conflict Management & Peace Science* 39, no. 3 (August 2021): 333–336, https://doi.org/10.1177/07388942211033229.

90. Suykens, "Comparing Rebel Rule," 150–152.

91. Hansen, *Al-Shabaab*, 91–92.

92. Barnett R. Rubin, "The Political Economy of War and Peace in Afghanistan," *World Development* 28, no. 10 (2000): 1797, https://doi.org/10.1016/S0305-750X(00)00054-1.

93. Bandula-Irwin et al., "Beyond Greed," 3–4.

94. Zachariah Mampilly, "Rebel Taxation: Between Moral and Market Economy," in *Rebel Economies: Warlords, Insurgents, Humanitarians*, ed. Nicola Di Cosmo et al. (Rowman & Littlefield, 2021), 77–100.

95. Revkin, "What Explains Taxation," 761; Breslwaski and Tucker, "Ideological motives," 333–336.

96. Suykens, "Comparing Rebel Rule," 150; Bandula-Irwin et al., "Beyond Greed," 8–11.

97. Bandula-Irwin et al., "Beyond Greed," 11–14.

98. Bandula-Irwin et al., 10.

99. Arjona, *Rebelocracy*, 185.

2. STUDYING GOVERNANCE BY ARMED GROUPS

1. An earlier version of this typology appeared in Marta Furlan, "Understanding Governance by Insurgent Non-State Actors: A Multi-Dimensional Typology," *Civil Wars* 22, no. 4 (June 2020): 478–511, https://doi.org/10.1080/13698249.2020.1785725.

2. Yelena Biberman and Megan Turnbull, "When Militias Provide Welfare: Lessons from Pakistan and Nigeria," *Political Science Quarterly* 133, no. 4 (December 2018): 713, https://doi.org/10.1002/polq.12832.

3. Bert Suykens, "Comparing Rebel Rule Through Revolution and Naturalization: Ideologies of Governance in Naxalite and Naga India," in *Rebel Governance in Civil War*, ed. Ana Arjona et al. (Cambridge University Press, 2015), 145–7.

4. Carter Malkasian, *The American War in Afghanistan: A History* (Oxford University Press, 2021), 35–52.

5. Jori Breslawski, "The Social Terrain of Rebel Held Territory," *Journal of Conflict Resolution* 65, nos. 2–3 (August 2020): 467–468, https://doi.org/10.1177/0022002720951857.

6. Jeremy Weinstein, *Inside Rebellion: The Politics of Insurgent Violence* (Cambridge University Press 2007), 165–7; Nelson Kasfir, "Guerrillas and Civilian Participation: The National Resistance Army in Uganda, 1981–6," *Journal of Modern African Studies* 43, no. 2 (June 2005): 273, https://www.jstor.org/stable/3876207.

7. Weinstein, *Inside Rebellion*, 165.

8. Nelson Kasfir, "Rebel Governance—Constructing a Field of Inquiry: Definitions, Scope, Patterns, Order, Causes," in Arjona et al., *Rebel Governance in Civil War*, 35.

9. Kasfir, "Rebel Governance," 163.

10. Kasfir, "Guerrillas and Civilian Participation," 273.

11. Breslawski, "The Social Terrain," 454.

12. Zachariah Mampilly, *Rebel Rulers* (Cornell University Press, 2011), 212.

13. Jonathan Spyer, "Facts on the Ground: The Growing Power of Hamas's Gaza Leadership," *Middle East Review of International Affairs* 16, no. 2 (June 2012): 44–51, https://ciaotest.cc.columbia.edu/journals/meria/v16i2/f_0029678_23996.pdf; Jeroen Gunning, *Hamas in Politics: Democracy, Religion, Violence* (Hurst, 2008), 98; Erika Schwarze, *Public Opinion and Political Response in Palestine: Leadership, Campaigns and Elections Since Arafat* (I. B. Tauris, 2016), 75–77.

14. Sukanya Podder, "Understanding the Legitimacy of Armed Groups: A Relational Perspective," *Small Wars and Insurgencies* 28, nos. 4–5 (July 2017): 689, https://doi.org/10.1080/09592318.2017.1322333.

15. Florian Weigand, "Afghanistan's Taliban: Legitimate Jihadists or Coercive Extremists?," *Journal of Intervention & Statebuilding* 11, no. 3 (August 2017): 361, https://doi.org/10.1080/17502977.2017.1353755.

16. Kasfir, "Rebel Governance," 38.

17. Kasfir, 272.

18. Marie Lecomte-Tilouine, "Terror in a Maoist Model Village in Mid-Western Nepal," in *Windows Into a Revolution: Ethnographies of Maoism in India and Nepal*, ed. Alpa Shah and Judith Pettigrew (Routledge, 2017), 208.

19. William Maley, *The Afghanistan Wars* (Palgrave Macmillan, 2009), 196.

20. Niels Terpstra and Georg Frerks, "Rebel Governance and Legitimacy: Understanding the Impact of Rebel Legitimation on Civilian Compliance with the LTTE Rule," *Civil Wars* 19, no. 3 (October 2017): 283, https://doi.org/10.1080/13698249.2017.1393265.

21. Mara Revkin and Ariel Ahram, "Perspectives on the Rebel Social Contract: Exit, Voice and Loyalty in the Islamic State in Iraq and Syria," *World Development* 132 (August 2020): 4–6, https://doi.org/10.1016/j.worlddev.2020.104981; Ana Arjona et al., "Introduction," in Arjona et al., *Rebel Governance in Civil War*, 11; Kasfir, "Guerrillas and Civilian Participation," 39; Kasper Hoffmann and Judith Verweijen, "Rebel Rule: A Governmentality Perspective," *African Affairs* 118, no. 471 (April 2019): 359–370, https://doi.org/10.1093/afraf/ady039; Terpstra and Frerks, "Rebel Governance," 289–297;

Podder, "Understanding Legitimacy," 687–691; Niels Terpstra and Georg Frerks, "Governance Practices and Symbolism: De Facto Sovereignty and Public Authority in 'Tigerland,'" *Modern Asian Studies* 52, no. 3 (May 2018): 1031–1041, https://doi.org/10.1017/S0026749X16000822.

22. John Young, *Peasant Revolution in Ethiopia: The Tigray People's Liberation Front, 1975–1991* (Cambridge University Press, 1997), 172–196.

23. Podder "Understanding Legitimacy," 688.

24. Weigand, "Afghanistan's Taliban," 361.

25. Stathis N. Kalyvas, *The Logic of Violence in Civil War* (Cambridge University Press, 2006), 101–104.

26. Kasper Hoffmann, "Myths Set in Motion: The Moral Economy of Mai Mai Governance," in Arjona et al., *Rebel Governance in Civil War*, 173–175.

27. Tim Glawion and Anne-Clémence Le Noan, "Rebel Governance or Governance in Rebel Territory? Extraction and Services in Ndele, Central African Republic," *Small Wars & Insurgencies* 34, no. 1 (November 2022): 25, https://doi.org/10.1080/09592318.2022.2137282.

28. Mampilly, *Rebel Rulers*, 156–157.

29. Mampilly, 163–165.

30. Brian Fishman, "Redefining the Islamic State: The Fall and Rise of Al-Qaeda in Iraq," National Security Studies Program Policy Paper (New America Foundation, August 2011), https://static.newamerica.org/attachments/4343-redefining-the-islamic-state/Fishman_Al_Qaeda_In_Iraq.023ac20877a64488b2b791cd7e313955.pdf.

31. William McCants, "Experts Weigh In (Part 6): Is ISIS Good at Governing?," Brookings, March 22, 2016, https://www.brookings.edu/blog/markaz/2016/03/22/experts-weigh-in-part-6-is-isis-good-at-governing/.

32. Ashley Jackson, *Life Under the Taliban Shadow Government* (Overseas Development Institute, June 2018), 12–24, https://odi.org/en/publications/life-under-the-taliban-shadow-government/; Jelte Johannes Schievels and Thomas Colley, "Explaining Rebel-State Collaboration in Insurgency: Keep Your Friends Close but Your Enemies Closer," *Small Wars & Insurgencies* 32, no. 8 (October 2020): 1337–1341, https://doi.org/10.1080/09592318.2020.1827847.

33. Kasfir, "Rebel Governance," 33–34.

34. Mampilly, *Rebel Rulers*, 193–204.

35. Roland Marchal, "The Rise of a Jihadist Movement in a Country at War: Harakat al-Shabaab al-Muajhidin in Somalia" (Research Report, Sciences Po, 2011), 73–74, https://sciencespo.hal.science/hal-03641269.

36. Suykens, "Comparing Rebel Rule," 140, 148–152.

37. Mampilly, *Rebel Rulers*, 82, 91; Terpstra and Frerks, "Rebel Governance," 290–291.

38. Terpstra and Frerks, "Rebel Governance," 295.

39. Terpstra and Frerks, 294–296.

40. Bruce Hoffman, *Inside Terrorism* (Columbia University Press, 2006), 137–145; Human Rights Watch, *Living in Fear: Child Soldiers and the Tamil Tigers in Sri Lanka* (Human

Rights Watch, November 2004), 16–17, 22, 47, https://www.hrw.org/sites/default/files/reports/srilanka1104.pdf.

41. Terpstra and Frerks, "Rebel Governance," 288.

42. Human Rights Watch, *Living in Fear*, 17.

43. Terpstra and Frerks, "Rebel Governance," 288.

44. Kristian Stokke, "Building the Tamil Eelam State: Emerging State Institutions and Forms of Governance in LTTE-Controlled Areas in Sri Lanka," *Third World Quarterly* 27, no. 6 (2004): 1035–1037, https://www.jstor.org/stable/4017738.

45. Stokke, "Building Tamil Eelam," 1035.

46. Stokke, "Building Tamil Eelam," 1028; Joanne Richards, "An Institutional History of the Liberation Tigers of Tamil Eelam (LTTE)," CCDP Working Paper No. 10 (Center of Conflict Development and Peacebuilding, October 2014), 45, https://repository.graduateinstitute.ch/record/292651?v=pdf; Suthaharan Nadarajah and Luxshi Vimalarajah, "The Politics of Transformation: the LTTE and the 2002–2006 Peace Process in Sri Lanka," Transition Series No. 4 (Berghof Foundation, April 2008), 33, https://berghof-foundation.org/library/the-politics-of-transformation-the-ltte-and-the-2002-2006-peace-process-in-sri-lanka.

47. Mampilly, *Rebel Rulers*, 116.

48. Terpstra and Frerks, "Governance Practices," 1017.

49. Mampilly, *Rebel Rulers*, 116–119; Stokke, "Building Tamil Eelam," 1027; "LTTE Opens First Thamileelam Court in Trincomalee District," *TamilNet*, December 2, 2002, https://www.tamilnet.com/art.html?catid=13&artid=7925; Nadarajah and Vimalarajah, "Politics of Transformation," 33.

50. Stokke, "Building Tamil Eelam," 1034; Mattukrishan Sarvananthan, *Economy of the Conflict Region in Sri Lanka: From Embargo to Repression* (East West Center, 2007), 49–50, https://www.eastwestcenter.org/publications/economy-conflict-region-sri-lanka-embargo-repression.

51. Peter Schalk, "Historisation of the Martial Ideology of the Liberation Tigers of Tamil Eelam (LTTE)," *South Asia: Journal of South Asian Studies* 20, no. 2 (May 2997): 39, https://doi.org/10.1080/00856409708723295; Terpstra and Frerks, "Rebel Governance," 298.

52. "Thamil Eelam Judiciary Said a Basis for Rebuilding North-East," *TamilNet*, October 30, 2003, https://www.tamilnet.com/art.html?catid=79&artid=10277.

53. Terpstra and Frerks, "Governance Practices," 1019.

54. Richards, "An Institutional History," 44, 46; Jayadeva Uyangoda, "Ethnic Conflict, the State and the Tsunami Disaster in Sri Lanka," *Inter-Asia Cultural Studies* 6, no. 3 (December 2010): 341–352, https://doi.org/10.1080/14649370500169979; Nadarajah and Vimalarajah, "Politics of Transformation," 33–34.

55. Mampilly, *Rebel Rulers*, 119–120.

56. Mampilly, 119–120.

57. Terpstra and Frerks, "Governance Practices," 1021.

58. Mampilly, *Rebel Rulers*, 119–120.

59. Mampilly, 120–123; Schievels and Colley, "Explaining Rebel-State Collaboration," 1335–1336.

60. Terpstra and Frerks, "Rebel Governance and Legitimacy," 289.

61. Terpstra and Frerks, 289.

62. Annette Idler and James J. F. Forest, "Behavioral Patterns Among (Violent) Non-State Actors: A Study of Complementary Governance," *Stability* 4, no. 1 (January 2015): 7–8, https://doi.org/10.5334/sta.er; Mapping Militants Project, "Revolutionary Armed Forces of Colombia—People's Army," Center for International Security and Cooperation, last modified July 1, 2019, https://mappingmilitants.org/profiles/revolutionary-armed -forces-of-colombia-peoples-army?highlight=farc.

63. Ana Arjona, "Wartime Institutions: A Research Agenda," *Journal of Conflict Resolution* 58, no. 8 (September 2014): 1365, https://doi.org/10.1177/0022002714547904.

64. Arjona, *Rebelocracy*, 188; Mampilly, *Rebel Rulers*, 2.

65. Thomas R. Cook, "The Financial Arm of the FARC: A Threat Finance Perspective," *Journal of Strategic Security* 4, no. 1 (Spring 2011): 21, http://dx.doi.org/10.5038/1944-0472 .4.1.2.

66. Ana Arjona, "Civilian Resistance to Rebel Governance," in Arjona et al., *Rebel Governance in Civil War*, 192–194.

67. Arjona, 192.

68. Alexandra Phelan, "Engaging Insurgency: The Impact of the 2016 Colombian Peace Agreement on FARC's Political Participation," *Studies in Conflict & Terrorism* 42, no. 9 (February 2918): 842, https://doi.org/10.1080/1057610X.2018.1432027.

69. Mapping Militants Project, "Revolutionary Armed Forces of Colombia—People's Army"; Chris Lee, "The FARC and the Colombian Left: Time for a Political Solution?," *Latin American Perspectives* 39, no. 1 (January 2012): 31, https://www.jstor.org/stable /23238966.

70. Lee, "The FARC," 33; "Nace el Movimiento Bolivariano de las FARC," *El Tiempo*, April 29, 2000, https://www.eltiempo.com/archivo/documento/MAM-1291569.

71. Nelson Bocanegra and Julia Symmes Cobb, "After Decades of War, Colombia's FARC Rebels Debut Political Party," Reuters, August 27, 2017, https://www.reuters.com/article /us-colombia-peace-politics/after-decades-of-war-colombias-farc-rebels-debut -political-party-idUSKCN1B705U/.

72. René Provost, *Rebel Courts: The Administration of Justice by Armed Insurgents* (Oxford University Press, 2021), 25.

73. Timothy Wickham-Crowley, "Del Gobierno de Abajo al Gobierno de Arriba . . . and Back: Transitions To and From Rebel Governance in Latin America: 1956–1999," in Arjona et al., *Rebel Governance in Civil War*, 58.

74. Cook "Financial Arm," 24.

75. Weinstein, *Inside Rebellion*, 291.

76. Diana Rodriguéz-Franco, "Internal Wars, Taxation and State Building," *American Sociological Review* 81, no. 1 (December 2015): 204, https://doi.org/10.1177/0003122415615903.

77. Arjona, "Civilian Resistance," 190; Cook, "Financial Arm," 24.

78. Renée Provost, "FARC Justice: Rebel Rule of Law," *UC Irvine Law Review* 8, no. 2 (March 2018): 248, https://escholarship.org/uc/item/72q1w1ho.

79. Arjona, *Rebelocracy*, 185.

80. Arjona, *Rebelocracy*, 189–190; Ana Arjona, "Institutions, Civilian Resistance, and Wartime Social Order: A Process-Driven Natural Experiment in the Colombian Civil War," *Latin America Politics and Society* 58, no. 3 (Fall 2016): 109–112, https://www.jstor.org/stable/24766058.

81. Weinstein, *Inside Rebellion*, 288; Arjona, "Civilian Resistance," 193–194; Arjona, "Institutions," 110; Rodriguéz-Franco, "Internal Wars," 204.

82. Arjona, "Institutions," 111.

83. Arjona, 110.

84. "Relatos de pesadillas que vivieron niños reclutados por FARC. ELN y paramilitares," BLU Radio, February 10, 2018, https://www.bluradio.com/nacion/relatos-de-pesadillas-que-vivieron-ninos-reclutados-por-farc-eln-y-paramilitares.

85. Arjona, *Rebelocracy*, 176–177.

86. Weinstein, *Inside Rebellion*, 289–290.

87. Weinstein, 291

88. Arjona, "Institutions," 109.

89. Arjona, 109.

90. Kayla Koontz, "Borders Beyond Borders: The Many (Many) Kurdish Political Parties of Syria," Policy Paper 2019-21 (Middle East Institute, October 2019), 5, https://www.mei.edu/publications/borders-beyond-borders-many-many-kurdish-political-parties-syria.

91. Pinar Dinc, "The Kurdish Movement and the Democratic Federation of Northern Syria: An Alternative to the (Nation-)State Model?," *Journal of Balkan and Near Eastern Studies* 22, no. 1 (January 2020): 51, https://doi.org/10.1080/19448953.2020.1715669.

92. Harriet Allsopp, *The Kurds of Syria: Political Parties and Identity in the Middle East* (I. B. Tauris, 2014), 181; Joost Jongerden, "Governing Kurdistan: Self-Administration in the Kurdistan Regional Government in Iraq and the Democratic Federation of Northern Syria," *Ethnopolitics* 18, no. 1 (November 2018): 62, https://doi.org/10.1080/17449057.2018.1525166; Cengiz Gunes, *The Kurds in a New Middle East: The Changing Geopolitics of Regional Conflict* (Palgrave Macmillan, 2019), 69.

93. Jongerden, "Governing Kurdistan," 66–67; Rana Khalaf, *Governing Rojava: Layers of Legitimacy in Syria* (Chatham House, 2016), 10–17; Justine Clark and Mohammad Abdulsattar Ibrahim, "The State of Rojava: A Month-Long Reporting Series from Syria Direct," *Syria Direct*, November 5, 2017, https://syriadirect.org/news/the-state-of-rojava-a-month-long-reporting-series-from-syria-direct/; Nathalie Colasanti et al., "Grassroots Democracy and Local Government in Northern Syria: The Case of Democratic Confederalism," *Local Government Studies* 44, no. 6 (July 2018): 808–810, https://doi.org/10.1080/03003930.2018.1501366; Carne Ross, "Power to the People: A Syrian Experiment in Democracy," *Financial Times*, October 23, 2015, https://www.ft.com/content/50102294-77fd-11e5-a95a-27d368e1ddf7.

94. Fabrice Balanche, "Rojava's Sustainability and the PKK's Regional Strategy," Policy Watch 2680 (Washington Institute for Near East Policy, August 24, 2016), https://www .washingtoninstitute.org/policy-analysis/view/rojavas-sustainability-and-the-pkks -regional-strategy; Jongerden, "Governing Kurdistan," 71; Clark and Ibrahim, "State of Rojava."

95. Gunes, *The Kurds*, 69.

96. Gunes, *The Kurds*, 61–62; Clark and Ibrahim, "State of Rojava"; "Final Statement of Autonomous Administration of North, East Syria," *Hawar News*, September 7, 2018, https://hawarnews.com/en/haber/final-statement-of-autonomous-administration-of -north-east-syria-h3608.html.

97. "Social Contract of the Democratic Federation of Northern Syria," Internationalist Commune of Rojava, accessed February 11, 2025, article 16, https://internationalist commune.com/social-contract/.

98. Colasanti et al., "Grassroots Democracy," 812.

99. Burcu Özçelik, "Explaining the Kurdish Democratic Union Party's Self-Governance Practices in Northern Syria, 2012–18," *Government and Opposition* 55, no. 4 (October 2020): 701, https://doi.org/10.1017/gov.2019.1; Dinc, "Kurdish Movement," 54–55.

100. Ross, "Power to the People"; Jongerden, "Governing Kurdistan," 71; Colasanti et al., "Grassroots Democracy," 814; Gunes, *The Kurds*, 72.

101. Bahar Şimşek and Joost Jongerden, "Gender Revolution in Rojava: The Voices Beyond Tabloid Geopolitics," *Geopolitics* 26, no. 4 (October 2018): 1034–1040, https://doi.org/10 .1080/14650045.2018.1531283.

102. Jongerden, "Governing Kurdistan," 70.

103. Özçelik, "Explaining the Kurdish," 699–701; Clark and Ibrahim, "The State of Rojava."

104. Khalaf, *Governing Rojava*, 6.

105. Khalaf, 11.

106. Dinc, "Kurdish Movement," 56; Michiel Leezenberg, "The Ambiguities of Democratic Autonomy: The Kurdish Movement in Turkey and Rojava," *Southeast European and Black Sea Studies* 16, no. 4 (October 2016): 683, https://doi.org/10.1080/14683857.2016 .1246529.

107. Özçelik, "Explaining the Kurdish," 698; Kheder Khaddour, "How Regional Security Concerns Uniquely Constrain Governance in Northeastern Syria," Carnegie Endowment for International Peace Middle East Center, March 23, 2017, https://carnegie-mec .org/2017/03/23/how-regional-security-concerns-uniquely-constrain-governance-in -northeastern-syria-pub-68380.

108. International Crisis Group, "The PKK's Fateful Choice in Northern Syria," Middle East Report No. 176 (International Crisis Group, May 2017), 16, https://www.crisisgroup.org /middle-east-north-africa/eastern-mediterranean/syria/176-pkk-s-fateful-choice -northern-syria.

109. Özçelik, "Explaining the Kurdish," 701–703; Amnesty International, *"We Had Nowhere to Go": Forced Displacement and Demolitions in Northern Syria* (Amnesty International, October 2015), https://www.amnesty.org/en/documents/mde24/2503/2015/en/; Koontz, "Borders," 9–10; Human Rights Watch, *Under Kurdish Rule: Abuses in PYD-Run*

Enclaves of Syria (Human Rights Watch, June 2014), 19–22, 34–44, https://www.hrw.org /report/2014/06/19/under-kurdish-rule/abuses-pyd-run-enclaves-syria.

110. Khalaf, *Governing Rojava*, 15.

111. Kheder Khaddour and Kevin Mazur, "Eastern Expectations: The Changing Dynamics in Syria's Tribal Regions," Carnegie Endowment for International Peace, February 28, 2017, https://carnegie-mec.org/2017/02/28/eastern-expectations-changing-dynamics-in -syria-s-tribal-regions-pub-68008; Khaddour, "Regional Security."

112. International Crisis Group, "PKK's Fateful Choice," 16.

113. International Crisis Group, 16.

114. Haian Dukhan, "Critical Analysis of Attempts to Coopt the Tribes in Syria," London School of Economics, May 2, 2019, https://blogs.lse.ac.uk/crp/2019/05/02/critical -analysis-of-attempts-to-co-opt-the-tribes-in-syria/.

115. Dukhan, "Critical Analysis."

116. International Crisis Group, "PKK's Fateful Choice," 6, 10–16; Khaddour, "Regional Security"; Khaddour and Mazur, "Eastern Expectations"; International Crisis Group, "Fighting ISIS: The Road to and Beyond Raqqa," Middle East Briefing No. 53 (International Crisis Group, April 2017), 3–5, https://www.crisisgroup.org/middle-east-north -africa/eastern-mediterranean/syria/b053-fighting-isis-road-and-beyond-raqqa.

117. International Crisis Group, "Flight of Icarus? The PYD's Precarious Rise in Syria," (Middle East Report No. 151, May 2014), 13, https://www.crisisgroup.org/middle-east -north-africa/eastern-mediterranean/syria/flight-icarus-pyd-s-precarious-rise-syria.

118. International Crisis Group, "Flight of Icarus?," 16–22; Khaddour, "Regional Security."

119. Khaddour, "Regional Security."

120. Khalaf, *Governing Rojava*, 19; Schievels and Colley, "Explaining," 1341–1348.

121. International Crisis Group, "Flight of Icarus?," 9.

122. Schievels and Colley, "Explaining," 1348.

123. Ercan Ayboga, "Consensus Is Key: New Justice System in Rojava," *New Compass*, October 13, 2014, http://new-compass.net/articles/consensus-key-new-justice-system -rojava.

124. Khalaf, *Governing Rojava*, 17.

3. SALAFI-JIHADISM AND GOVERNANCE

1. Shiraz Maher, *Salafi-Jihadism: The History of an Idea* (Oxford University Press, 2016), 7.

2. Abdulbasit Kassim, "Defining and Understanding the Religious Philosophy of *Jihadi-Salafism* and the Ideology of Boko Haram," *Politics, Religion & Ideology* 16, nos. 2–3 (September 2015): 175–176, https://doi.org/10.1080/21567689.2015.1074896.

3. Gilles Kepel, *Jihad: The Trail of Political Islam* (Harvard University Press, 2002), 259; Roel Meijer, "Introduction," in *Global Salafism: Islam's New religious Movement*, ed. Roel Meijer (Oxford University Press, 2013), 1–31; Olivier Roy, *Globalised Islam* (Hurst & Co., 2004), 243–245; Bernard Haykel, "On the Nature of Salafi Thought and Action,"

in Meijer, *Global Salafism*, 39–40; Quintan Wicktorowicz, "Anatomy of the Salafi Movement," *Studies in Conflict & Terrorism* 29, no. 3 (April 2005): 207–208, https://web.archive.org/web/20190712124836id_/http://www.clagsborough.uk:80/anatomy_of_the_salafi_movement.pdf.

4. Reza Pankhurst, *The Inevitable Caliphate? A History of the Struggle for Global Islamic Union, 1942 to the Present* (Oxford University Press, 2013), 140; Roy Jackson, "Authority," in *Islamic Political Thought: An Introduction,* ed. Gerhard Bowering (Princeton University Press, 2015), 25–36; John A. Turner, *Religious Ideology and the Roots of the Global Jihad* (Palgrave Macmillan, 2014), 53.

5. Brynjar Lia, "Understanding Jihadi Proto-States," *Perspectives on Terrorism* 9, no. 4 (August 2015): 32, https://pt.icct.nl/article/understanding-jihadi-proto-states.

6. Wicktorowicz, "Anatomy," 217–228.

7. While Wicktorowicz's distinction is extremely useful in shedding light on the diversity within the Salafi movement, it should not be understood in rigid terms, since similarities across the categories and differences within each category do exist. See Joas Wagemakers, "A Purist Jihadi-Salafi: The Ideology of Abu Muhammad al-Maqdisi," *British Journal of Middle Eastern Studies,* 36, no. 2 (August 2009): 284, https://www.jstor.org/stable/40593257.

8. Kassim, "Defining and Understanding," 176.

9. Reuven Firestone, "'Jihadism' as a New Religious Movement," in *Cambridge Companion to New Religious Movements,* ed. Olav Hammer and Mikael Rothstein (Cambridge University Press, 2012), 264.

10. Firestone, 146.

11. Jack Barclay, "Tawhid al-Hakimiyah: A Jihadi Achilles Heel?," *Terrorism Monitor* 8, no. 29 (July 2010): 6–9, https://jamestown.org/program/tawhid-al-hakimiyah-a-jihadi-achilles-heel/.

12. Abdul Hassan al-Mawardi, *Al-Ahkam as-Sultaniyyah: The Laws of Islamic Governance,* trans. Asadullah Yate (Ta-Ha Publishers, 1996), 270.

13. Maher, *Salafi-Jihadism*, 185.

14. Maher, 200.

15. Hassan Hassan, "The Sectarianism of the Islamic State: Ideological Roots and Political Context" (Carnegie Endowment for International Peace, June 2016), 8, https://carnegieendowment.org/research/2016/12/the-sectarianism-of-the-islamic-state-ideological-roots-and-political-context?lang=en.

16. Maher, *Salafi-Jihadism*, 205.

17. Maher, 111.

18. Maher, 114.

19. Joas Wagemakers, "Framing the 'Threat to Islam': *Al-Wala wa al-Bara'* in Salafi Discourse," *Arab Studies Quarterly* 30, no. 4 (Fall 2008): 3, https://www.jstor.org/stable/41858559.

20. Maher, *Salafi-Jihadism*, 138–140; Wagemakers, "Framing," 7.

21. Wagemakers, "Framing," 6–7.

22. Maher, *Salafi-Jihadism*, 73.
23. Wicktorowicz, "Anatomy," 228–34; Reuven Paz, "Debates Within the Family," in Meijer, *Global Salafism*, 270.
24. Maher, *Salafi-Jihadism*, 89; Kassim, "Defining and Understanding," 187.
25. Maher, *Salafi-Jihadism*, 83,
26. Seyyed Hossein Nasr, *The Study Quran* (HarperCollins, 2015), 492.
27. Maher, *Salafi-Jihadism*, 32.
28. Firestone, " 'Jihadism,' " 275; Kassim, "Defining and Understanding," 179–187.
29. Wicktorowicz, "Anatomy," 228–234.
30. See Fawaz Gerges, *The Far Enemy: Why Jihad Went Global* (Cambridge University Press, 2005).
31. I followed the conceptualization of ideology advanced by Francisco Gutiérrez-Sanín and Elisabeth Jean Wood, "Ideology in Civil War: Instrumental Adoption and Beyond," *Journal of Peace Research* 51, no. 2 (March 2014): 215, https://doi.org/10.1177/0022343313514073.
32. Seth G. Jones and Patrick B. Johnston, "The Future of Insurgency," *Studies in Conflict and Terrorism* 36, no. 1 (June 2012): 2, https://doi.org/10.1080/1057610X.2013.739077.
33. Daniel Byman, "Fighting *Salafi-Jihadist* Insurgencies: How Much Does Religion Really Matter?," *Studies in Conflict & Terrorism,* 36, no. 5 (April 2013): 356–357, https://doi.org/10.1080/1057610X.2013.775417; Mohamed-Ali Adraoui, "Border and Sovereignty in Islamist and Jihadist Political Thought: Past and Present," *International Affairs* 93, no. 4 (July 2017): 920, https://doi.org/10.1093/ia/iix123.
34. Roy, *Globalised Islam*, 288.
35. David Kilcullen, "Countering Global Insurgency," *Journal of Strategic Studies* 28, no. 4 (January 2007): 604, https://doi.org/10.1080/01402390500300956.
36. Michael W. S. Ryan, *Decoding Al-Qaeda's Strategy: The Deep Battle Against America* (Columbia University Press, 2013), 8; Mark Stout, "In Search of Salafi-Jihadist Strategic Thought: Mining the Words of the Terrorists," *Studies in Conflict & Terrorism* 32, no. 10 (September 2009): 879–883, https://doi.org/10.1080/10576100903185578; Kenneth Payne, "Building the Base: Al Qaeda's Focoist Strategy," *Studies in Conflict & Terrorism* 34, no. 2 (2011): 127–140, https://doi.org/10.1080/1057610X.2011.538832.
37. Payne, "Building the Base," 127; Ayman al-Zawahiri, *Knights Under the Prophet's Banner,* trans. Laura Mansfield, in Laura Mansfield, *His Own Words: A Translation of the Writings of Dr Aymann al-Zawahiri* (Lulu Press, 2006).
38. Al-Zawahiri, *Knights*; Simon Staffell and Akil N. Awan, "Introduction," in *Jihadism Transformed: Al-Qaeda and Islamic State's Battle of Ideas,* ed. Simon Staffell and Akil N. Awan (Hurst & Co., 2016), 18; Ryan, *Decoding Al-Qaeda's Strategy*, 72, 181.
39. Ayman al-Zawahiri, *General Guidelines for Jihad* (As-Sahab Media, 2013), 1.
40. Al-Zawahiri, 1–3.
41. Ayman al-Zawahiri, "Letter to Abu Musʿab al-Zarqawi," July 9, 2005, Combating Terrorism Center at West Point, accessed September 25, 2023, https://ctc.westpoint.edu/harmony-program/zawahiris-letter-to-zarqawi-original-language-2/.

42. Al-Zawahiri, "Letter to al-Zarqawi."
43. Abu Bakr Naji, *The Management of Savagery*, trans. William McCants (John M. Olin Institute for Strategic Studies at Harvard University, 2006), 36, 39–42.
44. Naji, 42–57.
45. Naji, 36, 117.
46. Naji, 27–28.
47. Ryan, *Decoding Al-Qaeda's Strategy*, 7, 12, 92, 148.
48. Abu 'Ubayd al-Qurashi, "Revolutionary Wars," trans. Michael W. S. Ryan, in Ryan, *Decoding Al-Qaeda's Strategy*, 269–279.
49. Al-Qurashi, "Revolutionary Wars," 272–273.
50. 'Abd al- 'Aziz al-Muqrin, *A Practical Course for Guerrilla Warfare*, trans. Norman Cigar, in Norman Cigar, *Al-Qaida's Doctrine for Insurgency: Abd Al-Aziz Al-Muqrin's A Practical Course for Guerrilla Warfare* (Potomac Books, 2009), 92.
51. Al-Muqrin, 94–102.
52. Al-Muqrin, 105.
53. Al-Muqrin, 98–99, 105.
54. Payne, "Building the Base," 131–136.
55. Brynjar Lia, *Architect of Global Jihad: The Life of Al Qaeda Strategist Abu Mus'ab Al-Suri* (Columbia University Press, 2008), 381; Ryan, *Decoding Al-Qaeda's Strategy*, 230.
56. Usama bin Laden, "Letter to Nasir al-Wuhayshi," undated, presumably early 2011, Combating Terrorism Center at West Point, accessed September 25, 2023, https://ctc.westpoint.edu/harmony-program/letter-to-nasir-al-wuhayshi-original-language-2/.
57. Bin Laden, "Letter to al-Wuhayshi."
58. Usama bin Laden, "Letter to Abu Mus'ab 'Abd Al-Wadud from Zamray," undated, presumably, October 2010, Office of the Director of National Intelligence, accessed September 25, 2023, https://www.dni.gov/files/documents/ubl2017/english/Letter%20to%20Abu-Musa%20b%20Abd-al-Wadud.pdf.
59. Al-Zawahiri, *General Guidelines*, 210–214.
60. Abu Muhammad al-Julani, "Oh People of al-Sham," 2012, Jihadology, accessed on September 25, 2023, https://azelin.files.wordpress.com/2012/12/abc5ab-mue1b8a5ammad-al-jawlc481nc4ab-al-golani-220h-people-of-ash-shc481m-we-sacrifice-our-souls-for-you22-en.pdf.
61. Al-Julani, "Oh People."
62. Nasir al-Wuhayshi, "First Letter from Abu Basir to the Emir of al-Qaida in the Islamic Maghreb," May 21, 2012, in Associated Press, "al-Qaida Papers," republished by *Long War Journal*, https://www.longwarjournal.org/images/al-qaida-papers-how-to-run-a-state.pdf.
63. Al-Wuhayshi, "First Letter from Abu Basir."
64. Abdelmalek Droukdel, "Letter from Abu Mus'ab 'Abdel-Wudoud to His Brother Emirs and Members of the Shura Council of the Organization and Ansar ed-Din in the Great Desert," undated, presumably July 2012, in Associated Press, "Al-Qaida Papers: Al-Qaida's Sahara Playbook," https://www.documentcloud.org/documents/838898-aqp-sahara-playbook.html.

65. Droukdel, "Letter from Abu Mus'ab 'Abdel-Wudoud."

66. Droukdel, "Letter from Abu Mus'ab 'Abdel-Wudoud."

67. Rashmi Singh, "A Preliminary Typology Mapping Patterns of Learning and Innovation by Modern Jihadist Groups," *Studies in Conflict & Terrorism* 40, no. 7 (September 2016): 633, http://dx.doi.org/10.1080/1057610X.2016.1237228; Seth G. Jones et al., *The Evolution of the Salafi-Jihadist Threat* (Center for Strategic and International Studies, November 2018), 6–11, https://csis-website-prod.s3.amazonaws.com/s3fs-public /publication/181221_EvolvingTerroristThreat.pdf.

68. Byman, "Fighting *Salafi-Jihadist*," 362.

69. Uriya Shavit, "Is Shura a Muslim Form of Democracy? Roots and Systemization of a Polemic," *Middle Eastern Studies* 46, no. 3 (August 2010): 359, https://doi.org/10.1080 /00263200902917085.

70. Shavit, 360–362.

71. Kassim, "Defining and Understanding," 178.

72. Al-Julani, "Oh People"; Al-Muqrin, *Practical Course,* 99; al-Wuhayshi, "First Letter from Abu Basir."

73. Bruce Hoffman, *Inside Terrorism* (Columbia University Press, 2006), 90.

74. Al-Zawahiri, "Letter to al-Zarqawi."

75. Byman, "Fighting *Salafi-Jihadist*," 361.

76. Sayyid Qutb, *Milestones* (Islamic Book Service, 2005), 127.

77. Syed Z. Abedin and Saleha M. Abedin, "Minorities," in *The Oxford Encyclopedia of the Islamic World*, ed. John L. Esposito (Oxford University Press, 2009), https://www .oxfordreference.com/display/10.1093/acref/9780195305135.001.0001/acref-9780195305135-e-0536; Andrea Nusse, *Muslim Palestine: The Ideology of Hamas* (RoutledgeCurzon, 2003), 75; Paul L. Heck, "Taxation," in *Encyclopaedia of the Qur'an*, ed. Jane Dammen McAuliffe (Brill, 2006), 196–199.

78. Heck, "Taxation"; Nusse, *Muslim Palestine*, 76.

79. Malise Ruthven, *Islam in the World* (Penguin, 2000), 329.

80. Chelsea Daymon and Devorah Margolin, *Women in American Violent Extremism: An Examination of Far-Right and Salafi-Jihadist Movements* (Program on Extremism at George Washington University, June 2022), 36, https://extremism.gwu.edu/sites/g/files /zaxdzs5746/files/Women-in-American-Violent-Extremism_Daymon-and-Margolin _June-2022.pdf; Nelly Lahoud, "The Neglected Sex: The Jihadis' Exclusion of Women from Jihad," *Terrorism and Political Violence* 26, no. 5 (February 2014): 783–789, 792–794 https://doi.org/10.1080/09546553.2013.772511; Seran de Leede, "Women in Jihad: A Historical Perspective," ICCT Policy Brief (International Center on Counter Terrorism, September 2018), https://www.jstor.org/stable/resrep19608.

81. Daymon and Margolin, "Women," 31.

82. Sayed Khatab, *The Political Thought of Sayyid Qutb: The Theory of Jahiliyyah* (Routledge, 2006), 109.

83. Maher, *Salafi-Jihadism*, 49.

84. Naji, *Management of Savagery*, 35.

85. Naji, 35.

4. RESTORING THE CALIPHATE IN SYRIA AND IRAQ

1. Jeffrey White, "The Death of Zarqawi: Organizational and Operational Implications for the Insurgency," Washington Institute for Near East Policy, June 8, 2006, https://www.washingtoninstitute.org/policy-analysis/death-zarqawi-organizational-and-operational-implications-insurgency; Brian Fishman, "After Zarqawi: The Dilemmas and Future of Al Qaeda in Iraq," *The Washington Quarterly* 29, no. 4 (January 2010): 25–29, https://doi.org/10.1162/wash.2006.29.4.19.

2. Daniel Byman, "ISIS Goes Global: Fight the Islamic State by Targeting Its Affiliates," *Foreign Affairs*, March–April 2016, https://www.foreignaffairs.com/articles/middle-east/isis-goes-global.

3. Gordon Corera, "Unraveling Zarqawi's al-Qaeda connection," *Terrorism Monitor* 2, no. 24 (May 2005), https://jamestown.org/program/unraveling-zarqawis-al-qaeda-connection/.

4. Andrea Plebani, "The Unfolding Legacy of al-Qaeda in Iraq: From al-Zarqawi to the New Islamic Caliphate," in *New (and Old) Patterns of Jihadism: Al-Qa'ida, the Islamic State and Beyond*, ed. Andrea Plebani (ISPI, 2014), 6.

5. Charles Lister, "Profiling the Islamic State," Brookings Doha Center Analysis Paper No. 13 (Brookings Institution, November 2014), 7–9, https://www.brookings.edu/wp-content/uploads/2014/12/en_web_lister.pdf.

6. Fishman, "After Zarqawi," 25.

7. Miranda Sissons and Abdulrazzaq al-Saiedi, *A Bitter Legacy: Lessons of De-Baathification in Iraq* (International Center for Transitional Justice, March 2013), 9–18, https://www.ictj.org/sites/default/files/ICTJ-Report-Iraq-De-Baathification-2013-ENG.pdf; "Shia Alliance Wins Iraq Elections," *Guardian*, January 20, 2006, https://www.theguardian.com/world/2006/jan/20/iraq.

8. Matthew Bamber-Zyrd, "Cyclical Jihadist Governance: The Islamic State Governance Cycle in Iraq and Syria," *Small Wars & Insurgencies* 33, no. 8 (September 2022): 1323, https://doi.org/10.1080/09592318.2022.2116182.

9. Bamber-Zyrd, 1324.

10. Cole Bunzel, "From Paper State to Caliphate: The Ideology of the Islamic State," Analysis Paper No. 19 (Brookings Project on US Relations with the Islamic Word, March 2015), 17–24, https://www.brookings.edu/research/from-paper-state-to-caliphate-the-ideology-of-the-islamic-state.

11. Brian Fishman, "Redefining the Islamic State: The Fall and Rise of Al-Qaeda in Iraq," National Security Studies Program Policy Paper Policy Paper (New America Foundation, August 2011), https://static.newamerica.org/attachments/4343-redefining-the-islamic-state/Fishman_Al_Qaeda_In_Iraq.023ac20877a64488b2b791cd7e313955.pdf.

12. Bamber-Zyrd, "Cyclical Jihadist Governance," 1324; Najim Abed Al-Jabouri and Sterling Jensen, "The Iraqi and AQI Roles in the Sunni Awakening," *PRISM* 2, no. 1 (December 2010): 4–8, https://www.jstor.org/stable/10.2307/26469091.

13. Myriam Benraad, "Iraq's Tribal 'Sahwa': Its Rise and Fall," *Middle East Policy* 18, no. 1 (March 2011): 121–131, https://doi.org/10.1111/j.1475-4967.2011.00477.x; Fawaz Gerges,

ISIS: A History (Princeton University Pres, 2016), 88, 103–104; Al-Jabouri and Jensen, "Iraqi and AQI Roles," 8–11; Hosham Dawod, "Iraqi Tribes in the Land of Jihad," in *Tribes and Global Jihadism*, ed. Virginie Collombier and Olivier Roy (Oxford University Press, 2017), 28.

14. Plebani, "Unfolding Legacy," 10.

15. Gerges, *ISIS*, 119–120, 125, 148–149; Abdul Basir Yosufi, "The Rise and Consolidation of Islamic State: External Intervention and Sectarian Conflict," *Connections* 15, no. 4 (Fall 2016): 102–108, https://www.jstor.org/stable/26326461; Michael Weiss and Hassan Hassan, *ISIS: Inside the Army of Terror* (Regan Arts, 2015), 117–118.

16. Gerges, *ISIS*, 99, 118; Jessica Lewis, "Al-Qaeda in Iraq Resurgent: The Breaking Walls Campaign, Part I," Middle East Security Report 14 (Institute for the Study of War, September 2013), 9, https://www.understandingwar.org/report/al-qaeda-iraq-resurgent.

17. Gerges, *ISIS*, 175–177.

18. Gerges, 122–124; Lewis, "Al-Qaeda in Iraq Resurgent," 9–19.

19. Lewis, "Al-Qaeda in Iraq Resurgent," 7–8, 30–31; Jessica Lewis, "Al-Qaeda in Iraq Resurgent Part II," Middle East Security Report 15 (Institute for the Study of War, October 2013), 7, https://www.understandingwar.org/report/al-qaeda-iraq-resurgent-part-ii.

20. Mathilde Becker Aarseth, *Mosul Under ISIS: Eyewitness Accounts of Life in the Caliphate* (I. B. Tauris, 2021), 35; Lewis, "Al-Qaeda in Iraq Resurgent," 8–9.

21. Stathis N. Kalyvas, "Is ISIS a Revolutionary Group and if Yes, What Are the Implications?," *Perspectives on Terrorism* 9, no. 4 (August 2015): 42–47, https://www.jstor.org/stable/26297413.

22. Bamber-Zyrd, "Cyclical Jihadist Governance," 1327–1328; Gerges, *ISIS*, 126–128; Lewis, "Al-Qaeda in Iraq Resurgent Part II," 29; Kareem Shaheen, "IS Controls '50% of Syria' After Seizing Historic City of Palmyra," *Guardian*, May 21, 2015, https://www.theguardian.com/world/2015/may/21/isis-palmyra-syria-islamic-state.

23. Aaron Y. Zelin, "The War Between IS and al-Qaeda for Supremacy of the Global Jihadist Movement," Research Notes No. 20 (Washington Institute for Near East Policy, June 2014), 6, https://www.washingtoninstitute.org/sites/default/files/pdf/ResearchNote_20_Zelin.pdf.

24. Tim Arango, "ISIS Fighters Seize Control of Government Headquarters in Ramadi, Iraq," *New York Times*, May 15, 2015, https://www.nytimes.com/2015/05/16/world/middleeast/isis-fighters-seize-government-headquarters-in-ramadi-iraq.html.

25. Bamber-Zyrd, "Cyclical Jihadist Governance," 1328.

26. Bamber-Zyrd, 1328.

27. Timothy Clancy, "Theory of an Emerging-State Actor: The Islamic State of Iraq and Syria (ISIS) Case," *Systems* 6, no. 16 (May 2018): 13–22, https://doi.org/10.3390/systems6020016.

28. Audrey Kurth Cronin, "ISIS Is Not a Terrorist Group," *Foreign Affairs*, March–April 2015, https://www.foreignaffairs.com/articles/middle-east/2019-02-18/isis-not-terrorist-group.

29. Cronin.

30. Becker Aarseth, *Mosul*, 37.

31. Burak Kadercan, "Territorial Logic of the Islamic State: An Interdisciplinary Approach," *Territory, Politics, Governance* 9, no. 1 (March 2019): 103, https://doi.org/10.1080/21622671 .2019.1589563.

32. Mara Revkin, "ISIS's Social Contract," *Foreign Affairs*, January 10, 2016, https://www .foreignaffairs.com/articles/syria/2016-01-10/isis-social-contract.

33. Aymenn J. al-Tamimi, *The Islamic State and Its Treatment of 'Out Groups': A Comparative Analysis* (Center for Justice and Accountability, August 2023), 3–6, https://cja.org /wp-content/uploads/2023/09/Al-Tamimi_theislamicstateandoutgroups.pdf.

34. Islamic State, "Ultimatum for the Christians in Mosul," Aymmenjawad.org, Archive of Islamic State Documents, Specimen S, January 27, 2015, http://www.aymennjawad .org/2015/01/archive-of-islamic-state-administrative-documents.

35. Hamoud Almousa, "Christians of Raqqa in a Succession of ISIS," Raqqa Is Being Slaughtered Silently, November 23, 2015, accessed September 25, 2023, https://www.raqqa-sl .com/en/?p=1562 (site discontinued); Harout Akdedian, "On Violence and Radical Theology in the Syrian War: The Instrumentality of Spectacular Violence and Exclusionary Practices from Comparative and Local Standpoints," *Politics, Religion & Ideology* 20, no. 3 (August 2019): 374–375, https://doi.org/10.1080/21567689.2019.1656074; Islamic State, "Jizya Payment Receipt in Raqqa," Aymmenjawad.org, Archive of Islamic State Documents, Specimen 2X, January 27, 2015, http://www.aymennjawad.org/2015/01 /archive-of-islamic-state-administrative-documents.

36. Revkin, "ISIS's Social Contract."

37. Mara Revkin, "Does the Islamic State Have a 'Social Contract'? Evidence from Iraq and Syria," Working Paper No. 9 (Program on Governance and Local Development, 2016), 13–14, https://papers.ssrn.com/sol3/papers.cfm?abstract_id=3732239.

38. Mike Giglio and Munzer al-Awad, "This Is What It's Like to Be Christian and Live Under ISIS," *BuzzFeed News*, January 9, 2016, https://www.buzzfeednews.com/article /mikegiglio/this-is-what-its-like-to-be-christian-and-live-under-isis.

39. Islamic State, "The Original Fatwa on Yezidis," Aymmenjawad.org, Archive of Islamic State Documents, Specimen 43T, August 9, 2014, https://www.aymennjawad.org/2017 /08/archive-of-islamic-state-administrative-documents-3; Vicken Cheterian, "ISIS Genocide Against the Yazidis and Mass Violence in the Middle East," *British Journal of Middle Eastern Studies* 48, no. 4 (October 2019): 629–635, https://doi.org/10.1080 /13530194.2019.1683718; Becker Aarseth, *Mosul*, 37.

40. Islamic State, *Dabiq*, no. 4 (July 2014): 14–15, https://jihadology.net/2014/07/27/al -%e1%b8%a5ayat-media-center-presents-a-new-issue-of-the-islamic-states-magazine -dabiq-2/.

41. Mara Revkin, "The Legal Foundations of the Islamic State," Analysis Paper No. 23 (Brookings Project on US Relations with the Islamic World, July 2016), 16, https://www .brookings.edu/wp-content/uploads/2016/07/Brookings-Analysis-Paper_Mara-Revkin _Web.pdf.

42. United Nations Human Rights Council, " 'They Came to Destroy': ISIS Crimes Against the Yezidis," A/HRC/32/CRP.2 (June 15, 2016), 8, https://www.ohchr.org/sites/default /files/Documents/HRBodies/HRCouncil/CoISyria/A_HRC_32_CRP.2_en.pdf.

43. United Nations Human Rights Council, 18.

44. Islamic State, "Notice on Buying Sex Slaves, Homs Province," Aymmenjawad.org, Archive of Islamic State Documents, Specimen 13Y, June 15, 2015, http://www .aymennjawad.org/2016/01/archive-of-islamic-state-administrative-documents-1; Islamic State, "Proof of Ownership of a Sex Slave, Mosul," Aymmenjawad.org, Archive of Islamic State Documents, Specimen 36L, August 16, 2016, http://www.aymennjawad .org/2016/09/archive-of-islamic-state-administrative-documents-2; Islamic State, "Transactions for Sabaya, Wilayat al-Jazeera," Aymmenjawad.org, Archive of Islamic State Documents, Specimen 44B, June 16, 2016, https://www.aymennjawad.org/2017/08 /archive-of-islamic-state-administrative-documents-3; Mara Revkin and Elisabeth Jean Wood, "The Islamic State's Patterns of Sexual Violence: Ideology and Institutions, Policies and Practices," *Journal of Global Security Studies* 6, no. 2 (July 2020): 1–20, https:// doi.org/10.1093/jogss/ogaa038.

45. Islamic State, "Regulations on Sale of Child Sabaya with Prices, Wilayat al-Jazeera," Aymmenjawad.org, Archive of Islamic State Documents, Specimen 44C, July 11, 2015, https://www.aymennjawad.org/2017/08/archive-of-islamic-state-administrative -documents-3.

46. Gina Vale, "Liberated, Not Free: Yazidi Women After Islamic State Captivity," *Small Wars & Insurgencies,* 31, no. 3 (April 2020): 520–523, https://doi.org/10.1080/09592318 .2020.1726572.

47. Salah Hassan Baban, "Sold, Whipped and raped: A Yazidi Woman Remembers ISIL Captivity," *Al Jazeera,* October 16, 2020, https://www.aljazeera.com/features/2020/10 /16/separation-from-my-children-was-more-painful-than.

48. Rukmini Callimachi, "ISIS Enshrines a Theology of Rape," *New York Times,* August 13, 2015, https://www.nytimes.com/2015/08/14/world/middleeast/isis-enshrines-a-theology -of-rape.html.

49. Haroro J. Ingram et al., *The ISIS Reader: Milestone Texts of the Islamic State Movement* (Oxford University Press, 2020), 177–198.

50. Islamic State, *Dabiq,* no. 13 (January 2016): 45, https://jihadology.net/wp-content /uploads/_pda/2016/01/the-islamic-state-e2809cdacc84biq-magazine-13e280b3 .pdf.

51. "Iraq: ISIS Abducting, Killing, Expelling Minorities," Human Rights Watch, July 19, 2014, https://www.hrw.org/news/2014/07/19/iraq-isis-abducting-killing-expelling-mi norities.

52. "Iraqi Court Sentences 24 to Death Over Speicher Massacre," Middle East Monitor, July 9, 2015, https://www.middleeastmonitor.com/news/middle-east/19749-iraqi-court -sentences-24-to-death-over-speicher-massacre.

53. Kristen Chick, "Their Town Now Liberated, Iraqi Christians Talk of Life Under ISIS," *Christian Science Monitor,* November 28, 2016, https://www.csmonitor.com/World /Middle-East/2016/1128/Their-town-now-liberated-Iraqi-Christians-talk-of-life -under-ISIS.

54. Jenna Lefler, "Life Under ISIS in Mosul," Institute for the Study of War, July 28, 2014, http://www.iswresearch.org/2014/07/life-under-isis-in-mosul.html.

55. Hamoud Almousa, "ISIS's Bureaus (Diwan), Between Structures of a State and Sources to Make Money," Raqqa Is Being Slaughtered Silently, March 31, 2016, accessed September 25, 2023, https://www.raqqa-sl.com/en/?p=1755 (site discontinued); Islamic State, "Ultimatum to Confiscate Property of Those Who Have Illegally Left Islamic State Territory," Aymmenjawad.org, Archive of Islamic State Documents, Specimen 25I, August 2016, http://www.aymennjawad.org/2016/09/archive-of-islamic-state-administrative-documents-2.

56. "Inside Mosul: What's Life Like Under Islamic State?," BBC, June 9, 2015, https://www.bbc.com/news/world-middle-east-32831854.

57. Becker Aarseth, Mosul, 50.

58. Islamic State, Dabiq, no. 2 (July 2014): 14–17, https://jihadology.net/wp-content/uploads/_pda/2014/07/islamic-state-e2809cdc48ibiq-magazine-2e280b3.pdf.

59. Carla Del Ponte et al., "Rule of Terror," Cairo Review of Global Affairs 19 (Fall 2015): 54, https://www.thecairoreview.com/essays/rule-of-terror/; Charles Caris and Samuel Reynolds, "ISIS Governance in Syria," Middle East Security Report No. 22 (Institute for the Study of War, July 2014), 11, https://www.understandingwar.org/report/isis-governance-syria.

60. Del Ponte et al., "Rule of Terror," 55.

61. Benjamin Ishakhan and Sofya Shahad, "The Islamic State's Destruction of Yezidi Heritage: Responses, Resilience, and Reconstruction After Genocide," Journal of Social Archaeology 20, no. 1 (November 2019): 11–14, http://dx.doi.org/10.1177/1469605319884137.

62. Islamic State, "Notification to Kurds Wishing to Reside in Raqqa Province," Aymmenjawad.org, Archive of Islamic State Documents, Specimen 37R, December 1, 2015, https://www.aymennjawad.org/2016/09/archive-of-islamic-state-administrative-documents-2.

63. Islamic State, "Denial of Expelling Kurds from Ninawa Province," Aymmenjawad.org, Archive of Islamic State Documents, Specimen 8Y, July 25, 2014, https://www.aymennjawad.org/2015/01/archive-of-islamic-state-administrative-documents.

64. Islamic State, "Notification for Kurds to Leave Raqqa City," Aymmenjawad.org, Archive of Islamic State Documents, Specimen 5M, undated, https://www.aymennjawad.org/2015/01/archive-of-islamic-state-administrative-documents.

65. Kevin Sullivan and Karla Adam, "Hoping to Create a New Society, the Islamic State Recruits Entire Families," Washington Post, December 24, 2014, https://www.washingtonpost.com/world/national-security/hoping-to-create-a-new-homeland-the-islamic-state-recruits-entire-families/2014/12/24/dbffceec-8917-11e4-8ff4-fb93129c9c8b_story.html?utm_term=.71bc49832e1b; Olivier Arvisais and Mathieu Guidère, "Education in Conflict: How Islamic State Established Its Curriculum," Journal of Curriculum Studies 52, no. 4 (May 2020): 510, https://doi.org/10.1080/00220272.2020.1759694.

66. Islamic State, "Opening of College for Sharia Sciences in Ninawa," Aymmenjawad.org, Archive of Islamic State Documents, Specimen 27V, unintelligible date, https://www.aymennjawad.org/2016/09/archive-of-islamic-state-administrative-documents-2.

67. The niqab is a veil covering the head and the face that is worn with the abaya, a loose garment that covers the body from head to feet.

68. Islamic State, *al-Naba*, no. 23 (March 2016): 15, https://jihadology.net/wp-content /uploads/_pda/2016/03/the-islamic-state-e2809cal-nabacc84_-newsletter-2322.pdf; Islamic State, "Prohibition on Shaving Beards," Aymmenjawad.org, Archive of Islamic State Documents, Specimen 6J, June 20, 2015, http://www.aymennjawad.org/2015/01 /archive-of-islamic-state-administrative-documents. See also Islamic State fatwas no. 40 and 44 (December 17, 2014), 55 (January 17, 2014), and 56 (January 19, 2015), in Islamic State, "32 Islamic State Fatwas," trans. Cole Bunzel, Jihadica, March 2, 2015, http://www.jihadica.com/32-islamic-state-fatwas/.

69. *BBC*, "Inside Mosul."

70. Rukmini Callimachi, "For Women Under ISIS, a Tyranny of Dress Code and Punishment," *New York Times*, December 12, 2016, https://www.nytimes.com/2016/12/12/world /middleeast/islamic-state-mosul-women-dress-code-morality.html.

71. Del Ponte et al., "Rule of Terror," 59.

72. Islamic State, "On Movement of Women and the Garages: Raqqa Province," Aymmenjawad.org, Archive of Islamic State Documents, Specimen M, undated, http://www .aymennjawad.org/2015/01/archive-of-islamic-state-administrative-documents; Islamic State, fatwa no. 45 (December 17, 2014), in Islamic State, "32 Islamic State Fatwas"; Islamic State, "Fatwa on Women's Travel: Al-Buhuth wa al-Eftaa Committee," Aymmenjawad.org, Archive of Islamic State Documents, Specimen 1Y, February 25, 2014, http://www.aymennjawad.org/2015/01/archive-of-islamic-state-administrative -documents.

73. Adnan R. Khan, "Life Under ISIS: Four Stories of Terror Endured," *Maclean's*, December 14, 2016, https://www.macleans.ca/news/world/life-under-isis-four-stories-of-terror -endured/.

74. Islamic State, "On Movement."

75. Islamic State, "Establishment of the Islamic Court, Deir ez-Zor City," Aymmenjawad .org, Archive of Islamic State Documents, Specimen 5Q, October 2013, http://www .aymennjawad.org/2015/01/archive-of-islamic-state-administrative-documents; Eric Robinson et al., *When the Islamic State Comes to Town* (RAND, 2017), 107.

76. Islamic State, "Willingness to Address Grievances of People Against Personnel Tel Abiyad," Aymmenjawad.org, Archive of Islamic State Documents, Specimen 38K, March 8, 2014, http://www.aymennjawad.org/2016/09/archive-of-islamic-state-admin istrative-documents-2.

77. Caris and Reynolds, "ISIS Governance," 19.

78. Nadia Kaneva and Andrea Stanton, "An Alternative Vision of Statehood: Islamic State's Ideological Challenge to the Nation State," *Studies in Conflict & Terrorism* 46, no. 5 (June 2020): 652, https://doi.org/10.1080/1057610X.2020.1780030.

79. Author interview, IS03, March 2023.

80. Author interview, IS02, February 2023.

81. Ingram et al., *ISIS Reader*, 161–176.

82. Kaneva and Stanton, "Alternative Vision," 640–641.

83. Kaneva and Stanton, 641.

84. Revkin, "Legal Foundations," 14–15.

85. Revkin, "Does the Islamic State," 11; Mara Revkin and Ariel Ahram, "Perspectives on the Rebel Social Contract: Exit, Voice and Loyalty in the Islamic State in Iraq and Syria," *World Development*, no. 132 (August 2020): 4–6, https://doi.org/10.1016/j.worlddev.2020.104981.

86. Revkin, "Does the Islamic State," 12.

87. Associated Press, "Only Days After Fall of Mosul, Iraqis Return to Find Lower Prices, Restored Services and More," Fox News, December 5, 2014, https://www.foxnews.com/world/only-days-after-fall-of-mosul-iraqis-return-to-find-lower-prices-restored-services-and-more.

88. Rebecca Collard, "Life in Mosul Gets Back to Normal," *Time*, June 19, 2014, https://time.com/290138/mosul-isis-iraq-syria/.

89. Associated Press, "Only Days."

90. Mara Revkin, "Competitive Governance and Displacement Decisions Under Rebel Rule: Evidence from the Islamic State in Iraq," *Journal of Conflict Resolution* 65, no. 1 (August 2020): 12–16, https://dx.doi.org/10.2139/ssrn.3365503.

91. Tim Arango, "ISIS Transforming Into Functioning State that Uses Terror as Tool," *New York Times*, July 21, 2015, https://www.nytimes.com/2015/07/22/world/middleeast/isis-transforming-into-functioning-state-that-uses-terror-as-tool.html.

92. "In ISIL-Controlled Territory, 8 Million Civilians Living in 'State Of Fear'—UN Expert," UN News, July 31, 2015, https://news.un.org/en/story/2015/07/505512-isil-controlled-territory-8-million-civilians-living-state-fear-un-expert.

93. Joby Warrick, *Black Flags: The Rise of ISIS* (Doubleday, 2016), 670–671; Mara Revkin and William McCants, "Experts Weigh In: Is ISIS Good at Governing?," Brookings, November 20, 2015, https://www.brookings.edu/blog/markaz/2015/11/20/experts-weigh-in-is-isis-good-at-governing/; Eric Robinson, "Cutting the Islamic State's Money Supply," *National Interest*, July 20, 2016, https://nationalinterest.org/blog/the-buzz/cutting-the-islamic-states-money-supply-17046.

94. "Iraq: ISIS Ruel Marked by Executions, Cruelty," Human Rights Watch, July 10, 2016, https://www.hrw.org/news/2016/07/10/iraq-isis-rule-marked-executions-cruelty.

95. Deborah Amos, "Under ISIS, Life in Mosul Takes a Turn for the Bleak," *National Public Radio*, March 21, 2015, https://www.npr.org/sections/parallels/2015/03/21/394322708/under-isis-life-in-mosul-takes-a-turn-for-the-bleak.

96. Khan, "Life Under ISIS."

97. Robinson et al., *When the Islamic State*, 12; Sarah Almukhtar, "Life Under the Islamic State: Fines, Taxes and Punishments," *New York Times*, May 26, 2016, https://www.nytimes.com/interactive/2016/05/26/world/middleeast/isis-taxes-fines-revenue.html; Islamic State, "Hisba Regulations Against Smoking, Hit, Anbar Province," Specimen Q, November 2, 2014, reproduced in Aymmen Jawad Al-Tamimi, "The Archivist: 26 Unseen Islamic State Administrative Documents: Overview, Translation & Analysis," Jihadology, August 24, 2015, https://jihadology.net/2015/08/24/the-archivist-26-unseen-islamic-state-administrative-documents-overview-translation-analysis/.

98. Erika Solomon, "Fines, Sell-Offs and Subsidy Cuts: Life Under Cash-Squeezed Isis," *Financial Times*, February 27, 2015, https://www.ft.com/content/15b493ca-bdbb-11e4 -9d09-00144feab7de.

99. Islamic State, "Promise Not to Commit a Certain Offense Again," Aymmenjawad.org, Archive of Islamic State Documents, Specimen 18R, undated, https://www.aymennjawad .org/2016/01/archive-of-islamic-state-administrative-documents-1.

100. Islamic State, "Reprimand Penalties for Various Offences," Aymmenjawad.org, Archive of Islamic State Documents, Specimen 13S, 2014, http://www.aymennjawad.org/2016/01 /archive-of-islamic-state-administrative-documents-1; Islamic State, "Confiscation Slip, Diwan al-Hisba, Qayyara Office," Aymmenjawad.org, Archive of Islamic State Documents, Specimen 24T, June 5, 2016, http://www.aymennjawad.org/2016/09/archive -of-islamic-state-administrative-documents-2.

101. Islamic State, "Confiscation of a Person's Property in Deir ez-Zor Province for not Pay- ing Zakat," Specimen I, dubious date, reproduced in Aymmen Jawad Al-Tamimi, "The Archivist: 26 Unseen Islamic State Administrative Documents: Overview, Translation & Analysis," Jihadology, August 24, 2015, https://jihadology.net/2015/08/24/the-archivist -26-unseen-islamic-state-administrative-documents-overview-translation-analysis/.

102. Matthew Rosenberg et al., "Predatory Islamic State Wrings Money from Those It Rules," *New York Times*, November, 29, 2015, https://www.nytimes.com/2015/11/30/world /middleeast/predatory-islamic-state-wrings-money-from-those-it-rules.html.

103. Islamic State, "Statement on Punishment for Theft, Deir ez-Zor Province," Aymmen- jawad.org, Archive of Islamic State Documents, Specimen 6F, undated, http://www .aymennjawad.org/2015/01/archive-of-islamic-state-administrative-documents.

104. *BBC*, "Inside Mosul."

105. "Women Under ISIL: The Torturers," *Al Jazeera*, November 27, 2019, https://www .aljazeera.com/indepth/features/women-isil-torturers-191124095032690.html.

106. Azadeh Moaveni, "ISIS Women and Enforcers in Syria Recount Collaboration, Anguish and Escape," *New York Times*, November 21, 2015, https://www.nytimes.com/2015/11/22 /world/middleeast/isis-wives-and-enforcers-in-syria-recount-collaboration-anguish -and-escape.html.

107. Callimachi, "For Women."

108. Matthew Rosenberg et al., "A System of Extortion Mimicking a Real State With Reve- nue Raised in Taxes and Fines," *New York Times*, November 29, 2015, https://www .pulitzer.org/finalists/new-york-times-staff-1.

109. Del Ponte et al., "Rule of Terror," 60–61.

110. "80 Executions During the 22nd Month," Syrian Observatory for Human Rights, April 29, 2016, https://www.syriahr.com/en/46213/.

111. "Women Under ISIL: The Teacher," *Al Jazeera*, December 11, 2019, https://www.aljazeera .com/indepth/features/women-isil-teacher-191126053801151.html.

112. Rasha al-Aqeedi, "Hisba in Mosul: Systematic Oppression in the Name of Virtue," Occasional Paper (Program on Extremism at George Washington University, Febru- ary 2016), https://extremism.gwu.edu/sites/g/files/zaxdzs5746/files/downloads/Al%20 Aqeedi.pdf.

113. Caris and Reynolds, "ISIS Governance," 15–16.

114. John Rossomando, "ISIS Inflicts Saudi-style Religious Police on Syrians," Investigative Project on Terrorism, March 4, 2014, http://www.investigativeproject.org/4303/isis -inflicts-saudi-stylereligious-police-on.

115. Caris and Reynolds, "ISIS Governance," 16.

116. Sarah Birke, "How ISIS Rules," *New York Review of Books*, December 9, 2014, https:// www.nybooks.com/daily/2014/12/09/how-isis-rules/; Rossomando, "ISIS Inflicts"; Dominique Soguel, "Heard at Syria's Border: Life in the Islamic State Is Orderly, but Brutal," *Christian Science Monitor*, September 21, 2014, https://www.csmonitor.com /World/Middle-East/2014/0921/Heard-at-Syria-s-border-Life-in-the-Islamic-State-is -orderly-but-brutal; Ariel Ahram, "Sexual Violence, Competitive State Building, and Islamic State in Iraq and Syria," *Journal of Intervention and Statebuilding*, 13, no. 2 (November 2018): 188, https://doi.org/10.1080/17502977.2018.1541577.

117. Michael Weddegjerde Skjelderup, "Jihadi Governance and Traditional Authority Struc- tures: Al-Shabaab and Clan Elders in Southern Somalia, 2008–2012," *Small Wars & Insurgencies* 31, no. 6 (August 2020): 1181, https://doi.org/10.1080/09592318.2020.1780686.

118. Christopher Anzalone, "Organising Sharia Politics and Governing Violence: Al- Shabaab's Rebel Proto-State in Somalia," in *The Rule Is for None but Allah: Islamist Approaches to Governance*, ed. Joana Cook and Shiraz Maher (Hurst & Co., 2023), 108.

119. Birke, "How ISIS Rules."

120. Revkin, "Competitive Governance," 14–15.

121. Islamic State, "Fatwa on Selling Passports," Aymmenjawad.org, Archive of Islamic State Documents, Specimen 2B, December 20, 2014, https://www.aymennjawad.org/2015/01 /archive-of-islamic-state-administrative-documents.

122. Islamic State, "Conditions for Travel Outside of Mosul," Aymmenjawad.org, Archive of Islamic State Documents, Specimen 6G, undated, http://www.aymennjawad.org/2015 /01/archive-of-islamic-state-administrative-documents.

123. Revkin, "Competitive Governance," 19.

124. Islamic State, "Qur'an Memorization Competition (Raqqa Province)," Aymmenjawad .org, Archive of Islamic State Documents, Specimen I, September 2014, http://www .aymennjawad.org/2015/01/archive-of-islamic-state-administrative-documents; Aaron Y. Zelin, "Al-Qaeda in Syria: A Closer Look at ISIS (Part I)," Policy Watch 2137 (Washington Institute for Near East Policy, September 10, 2013), https://www .washingtoninstitute.org/policy-analysis/al-qaeda-syria-closer-look-isis-part-i; Jessica Lewis, "The Islamic State: A Counter-Strategy for a Counter-State," Middle East Security Report 21 (Institute for the Study of War, July 2014), 18, https://www .understandingwar.org/sites/default/files/Lewis-Center%20of%20gravity.pdf; Gina Vale, *Cubs in the Lions' Den: Indoctrination and Recruitment of Children Within Islamic State Territory* (International Centre for the Study of Radicalisation, July 2018), 20–21, https://icsr.info/wp-content/uploads/2018/07/Cubs-in-the-Lions-Den-Indoctrination- and-Recruitment-of-Children-Within-Islamic-State-Territory.pdf; Caris and Reynolds, "ISIS Governance," 15; Islamic State, "Competitions and Prizes Urum al-Kubra (Aleppo Province)," Aymmenjawad.org, Archive of Islamic State Documents, Specimen 13U,

December 2013, http://www.aymennjawad.org/2016/01/archive-of-islamic-state-admin istrative-documents-1; Islamic State, "Certificate for Passing Shari'i Course, Ninawa," Aymmenjawad.org, Archive of Islamic State Documents, Specimen 41F, August 28, 2017, https://www.aymennjawad.org/2017/08/archive-of-islamic-state-administrative -documents-3.

125. Vale, *Cubs in the Lions' Den*, 16–19; Aaron Y. Zelin, "46 Scenes from the Islamic State in Syria," *BuzzFeed*, October 12, 2013, https://www.buzzfeed.com/aaronyzelin/46-scenes -from-the-islamic-state-in-syria-dski.

126. Islamic State, "Friday Sermon for Ninawa Province Mosques," Aymmenjawad.org, Archive of Islamic State Documents, Specimen 1Q, February 2, 2015, http://www .aymennjawad.org/2015/01/archive-of-islamic-state-administrative-documents.

127. Revkin, "Legal Foundations," 29–30; Becker Aarseth, *Mosul*, 55.

128. Revkin, "Legal Foundations," 11.

129. Revkin and McCants, "Experts Weigh In."

130. Revkin, "Legal Foundations," 30–31; Revkin, "Does the Islamic State," 19.

131. Revkin and Ahram, "Perspectives," 6.

132. Revkin, "Does the Islamic State," 19.

133. Graeme Wood, "What ISIS Really Wants," *Atlantic*, March 2015, https://www.theatlantic .com/magazine/archive/2015/03/what-isis-really-wants/384980/; Ken Chitwood, "What Is a Caliph? The Islamic State Tries to Boost Its Legitimacy by Hijacking a Historic Insti- tution," *Conversation*, November 14, 2019, https://theconversation.com/what-is-a -caliph-the-islamic-state-tries-to-boost-its-legitimacy-by-hijacking-a-historic -institution-126175; William McCants, "How ISIS Got Its Flag," *Atlantic*, September 22, 2015, https://www.theatlantic.com/international/archive/2015/09/isis-flag-apocalypse /406498/.

134. Mona Hassan, *Longing for the Lost Caliphate: A Transregional History* (Princeton Uni- versity Press, 2016), 13.

135. Aaron Y. Zelin, "The Islamic State's Territorial Methodology," Research Notes No. 29 (Washington Institute for Near East Policy, January 2016), 10–15, https://www .washingtoninstitute.org/sites/default/files/pdf/ResearchNote29-Zelin.pdf; Gina Vale, "Piety Is in the Eye of the Bureaucrat: The Islamic State's Strategy of Civilian Control," *CTC Sentinel* 13, no. 1 (January 2020): 38, https://ctc.westpoint.edu/wp-content/uploads /2020/01/CTC-SENTINEL-012020.pdf; Jennifer Boutz et al., "Exploiting the Prophet's Authority: How Islamic State Propaganda Uses *Hadith* Quotation to Assert Legiti- macy," *Studies in Conflict & Terrorism* 42, no. 11 (February 2018): 974–977, https://doi .org/10.1080/1057610X.2018.1431363.

136. Thanassis Cambanis and Rebecca Collard, "How ISIS Runs a City," *Time*, February 26, 2015, https://time.com/3720063/isis-government-raqqa-mosul/.

137. Author interview, IS03, March 2023.

138. Truls Hallberg Tønnessen, "The Group that Wanted to Be a 'State': The Rebel Gover- nance of the Islamic State," in *Islamists and the Politics of the Arab Uprisings: Gover- nance, Pluralization and Contention*, ed. Hendrik Kraetzschmar and Paola Rivetti (Edinburgh University Press, 2018), 63.

139. Tønnessen, 63.

140. William McCants, *The ISIS Apocalypse: The History, Strategy, and Doomsday Vision of the Islamic State* (St. Martin's Press, 2015), 89.

141. Revkin, "ISIS's Social Contract."

142. Caris and Raynolds, "ISIS Governance," 23.

143. Lina Khatib, *The Islamic State's Strategy* (Carnegie Endowment for International Peace, June 2015), 7, https://carnegieendowment.org/research/2015/06/the-islamic-states -strategy-lasting-and-expanding?lang=en; Revkin, "Legal Foundations," 23; Katie Walmsley, "'If Not Us, Then Who?' In the Bull's-Eye of ISIS," *CNN*, March 14, 2015, https://edition.cnn.com/2015/03/14/intl_world/iyw-aid-workers-in-danger/index.html.

144. Hamoud Almousa, "The Truth of the Islamic State's Governance," Raqqa Is Being Slaughtered Silently, August 1, 2016, accessed September 25, 2023, https://www.raqqa -sl.com/en/?p=1907 (site discontinued).

145. Eva Svoboda, "Aid and the Islamic State," Overseas Development Institute and IRIN News, December 2014, https://reliefweb.int/sites/reliefweb.int/files/resources/9390.pdf.

146. Walmsley, "'If Not Us.'"

147. Bamber-Zyrd, "Cyclical Jihadist Governance," 1334; Craig Whiteside and Anas Elallame, "Accidental Ethnographers: The Islamic State's Tribal Engagement Experiment," *Small Wars & Insurgencies* 31, no. 2 (February 2020): 231, https://doi.org/10.1080 /09592318.2020.1713529.

148. Whiteside and Elallame, "Accidental Ethnographers," 229.

149. Whiteside and Elallame, 229.

150. Islamic State, *Dabiq*, no. 1 (July 2014): 12, https://jihadology.net/2014/07/05/al -%e1%b8%a5ayat-media-center-presents-a-new-issue-of-the-islamic-states-magazine -dabiq-1/.

151. Author interview, IS05, April 2023.

152. Rudayna al-Baalbaky and Ahmad Mhidi, *Tribes and the Rule of the "Islamic State": The Case of the Syrian City of Deir Ez-Zor* (Issam Fares Institute for Public Policy and International Affairs; Konrad Adenauer Stiftung, December 2018), 32, https://www.aub .edu.lb/ifi/Documents/publications/research_reports/2018-2019/20181221_tribes_and _islamic_state.pdf; Haian Dukhan and Sinan Hawat, "The Islamic State and the Arab Tribes in Eastern Syria," in *Caliphates and Islamic Global Politics*, ed. Timothy Poirson and Robert L. Oprisko (E-International Relations, 2014), 51–52.

153. Islamic State, *Dabiq*, no. 1, 13–14.

154. Islamic State, 14.

155. Haian Dukhan et al., "The Kin Who Count: Mapping Raqqa's Tribal Typology," Middle East Institute, March 24, 2021, https://www.mei.edu/publications/kin-who-count -mapping-raqqas-tribal-topology.

156. Brynjar Lia, "The Islamic State's Tribal Policies in Syria and Iraq," *Third World Thematics* 6, nos. 1–3 (November 2022): 42, https://doi.org/10.1080/23802014.2022.2147990.

157. Al-Baalbaky and Mhidi, "Tribes," 36; Dawod, "Iraqi Tribes," 29–30.

158. Khaddour and Mazur, "Eastern Expectations."

159. Al-Baalbaky and Mhidi, "Tribes," 32.

160. Al-Baalbaky and Mhidi, 32.

161. Walid al-Nofal and Madeline Edwards, "'Blood for Blood': Murder, Retribution Killings Mire Syria's Eastern Desert as Tribes Avenge Islamic State-Era Abuses," *Syria Direct*, August 22, 2018, https://syriadirect.org/news/'blood-for-blood'-murder -retribution-killings-mire-syria's-eastern-desert-as-tribes-avenge-islamic-state-era -abuses/; Liz Sly, "Syria Tribal Revolt Against Islamic State Ignored, Fueling Resentment," *Washington Post*, October 20, 2014, https://www.washingtonpost.com/world /syria-tribal-revolt-against-islamic-state-ignored-fueling-resentment/2014/10/20 /25401beb-8de8-49f2-8e64-c1cfbee45232_story.html.

162. Patrick Cockburn, "For This Iraqi Tribe Massacred by Isis, Fear of the Group's Return Is a Constant Reality," *Independent*, July 4, 2018, https://www.independent.co.uk/news /world/middle-east/iraq-tribe-isis-massacre-war-hit-albu-nimr-baghdad-sunni -a8431466.html.

163. Cockburn.

164. Lia, "Islamic State's Tribal Policies," 42.

165. Solomon, "Fines"; Aryn Baker, "Why Bashar Assad Won't Fight ISIS," *Time*, February 26, 2015, https://time.com/3719129/assad-isis-asset/; Barak Mendelsohn, "The Limits of Ideologically-Unlikely Partnerships: Syria's Support for Jihadi Terrorist Groups," *Studies in Conflict & Terrorism* 46, no. 9 (January 2021): 1668–1671, https://doi.org/10 .1080/1057610X.2020.1868094.

166. Baker, "Why Bashar Assad."

167. Baker.

168. Baker.

169. Solomon, "Fines."

170. Baker, "Why Bashar Assad."

171. Aymenn Jawad al-Tamimi, "'Principles in the Administration of the Islamic State'— Full Text and Translation," Aymennjawad.org, December 7, 2015, https://www .aymennjawad.org/18215/principles-in-the-administration-of-the-islamic.

172. Matthew Bamber, "'Without Us There Would Be No Islamic State': The Role of Civilian Employees in the Caliphate," *CTC Sentinel* 14, no. 9 (November 2021): 34, https:// ctc.westpoint.edu/wp-content/uploads/2021/11/CTC-SENTINEL-092021.pdf.

173. William A. Wagstaff and Danielle F. Jung, "Competing for Constituents: Trends in Terrorist Service Provision," *Terrorism & Political Violence* 32, no. 2 (September 2017): 294, https://doi.org/10.1080/09546553.2017.1368494.

174. Muhammad al-Ubaydi et al., *The Group that Calls Itself a State: Understanding the Evolution and Challenges of the Islamic State* (Combating Terrorism Center at West Point, December 2014), 67, https://ctc.westpoint.edu/the-group-that-calls-itself-a-state -understanding-the-evolution-and-challenges-of-the-islamic-state/.

175. Islamic State, "Notice to the Employees of the Gasworks in Ramadi," Aymmenjawad .org, Archive of Islamic State Documents, Specimen 4Z, June 10, 2015, http://www .aymennjawad.org/2015/01/archive-of-islamic-state-administrative-documents.

176. Robinson et al., *When the Islamic State*, 108; Mariam Karouny, "In Northeastern Syria, Islamic State Builds a Government," Reuters, September 4, 2014, https://www.reuters

.com/article/us-syria-crisis-raqqa-insight/in-northeast-syria-islamic-state-builds-a
-government-idUSKBN0GZ0D120140904.

177. Robinson et al., *When the Islamic State*, 186.

178. Karouny, "In Northeastern Syria."

179. Islamic State, "Call for Staff of Raqqa National Hospital to Return to Work," Aymmen-jawad.org, Archive of Islamic State Documents, Specimen 10Q, undated, http://www
.aymennjawad.org/2015/01/archive-of-islamic-state-administrative-documents.

180. Solomon, "Fines."

181. Ben Hubbard, "Life in a Jihadist Capital: Order with a Darker Side," *New York Times*,
July 23, 2014, https://www.nytimes.com/2014/07/24/world/middleeast/islamic-state
-controls-raqqa-syria.html?_r=0.

182. Aymenn Jawad al-Tamimi, "A Caliphate Under Strain: The Documentary Evidence,"
CTC Sentinel 9, no. 4 (April 2016): 3, https://ctc.westpoint.edu/a-caliphate-under-strain
-the-documentary-evidence/.

183. Youmna al-Dimashqi, "Conversations: Life as a Paramedic During ISIS' Rule of Raqqa,"
New Humanitarian, December 7, 2017, https://deeply.thenewhumanitarian.org/syria
/articles/2017/12/07/conversations-life-as-a-paramedic-during-isis-rule-of-raqqa.

184. "Women Under ISIL: The Nurse," *Al Jazeera*, December 18, 2019, https://www.aljazeera
.com/indepth/features/women-isil-nurse-191125091344781.html.

185. Islamic State, "Ultimatum for Medical Professionals and Academics to Return to IS-Held Areas, Ninawa Province," Aymmenjawad.org, Archive of Islamic State Docu-ments, Specimen 5I, May 18, 2015, http://www.aymennjawad.org/2015/01/archive-of
-islamic-state-administrative-documents.

186. Islamic State, "Ultimatum for Owner of Medical Establishment to Return, Hasakah
Province," Aymmenjawad.org, Archive of Islamic State Documents, Specimen 8O,
August 26, 2015, http://www.aymennjawad.org/2015/01/archive-of-islamic-state
-administrative-documents.

187. Islamic State, "Notification from the Diwan al-Siha in Aleppo Province," Aymmen-jawad.org, Archive of Islamic State Documents, Specimen 13T, January 2015, http://
www.aymennjawad.org/2016/01/archive-of-islamic-state-administrative-docum
ents-1.

188. Tessa Fox, "Iraq Government Employees Face Prosecution for Working Under ISIL,"
Al Jazeera, July 9, 2019, https://www.aljazeera.com/news/2019/7/9/iraq-government
-employees-face-prosecution-for-working-under-isil.

189. Islamic State, "Repentance Cards, North Baghdad Province," Aymmenjawad.org,
Archive of Islamic State Documents, Specimen 12L, August–September 2014, http://
www.aymennjawad.org/2016/01/archive-of-islamic-state-administrative-documents-1.

190. "IS Organization Starts to Distribute Applications for 'Employing Teachers,'" Syrian
Observatory for Human Rights, February 26, 2015, https://www.syriahr.com/en/13576
/; Arvisais, Guidère, "Education."

191. Islamic State, *Dabiq*, no. 10 (July 2015): 62, https://jihadology.net/wp-content/uploads/
_pda/2015/07/the-islamic-state-e2809cdc481biq-magazine-1022.pdf.

192. Islamic State, "Training Session for Teachers in Aleppo Province, May 2014," Aymmen-jawad.org, Archive of Islamic State Documents, Specimen 3A, May 2014, http://www.aymennjawad.org/2015/01/archive-of-islamic-state-administrative-documents; Islamic State, "Sharia Session for Teachers, Raqqa Province," Aymmenjawad.org, Archive of Islamic State Documents, Specimen L, undated, http://www.aymennjawad.org/2015/01/archive-of-islamic-state-administrative-documents.

193. Author interview, ISo3, March 2023.

194. Islamic State, "Educational Plans of Diwan al-Ta'aleen in Raqqa Province," Aymmen-jawad.org, Archive of Islamic State Documents, Specimen G, undated, https://www.aymennjawad.org/2015/01/archive-of-islamic-state-administrative-documents.

195. Hamoud Almousa, "Conversations: In Raqqa, Pharmacists Take an ISIS 'Re-Education Course,'" Raqqa Is Being Slaughtered Silently, January 18, 2015, accessed September 25, 2023, https://www.raqqa-sl.com/en/?p=312 (site discontinued).

196. Bram Jansen et al., "Life Under the Islamic State," Associated Press, June 4, 2015, http://interactives.ap.org/2015/inside-islamic-state/.

197. Bamber, "Without Us," 34–35.

198. Islamic State, "Summary of Various General Administrative Decisions from the Del-egated Committee," Aymmenjawad.org, Archive of Islamic State Documents, Speci-men 25J, August–September 2015, https://www.aymennjawad.org/2016/09/archive-of-islamic-state-administrative-documents-2.

199. Aymenn Jawad al-Tamimi, "The Internal Structure of the Islamic State's Hisba Appa-ratus," Middle East Center for Reporting and Analysis, June 1, 2018, https://www.mideastcenter.org/islamic-state-hisba-apparat.

200. Caris and Reynolds, "ISIS Governance," 19; Islamic State, *Dabiq*, no. 4, 19.

201. Birke, "How ISIS Rules"; Rossomando, "ISIS Inflicts"; Soguel, "Heard at Syria's Bor-der"; Ahram, "Sexual Violence," 188.

202. Hassan Hassan, "We Have Not Yet Seen the Full Impact of ISIS Sleeper Cells Coming Back to Life," *National*, April 18, 2018, https://www.thenational.ae/opinion/comment/we-have-not-yet-seen-the-full-impact-of-isis-sleeper-cells-coming-back-to-life-1.722796; Hassan Hassan, "Out of the Desert: ISIS's Strategy for a Long War," Policy Paper No. 8 (Middle East Institute, September 2018), 16, https://www.mei.edu/sites/default/files/2018-11/PP10_Hassan_ISISCT.pdf; Anne Speckhard and Ahmet S. Yayla, "The ISIS Emni: Origins and Inner Workings of ISIS's Intelligence Apparatus," *Per-spectives on Terrorism* 11, no. 1 (February 2017): 3–10, https://www.jstor.org/stable/26297733; Islamic State, "Amni Card, Mosul Area," Aymmenjawad.org, Archive of Islamic State Documents, Specimen 32C, June 25, 2014, http://www.aymennjawad.org/2016/09/archive-of-islamic-state-administrative-documents-2.

203. Islamic State, "Form to Record a Case, Islamic Court in Palmyra," Aymmenjawad.org, Archive of Islamic State Documents, Specimen 35C, undated, http://www.aymennjawad.org/2016/09/archive-of-islamic-state-administrative-documents-2.

204. Andrew F. March and Mara R. Revkin, "Caliphate of Law," *Foreign Affairs*, April 15, 2015, https://www.foreignaffairs.com/articles/syria/2015-04-15/caliphate-law; "ISIL Torture

and Detention Centers," Syrian Network for Human Rights, April 25, 2016, https://
sn4hr.org/blog/2016/04/25/21031/; Onur Burcak Belli et al., "The Business of the
Caliph," *Zeit*, December 3, 2014, https://www.zeit.de/feature/islamic-state-is-caliphate;
Islamic State, "Call for Submission of Complaints: Aleppo Province," Aymmenjawad
.org, Archive of Islamic State Documents, Specimen R, December 2014, http://www
.aymennjawad.org/2015/01/archive-of-islamic-state-administrative-documents;
Revkin, "Legal Foundations," 26.

205.   Zelin, "Territorial Methodology," 4.

206.   Islamic State, "List of Hudud Punishments (Aleppo Province)," Aymmenjawad.org,
Archive of Islamic State Documents, Specimen 1C, undated, http://www.aymennjawad
.org/2015/01/archive-of-islamic-state-administrative-documents; Syria Justice and
Accountability Centre, *Judge, Jury and Executioner: The ISIS Bureau of Justice and
Grievances* (Syria Justice and Accountability Centre, January 2020), 11, https://
syriaaccountability.org/judge-jury-and-executioner-the-isis-bureau-of-justice-and
-grievances/.

207.   Islamic State, "Note on Punishing Those Who Try to Flee to the Abode of Kufr," Aym-
menjawad.org, Archive of Islamic State Documents, Specimen 34V, unclear date, http://
www.aymennjawad.org/2016/09/archive-of-islamic-state-administrative-documents
-2; Islamic State, "Court Judgement of Death Penalty for Blasphemy," Aymmenjawad
.org, Archive of Islamic State Documents, Specimen 14D, August 29, 2015, http://www
.aymennjawad.org/2016/01/archive-of-islamic-state-administrative-documents-1.

208.   Islamic State, *Dabiq*, no. 2, 33–34.

209.   Islamic State, *Dabiq*, no. 7 (February 2015): 42–43, https://jihadology.net/wp-content
/uploads/_pda/2015/02/the-islamic-state-e2809cdc481biq-magazine-722.pdf.

210.   "Women Under ISIL: The Wives," *Al Jazeera*, December 4, 2019, https://www.aljazeera
.com/features/2019/12/4/women-under-isil-the-wives.

211.   UN-Habitat, *City Profile of Mosul, Iraq: Multi-Sector Assessment of a City Under Siege*
(United Nations Human Settlements Programme in Iraq, 2016), 6, 73, 88, https://
unhabitat.org/city-profile-of-mosul-iraq-multi-sector-assessment-of-a-city-under
-siege; Arvisais and Guidère, "Education," 504–505.

212.   Futoun al-Sheikh et al., "Every Child Left Behind in the Islamic State's New Elementary School," *Syria Direct*, October 27, 2015, https://syriadirect.org/?s=Every+Child+Left
+Behind+in+the+Islamic+State%E2%80%99s+New+Elementary+School.

213.   Islamic State, "Opening of Schools in Raqqa for Children of English-Speaking Foreign
Fighters," Aymmenjawad.org, Archive of Islamic State Documents, Specimen 1W,
undated,   http://www.aymennjawad.org/2015/01/archive-of-islamic-state-adminis
trative-documents; Islamic State, "Opening of Kindergarten Center, Raqqa Province," Aymmenjawad.org, Archive of Islamic State Documents, Specimen 2W,
April 4, 2015, http://www.aymennjawad.org/2015/01/archive-of-islamic-state-adm
inistrative-documents.

214.   Mona Alami, "ISIS's Governance Crisis (Part II): Social Services," Atlantic Council, December 24, 2014, https://www.atlanticcouncil.org/blogs/menasource/isis-s
-governance-crisis-part-ii-social-services/; Islamic State, "Opening of Sharia Institute

for Men," Aymmenjawad.org, Archive of Islamic State Documents, Specimen D, undated, http://www.aymennjawad.org/15961/aspects-of-islamic-state-is-adminis tration-in.

215. Hamoud Almousa, "ISIS Curriculum and Educational System," Raqqa Is Being Slaugh- tered Silently, September 18, 2016, accessed September 25, 2023, https://www.raqqa-sl .com/en/?p=1959 (site discontinued); Islamic State, *Dabiq*, no. 9 (May 2015): 25–26, https://jihadology.net/2015/05/21/al-%e1%b8%a5ayat-media-center-presents-a-new -issue-of-the-islamic-states-magazine-dabiq-9/; Omar al-Jaffal, "Iraqi Hospitals Under IS Suffer Lack of Medicine, Staff," *Al-Monitor*, January 15, 2015, https://www .al-monitor.com/originals/2015/01/iraq-anbar-mosul-hospitals-islamic-state.html; Hamoud Almousa, "ISIS Nurses Told They Must Speak ENGLISH Under Rules Stricter than NHS," Raqqa Is Being Slaughtered Silently, April 9, 2015, accessed Sep- tember 25, 2023, https://www.raqqa-sl.com/en/?p=941 (site discontinued).

216. Islamic State, *Dabiq*, no. 9, 25–26; al-Jaffal, "Iraqi Hospitals."

217. Almousa, "ISIS Nurses."

218. Hamoud Almousa, "The Truth of the Islamic State's Governance," Raqqa Is Being Slaughtered Silently, August 1, 2016, accessed September 25, 2023, https://www.raqqa -sl.com/en/?p=1907 (site discontinued).

219. Islamic State, "Announcement of Beginning of School Term with List of Schools," Aym- menjawad.org, Archive of Islamic State Documents, Specimen H, undated, http://www .aymennjawad.org/2015/01/archive-of-islamic-state-administrative-documents; Hamoud Almousa, "Inside the Islamic State Capital: No End in Sight to Its Grim Rule," Raqqa Is Being Slaughtered Silently, February 22, 2015, accessed September 25, 2023, https:// www.raqqa-sl.com/en/?p=634 (site discontinued); Hamoud Almousa, "Teachers Are the Victims of ISIS After the Educational Process," Raqqa Is Being Slaughtered Silently, March 2, 2015, accessed September 25, 2023, https://www.raqqa-sl.com/en/?p =707 (site discontinued); Mathilde Becker Aarseth, "Resistance in the Caliphate's Class- rooms: Mosul Civilians vs IS," *Middle East Policy* 25, no. 1 (March 2018): 50–52, https:// doi.org/10.1111/mepo.12324.

220. Islamic State, "Educational Regulations Notification Distributed in Aleppo Province," Aymmenjawad.org, Archive of Islamic State Documents, Specimen 3F, undated, http:// www.aymennjawad.org/2015/01/archive-of-islamic-state-administrative-documents; Caris and Reynolds, "ISIS Governance," 17; Becker Aarsath, *Mosul*, 72.

221. Islamic State, "'I Am Muslim'—Primary School Textbook for Reading," Aymmenjawad .org, Archive of Islamic State Documents, Specimen 6X, undated, http://www .aymennjawad.org/2015/01/archive-of-islamic-state-administrative-documents.

222. Arvisais and Guidère, "Education," 509–512; Becker Aarseth, "Resistance," 51–52; Islamic State, "Mathematics & Arabic Language Text Books Issued by Diwan al-Ta'aleem for First Grade, Primary School, Year 1436 AH," Aymmenjawad.org, Archive of Islamic State Documents, Specimen 1X, January, 27, 2015, http://www.aymennjawad.org/2015 /01/archive-of-islamic-state-administrative-documents; Islamic State, "Islamic State Diwan al-Ta'aleem Primary School Level One Textbook (Grades 1–3) on Creed and Jurisprudence," Aymmenjawad.org, Archive of Islamic State Documents, Specimen 2O,

undated, http://www.aymennjawad.org/2015/01/archive-of-islamic-state-administra
tive-documents; Casey Tolan, "These Are the Textbooks Supposedly Used by the
Islamic State," *Splinter*, October 28, 2015, https://splinternews.com/these-are-the-text
books-supposedly-used-by-the-islamic-1793852375.

223. Islamic State, "Excerpt on a Text on Creed and Jurisprudence for Primary School Children," Aymmenjawad.org, Archive of Islamic State Documents, Specimen 3M,
undated, http://www.aymennjawad.org/2015/01/archive-of-islamic-state-administra
tive-documents.

224. Mark Molloy, "Islamic State Textbooks Featuring Tanks and Guns Used to Teach Children Maths in School," *Telegraph*, February 16, 2017, https://www.telegraph.co.uk
/news/2017/02/16/isis-textbooks-featuring-guns-tanks-used-teach-children-maths/.

225. *Al Jazeera*, "The Teacher."

226. Islamic State, "Notice to Members of Ramadi Teaching Hospital," Aymmenjawad.org,
Archive of Islamic State Documents, Specimen 4B, May 18, 2015, http://www
.aymennjawad.org/2015/01/archive-of-islamic-state-administrative-documents.

227. Almousa, "ISIS's Bureaus"; Hamoud Almousa, "Health Sector a New Victim of ISIS
Economy in Tell Abiad," Raqqa Is Being Slaughtered Silently, March 13, 2015, accessed
September 25, 2023, https://www.raqqa-sl.com/en/?p=794 (site discontinued); Islamic
State, "Childbirth Operations in Deir ez-Zor Province," Aymmenjawad.org, Archive
of Islamic State Documents, Specimen A, October 26, 2014, http://www.aymennjawad
.org/2015/01/archive-of-islamic-state-administrative-documents; Islamic State, *Dabiq*,
no. 9, 25–26; Becker Aarseth, *Mosul*, 103–105.

228. Georgia J. Michlig et al., "Providing Healthcare Under ISIS: A Qualitative Analysis of
Healthcare Worker Experiences in Mosul, Iraq Between June 2014 and June 2017," *Global
Public Health* 14, no. 10 (April 2019): 7, https://doi.org/10.1080/17441692.2019.1609061.

229. Michlig et al., 4–5.

230. Islamic State, "Ban on Importing Iranian Food and Medical Goods," Aymmenjawad
.org, Archive of Islamic State Documents, Specimen 4X, May 28, 2015, http://www
.aymennjawad.org/2015/01/archive-of-islamic-state-administrative-documents.

231. "Daily Life in the Caliphate," Human Rights Watch, December 8, 2015, https://www
.hrw.org/news/2015/12/08/daily-life-caliphate-0.

232. Almousa, "The Truth"; Aymenn al-Tamimi, "Critical Analysis of the Islamic State's
Health Department," Jihadology, August 27, 2015, https://jihadology.net/2015/08/27/the
-archivist-critical-analysis-of-the-islamic-states-health-department/.

233. Hubbard et al., "Life"; Kelly Phillips Erb, "Islamic State Warns Christians Convert, Pay
Tax, Leave Or Die," *Forbes*, July 19, 2014, https://www.forbes.com/sites/kellyphillipserb
/2014/07/19/islamic-state-warns-christians-convert-pay-tax-leave-or-die/#1af0149e2c25;
Richard Spencer, "Militant Islamist Group in Syria Orders Christians to Pay Protection
Tax," *Telegraph*, February 27, 2014, https://www.telegraph.co.uk/news/worldnews
/middleeast/syria/10666257/Militant-Islamist-group-in-Syria-orders-Christians-to-pay
-protection-tax.html; Gerges, *ISIS*, 201; Revkin, "Legal Foundations," 16.

234. Al-Ubaydi et al., "Group," 61; "Islamic State Imposes Taxes (Zakat) on the Rich," Syrian Observatory for Human Rights, December 21, 2014, http://www.syriahr.com/en/

?p=8268; Islamic State, "Zakat Receipts, al-Ba'aj and Tel Abtah," Aymmenjawad.org, Archive of Islamic State Documents, Specimen 31J, undated, http://www.aymennjawad .org/2016/09/archive-of-islamic-state-administrative-documents-2.

235. Islamic State, "On Zakat al-Fitr, Aleppo Province," Aymmenjawad.org, Archive of Islamic State Documents, Specimen 2U, undated, http://www.aymennjawad.org/2015 /01/archive-of-islamic-state-administrative-documents.

236. Almousa, "ISIS's Bureaus"; "IS Militants Collect 'al-Zakat Money' from the Owner of Stores in the Town of al-Bsiri," Syrian Observatory for Human Rights, January 30, 2015, http://www.syriahr.com/en/?p=11120.

237. Syrian Observatory for Human Rights, "IS Militants."

238. Islamic State, "Note for Providing Aid to Displaced Persons from Salah al-Din Province," Aymmenjawad.org, Archive of Islamic State Documents, Specimen 40L, undated, https://www.aymennjawad.org/2017/08/archive-of-islamic-state-administrative -documents-3.

239. Islamic State, *Dabiq*, no. 2, 36.

240. Revkin, "Legal Foundations," 20.

241. Revkin, "ISIS's Social Contract."

242. Ayse Lokmanoglu and Alexandra Phelan, "Monetary Economics, Illicit Economies, and Legitimation: The Case of Islamic State," in *The Rule Is for None but Allah: Islamist Approaches to Governance*, ed. Joana Cook and Shiraz Maher (Hurst & Co., 2023), 180–181.

243. Belli et al., "Business"; Charles Lister, "ISIS's Extortion and 'Taxation' Are Lucrative and Hard to Suppress," *New York Times*, November 20, 2015, https://www.nytimes.com /roomfordebate/2015/11/20/draining-isis-coffers/isis-extortion-and-taxation-are -lucrative-and-hard-to-suppress.

244. Islamic State, "Water and Municipality Services Tax Receipt, Euphrates Province," Aymmenjawad.org, Archive of Islamic State Documents, Specimen 29V, undated, http://www.aymennjawad.org/2016/09/archive-of-islamic-state-administrative -documents-2.

245. Hubbard et al., "Life"; Islamic State, "Shops and Cleaning Services, Manbij," Aymmenjawad.org, Archive of Islamic State Documents, Specimen 2S, September 2014, http:// www.aymennjawad.org/2015/01/archive-of-islamic-state-administrative-documents; Islamic State, "City Cleaning Receipt, Mosul," Aymmenjawad.org, Archive of Islamic State Documents, Specimen 6M, July 19, 2015, http://www.aymennjawad.org/2015/01 /archive-of-islamic-state-administrative-documents.

246. Hamoud Almousa, "Raqqa: 'It Is a Very Sad Life Under ISIL,'" Raqqa Is Being Slaughtered Silently, January 9, 2015, accessed September 25, 2023, https://www.raqqa-sl.com /en/?p=412 (site discontinued); Islamic State, "Electricity Prices in Raqqa," Aymmenjawad.org, Archive of Islamic State Documents, Specimen 9K, July 11, 2015, http:// www.aymennjawad.org/2015/01/archive-of-islamic-state-administrative-documents; Birke, "How ISIS Rules"; Islamic State, "Payment of 800 Syrian Pounds for Phone Subscription Service, Aleppo Province," Aymmenjawad.org, Archive of Islamic State Documents, Specimen 38N, undated, http://www.aymennjawad.org/2016/09/archive

-of-islamic-state-administrative-documents-2; Islamic State, "Electricity Generator Operating Hours and Fees," Aymmenjawad.org, Archive of Islamic State Documents, Specimen 6C, July 6, 2015, http://www.aymennjawad.org/2015/01/archive-of -islamic-state-administrative-documents.

247.   Islamic State, "Educational Regulations"; Almousa, "The Truth"; Almousa, "Health Sector"; Islamic State, "Childbirth Operations."

248.   Islamic State, fatwas no. 42 and 43 (December 17, 2014), in Islamic State, "32 Islamic State Fatwas"; Islamic State, "Prohibition on Gender Mixing, Manbij, Aleppo Province," Aymmenjawad.org, Archive of Islamic State Documents, Specimen 7Y, February 28, 2014, http://www.aymennjawad.org/2015/01/archive-of-islamic-state-administrative -documents.

249.   Islamic State, "On Movement"; Islamic State, "Conditions for Travel"; Islamic State, "Early Rulings Imposed in Mosul," Aymmenjawad.org, Archive of Islamic State Documents, Specimen 10M, June 18, 2014, http://www.aymennjawad.org/2015/01/archive-of -islamic-state-administrative-documents.

250.   Islamic State, "Call for Shops to Close During Prayer Time, Raqqa Province, Northern Region," Aymmenjawad.org, Archive of Islamic State Documents, Specimen 38M, April 30, 2014, http://www.aymennjawad.org/2016/09/archive-of-islamic-state-adm inistrative-documents-2; Islamic State, "Order to Close Shops During Prayer Time, Ramadi," Aymmenjawad.org, Archive of Islamic State Documents, Specimen 10G, May 29, 2015, http://www.aymennjawad.org/2015/01/archive-of-islamic-state-admi nistrative-documents.

251.   Hassan Hassan, "What ISIS Did to My Village," *Atlantic*, April 27, 2019, https://www .theatlantic.com/ideas/archive/2019/04/isis-i-study-today-not-isis-my-past/588088/; Nabih Bulos, "Life Under Islamic State Was Strict and Brutal, but Some Moments Didn't Seem So Bad, Sunni Iraqis say," *Los Angeles Times*, October 28, 2016, https://www .latimes.com/world/middleeast/la-fg-iraq-sunni-villages-20161027-story.html.

252.   Islamic State, "Increasing Penalty for Smoking, Aleppo Province," Aymmenjawad.org, Archive of Islamic State Documents, Specimen 14K, March 2016, http://www .aymennjawad.org/2016/01/archive-of-islamic-state-administrative-documents-1; Islamic State, fatwas no. 49 and 50 (December 28, 2014), in Islamic State, "32 Islamic State Fatwas."

253.   Islamic State, "Leave Permit, Aleppo Province," Aymmenjawad.org, Archive of Islamic State Documents, Specimen 12O, undated, http://www.aymennjawad.org/2016/01 /archive-of-islamic-state-administrative-documents-1; Islamic State, fatwas no. 48 (December 20, 2014), 37 (December 16, 2014), and 40 (December 17, 2014), in Islamic State, "32 Islamic State Fatwas"; Islamic State, "Permission Slip for Travel to Kuwait," Aymmenjawad.org, Archive of Islamic State Documents, Specimen 2J, October 25, 2014, http://www.aymennjawad.org/2015/01/archive-of-islamic-state-administrative -documents; Islamic State, "Medical Leave Permit," Aymmenjawad.org, Archive of Islamic State Documents, Specimen 40V, October 29, 2016, https://www.aymennjawad .org/2017/08/archive-of-islamic-state-administrative-documents-3; Islamic State, "Document to Pass Through Hasakah Province Checkpoints," Aymmenjawad.org, Archive

of Islamic State Documents, Specimen 14I, undated, http://www.aymennjawad.org/2016 /01/archive-of-islamic-state-administrative-documents-1; Islamic State, "Travel Slip from 'Euphrates Province' to Damascus," Aymmenjawad.org, Archive of Islamic State Documents, Specimen 14N, undated, http://www.aymennjawad.org/2016/01/archive -of-islamic-state-administrative-documents-1; Islamic State, "Travel Document, Deir az-Zor Province," Aymmenjawad.org, Archive of Islamic State Documents, Specimen 26K, undated, http://www.aymennjawad.org/2016/09/archive-of-islamic-state -administrative-documents-2.

254.   " 'Islamic State' Storms Internet Cafes in the City of al- Raqqa, While Closes Others in 'al-Furat State' and Asks Their Owners to Issue Licences," Syrian Observatory for Human Rights, August 3, 2015, http://www.syriahr.com/en/?p=27749; "After al-Raqqa and 'al-Forat State' ISIS Closes the Internet Cafes in al-Mayadin Around Its Headquarters," Syrian Observatory for Human Rights, August 8, 2015, http://www.syriahr.com /en/?p=28275; Islamic State, "Notice to Internet Cafes, Raqqa Province," Aymmenjawad .org, Archive of Islamic State Documents, Specimen 6L, July 19, 2015, http://www .aymennjawad.org/2015/01/archive-of-islamic-state-administrative-documents; Islamic State, "Restrictions on Phone Use, Fallujah," Aymmenjawad.org, Archive of Islamic State Documents, Specimen 15J, May 31, 2016, http://www.aymennjawad.org/2016/01 /archive-of-islamic-state-administrative-documents-1; "Mosul Diaries: Poisoned by Water," *BBC*, December 19, 2014, https://www.bbc.com/news/world-middle-east -29600573; Islamic State, "Further Internet Restrictions in Mosul," Aymmenjawad.org, Archive of Islamic State Documents, Specimen 18V, July 19, 2016, http://www.aymennja wad.org/2016/01/archive-of-islamic-state-administrative-documents-1; Islamic State, "Regulations on Internet Connections, 'Euphrates Province'—Albukamal," Aymmenjawad.org, Archive of Islamic State Documents, Specimen 7I, undated, http://www .aymennjawad.org/2015/01/archive-of-islamic-state-administrative-documents; Islamic State "Application Form to Obtain Licensing for an Internet Hall, Mosul," Aymmenjawad.org, Archive of Islamic State Documents, Specimen 22L, January 11, 2016, http://www.aymennjawad.org/2016/01/archive-of-islamic-state-administrative -documents-1.

255.   Islamic State, "Imposition of the Niqab in Raqqa," Aymmenjawad.org, Archive of Islamic State Documents, Specimen 12V, January 2014, http://www.aymennjawad.org /2016/01/archive-of-islamic-state-administrative-documents-1; Islamic State, "Restrictions on Women's Clothing, Tel Abiyad, Raqqa Province," Aymmenjawad.org, Archive of Islamic State Documents, Specimen 1I, December 2013, http://www.aymennjawad .org/2015/01/archive-of-islamic-state-administrative-documents.

256.   Islamic State, "Prohibition on Shaving"; Hassan, "What ISIS Did"; Islamic State, fatwa no. 55.

257.   Islamic State, "Employment Opportunities with the Diwan al-Zakat in Raqqa Province," Aymmenjawad.org, Archive of Islamic State Documents, Specimen J, December 3, 2014, http://www.aymennjawad.org/2015/01/archive-of-islamic-state-administrative -documents; Islamic State, "Employment Opportunities with the Diwan al-Hisba, Raqqa Province," Aymmenjawad.org, Archive of Islamic State Documents, Specimen K,

undated, http://www.aymennjawad.org/2015/01/archive-of-islamic-state-administrative
-documents.

258.   Islamic State, "Recruiting for the Diwan al-Ta'aleem, Ninawa Province," Aymmenjawad
.org, Archive of Islamic State Documents, Specimen 17C, undated, http://www
.aymennjawad.org/2016/01/archive-of-islamic-state-administrative-documents-1.

259.   Laith Alkhouri and Alex Kassirer, "Governing the Caliphate: The Islamic State Picture,"
CTC Sentinel 8, no. 8 (August 2015): 20, https://ctc.westpoint.edu/governing-the
-caliphate-the-islamic-state-picture/.

260.   Abu Bakr al-Baghdadi, "Audio Message to the Mujahidin and the Muslim Ummah in
the Month of Ramadan," July 1, 2014, accessed September 25, 2023, https://kyleorton1991
.wpcomstaging.com/2014/07/02/the-leader-of-the-islamic-state-explains-the
-caliphates-vision/ (site discontinued).

261.   Erkan Toguslu, "Caliphate, *Hijra* and Martyrdom as Performative Narrative in ISIS
Dabiq Magazine," *Politics, Religion & Ideology* 20, no. 1 (December 2018): 112, https://
doi.org/10.1080/21567689.2018.1554480.

262.   Islamic State, "Form for Reception of Newcomers, Ramadi Area," Aymmenjawad.org,
Archive of Islamic State Documents, Specimen 13J, undated, http://www.aymennjawad
.org/2016/01/archive-of-islamic-state-administrative-documents-1.

263.   Al-Ubaydi et al., "The Group," 75.

5. BUILDING AN ISLAMIST POLITY IN NORTHWESTERN SYRIA

1.   Charles Lister, "Profiling the Islamic State," Brookings Doha Center Analysis Paper
No. 13 (Brookings Institution, November 2014), 5, https://www.brookings.edu/wp
-content/uploads/2016/07/iwr_20160728_profiling_nusra.pdf.

2.   Raymond Hinnebusch et al., "Civil Resistance in the Syrian Uprising: From Peaceful
Protest to Sectarian Civil War," in *Civil Resistance in the Arab Spring: Triumphs and
Disasters*, ed. Adam Roberts et al. (Oxford University Press, 2016), 223–247.

3.   Hinnebusch et al., "Civil Resistance," 223–247.

4.   Hinnebusch et al., 223–247.

5.   Adam Roberts, "The Fate of the Arab Spring: Ten Propositions," *Asian Journal of Middle Eastern and Islamic Studies* 12, no. 3 (January 2019): 283, https://doi.org/10.1080
/25765949.2018.1546977.

6.   Roberts, "Fate," 283.

7.   "The Best of Bad Options for Syria's Idlib," Middle East Report No. 197 (International
Crisis Group, March 2019), 7, https://www.crisisgroup.org/middle-east-north-africa
/eastern-mediterranean/syria/197-best-bad-options-syrias-idlib.

8.   Fawaz Gerges, *ISIS: A History* (Princeton University Pres, 2016), 187–188.

9.   Aaron Y. Zelin, "Jihadi 'Counterterrorism': Hayat Tahrir al-Sham Versus the Islamic
State," *CTC Sentinel* 16, no. 2 (February 2023): 14.

10.   Seth G. Jones, *A Persistent Threat: The Evolution of al-Qa'ida and Other Salafi-Jihadists*
(RAND, 2014), 7–24; Mohamed-Ali Adraoui, "The Case of Jabhat al-Nusra in the

Syrian Conflict 2011–2016: Towards a Strategy of Nationalization?," *Mediterranean Politics* 24, no. 2 (October 2017): 260–267, https://doi.org/10.1080/13629395.2017 .1392709.

11. Aymenn Jawad al-Tamimi, *From Jabhat al-Nusra to Hay'at Tahrir al-Sham: Evolution, Approach and Future* (Konrad Adenauer Stiftung, December 2017), 6, https://www.kas .de/c/document_library/get_file?uuid=8cfa4cdb-e337-820d-d0bd-4cd998f38612 &groupId=252038.

12. Aaron Y. Zelin, "The War Between IS and al-Qaeda for Supremacy of the Global Jihadist Movement," Research Notes No. 20 (Washington Institute for Near East Policy, June 2014), 4–6, https://www.washingtoninstitute.org/sites/default/files/pdf /ResearchNote_20_Zelin.pdf.

13. Abu Mohammad al-Julani, interview by Martin Smith, *Frontline*, PBS, February 2021, https://www.pbs.org/wgbh/frontline/interview/abu-mohammad-al-jolani/.

14. Center for International Security and Cooperation, "Hayat Tahrir al-Sham," CSIS Terrorism Backgrounder, October 4, 2018, https://www.csis.org/programs/former -programs/warfare-irregular-threats-and-terrorism-program-archives/terrorism -backgrounders/hayat-tahrir.

15. Al-Tamimi, "From Jabhat al-Nusra," 8; Charles Lister, "Hayat Tahrir al-Sham: To Unite or to Divide the Ranks?," in *How al-Qaeda Survived Drones, Uprisings and the Islamic State*, ed. Aaron Zelin (Washington Institute for Near East Policy, 2017), 21–24.

16. Al-Tamimi, 8.

17. Al-Tamimi, 9–10.

18. Al-Tamimi, 11.

19. Al-Tamimi, 12–13.

20. Aymenn Jawad al-Tamimi, "Idlib and Its Environs," Policy Notes No. 75 (Washington Institute for Near East Policy, February 2020), 3–4, https://www.washingtoninstitute .org/sites/default/files/pdf/PolicyNote75-Tamimi.pdf.

21. Jerome Drevon and Patrick Haenni, "How Global Jihad Relocalises and Where It Leads: The Case of HTS, the Former AQ Franchise in Syria," RSC Working Paper 2021/08 (European University Institute, August 2021), 2, https://hdl.handle.net/1814/69795.

22. Al-Tamimi, "From Jabhat al-Nusra," 16–17.

23. Silvia Carenzi, "How Do Non-State Actors Seek Legitimacy? The Case of Idlib," Italian Institute for International Political Studies, September 15, 2022, https://www .ispionline.it/en/publication/how-do-non-state-actors-seek-legitimacy-case-idlib -36156.

24. Haid Haid, "HTS Attempts State-Building as Survival Strategy in Idlib," *Arab News*, April 24, 2019, https://www.arabnews.com/node/1487521; Dareen Khalifa, "Idlib and the Hayat Tahrir al-Sham Conundrum in Syria," in *The Rule Is for None but Allah: Islamist Approaches to Governance*, ed. Joana Cook and Shiraz Maher (Hurst & Co., 2023), 258.

25. Nisreen Al-Zaraee and Kareem Shaar, "The Economics of Hayat Tahrir al-Sham," Middle East Institute, June 21, 2021, https://www.mei.edu/publications/economics-hayat -tahrir-al-sham.

26. Thomas Pierret and Laila Alrefaai, "Religious Governance in Syria Amid Territorial Fragmentation," in *Return to Islamic Institutions in Arab States: Mapping the Dynamics*

of Control, Co-Option and Contention, ed. Frederic Wehrey (Carnegie Endowment for International Peace, 2021), 12, https://hal.science/hal-03259910/document.

27. Drevon and Haenni, "Global Jihad Relocalises," 8.

28. Christopher Solomon, "HTS: Evolution of a Jihadi Group," Wilson Center, July 13, 2022, https://www.wilsoncenter.org/article/hts-evolution-jihadist-group; Carenzi, "Non-State Actors."

29. "Syria Update," Center for Operational Analysis and Research, July 27, 2020, https:// coar-global.org/2020/07/27/potemkin-parliament-baathists-consolidate-control-as -access-to-power-shifts/.

30. Emman El-Badawi et al., *Inside the Jihadi Mind: Understanding Ideology and Propaganda* (Tony Blair Institute for Global Change, October 2015), 49, https://institute. global/insights/geopolitics-and-security/inside-jihadi-mind-understanding-ideology -and-propaganda.

31. Marwan Hisham and Molly Crabapple, *Brothers of the Gun: A Memoir of the Syrian War* (Oneworld, 2018), 108.

32. Rania Abouzeid, "Interview with Official of Jabhat al-Nusra Syria's Islamist Militia Group," *Time*, December 25, 2012, http://world.time.com/2012/12/25/interview-with-a -newly-designated-syrias-jabhat-al-nusra/.

33. "The Druze: Solidarity and Allegiance in Syria," Tony Blair Institute for Global Change, October 30, 2014, https://www.institute.global/insights/geopolitics-and-security/druze- solidarity-and-allegiance-syria; Aymenn al-Tamimi, "Hayat Tahrir al-Sham's Abu al- Fatah al-Farghali on Minority Sects," Aymmenjawad.org, June 17, 2021, https://www .aymennjawad.org/2021/06/hayat-tahrir-al-sham-abu-al-fatah-al-farghali-on.

34. Yvette Talhami, "The *Fatwas* and the Nusayri/Alawis of Syria," *Middle Eastern Studies* 46, no. 2, (April 2010): 179–180, https://doi.org/10.1080/00263200902940251.

35. Nour Matraji and Richard Hall, "The Other Islamic State: Al-Qaeda Is Still Fighting for an Emirate of Its Own," Public Radio International, May 2, 2016, https://www.pri.org /stories/2016-04-29/other-islamic-state-al-qaeda-still-fighting-emirate-its-own; "You Can Still See Their Blood," Human Rights Watch, October 10, 2013, https://www.hrw.org /report/2013/10/10/you-can-still-see-their-blood/executions-indiscriminate-shootings -and-hostage.

36. Human Rights Watch, "You Can Still See."

37. Human Rights Watch.

38. Lister, "Profiling Jabhat al-Nusra," 25.

39. Charles Lister, *The Syrian Jihad: Al-Qaeda, the Islamic State and the Evolution of an Insurgency* (Oxford University Press, 2015), 354.

40. Aymenn Jawad al-Tamimi, "Jabhat al-Nusra and the Druze of Idlib Province," *Syria Comment*, January 24, 2015, https://www.joshualandis.com/blog/jabhat-al-nusra-druze -idlib-province/.

41. "Idlib Druze Agree to Forced Conversion, Destroyed Shrines Under Nusra Rule," *Syria Direct*, March 17, 2015, https://syriadirect.org/news/idlib-druze-agree-to-forced -conversion-destroyed-shrines-under-nusra-rule/.

42. *Syria Direct*, "Idlib Druze."

43. Al-Tamimi, "Jabhat al-Nusra and the Druze"; Aymenn Jawad al-Tamimi, "Additional Notes on the Druze of Jabal al-Summaq," Aymennjawad.org, October 6, 2015, http://www.aymennjawad.org/2015/10/additional-notes-on-the-druze-of-jabal-al-summaq.

44. Aymenn Jawad al-Tamimi, "The Massacre of Druze Villagers in Qalb Lawza, Idlib Province," *Syria Comment*, June 15, 2015, https://www.joshualandis.com/blog/the-massacre-of-druze-villagers-in-qalb-lawza-idlib-province/; Ibrahim al-Assim and Randa Slim, "The Syrian Druze at Crossroads," Middle East Institute, July 13, 2015, https://www.mei.edu/publications/syrian-druze-crossroads; Daveed Gartenstein-Ross, "Druze Clues," Foundation for the Defense of Democracies, October 6, 2015, https://www.fdd.org/analysis/2015/10/06/druze-clues/; Lister, *Syrian Jihad*, 360.

45. Nour Samaha, "Trapped Between Assad, Israel, and al-Qaeda," *Foreign Policy*, June 22, 2015, https://foreignpolicy.com/2015/06/22/druze-syria-assad-israel-netanyahu/.

46. The Kharijites were the first identifiable sect in Islam. The extreme position of the Kharijites was that Muslims who commit grave sins effectively reject their religion, thus entering the rank of apostates and deserving death. This position was considered excessively restrictive by most Muslims. Most recently, the term "Kharijites" was disparagingly used to refer to the Islamic State.

47. Gartenstein-Ross, "Druze Clues."

48. Islamic State, *Dabiq*, no. 10, 8.

49. Al-Tamimi, "Jabhat al-Nusra and the Druze."

50. *Syria Direct*, "Idlib Druze."

51. Ammar Hamou and Avery Edelman, "Property Seizures by Hardline Rebels Stoke Fears Among Idlib Province's Fading Christian Community," *Syria Direct*, December 13, 2018, https://syriadirect.org/property-seizures-by-hardline-rebels-stoke-fears-among-idlib-provinces-fading-christian-community/; "Syrian Christians Face New Threat from Rebel Alliance," National Public Radio, July 3, 2015, https://www.npr.org/2015/07/03/419824382/syrian-christians-face-new-threat-from-rebel-alliance.

52. Hamou and Edelman, "Property Seizures."

53. "Islamic Terror Group Confiscating Christian-Owned Properties in Syria," Syrian Observatory for Human Rights, May 5, 2020, https://www.syriahr.com/en/163224/; "HTS Confiscates No Less than 550 Homes and Businesses Belonging to Christians in Idlib," Syrians for Truth & Justice, January 14, 2020, https://stj-sy.org/en/hts-confiscates-no-less-than-550-homes-and-businesses-belonging-to-christians-in-idlib/; "Details of the Salvation Government's Confiscation of Christian Property in Idlib" [in Arabic], *Orient Net*, November 22, 2018, https://orient-news.net/ar/news_show/156949/0/إدلب-في-المسيحيين-أملاك-الإنقاذ-حكومة-مصادرة-تفاصيل.

54. Syrians for Truth & Justice, "HTS Confiscates."

55. Hamou and Edelman, "Property Seizures."

56. Syrians for Truth & Justice, "HTS Confiscates"; Daniele Rocchi, "Syria: Idlib, Christians' Christmas Under al-Qaeda Rule, with No Lights but with the Light," *Agensir*, December 23, 2019, https://archivio.agensir.it/2019/12/23/syria-idlib-christians-christmas-under-al-qaeda-rule-with-no-lights-but-with-the-light/.

57. Rocchi, "Syria."

58. Rocchi.

59. Sultan al-Kanj, "Syrian Jihadi Leader Golani Meets with Idlib's Christians," *Al-Monitor*, July 27, 2022, https://www.al-monitor.com/originals/2022/07/syrian-jihadi-leader-golani-meets-idlibs-christians.

60. Al-Julani, interview by Martin Smith.

61. Al-Kanj, "Syrian Jihadi Leader."

62. Khaled al-Khateb, "Christians in Syria's Idlib Hold Major Mass," *Al-Monitor*, September 4, 2022, https://www.al-monitor.com/originals/2022/09/christians-syrias-idlib-hold-major-mass.

63. Al-Khateb.

64. Video of the visit was available as of September 2023 at https://amjaad.video/watch/Lc5WsU8MbcKbDdS, but it appears that this site has since been disabled.

65. "Will HTS Give Back Seized Druze Properties in Jabal al-Summaq?," *Syria Report*, June 14, 2022, https://hlp.syria-report.com/hlp/will-hts-give-back-seized-druze-properties-in-jabal-al-summaq/.

66. Ninar Khalifa, "Idlib's Druze Complain of Persecution," Syrians for Truth & Justice, November 24, 2022, https://stj-sy.org/en/idlibs-druze-complain-of-persecution/.

67. Mohammed Hardan, "Syrian Jihadi Leader Courts Druze Community in Idlib," *Al-Monitor*, June 16, 2022, https://www.al-monitor.com/originals/2022/06/syrian-jihadi-leader-courts-druze-community-idlib.

68. "The Most Notable Hayat Tahrir al-Sham Violations Since the Establishment of Jabhat al-Nusra to Date," Syrian Network for Human Rights, January 31, 2022, https://snhr.org/wp-content/pdf/english/The_Most_Notable_Hayat_Tahrir_al_Sham_Violations_Since_the_Establishment_of_Jabhat_al_Nusra_to_Date_1_en.pdf.

69. "Idlib . . . Women Dress Code and the Suffocating Laws of Hayat Tahrir al-Sham," Rozana Radio, May 25, 2020, https://www.rozana.fm/english/article/96107-idlib%E2%80%A6-women-dress-code-and-the-suffocating-laws-of-hay%E2%80%99at-tahrir-al-sham.

70. Rozana Radio, "Idlib."

71. Rozana Radio.

72. Drevon, Haenni, "Global Jihad Relocalises," 16.

73. International Crisis Group, "Best of Bad Options"; Zaina Erhaim and Jomana Qaddour, "Women in Idlib Challenge Islamic Extremists," Middle East Institute, July 26, 2017, https://www.mei.edu/publications/women-idlib-challenge-islamic-extremists; Leila Shami, "Women Are at the Forefront of Challenging Extremism in Idlib," Chatham House, July 2018, https://syria.chathamhouse.org/research/women-are-at-the-forefront-of-challenging-extremism-in-idlib; Madeline Edwards and Mohammad Abdulssattar Ibrahim, "Widows in Syria's Idlib Told to Move in With Male Guardian," *Middle East Eye*, December 15, 2017, https://www.middleeasteye.net/news/widows-syrias-idlib-told-move-male-guardian.

74. "Syria: Extremists Restricting Women's Rights," Human Rights Watch, January 13, 2014, https://www.hrw.org/news/2014/01/13/syria-extremists-restricting-womens-rights.

75. Edwards and Ibrahim, "Widows."

76. Edwards and Ibrahim.

77. Mouneb Taim, "Syrian Jihadist Group HTS Accused of Blocking Married Women from Studying," *Al-Monitor*, September 3, 2022, https://www.al-monitor.com/originals/2022/08/syrian-jihadist-group-hts-accused-blocking-married-women-studying.

78. International Crisis Group, "Best of Bad Options."

79. International Crisis Group.

80. Rose Chacko, "Ghalia Rahhal: The Idlib-Based Women's Rights Defender Fighting for Female Empowerment," *New Arab*, June 17, 2022, https://www.newarab.com/features/mazaya-female-led-initiative-promotes-womens-empowerment; Erhaim and Qaddour, "Women in Idlib"; Shami, "Women at the Forefront"; Alaa Nassar and Alice al-Maleh, "Civil Society Activist Defies War and Islamist Intimidation in Her Efforts to Empower Women," *Syria Direct*, April 25, 2018, https://syriadirect.org/civil-society-activist-defies-war-and-islamist-intimidation-in-her-efforts-to-empower-women/#.WuMjbjJqbP8.twitter.

81. Nassar and al-Maleh, "Civil Society."

82. Ghalia Rahhal, "I Have Huge Faith in Syrian Women," Syria Campaign, March 8, 2022, https://diary.thesyriacampaign.org/i-have-huge-faith-in-syrian-women/.

83. Khaled al-Khateb, "Al-Qaeda-Linked Leader Again Descends on Idlib Streets to Polish His Image," *Al-Monitor*, February 2, 2021, https://www.al-monitor.com/originals/2021/02/syria-idlib-hts-leader-public-appearance-terrorist-list.html.

84. Aaron Y. Zelin, "A Timeline of Abu Muhammad al-Jawlani's Appearances," Jihadology, May 27, 2020, https://jihadology.net/2020/05/27/a-timeline-of-abu-muhammad-al-jawlanis-appearances/; Mohammed Hardan, "HTS Leader Tours Idlib on Eid al-Fitr," *Al-Monitor*, May 11, 2022, https://www.al-monitor.com/originals/2022/05/hts-leader-tours-idlib-eid-al-fitr.

85. Zelin, "Timeline."

86. Sultan al-Kanj, "Hayat Tahrir al-Sham Leader Seeks More Support in Syria's Idlib," *Al-Monitor*, April 8, 2022, https://www.al-monitor.com/originals/2022/04/hayat-tahrir-al-sham-leader-seeks-more-popular-support-syrias-idlib.

87. Aaron Y. Zelin, "Jawlani's 'State of the Union,'" Jihadica, August 29, 2022, https://www.jihadica.com/jawlanis-state-of-the-union/.

88. "Formation of the 'Salvation Government' in Northern Syria" [in Arabic], *Enab Baladi*, November 2, 2017, https://www.enabbaladi.net/archives/181916.

89. Drevon and Haenni, "Global Jihad Relocalises," 6.

90. Drevon and Haenni, 8.

91. International Crisis Group, "Best of Bad Options."

92. Pierret and Alrefaai, "Religious Governance," 60.

93. Orwa Ajjoub, "HTS Is Not al-Qaeda, but It Is Still an Authoritarian Regime to Be Reckoned With," Middle East Institute, June 24, 2021, https://www.mei.edu/publications/hts-not-al-qaeda-it-still-authoritarian-regime-be-reckoned.

94. Regine Schwab, "Governance of Jabhat Al-Nusra," paper presented at the Islamist Rebel Governance Workshop, Graduate Institute of International and Development Studies, Geneva, October 8, 2020.

95. Haid, "HTS Attempts State-Building."

96. Haid.

97. Aymenn Jawad al-Tamimi, "A Hay'at Tahrir al-Sham Perspective on Democracy," Aymennjawad.org, February 9, 2019, http://www.aymennjawad.org/2019/02/a-hayat-tahrir-al-sham-perspective-on-democracy.

98. Al-Tamimi.

99. Author Interview, HTS02, March 2023.

100. Ayman al-Dassouky, "The Role of Jihadi Movements in Syrian Local Governance," Omran for Strategic Studies (July 2017): 10, https://omranstudies.org/publications/papers/the-role-of-jihadi-movements-in-syrian-local-governance.html.

101. Jabhat al-Nusra, "Educational Regulations Imposed in Darkush (Idlib, Sahel Area)," Aymennjawad.org, Archive of Jabhat al-Nusra Dar al-Qaḍa Documents, Specimen I, September 12, 2014, http://www.aymennjawad.org/2015/03/archive-of-jabhat-al-nusra-dar-al-qaa-documents.

102. Jabhat al-Nusra, "Closing Shops During Prayer Time: Kafr Hamra, Aleppo," Aymennjawad.org, Archive of Jabhat al-Nusra Dar al-Qaḍa Documents, Specimen F, December 24, 2014, http://www.aymennjawad.org/2015/03/archive-of-jabhat-al-nusra-dar-al-qaa-documents; Jabhat al-Nusra, "Shop Closed for Being Open During Prayer Time, Sarmada, Idlib," Aymennjawad.org, Archive of Jabhat al-Nusra Dar al-Qaḍa Documents, Specimen K, undated, http://www.aymennjawad.org/2015/03/archive-of-jabhat-al-nusra-dar-al-qaa-documents.

103. Al-Dassouky, "Role of Jihadi Movements," 8.

104. "Tahrir al-Sham Unleashes the Hand of the Goodwill Corps in Idlib . . . Smuggling Cigarettes, Islamic Dress and Mixing Are Its Main Goals . . .?!" [in Arabic], Shaam Network, April 10, 2017, http://www.shaam.org/news/syria-news/في-الخير-سواعد-يد-تطلق-الشام-تحرير-إدلب-وتهريب-الدخان-واللباس-الشرعي-والاختلاط-أبرز-أهدافها؟.html.

105. Jabhat al-Nusra, "Closing of Entertainment Stores with Billiards, Tabel Football & Computer Games—Houreitan, Aleppo Province," Aymennjawad.org, Archive of Jabhat al-Nusra Dar al-Qaḍa Documents, Specimen B, December 28, 2014, http://www.aymennjawad.org/2015/03/archive-of-jabhat-al-nusra-dar-al-qaa-documents.

106. Human Rights Watch, "Extremists."

107. Human Rights Watch.

108. Elizabeth Tsurkov, "The Breaking of Syria's Rebellion," Forum for Regional Thinking, July 10, 2018, https://www.regthink.org/en/articles/the-breaking-of-syrias-rebellion; Syrian Network for Human Rights, "Most Notable"; Khaled al-Khateb, "Idlib Residents Demand Release of Detainees in Jihadist Group's Prisons," Al-Monitor, January 26, 2022, https://www.al-monitor.com/originals/2022/01/idlib-residents-demand-release-detainees-jihadist-groups-prisons; al-Tamimi, "Idlib and Its Environs," 9; Sadiq Abdul Rahman, "From the Events of Four Days in Saraqib" [in Arabic], al-Jumhuriya, July 25, 2017, https://aljumhuriya.net/ar/2017/07/25/38504/.

109. Al-Tamimi, "Idlib and Its Environs," 9; Paul McLoughlin, "Syria Weekly: Idlib Civilians Demand No Assad, No Jolani," New Arab, November 8, 2019, https://english.alaraby.co.uk/english/indepth/2019/11/9/syria-weekly-idlib-civilians-demand-no-assad-no-jolani.

110. Isak Svensson et al., *Confronting the Caliphate: Civil Resistance in Jihadi Proto-States* (Oxford University Press, 2022), 171.

111. "Syria: Arrests, Torture by Armed Group," Human Rights Watch, January 28, 2019, https://www.hrw.org/news/2019/01/28/syria-arrests-torture-armed-group.

112. Syrian Network for Human Rights, "Most Notable."

113. Syrian Network for Human Rights.

114. Svensson et al., *Confronting the Caliphate*, 167.

115. Svensson et al., 168.

116. Matraji and Hall, "The Other Islamic State."

117. Matraji and Hall.

118. Haid Haid, *HTS's Offline Propaganda: Infrastructure, Engagement and Monopoly* (International Centre for the Study of Radicalisation, September 2019), 14–15, https://icsr.info/wp-content/uploads/2019/09/ICSR-Report-HTS's-Offline-Propaganda-Infrastructure-Engagement-and-Monopoly.pdf; *Shaam Network*, "Tahrir al-Sham Unleashes."

119. Ahmad Obeid, "Inside HTS' Most Dangerous Prison," *Syria Untold*, October 9, 2020, https://syriauntold.com/2020/10/09/inside-hts-most-dangerous-prison/.

120. Waleed Abu al-Khair, "Anger in Idlib Over the Return of Tahrir al-Sham's al-hesba," Diyaruna, May 4, 2020, https://diyaruna.com/en_GB/articles/cnmi_di/features/2020/05/14/feature-02.

121. Syrian Network for Human Rights, "Most Notable."

122. Abu al-Khair, "Anger in Idlib."

123. Abu al-Khair.

124. Mohammed Hardan, "Syrian Jihadist Group in Idlib Replaces Security Squad with 'Moral Police,'" *Al-Monitor*, September 13, 2021, https://www.al-monitor.com/originals/2021/09/syrian-jihadist-group-idlib-replaces-security-squad-moral-police.

125. Haid, *HTS's Offline Propaganda*, 8–9.

126. Miron Lakomy, "Crouching *Shahid*, Hidden *Jihad*: Mapping the Online Propaganda Campaign of the Hayat Tahrir al-Sham-Affiliated Ebaa News Agency," *Behavioral Sciences of Terrorism and Political Aggression* 15, no. 3 (September 2021): 364–383, https://doi.org/10.1080/19434472.2021.1977372.

127. Haid, *HTS's Offline Propaganda*, 9–10.

128. Jabhat al-Nusra, "Warning Against Eating in Public During Daytime in Ramadan, Hureitan, Aleppo Province," Aymennjawad.org, Archive of Jabhat al-Nusra Dar al-Qaḍa Documents, Specimen 1A, June 15, 2015, http://www.aymennjawad.org/2015/03/archive-of-jabhat-al-nusra-dar-al-qaa-documents.

129. Jabhat al-Nusra.

130. Haid, *HTS's Offline Propaganda*, 16–17.

131. Lina Rafaat and Charles Lister, "From Goods and Services to Counterterrorism: Local Messaging in Hay'at Tahrir al-Sham Propaganda," Jihadica, September 12, 2018, http://www.jihadica.com/from-goods-and-services-to-counterterrorism/.

132. Yasir Abbas, "Another 'State' of Hate: Al-Nusra's Quest to Establish an Islamic Emirate in the Levant," Hudson Institute, April 29, 2016, https://www.hudson.org/research

/12454-another-state-of-hate-al-nusra-s-quest-to-establish-an-islamic-emirate-in-the -levant.

133. Marta Furlan, "Rebel Governance at the Time of Covid-19: Emergencies as Opportunities for Rebel Rulers," *Studies in Conflict & Terrorism* 46, no. 8 (September 2020): 1446–1451, https://doi.org/10.1080/1057610X.2020.1816681.

134. Rafaat and Lister, "From Goods and Services."

135. "Idlib Is a Bright Example of Contemporary Revolutions," *Ebaa*, June 30, 2018, https:// ebaa.news/visuals/report-vid/2018/06/4631/.

136. Gerges, *ISIS*, 186.

137. Haid, *HTS's Offline Propaganda*, 19–20.

138. Hay'at Tahrir al-Sham, "Coverage of the Opening of an Exhibition to Better Understand the Holy Prophet," Jihadology, December 1, 2020, https://jihadology.net/2020/12 /01/new-video-message-from-hayat-tahrir-al-sham-coverage-of-the-opening-of-an-e xhibition-to-better-understand-the-holy-prophet/.

139. Lister, "Profiling Jabhat al-Nusra," 36.

140. Lister, 25.

141. Lister, 17.

142. Gerges, *ISIS*, 186; Gaith Abdul-Ahad, "Syria's al-Nusra front—Ruthless, Organised and Taking Control," *Guardian*, July 10, 2013, https://www.theguardian.com/world/2013/jul /10/syria-al-nusra-front-jihadi.

143. Jennifer Cafarella, "Jabhat al-Nusra in Syria: An Islamic Emirate for al-Qaeda," Middle East Security Report No. 25 (Institute for the Study of War, December 2014), 37, https://www.understandingwar.org/sites/default/files/JN%20Final.pdf.

144. Cafarella, "Jabhat al-Nusra," 38; Lister, "Profiling Jabhat al-Nusra," 12; Joana Cook et al., "Jurisprudence Beyond the State: An Analysis of Jihadist 'Justice' in Yemen, Syria and Libya," *Studies in Conflict and Terrorism* 46, no. 5 (June 2020): 566, https://doi.org/10 .1080/1057610X.2020.1776958; Hussam Hamdan, "The Sharia Board in Aleppo . . . Multiple Roles," *Al Jazeera*, June 12, 2013, https://www.aljazeera.net/news/reportsan dinterviews/2013/6/12/الهيئة-الشرعية-بحلب-أدوار-متعددة; Liz Sly, "Islamic Law Comes to Rebel-Held Areas of Syria," *Washington Post*, March 19, 2013, https://www.washingtonpost .com/world/middle_east/islamic-law-comes-to-rebel-held-syria/2013/03/19/b310532e -90af-11e2-bdea-e32ad90da239_story.html.

145. Benedetta Berti, "From Cooperation to Competition: Localization, Militarization and Rebel Co-Governance Arrangements in Syria," *Studies in Conflict & Terrorism* 46, no. 2 (June 2020): 216, https://doi.org/10.1080/1057610X.2020.1776964.

146. Cafarella, "Jabhat al-Nusra," 38.

147. Hamdan, "Sharia Board in Aleppo."

148. Cook et al., "Jurisprudence Beyond the State," 566; Hamdan, "Sharia Board in Aleppo"; Regine Schwab, "Insurgent Courts in Civil Wars: The Three Pathways of (Trans)Formation in Today's Syria (2012–17)," *Small Wars & Insurgencies* 29, no. 4 (August 2018): 813, https://doi.org/10.1080/09592318.2018.1497290.

149. Hamdan, "Sharia Board in Aleppo."

150. Cafarella, "Jabhat al-Nusra," 39.

151. Cafarella, 39.

152. Schwab, "Insurgent Courts," 808.

153. Maxwell Martin, "Al-Qaeda's Syrian Judiciary—Is It Really What al-Jolani Makes It Out to Be?," *Syria Comment*, November 9, 2014, https://www.joshualandis.com/blog /al-qaedas-syrian-judiciary-really-al-jolani-makes/.

154. Berti, "From Cooperation to Competition," 216.

155. Lister, *Syrian Jihad*, 243.

156. Cafarella, "Jabhat al-Nusra," 41; Lister, "Profiling Jabhat al-Nusra," 12; Berti, "From Cooperation to Competition," 215–218.

157. Schwab, "Insurgent Courts," 812.

158. Al-Tamimi, "From Jabhat al-Nusra," 14.

159. Sam Heller, "Keeping the Lights on in Rebel Idlib," Century Foundation, November 29, 2016, https://tcf.org/content/report/keeping-lights-rebel-idlib/.

160. Ibrahim al-Assil, "Al-Qaeda Affiliate and Ahrar al-Sham Compete for Control in Idlib," Middle East Institute, June 29, 2017, https://www.mei.edu/publications/al-qaeda -affiliate-and-ahrar-al-sham-compete-control-idlib.

161. Ajjoub, "HTS Is Not al-Qaeda."

162. Al-Dassouky, "Role of Jihadi Movements," 8–9, 12–13.

163. Gregory Waters, "The Promise of Local Councils: A Future for Syrians, by Syrians," *International Review*, November 21, 2017, https://international-review.org/promise-local -councils-future-syrians-syrians/; Agnès Favier, "Local Governance Dynamics in Opposition-Controlled Areas in Syria," in *Inside Wars: Local Dynamics of Conflicts in Syria and Libya*, ed. Luigi Narbone et al. (European University Institute, 2016), 7.

164. Aymenn Jawad al-Tamimi, "The Local Council in Kukanaya: Interview," Aymennjawad .org, January 3, 2020, http://www.aymennjawad.org/2020/01/the-local-council-in -kukanaya-interview.

165. Aymenn Jawad al-Tamimi, "The Harem Town Council: Interview," Aymennjawad.org, December 25, 2019, http://www.aymennjawad.org/2019/12/the-harem-town-council -interview.

166. "The Saraqib Power Station Supplies Electricity to the Homes of the Village of Maard-absa" [in Arabic], Radio al-Kul, March 30, 2017, https://www.radioalkul.com/p103792/.

167. José Ciro Martínez and Brent Eng, "Stifling Stateness: The Assad Regime's Campaign Against Rebel Governance," *Security Dialogue* 49, no. 4 (2018): 242–243, https://doi.org /10.1177/0967010618768622; al-Dassouky, "Role of Jihadi Movements," 13–14; Heller, "Keeping the Lights On"; Waters, "Promise of Local Councils"; Berti, "From Coopera-tion to Competition," 217–218; Aymenn Jawad al-Tamimi, "Hayat Tahrir al-Sham and Civil Society in Jabal al-Summaq," *Syria Comment*, March 4, 2017, https://www .joshualandis.com/blog/hayat-tahrir-al-sham-civil-society-jabal-al-summaq/.

168. Hay'at Tahrir al-Sham, "Notice to Local Councils," Aymennjawad.org, Archive of Jabhat al-Nusra/Hay'at Tahrir al-Sham Service Documents, Specimen H, August 20, 2017, http://www.aymennjawad.org/2015/08/archive-of-jabhat-al-nusra-service-docu ments.

169. Al-Tamimi, "Hayat Tahrir al-Sham and Civil Society."

170. "Hayat Tahrir al-Sham/HTS Impose Control Over Service and Civil Institutions in Saraqib City, Idlib Countryside," Syrians for Truth and Justice, December 25, 2017, https://stj-sy.org/en/369/.

171. Syrians for Truth and Justice, "Hayat Tahrir al-Sham/HTS Impose Control."

172. Drevon and Haenni, "Consolidation."

173. Charles Lister, "The Fight for Supremacy in Northwest Syria and the Implications for global Jihad," *CTC Sentinel* 14, no. 7 (September 2021): 49, https://ctc.westpoint .edu/twenty-years-after-9-11-the-fight-for-supremacy-in-northwest-syria-and-the-im plications-for-global-jihad/.

174. International Crisis Group, "Best of Bad Options."

175. Khaled al-Khateb, "Reshuffle of HTS-Linked Government Fails to Bring Hope in Idlib," *Al-Monitor*, December 29, 2019, https://www.al-monitor.com/pulse/originals/2019/12 /syria-idlib-hayat-tahrir-al-sham-government-protests.html; "The Salvation Government Announces the Names of the New Ministers in Its Third Session" [in Arabic], *SMART News*, December 16, 2019, https://smartnews-agency.com/ar/wires/2019-12-16 حكومة-الإنقاذ-تعلن-أسماء-الوزراء-الجدد-في-دورتها-الثالثة-.

176. Khaled al-Khateb, "Hayat Tahrir al-Sham in Consultations on Planned Military and Civil Administrations in Idlib," Chatham House, February 21, 2019, https://kalam .chathamhouse.org/articles/hayat-tahrir-al-sham-in-consultations-on-planned -military-and-civil-administrations-in-idlib/.

177. Aaron Y. Zelin, "Hanging On in Idlib: Hayat Tahrir al-Sham's Expanding Tribal Engagement," Washington Institute for Near East Policy, June 11, 2021, https://www .washingtoninstitute.org/policy-analysis/hanging-idlib-hayat-tahrir-al-shams -expanding-tribal-engagement; Mohammed Hardan, "Syrian Tribe Forms Shura Council in Idlib with Blessing from Jihadist Group," *Al-Monitor*, September 8, 2021, https://www.al-monitor.com/originals/2021/09/syrian-tribe-forms-shura-council -idlib-blessing-jihadist-group.

178. Zelin, "Hanging On."

179. Drevon and Haenni, "Global Jihad Relocalises," 7.

180. Author interview, HTS03, May 2023.

181. Author interview, HTS07, July 2023.

182. Mohammed Hardan, "HTS Finesses Tribes in Syria's Idlib," *Al-Monitor*, May 6, 2021, https://www.al-monitor.com/originals/2021/05/hts-finesses-tribes-syrias-idlib.

183. Zelin, "Timeline"; Hazar Hashmi (@Hazo9Hjhachmn6), "The meeting of sheikh al-Julani with the sheikhs of the tribes," Twitter, May 23, 2020, https://twitter .com /Hazo9 Hjhachmm9 /status /1264193921413980160 ?s =19; "Al-Julani's Frequent Appearances Between Propaganda and Targeted Messages" [in Arabic], Jusoor for Studies, May 25, 2020, https://www.jusoor.co/public/details/693/ظهور-الجولاني-المتكرّر-بين-الدعاية-والرسائل-الموجهة/ar; "Security Deployment of 'Tahrir al-Sham' in Idlib . . . al-Julani in the Camps" [in Arabic], *Enab Baladi*, May 16, 2020, https://www.enabbaladi.net/archives/384887/amp.

184. Zelin, "Timeline."

185. Elizabeth Tsurkov, "Hayat Tahrir al-Sham (Syria)," in *Guns and Governance: How Europe Should Talk with Non-State Armed Groups in the Middle East* (European

Council on Foreign Relations, 2020), https://ecfr.eu/special/mena-armed-groups/hayat
-tahrir-al-sham-syria/; Drevon and Haenni, "Global Jihad Relocalises," 7–8; Khalifa,
"Idlib and the Hayat Tahrir al-Sham," 259.

186. Dareen Khalifa "The Jihadist Factor in Syria's Idlib: A Conversation with Abu Muhammad al-Julani," International Crisis Group, February 20, 2020, https://www.crisisgroup
.org/middle-east-north-africa/east-mediterranean-mena/syria/jihadist-factor-syrias
-idlib-conversation-abu-muhammad-al-jolani.

187. "Coronavirus and the Salvation Government—Hayat Tahrir al-Sham," Jihadology,
July 9, 2020, https://jihadology.net/coronavirus-and-the-salvation-government-hayat
-tahrir-al-sham/.

188. "First Batch of Covid-19 Vaccines Arrives in Northwest Syria," Reuters, April 1, 2021,
https://www.reuters.com/world/middle-east/first-batch-covid-19-vaccines-arrives
-northwest-syria-2021-04-21/; "First Batch of Covid-19 Jabs Arrives in Northwest Syria,"
TRT World, April 22, 2021, https://www.trtworld.com/magazine/first-batch-of-covid-19
-jabs-arrive-in-northwestern-syria-46124; Gaith Alsayed, "Vaccine Campaign Begins
Amid Virus Surge in Rebel-Held Syria," Associated Press, May 2, 2021, https://apnews
.com/article/syria-europe-middle-east-coronavirus-health-bd6b38e4608915e91c7b5f3
406211825.

189. "Updates on Covid-19 Vaccination in Syria, August 2021," World Health Organization,
August 11, 2021, http://www.emro.who.int/syria/news/updates-on-covid-19-vaccination
-in-syria-august-2021.html?format=html.

190. "North-West Syria Receives Covid-19 Vaccines Amid Delta Variant Surge," New Arab,
September 7, 2021, https://english.alaraby.co.uk/news/northwest-syria-receives-covax
-delivery-amid-delta-surge.

191. Khaled al-Khateb, "Syrian Jihadist Group Opens Food Market in North of Idlib," Al-
Monitor, December 26, 2021, https://www.al-monitor.com/originals/2021/12/syrian
-jihadist-group-opens-food-market-north-idlib.

192. "Idlib Local Authorities Continue to Improve New Water-Pump Station," Levant 24,
August 1, 2022, https://levant24.com/news/2022/08/idlib-local-authorities-continue-to
-improve-new-water-pump-station/.

193. Khalifa, "Idlib and Hayat Tahrir al-Sham," 260.

194. Khalifa, 260.

195. Jalal Suleiman, "Jihadi Group in Syria's Idlib Seeks Control of NGOs," Al-Monitor,
June 8, 2022, https://www.al-monitor.com/originals/2022/06/jihadi-group-syrias-idlib
-seeks-control-ngos.

196. Suleiman.

197. "Civil Organizations in Idlib: Does Hayat Tahrir al-Sham Employ Civil and Relief Work
for Its Own Benefit?," Al-Hal Net, May 19, 2022, https://t.ly/O47W.

198. Suleiman, "Jihadi Group."

199. "Idlib Follows Suit in Adopting Turkish Lira to Shield Region from Plummeting Syrian Pound," Daily Sabah, June 16, 2020, https://www.dailysabah.com/business/economy
/idlib-follows-suit-in-adopting-turkish-lira-to-shield-region-from-plummeting
-syrian-pound.

200. Lister, "Fight for Supremacy," 49–50.
201. Mohammed Hardan, "Turkey Offers to Supply Electricity to Idlib," *Al-Monitor*, May 7, 2021, https://www.al-monitor.com/originals/2021/05/turkey-offers-supply-electricity -idlib.
202. "Turkey Admits Telecommunication Towers Into Idlib Governorate," *Enab Baladi*, July 7, 2018, https://english.enabbaladi.net/archives/2018/07/turkey-admits-telecommunication -towers-into-idlib-governorate/.
203. Lister, "Fight for Supremacy," 50.
204. Ben Hubbard, "Islamist Rebels Create Dilemma on Syria Policy," *New York Times*, April 27, 2013, https://www.nytimes.com/2013/04/28/world/middleeast/islamist-rebels -gains-in-syria-create-dilemma-for-us.html; Abdul-Ahad, "Syria's al-Nusra."
205. Abdul-Ahad, "Syria's al-Nusra."
206. Mohammed Abdulssattar Ibrahim et al., "Free Syrian Police in Northwestern Syria to 'Dissolve' Amid HTS Takeover," *Syria Direct*, January 10, 2019, https://syriadirect.org /free-syrian-police-in-northwestern-syria-to-dissolve-amid-hts-takeover/.
207. Mohammed Abdulssattar Ibrahim, "HTS Takes Over Opposition Police Stations in Northern Syria," *Al-Monitor*, February 3, 2019 https://www.al-monitor.com/pulse/iw /originals/2019/01/syria-aleppo-hayat-tahrir-al-sham-control-free-syrian-police .html.
208. Ibrahim.
209. Ibrahim.
210. "Students in Idleb Protest Closure of Universities," *Syrian Observer*, March 7, 2019, https://syrianobserver.com/EN/news/49009/students-in-idleb-protest-closure-of -universities.html; "Syria's Idlib Enclave: How Does It Work?," France 24, June 28, 2019, https://www.france24.com/en/20190628-syrias-idlib-enclave-how-does-it-work.
211. Drevon and Haenni, "Global Jihad Relocalises," 19; Solomon, "HTS."
212. Ayammen Jawad al-Tamimi, "Education in Jabal al-Summaq: Interview," Aymennjawad .org, April 27, 2021, https://aymennjawad.org/2021/04/education-in-jabal-al-summaq -interview.
213. Author interview, HTS04, May 2023.
214. Author interview, HTS05, June 2023.
215. Jabhat al-Nusra, "Closing Down 'Free Police of Aleppo' Stations in North Aleppo Countryside," Aymennjawad.org, Archive of Jabhat al-Nusra Dar al-Qaḍa Documents, Specimen C, January 7, 2015, http://www.aymennjawad.org/2015/03/archive-of-jabhat -al-nusra-dar-al-qaa-documents.
216. Jabhat al-Nusra, "Opening New Police Stations in north Aleppo Countryside," Aymennjawad.org, Archive of Jabhat al-Nusra Dar al-Qaḍa Documents, Specimen D, January 10, 2015, http://www.aymennjawad.org/2015/03/archive-of-jabhat-al-nusra-dar-al -qaa-documents.
217. Harun al-Aswad, "Syrian Free Police Disband Following HTS Militant Takeover in Idlib," *Middle East Eye*, January 16, 2019, https://www.middleeasteye.net/news/syrian -free-police-disband-following-hts-militant-takeover-idlib.
218. Zelin, "Jihadi 'Counterterrorism,'" 14.

219. Zelin, 20.
220. Gerges, *ISIS*, 186; Abdul-Ahad, "Syria's al-Nusra."
221. Cafarella, "Jabhat al-Nusra," 37.
222. Cook et al., "Jurisprudence Beyond the State," 566–567.
223. Jabhat al-Nusra, "Prohibition on Detention and Arrest by Military Factions: Salqin, Idlib Province," Aymennjawad.org, Archive of Jabhat al-Nusra Dar al-Qaḍa Documents, Specimen O, April 1, 2015, http://www.aymennjawad.org/2015/03/archive-of -jabhat-al-nusra-dar-al-qaa-documents.
224. Jabhat al-Nusra, "Implementation of Death Penalty: Qisas [Retaliation]: Hureitan, Aleppo Province," Aymennjawad.org, Archive of Jabhat al-Nusra Dar al-Qaḍa Documents, May 5, 2015, http://www.aymennjawad.org/2015/03/archive-of-jabhat-al-nusra -dar-al-qaa-documents.
225. Jabhat al-Nusra, "Stoning to Death for Fornication and Homosexuality, Huretian, Aleppo Province," Aymennjawad.org, Archive of Jabhat al-Nusra Dar al-Qaḍa Documents, Specimen 1E, August 3, 2015, http://www.aymennjawad.org/2015/03/archive-of -jabhat-al-nusra-dar-al-qaa-documents; Jabhat al-Nusra, "Ruling for Execution of Two People for Fornication and Homosexuality, Hureitan, Aleppo Province," Aymennjawad .org, Archive of Jabhat al-Nusra Dar al-Qaḍa Documents, Specimen 1G, August 1, 2015, http://www.aymennjawad.org/2015/03/archive-of-jabhat-al-nusra-dar-al-qaa -documents; Jabhat al-Nusra, "Executions for Homosexuality, Hureitan, Aleppo Province," Aymennjawad.org, Archive of Jabhat al-Nusra Dar al-Qaḍa Documents, Specimen 1H, September 20, 2015, http://www.aymennjawad.org/2015/03/archive-of-jabhat -al-nusra-dar-al-qaa-documents.
226. Jabhat al-Nusra, "Ruling of Execution for Alleged Regime Collaborators for Apostasy, Hureitan, Aleppo Province," Aymennjawad.org, Archive of Jabhat al-Nusra Dar al-Qaḍa Documents, Specimen 1F, August 1, 2015, http://www.aymennjawad.org/2015/03 /archive-of-jabhat-al-nusra-dar-al-qaa-documents.
227. Jabhat al-Nusra, "Vacancies at the Dar al-Qada: Salqin, Idlib Province," Aymennjawad .org, Archive of Jabhat al-Nusra Dar al-Qaḍa Documents, Specimen T, April 11, 2015, http://www.aymennjawad.org/2015/03/archive-of-jabhat-al-nusra-dar-al-qaa-documents.
228. International Crisis Group, "Best of Bad Options."
229. Ali Darwish, "Innocent Here; Convicted There: Two Separate Judiciaries in Northern Syria," *Enab Baladi*, February 13, 2021, https://english.enabbaladi.net/archives/2021/02 /innocent-here-convict-there-two-separate-judiciaries-in-northern-syria/.
230. Heller, "Keeping the Lights On."
231. Al-Dassouky, "Role of Jihadi Movements," 9.
232. Sam Heller, "Syrian Jihadists Jeopardize Humanitarian Relief," Century Foundation, June 1, 2017, https://tcf.org/content/report/syrian-jihadists-jeopardize-humanitarian -relief/.
233. "Tahrir al-Sham Hands Over Its Services Institution to the Salvation Government" [in Arabic], *Enab Baladi*, November 7, 2017, https://www.enabbaladi.net/archives/182737.
234. International Crisis Group, "Best of Bad Options"; Jana al-Issa and Hassan Ibrahim, "Will Tahrir al-Sham Succeed Where Others Fail? Investment in Idlib Under the

Mantle of Salvation Govt," *Enab Baladi*, September 19, 2022, https://english.enabbaladi.net/archives/2022/09/investment-in-idlib-under-the-mantle-of-salvation-govt/.

235. The video can be accessed at https://www.youtube.com/watch?v=8aIoSAeZ4wQ.

236. Hadia Mansour, "Syria: Confusion Reigns in Kfar Nabel School System," Institute for War & Peace Reporting, June 19, 2015, https://iwpr.net/global-voices/syria-confusion-reigns-kfar-nabels-school.

237. Caroline Hayek, "Universities in Idlib Threatened by Hayat Tahrir al-Sham," *L'Orient-Le Jour*, February 5, 2019, https://www.lorientlejour.com/article/1155484/universities-in-idlib-threatened-by-hayat-tahrir-al-sham.html.

238. Hayek, "Universities in Idlib."

239. Hay'at Tahrir al-Sham, "Setting Up an Independent Higher Education Council," Aymennjawad.org, Archive of Jabhat al-Nusra/Hay'at Tahrir al-Sham Service Documents, Specimen L, July 26, 2017, https://www.aymennjawad.org/2015/08/archive-of-jabhat-al-nusra-service-documents.

240. Sultan al-Kanj, "Syria's Idlib University Bans Mixed-Gender Online Groups," *Al-Monitor*, June 22, 2021, https://www.al-monitor.com/originals/2021/06/syrias-idlib-university-bans-mixed-gender-online-groups.

241. Al-Tamimi, "Education in Jabal al-Summaq."

242. Al-Tamimi'; "'Legitimate, Modest Dress . . .' New Restrictions Imposed by the 'University of Idlib' on Its Students" [in Arabic], Halab Today Tv, March 6, 2019, https://halabtodaytv.net/archives/59735.

243. Halab Today Tv, "'Legitimate, Modest Dress.'"

244. Hay'at Tahrir al-Sham, "Notice from Salvation Government Ministry of Health," Aymennjawad.org, Archive of Jabhat al-Nusra/Hay'at Tahrir al-Sham Service Documents, Specimen Z, October 22, 2019, https://www.aymennjawad.org/2015/08/archive-of-jabhat-al-nusra-service-documents; "Destruction, Obstruction and Inaction: The Makings of a Health Crisis in Northern Syria," Physicians for Human Rights, December 15, 2021, https://phr.org/our-work/resources/syria-health-disparities/.

245. Zedoun Alzoubi et al., *Reinventing State: Health Governance in Syrian Opposition-Held Areas* (Friedrich Erbert Stiftung, November 2019), 31, https://library.fes.de/pdf-files/bueros/beirut/15765.pdf.

246. Christopher Anzalone, "The Multiple Faces of Jabhat al-Nusra/Jabhat Fath al-Sham in Syria's Civil War," *Insight Turkey* 18, no. 2 (2016): 45, https://www.insightturkey.com/commentaries/the-multiple-faces-of-jabhat-al-nusrajabhat-fath-al-sham-in-syrias-civil-war.

247. "Al-Nusra imposes Zakat on the Merchants of the Town of al-Dana in Idlib" [in Arabic], Radio al-Kul, June 29, 2015, https://www.radioalkul.com/%D8%A7%D9%84%D9%86%D8%B5%D8%B1%D8%A9-%D8%AA%D9%81%D8%B1%D8%B6-%D8%A7%D9%84%D8%B2%D9%83%D8%A7%D8%A9-%D8%B9%D9%84%D9%89-%D8%AA%D8%AC%D8%A7%D8%B1-%D8%A8%D9%84%D8%AF%D8%A9-%D8%A7%D9%84%D8%AF%D8%A7%D9%86%D8%A9-%D8%A7%D9%84%D8%AF%D8%A7%D9%86%D8%A9/.

248. Hay'at Tahrir al-Sham, "Distribution of Zakat Shares to the Beneficiaries in the Twon of Muhambal in the Western Idlib Countryside," Jihadology, November 13, 2019,

https://jihadology.net/2019/11/13/new-video-message-from-hayat-ta%E1%B8%A5rir-al
-sham-distribution-of-zakat-shares-to-the-beneficiaries-in-the-town-mu%E1%B8%A
5ambal-in-the-western-idlib-countryside/; Hay'at Tahrir al-Sham, "Distribution of
Zakat Shares to the Beneficiaries in the Town of Atimah," Jihadology, July 12, 2019,
https://jihadology.net/2019/07/12/new-video-message-from-hayat-ta%E1%B8%A5rir
-al-sham-distribution-of-zakat-shares-to-the-beneficiaries-in-the-town-of-a%E1%B9
%ADimah/.

249. Hay'at Tahrir al-Sham, "Distribution of Zakat Shares in Salqin City in Western Idlib,"
Jihadology, November 10, 2019, https://jihadology.net/2019/11/10/new-video-message
-from-hayat-ta%E1%B8%A5rir-al-sham-distribution-of-zakat-shares-to-the
-beneficiaries-in-salqin-city-in-western-idlib-countryside/?utm_source=rss&utm
_medium=rss&utm_campaign=new-video-message-from-hayat-ta%25e1%25b8%25
a5rir-al-sham-distribution-of-zakat-shares-to-the-beneficiaries-in-salqin-city-in-wes
tern-idlib-countryside.

250. Hay'at Tahrir al-Sham, "The Process of Collecting Zakat in the City of Idlib," Jihadology, June 14, 2019 https://jihadology.net/2019/06/14/new-video-message-from-hayat
-ta%e1%b8%a5rir-al-sham-the-process-of-collecting-zakat-in-the-city-of-idlib/; Hay'at
Tahrir al-Sham, "Collecting Zakat from Crops and Fruits From the Agricultural and
Orchard Owners," Jihadology, June 20, 2019, https://jihadology.net/2019/06/20/new
-video-message-from-hayat-ta%e1%b8%a5rir-al-sham-collecting-zakat-from-crops
-and-fruits-from-the-agricultural-and-orchard-owners/; Hay'at Tahrir al-Sham,
"Aspects of the Work of the Zakat Committee in the City of al-Dana: Collecting Zakat
From Shops in the City," Jihadology, May 30, 2019, https://jihadology.net/2019/05/30
/new-video-message-from-hayat-ta%e1%b8%a5rir-al-sham-aspects-of-the-work-of
-the-zakat-committee-in-the-city-of-al-dana-collecting-zakat-from-shops-in-the
-city/; Hay'at Tahrir al-Sham, "Emergency Response of the General Authority of Zakat:
Assistance for Our People from Ma'arat al-Nu'man and Its Countryside," Jihadology,
December 22, 2019, https://jihadology.net/2019/12/22/new-video-message-from-hayat-t
aḥrir-al-sham-emergency-response-of-the-general-authority-of-zakat-assistance-
for-our-people-from-maarat-al-numan-and-its-countryside/.

251. "With Support of the Salvation Government Turkey private Company Accomplishes
Last Stages of Providing Power Supply to Idlib," Syrian Observatory for Human Rights,
May 4, 2021, https://www.syriahr.com/en/215590/; Jabhat al-Nusra, "On Water and Pro-
vision of Bread, Khan Sheikhoun," Aymennjawad.org, Archive of Jabhat al-Nusra/
Hay'at Tahrir al-Sham Service Documents, Specimen B, June 2015, http://www
.aymennjawad.org/2015/08/archive-of-jabhat-al-nusra-service-documents.

252. "Voices of Idlib," International Crisis Group, July 11, 2018, https://www.crisisgroup.org
/da/node/5839.

253. International Crisis Group, "Best of Bad Options"; Ruwan Rujouleh, "Splitting Civil
Society from the Jihadists in Idlib," Policy Watch No. 2858 (Washington Institute for
Near East Policy, September 2017), https://www.washingtoninstitute.org/policy-analysis
/view/splitting-civil-society-from-the-jihadists-in-idlib; Alaa Nassar and Jodi Brignola,
" 'From the Gutter to the Rain': Inside HTS's Takeover of Northwestern Syria," Syria

Direct, February 25, 2019 https://syriadirect.org/news/from-the-gutter-to-the-rain
-inside-hts-takeover-of-northwestern-syria/.

254.   *Syrian Observer*, "Students in Idleb."

255.   Nassar and Brignola, " 'From the Gutter to the Rain.' "

256.   Svensson et al., *Confronting the Caliphate*, 171.

257.   Al-Dassouky, "Role of Jihadi Movements," 10.

258.   Haid Haid, *Resisting Hayat Tahrir al-Sham: Syrian Civil Society on the Frontlines* (Adopt
a Revolution, December 2017), 7, https://adoptrevolution.org/wp-content/uploads/2017
/12/2017_11_10_HTS_Studie-eng.pdf.

259.   Haid, 7.

260.   Lina Khatib, "Is the Syrian Regime 'Winning' the War?," *Asharq al-Awsat*, March 13,
2018, https://aawsat.com/english/home/article/1203536/lina-khatib/syrian-regime-winn
ing-war.

261.   Al-Zaraee and Shaar, "Economics of Hayat Tahrir al-Sham."

262.   Al-Zaraee and Shaar.

263.   Nassar and Brignola, " 'From the Gutter to the Rain' "; al-Khateb, "Reshuffle of HTS-
Linked Government."

264.   Nassar and Brignola, " 'From the Gutter to the Rain.' "

265.   Al-Zaraee and Shaar, "Economics of Hayat Tahrir al-Sham."

266.   Nassar and Brignola, " 'From the Gutter to the Rain' "; al-Khateb, "Reshuffle of HTS-
Linked Government."

267.   Jabhat al-Nusra, "Closing of Entertainment"; Jabhat al-Nusra, "Closing Shops During Prayer Time"; Hay'at Tahrir al-Sham, "Warning to Detain and Refer to Judiciary
Anyone Openly Breaking Fast During Ramadan Dar al-Qada in Salqin," Aymen-
njawad.org, Archive of Jabhat al-Nusra Dar al-Qaḍa Documents, Specimen 1K, 2017,
https://www.aymennjawad.org/2015/03/archive-of-jabhat-al-nusra-dar-al-qaa
-documents.

268.   *Shaam Network*, "Tahrir al-Sham Unleashes"; Matraji and Hall, "The Other Islamic
State."

6. RAISING THE BLACK FLAG IN YEMEN

1.   Gregory D. Johnsen, *The Last Refuge: Yemen, al-Qaeda, and America's War in Arabia*
(W. W. Norton, 2013), 196.

2.   Katherine Zimmerman, "Al Qaeda in Yemen: Countering the Threat from the Arabian
Peninsula," Critical Threats Project (American Enterprise Institute, October 2012), 2,
https://www.criticalthreats.org/analysis/al-qaeda-in-yemen-countering-the-threat
-from-the-arabian-peninsula; Elisabeth Kendall, "Al-Qaeda and Islamic State in
Yemen," in *Jihadism Transformed: Al-Qaeda and Islamic State's Global Battle of Ideas*,
ed. Simon Staffell and Akil Awan (Oxford University Press, 2016), 92; Thomas Hegghammer, *Jihad in Saudi Arabia* (Cambridge University Press, 2010), 206–213; Victoria
Clark, *Dancing on the Heads of Snakes* (Yale University Press, 2010), 216, 232–233.

3. Gabriel Koheler-Derrik, *A False Foundation? AQAP, Tribes and Ungoverned Spaces in Yemen* (Combating Terrorism Center at West Point, September 2011), 19–20, https://www.files.ethz.ch/isn/133147/CTC_False_Foundation2.pdf.

4. Michael Scheuer, "Yemen's Role in al-Qaeda's Strategy," Jamestown Foundation, February 7, 2008, https://jamestown.org/program/yemens-role-in-al-qaedas-strategy/.

5. "The Five Letters [to the African Corps]," Document#AFGP-2002-60053, 29–30, Harmony Database, Combating Terrorism Center at West Point, https://ctc.westpoint.edu/wp-content/uploads/2013/10/Five-Letters-to-the-Africa-Corps-Translation.pdf.

6. Abu Musab al-Suri, "The Muslims in Central Asia and the Upcoming Battle for Islam," Document#AFGP-2002-002871, Harmony Database, Combating Terrorism Center at West Point, 6, 25–26, https://ctc.westpoint.edu/harmony-program/the-muslims-in-central-asia-and-the-upcoming-battle-of-islam-original-language-2/. Al-Suri's thinking on Yemen is also reprinted in Al-Qaeda in the Arabian Peninsula, *Inspire*, no. 4 (January 2010): 34, https://jihadology.net/wp-content/uploads/_pda/2011/01/inspire-magazine-4.pdf.

7. Koheler-Derrik, *False Foundation?*, 36.

8. Johnsen, *Last Refuge*, 191–194, 235.

9. Johnsen, *Last Refuge*, 144, 181–186; Elisabeth Kendall, "Contemporary Jihadi Militancy in Yemen: How Is the Threat Evolving?," Policy Paper No. 7 (Middle East Institute, July 2018), 2, https://www.mei.edu/sites/default/files/publications/MEI%20Policy%20Paper_Kendall_7.pdf; Nadwa Al-Dawsari, *Foe Not Friend: Yemeni Tribes and al-Qaeda in the Arabian Peninsula* (Project on Middle East Democracy, February 2018), 7–10, https://mideastdc.org/wp-content/uploads/2018/02/Dawsari_FINAL_180201.pdf.

10. Sarah G. Phillips, "Making al-Qa'ida Legible: Counter-Terrorism and the Reproduction of Terrorism," *European Journal of International Relations* 25, no. 4 (April 2019): 1140, https://doi.org/10.1177/1354066119837335.

11. Jeb Boone and Shatha al-Harazi, "As Yemen Unites, Will Al Qaeda Fall?," *MinnPost*, April 20, 2011, www.minnpost.com/global-post/2011/04/yemen-unites-will-al-qaeda-fall; Jeremy Scahill, "Washington's War in Yemen Backfires," *Nation*, February 15, 2012, https://www.thenation.com/article/archive/washingtons-war-yemen-backfires/; Andrew Cockburn and Alex Potter, "Before the War," *Harper's Magazine*, June 25, 2015, https://harpers.org/2015/06/before-the-war; Casey L. Coombs and Hannah Poppy, "Is AQAP to Blame for the String of Assassinations in Yemen?," *CTC Sentinel* 7, no. 1 (January 2014): 18–20, https://ctc.westpoint.edu/is-aqap-to-blame-for-the-string-of-assassinations-in-yemen/.

12. Adam Roberts, "The Fate of the Arab Spring: Ten Propositions," *Asian Journal of Middle Eastern and Islamic Studies* 12, no. 3 (January 2019): 286, https://doi.org/10.1080/25765949.2018.1546977; Helen Lackner, "The Change Squares of Yemen: Civil Resistance in an Unlikely Context," in *Civil Resistance in the Arab Spring: Triumphs and Disasters*, ed. Adam Roberts et al. (Oxford University Press, 2016), 141–168.

13. Lackner, "Change Squares of Yemen," 141–168.

14. Marta Furlan, "State Weakness, al-Qaeda, and Rebel Governance," *Middle East Journal* 76, no. 1 (2022): 14–17, https://doi.org/10.3751/76.1.11; Maria-Louise Clausen, "Islamic

State in Yemen: A Rival to al-Qaeda?," *Connections* 16, no. 1 (2017): 53–55, https://www
.jstor.org/stable/26326470; Katherine Zimmerman, "AQAP Post-Arab Spring and the
Islamic State," in *How al-Qaeda Survived Drones, Uprisings, and the Islamic State*, ed.
Aaron Zelin (Washington Institute for Near East Policy, 2017), 45–46.

15.   William McCants, *The ISIS Apocalypse: The History, Strategy, and Doomsday Vision
of the Islamic State* (St. Martin's Press, 2015), 56.

16.   Al-Qaeda in the Arabian Peninsula, *Inspire*, no. 4, 23.

17.   Nasir al-Wuhayshi, "Letter to the Brother in Command (i.e., Usama Bin Ladin),"
undated, presumably early 2011, Office of the Director of National Intelligence, https://
www.dni.gov/files/documents/ubl2016/english/Letter%20from%20Basir%20to%20
the%20Brother%20in%20Command.pdf.

18.   Al-Wuhayshi.

19.   Bin Laden, "Letter to Nasir al-Wuhayshi."

20.   Thomas Joscelyn, "An al Qaeda Commander Comes Out from Shadow," *Long War
Journal*, December 16, 2015, https://www.longwarjournal.org/archives/2015/12/an-al
-qaeda-commander-comes-out-from-the-shadows.php.

21.   Al-Qaeda in the Arabian Peninsula, "Online Questions and Answers Session," translated by the International Centre for the Study of Radicalisation and Political Violence,
Jihadology, April 18, 2011, https://jihadology.net/wp-content/uploads/_pda/2011/04
/ghorfah-minbar-al-ane1b9a3c481r-presents-a-new-audio-message-from-al-qc481
_idah-in-the-arabian-peninsulas-shaykh-abc5ab-zc5abbayr-adc4abl-bc4abn
-abdullah-al-abc481b-en.pdf.

22.   Gaith Abdul-Ahad, "Al Qaeda in Yemen," *Frontline*, PBS, May 29, 2012, https://www
.pbs.org/wgbh/frontline/film/al-qaeda-in-yemen/transcript/.

23.   Al-Qaeda in the Arabian Peninsula, "News Report Issue #7," Jihadology, January 26, 2012,
2, https://jihadology.net/2012/01/26/madad-news-agency-presents-a-new-newsletter-from
-an%E1%B9%A3ar-al-shariah-in-yemen-news-report-issue-7%E2%80%B3/.

24.   Zimmerman, "Al Qaeda in Yemen," 4.

25.   Zimmerman, 6; "Behind Militia Lines in Jaar," *New Humanitarian*, March 27, 2012,
http://www.thenewhumanitarian.org/report/95176/yemen-behind-militia-lines-jaar.

26.   Charles Lister, "Jihadi Rivalry: The Islamic State Challenges al-Qaeda," Brookings Doha
Center Analysis Paper No. 16 (Brookings Institution, January 2016), 10, https://www
.brookings.edu/articles/jihadi-rivalry-the-islamic-state-challenges-al-qaida/.

27.   International Crisis Group, "Yemen's al-Qaeda: Expanding the Base," Middle East
Report No. 174 (International Crisis Group, February 2017), 7, https://www.crisisgroup
.org/middle-east-north-africa/gulf-and-arabian-peninsula/yemen/174-yemen-s-al
-qaeda-expanding-base.

28.   McCants, *ISIS Apocalypse*, 59.

29.   International Crisis Group, "Yemen's al-Qaeda," 8–9.

30.   Clark, *Yemen*, 51.

31.   Maysaa Shuja Al-Deen, "Yemen's War-Torn Rivalries for Religious Education," in
*Return to Islamic Institutions in Arab States: Mapping the Dynamics of Control, Co-
Option and Contention*, ed. Frederic Wehrey (Carnegie Endowment for International

Peace, 2021); Barak A. Salmoni et al., *Regime and Periphery in Northern Yemen: The Huthi Phenomenon* (RAND, 2010),11–14; Marie-Louisa Clausen, "Competing for Control Over the State: The Case of Yemen," *Small Wars and Insurgencies* 29, no. 3 (May 2018): 563–564, https://www.tandfonline.com/doi/epdf/10.1080/09592318.2018 .1455792?needAccess=true; International Crisis Group, "The Huthis: From Saada to Sanaa," Middle East Report No. 154 (International Crisis Group, June 2014), 1–5, https:// www.crisisgroup.org/middle-east-north-africa/gulf-and-arabian-peninsula/yemen /huthis-saada-sanaa.

32. Brian M. Perkins, "Yemen: Between Revolution and Regression," *Studies in Conflict and Terrorism* 40, no. 4 (July 2016): 300–301, https://doi.org/10.1080/1057610X.2016.1205368.

33. Ahmed Nagi, "Yemen's Houthis Used Multiple Identities to Advance," Carnegie Endowment for International Peace Middle East Center, March 19, 2019, https://carnegie-mec .org/2019/03/19/yemen-s-houthis-used-multipleidentities-to-advance-pub-78623.

34. International Crisis Group, "Yemen's al-Qaeda," 9.

35. Daniel Green, "Defeating al-Qaeda's Shadow Government in Yemen," Policy Focus No. 159 (Washington Institute for Near East Policy, September 2019), 38–39, https://www .washingtoninstitute.org/policy-analysis/defeating-al-qaedas-shadow-government -yemen-need-local-governance-reform; Bill Roggio, "Al Qaeda Seizes More Territory in Southern Yemen," *Long War Journal*, February 11, 2016, https://www.longwarjournal .org/archives/2016/02/al-qaeda-seizes-more-territory-in-southern-yemen.php.

36. *Yemen: Confronting al-Qaeda, Preventing State Failure: Hearing Before the Committee on Foreign Relations, United States Senate*, 111th Cong., 2nd Sess. (January 20, 2010), https://www.govinfo.gov/content/pkg/CHRG-111shrg62357/html/CHRG 111shrg62357 .htm; Gregory Johnsen, "Waning Vigilance: Al-Qaeda Resurgence in Yemen," Policy Watch No. 1551 (Washington Institute for Near East Policy, July 2009), https://www .washingtoninstitute.org/policy-analysis/waning-vigilance-al-qaedas-resurgence -yemen.

37. Michael Page et al., "Al Qaeda in the Arabian Peninsula: Framing Narratives and Prescriptions," *Terrorism & Political Violence* 23, no. 2 (March 2011): 157, https://doi.org/10 .1080/09546553.2010.526039.

38. Al-Qaeda in the Arabian Peninsula, "The Collapse of the Shia Imamate," Jihadology, April 17, 2015, 48, 58, https://jihadology.net/wp-content/uploads/_pda/2015/04/shaykh -hc48¹rith-al-nae¹ba93c48¹rc4ab-22the-collapse-of-the-shc4abah-imamate22.pdf.

39. Al-Qaeda in the Arabian Peninsula, *Inspire*, no. 4, 5.

40. Aaron Y. Zelin, "English Translation of 'Umar al-Jawfi's 'The Huthis and the Coming Project' from Issue #15 of al-Qa'idah in the Arabian Peninsula's Sada al-Malahim Magazine," Jihadology, January 13, 2011, https://jihadology.net/2011/01/13/english-transla tion-of-umar-al-jawfis-the-ḥuthis-and-the-coming-project-from-issue-15-of-al-qaida h-in-the-arabian-peninsulas-ṣada-al-malaḥim-magazine/.

41. Al-Qaeda in the Arabian Peninsula, "News Report Issue #7," 1.

42. Al-Qaeda in the Arabian Peninsula, "News Report Issue #9," Jihadology, February 20, 2012, 1, https://jihadology.net/2012/02/20/madad-news-agency-presents-a -new-newsletter-from-anṣar-al-shariah-in-yemen-news-report-issue-9/.

43. Al-Qaeda in the Arabian Peninsula, "Fatwa on Fighting the Shia Houthis in the Southern Arabian Peninsula," Jihadology, January 2012, https://jihadology.net/wp-content/uploads/_pda/2012/01/al-qc481_idah-in-the-arabian-peninsula-22on-fighting-the-shc4abah-e1b8a5c5abthc4abs-in-the-southern-arabian-peninsula22.pdf.

44. Al-Qaeda in the Arabian Peninsula, "News Report Issue #7," 1.

45. Rafid Fadhil Ali, "Al-Qaeda's in the Arabian Peninsula Growing War with North Yemen's Houthis Movement," *Terrorism Monitor* 9, no. 2 (January 2011), https://jamestown.org/program/al-qaeda-in-the-arabian-peninsulas-growing-war-with-north-yemens-houthist-movement/.

46. Bill Roggio, "AQAP Destroys Tombs in Southern Yemen," *Long War Journal*, June 15, 2012, https://www.longwarjournal.org/archives/2012/06/aqap_destroys_shrine.php.

47. Henri Neuendorf, "Al-Qaeda Militants Destroy Sufi Shrine in Yemen," *Artnet*, February 16, 2015, https://news.artnet.com/art-world/al-qaeda-militants-destroy-sufi-shrine-in-yemen-255050; Sam Hardy, "Landmark Sufi Shrine Destroyed by Islamists in Yemen," *Hyperallergic*, February 11, 2015, https://hyperallergic.com/181925/landmark-sufi-shrine-destroyed-by-islamists-in-yemen/.

48. Author interview, AQ05, June 2023.

49. Farea al-Muslimi, "How Sunni-Shia Sectarianism Is Poisoning Yemen," Carnegie Endowment for International Peace, December 29, 2015, https://carnegieendowment.org/middle-east/diwan/2015/12/how-sunni-shia-sectarianism-is-poisoning-yemen?lang=en&center=middle-east; Jack Freeman, "The al Houthi Insurgency in the North of Yemen: An Analysis of the Shabaab al Moumineen," *Studies in Conflict & Terrorism* 32, no. 11 (October 2009): 1012, https://doi.org/10.1080/10576100903262716.

50. Islamic State, *Dabiq*, no. 6, (February 2015): 21–23, https://jihadology.net/wp-content/uploads/_pda/2015/02/the-islamic-state-e2809cdc481biq-magazine-622.pdf.

51. Islamic State, *Dabiq*, no. 5 (November 2014): 20–33, https://jihadology.net/wp-content/uploads/_pda/2015/02/the-islamic-state-e2809cdc481biq-magazine-522.pdf.

52. Bel Trew, "Mukalla: Life After al-Qaeda in Yemen," *Independent*, August 17, 2018, https://www.independent.co.uk/news/world/middle-east/mukalla-yemen-al-qaeda-civil-war-after-jihadi-terror-group-a8495636.html; Joana Cook, *"Their Fate Is Tied to Ours": Assessing AQAP Governance and Implications for Security in Yemen* (International Centre for the Study of Radicalization, October 2019), 15, https://icsr.info/wp-content/uploads/2019/10/ICSR-Report-Their-Fate-is-Tied-to-Ours-Assessing-AQAP-Governance-and-Implications-for-Security-in-Yemen.pdf.

53. Saleh al-Batati, "When Al Qaeda Stormed My City: Reporter's Notebook," *New York Times*, April 10, 2015, https://www.nytimes.com/times-insider/2015/04/10/when-al-qaeda-stormed-my-city-reporters-notebook/.

54. Cook, *"Their Fate Is Tied to Ours,"* 21.

55. Amnesty International, *Conflict in Yemen: Abyan's Darkest Hour* (Amnesty International, December 2012), 22, https://www.amnesty.org/en/documents/mde31/010/2012/en/.

56. Trew, "Mukalla."

57. Fawaz al-Haidari, "Relief in Yemen's Mukalla After al-Qaeda's Rule," Agence France-Press, May 4, 2016, https://sg.news.yahoo.com/relief-yemens-mukalla-qaeda-rule-115221471.html.

58. Amnesty International, *Conflict in Yemen*, 22.

59. Amnesty International, 23.

60. Katherine Zimmerman, "AQAP: A Resurgent Threat," *CTC Sentinel* 8, no. 9 (September 2015): 21, https://ctc.westpoint.edu/aqap-a-resurgent-threat/.

61. Saleh al-Batati, "Yemen: The Truth Behind al-Qaeda's Takeover of Mukalla," *Al Jazeera*, September 16, 2015, https://www.aljazeera.com/news/2015/09/16/yemen-the-truth-behind-al-qaedas-takeover-of-mukalla/; Cook, *"Their Fate Is Tied to Ours,"* 19; Michael Horton, "The Hadramawt: AQAP and the Battle for Yemen's Wealthiest Governorate," *Terrorism Monitor* 13, no. 14 (July 2015), https://jamestown.org/program/the-hadramawt-aqap-and-the-battle-for-yemens-wealthiest-governorate/.

62. Al-Qaeda in the Arabian Peninsula, *al-Masra*, no. 7 (March 14, 2016): 3, https://jihadology.net/wp-content/uploads/_pda/2016/03/al-masracc84-newspaper-7.pdf.

63. Al-Batati, "The Truth Behind."

64. Ayisha Amr, "How al-Qaeda Rules in Yemen," *Foreign Affairs*, October 28, 2015, https://www.foreignaffairs.com/articles/yemen/2015-10-28/how-al-qaeda-rules-yemen.

65. Horton, "Hadramawt."

66. Al-Batati, "The Truth Behind."

67. Ben Hubbard, "Al-Qaeda Tries New Tactic to Keep Power: Sharing It," *New York Times*, June 10, 2015, https://www.nytimes.com/2015/06/10/world/middleeast/qaeda-yemen-syria-houthis.html; Tawfeek al-Ganad et al., *387 Days of Power: How al-Qaeda Seized, Held and Ultimately Lost a Yemeni City* (Sana'a Center for Strategic Studies, December 2020), 19, https://sanaacenter.org/files/387_Days_of_Power_en.pdf.

68. Zimmerman, "Resurgent Threat," 21; Cook, *"Their Fate Is Tied to Ours,"* 21.

69. Hubbard, "Al-Qaeda Tries New Tactic."

70. Faisal Edroos and Saleh al-Batati, "After al-Qaeda: No Signs of Recovery in Yemen's Mukalla," *Al Jazeera*, January 11, 2018, https://www.aljazeera.com/features/2018/1/11/after-al-qaeda-no-signs-of-recovery-in-yemens-mukalla.

71. Author interview, AQ04, June 2023.

72. Gaith Abdul Ahad, "Al-Qaida's Wretched Utopia and the Battle for Hearts and Minds," *Guardian*, April 30, 2012, https://www.theguardian.com/world/2012/apr/30/alqaida-yemen-jihadis-sharia-law.

73. Al-Qaeda in the Arabian Peninsula, "Al-Malahim Media's Lecture 'Loyalty to the Believers' Abu Zubayr Adil bin Abdullah al-Abab," Jihadology, August 17, 2010, 4, https://jihadology.net/2010/08/17/the-global-islamic-media-front-presents-a-translation-of-al-malaḥim-medias-lecture-loyalty-to-the-believers-by-abu-zubayr-adil-bin-abdullah-al-abab/.

74. Abu Zubair Adil al-'Abab, "Gains and Benefits of Ansar al-Sharia Control of Parts of the Wilayas of Abyan and Shabwa," July 6, 2012, 18, in Associated Press, "al-Qaida Papers," republished by *Long War Journal*, https://www.longwarjournal.org/images/al-qaida-papers-how-to-run-a-state.pdf.

75. Al-'Abab.

76. Al-Qaeda in the Arabian Peninsula, "News Report Issue #10," Jihadology, March 2, 2012, 1, https://jihadology.net/2012/03/02/madad-news-agency-presents-a-new-newsletter-from-anṣar-al-shariah-in-yemen-news-report-issue-10"/.

77. Al-Qaeda in the Arabian Peninsula, "The English Translation of Statement of Qaedat al-Jihad Organization in the Arabian Peninsula Statement of Denying the News of Forming a Political Party," Jihadology, January 2013, https://jihadology.net/wp-content/uploads/_pda/2013/01/al-qc481_idah-in-the-arabian-peninsula-denying-rumors-of-forming-a-political-party-en.pdf.

78. Amnesty International, *Conflict in Yemen*, 20.

79. *New Humanitarian*, "Behind Militia Lines in Jaar."

80. Robin Simcox, "Ansar al-Sharia and Governance in Southern Yemen," Hudson Institute, December 27, 2012, https://www.hudson.org/research/9779-ansar-al-sharia-and-governance-in-southern-yemen; Abdul-Ahad, "Al Qaeda in Yemen"; *New Humanitarian*, "Behind Militia Lines in Jaar;" Amnesty International, *Conflict in Yemen*, 20.

81. Al-Qaeda in the Arabian Peninsula, "Online Questions and Answers."

82. Amnesty International, *Conflict in Yemen*, 20.

83. Abdul-Ahad, "Al Qaeda in Yemen."

84. Amnesty International, *Conflict in Yemen*, 19.

85. Al-Qaeda in the Arabian Peninsula, "From the Shariah Court in the State of Abyan of the Imarah of Waqar on the Establishment of the Hadd Punishment of God on a Group of Spies," Jihadology, February 13, 2012, https://jihadology.net/2012/02/13/madad-news-agency-presents-a-new-statement-from-anṣar-al-shariah-in-yemen-from-the-shariah-court-in-the-state-of-abyan-of-the-imarah-of-waqar-on-the-establishment-of-the-ḥadd-pu/.

86. Amnesty International, *Conflict in Yemen*, 15–16.

87. Al-Qaeda in the Arabian Peninsula, "News Report Issue #21," Jihadology June 1, 2012, 3, https://jihadology.net/2012/06/01/madad-news-agency-presents-a-new-newsletter-from-anṣar-al-shariah-in-yemen-news-report-issue-21"/.

88. Abdul-Ahad, "Al-Qaida's Wretched Utopia."

89. "Jaar After the Withdrawal of Ansar al-Sharia" [in Arabic], Sky News Arabia, June 29, 2012, https://www.skynewsarabia.com/video/30677-الشريعة-أنصار-تنظيم-انسحاب-جعار.

90. Adam Baron, "Yemen's Defense Minister Visits Zinjibar, Jaar—Freed from al Qaida-Linked Militants' Control," *Miami Herald*, June 13, 2012, https://www.miamiherald.com/latest-news/article1940567.html.

91. Khaled Abdallah and Mohammed Mukhashaf, "Yemenis Say al Qaeda Gave Town Security, at a Cost," Reuters, June 17, 2012, https://www.reuters.com/article/uk-yemen-jaar-idUKBRE85G0B120120617.

92. Sudarsan Raghavan, "In Yemen, Tribal Militias in a Fierce Battle with al-Qaeda Wing," *Washington Post*, September 10, 2012, https://www.washingtonpost.com/world/middle_east/in-yemen-tribal-militias-in-a-fierce-battle-with-al-qaeda-wing/2012/09/10/occe6f1e-f2b2-11e1-b74c-84ed55e0300b_story.html.

93. Abdallah and Mukhashaf, "Yemenis Say."

94. Al-Qaeda in the Arabian Peninsula, *al-Masra*, no. 7, 3.

95. Edroos and al-Batati, "After al-Qaeda."

96. Al-Haidari, "Relief."

97. Al-Qaeda in the Arabian Peninsula, *al-Masra*, no. 8 (March 26, 2016): 7, https:// jihadology.net/wp-content/uploads/_pda/2016/03/al-masracc84-newspaper-8.pdf.

98. Zimmerman, "A Resurgent Threat," 21.

99. Zimmerman, 21.

100. Trew, "Mukalla."

101. "A Report from an al Qaeda-Controlled City in Yemen," France 24, July 8, 2015, https:// observers.france24.com/en/20150708-yemen-mukalla-al-qaeda-control.

102. France 24, "Report."

103. Al-Ganad et al., *387 Days of Power*, 17.

104. Al-Ganad et al., 17; Al-Qaeda in the Arabian Peninsula, "News Report Issue #15," Jihadology, April 9, 2012, 2, https://jihadology.net/2012/04/09/madad-news-agency -presents-a-new-newsletter-from-anṣar-al-shariah-in-yemen-news-report-issue-15"/.

105. Al-Qaeda in the Arabian Peninsula, "News Report Issue #15," 2.

106. Kendall, "Al-Qaeda and Islamic State in Yemen," 94.

107. Kendall, 95.

108. See Al-Qaeda in the Arabian Peninsula, "Eyes on the Event #10," Jihadology, April 22, 2012, https://jihadology.net/2012/04/22/madad-news-agency-presents-a-new-video -message-from-anṣar-al-shariah-in-yemen-eyes-on-the-event-10"/; Al-Qaeda in the Arabian Peninsula, "Eyes on the Event #3," Jihadology, February 3, 2012, https:// jihadology.net/2012/02/03/madad-news-agency-presents-a-new-video-message-from -anṣar-al-shariah-in-yemen-eyes-on-the-event-3"/; Al-Qaeda in the Arabian Peninsula, "Eyes on the Event# 1," Jihadology, November 2, 2011, https://jihadology.net/2011/11/02 /madad-news-agency-presents-a-new-video-message-from-an%e1%b9%a3ar-al -shariah-in-yemen-eye-on-the-event-1/.

109. Al-Qaeda in the Arabian Peninsula, "News Report Issue #22," Jihadology, June 4, 2012, 4, https://jihadology.net/2012/06/04/madad-news-agency-presents-a-new-newsletter -from-anṣar-al-shariah-in-yemen-news-report-issue-22"/.

110. Al-Qaeda in the Arabian Peninsula, "News Report Issue #14," Jihadology, March 19, 2012, 2, https://jihadology.net/2012/03/19/madad-news-agency-presents -a-new-newsletter-from-anṣar-al-shariah-in-yemen-news-report-issue-14"/.

111. Al-Qaeda in the Arabian Peninsula, "News Report Issue #1," Jihadology, October 25, 2011, 2, https://jihadology.net/2011/10/25/madad-news-agency-presents-a-new-newsletter -from-anṣar-al-shariah-in-yemen-news-report-issue-1/.

112. Thomas Joscelyn, "AQAP Provides Social Services, Implements Sharia While Advancing in Southern Yemen," *Long War Journal*, February 3, 2016, https://www .longwarjournal.org/archives/2016/02/aqap-provides-social-services-implements -sharia-while-advancing-in-southern-yemen.php.

113. Kendall, "Al-Qaeda and Islamic State in Yemen," 96.

114. Al-Qaeda in the Arabian Peninsula, *al-Masra*, no. 10 (April 15, 2016): 3, https://jihadology .net/wp-content/uploads/_pda/2016/04/al-masracc84-newspaper-10.pdf.

115. Saleh al-Batati and Eric Schmitt, "Yemenis See Turning Point After Ousting Qaeda Militants in South," *New York Times*, October 7, 2017, https://www.nytimes.com/2017/10/07/world/middleeast/yemen-al-qaeda.html.

116. Edroos and al-Batati, "After al-Qaeda."

117. Al-Qaeda in the Arabian Peninsula, "Eyes on the Event #5," Jihadology, March 3, 2012, https://jihadology.net/2012/03/03/madad-news-agency-presents-a-new-video-message-from-anṣar-al-shariah-in-yemen-eyes-on-the-event-5″/; Abdul-Ahad, "Al Qaeda in Yemen."

118. Kendall, "Contemporary Jihadi Militancy," 9.

119. Kendall, 9.

120. Al-Qaeda in the Arabian Peninsula, "News Report Issue #15," 2.

121. Al-Qaeda in the Arabian Peninsula, *al-Masra*, no. 7, 8.

122. Kendall, "Contemporary Jihadi Militancy," 8–9.

123. Al-Qaeda in the Arabian Peninsula, "Online Questions and Answers."

124. Al-Adab, "Gains and benefits," 19.

125. Al-Adab, 22.

126. Amnesty International, *Conflict in Yemen*, 20.

127. Kendall, "Al-Qaeda and Islamic State in Yemen," 98.

128. Kendall, 98.

129. Sarah Moughty, "Gaith Abdul Ahad's Journey 'Into Al-Qaeda Heartland,'" *Frontline*, PBS, May 29, 2012, https://www.pbs.org/wgbh/frontline/article/ghaith-abdul-ahads-journey-into-al-qaeda-heartland/.

130. Simcox, "Ansar al-Sharia and Governance"; Abdul-Ahad, "Al Qaeda in Yemen"; Loidolt, "Managing the Global and Local."

131. Clausen, "Islamic State in Yemen," 55.

132. Sarah Phillips, "Al Qaeda and the Struggle for Yemen," *Survival* 53, no. 1 (2011): 105, https://www.tandfonline.com/doi/epdf/10.1080/00396338.2011.555605?needAccess=true; Moughty, "Gaith Abdul Ahad's Journey."

133. Sarah Phillips, "What Comes Next in Yemen? Al-Qaeda, the Tribes and State-Building," in *Yemen on the Brink*, ed. Christopher Boucek and Marina Ottaway (Carnegie Endowment for International Peace, 2010), 80–88; Phillips, "Al Qaeda and the Struggle for Yemen," 103.

134. Marieke Brandt, "The Global and the Local: Al-Qaeda and Yemen's Tribes," in *Tribes and Global Jihadism*, ed. Virginie Collombier and Olivier Roy (Oxford University Press, 2017), 114; Sarah Phillips and Rodger Shanahan. "Al-Qa'ida, Tribes and Instability in Yemen," Analysis (Lowy Institute for International Policy, November 2009), 4–8, https://www.jstor.org/stable/resrep10126.

135. Phillips, "Al Qaeda and the Struggle for Yemen," 106.

136. Michael Horton, "Fighting the Long War: The Evolution of al-Qa'ida in the Arabian Peninsula," *CTC Sentinel*, 10, no. 1 (January 2017): 17–18, https://ctc.westpoint.edu/fighting-the-long-war-the-evolution-of-al-qaida-in-the-arabian-peninsula/; Brandt, "The Global and the Local," 112.

137. Horton, "Fighting the Long War," 19–20; Kendall, "Contemporary Jihadi Militancy," 6–7.

138. Author interview, AQ02, April 2023.

139. Horton, "Fighting the Long War," 19–20.

140. International Crisis Group, "Yemen's al-Qaeda," 14.

141. Hussam Radman, *Al-Qaeda's Strategic Retreat in Yemen* (Sana'a Center for Strategic Studies, April 2019), 6, https://sanaacenter.org/publications/analysis/7306.

142. Al-Dawsari, "Foe Not Friend," 21.

143. International Crisis Group, "Yemen's al-Qaeda," 14.

144. Green, "Defeating al-Qaeda's Shadow Government," 37.

145. Kendall, "Contemporary Jihadi Militancy," 7.

146. Al-Batati, "Yemen."

147. Al-Batati.

148. Kendall, "Al-Qaeda and Islamic State," 96; Amr, "Al-Qaeda Rules in Yemen."

149. Elisabeth Kendall, "How Can al-Qaeda in the Arabian Peninsula Be Defeated?," *Washington Post*, May 3, 2016 https://www.washingtonpost.com/news/monkey-cage/wp/2016/05/03/how-can-al-qaeda-in-the-arabian-peninsula-be-defeated/?utm_term=.180b422c87e2.

150. International Crisis Group, *Exploiting Disorder: Al-Qaeda and the Islamic State*, Special Report No. 1 (International Crisis Group, March 2016), 31, https://www.crisisgroup.org/global/exploiting-disorder-al-qaeda-and-islamic-state.

151. Al-Qaeda in the Arabian Peninsula, "News Report Issue #16," Jihadology, May 8, 2012, 2, https://jihadology.net/2012/05/08/madad-news-agency-presents-a-new-newsletter-from-anṣar-al-shariah-in-yemen-news-report-issue-16-17″/.

152. Clausen, "Islamic State in Yemen," 59–61.

153. Al-Qaeda in the Arabian Peninsula, "Denying a Relationship with the Bombings of the Huthi Mosques in Sana'a," Jihadology, March 20, 2015, https://jihadology.net/2015/03/20/al-malaḥim-media-presents-a-new-statement-from-al-qaidah-in-the-arabian-peninsula-denying-a-relationship-with-the-bombings-of-the-ḥuthi-mosques-in-ṣanaa/.

154. Islamic State, *Dabiq*, no. 10, 67.

155. Islamic State, 67.

156. Al-Qaeda in the Arabian Peninsula, "Message from Shaykh Muhammad al-Haniq Following His Visit to the Emirate of Waqar in the State of Abyan," Jihadology, March 22, 2012, https://jihadology.net/2012/03/22/madad-news-agency-presents-a-new-video-message-from-shaykh-muḥammad-al-ḥaniq-message-following-his-visit-to-the-emirate-of-waqar-in-the-state-of-abyan/.

157. Abdul-Ahad, "Al-Qaida's Wretched Utopia."

158. Christopher Swift, "Arc of Convergence: AQAP, Ansar al-Shari'a and the Struggle for Yemen," *CTC Sentinel* 5, no. 6 (June 2012): 3, https://ctc.westpoint.edu/arc-of-convergence-aqap-ansar-al-sharia-and-the-struggle-for-yemen/.

159. Al-Qaeda in the Arabian Peninsula, "Do They Then Seek the Judgement of the Days of Ignorance?," Jihadology, April 13, 2013, https://jihadology.net/wp-content/uploads/_pda/2013/04/shaykh-ibrc481hc4abm-bin-sulaymc481n-al-rubaysh-22do-they-then-seek-the-judgement-of-the-days-of-ignorance22-en.pdf.

160. Al-Qaeda in the Arabian Peninsula, "Eyes on the Event #3."

161.   Abdul-Ahad, "Al-Qaida's Wretched Utopia."

162.   Amnesty International, *Conflict in Yemen*, 14.

163.   Green, "Defeating al-Qaeda's Shadow Government," 19.

164.   Cook, *"Their Fate Is Tied to Ours,"* 18.

165.   Abdul-Ahad, "Al-Qaida's Wretched Utopia."

166.   Al-'Abab, "Gains and Benefits," 21.

167.   Al-Qaeda in the Arabian Peninsula, "News Report Issue #17," Jihadology, May 8, 2012, 2, https://jihadology.net/2012/05/08/madad-news-agency-presents-a-new-newsletter -from-anṣar-al-shariah-in-yemen-news-report-issue-16-17″/; Al-Qaeda in the Arabian Peninsula, "News Report Issue #11," Jihadology, March 5, 2012, 1, https://jihadology.net /2012/03/05/madad-news-agency-presents-a-new-newsletter-from-anṣar-al-shariah-i n-yemen-news-report-issue-11″/; Al-Qaeda in the Arabian Peninsula, "News Report Issue #4," Jihadology, January 19, 2012, https://jihadology.net/2012/01/19/madad-news -agency-presents-a-new-newsletter-from-anṣar-al-shariah-in-yemen-news-report-iss ue-4″/.

168.   International Crisis Group, "Yemen's al-Qaeda," 12.

169.   "Jaar's Experience of Living Under the Control of Ansar al-Sharia," *Al Jazeera*, June 22, 2012, https://www.youtube.com/watch?v=Q7b8M-_oejQ."

170.   Al-'Abab, "Gains and Benefits," 23.

171.   Al-'Abab, 23.

172.   Al-Qaeda in the Arabian Peninsula, "News Report Issue #24," Jihadology, September 7, 2012, https://jihadology.net/2012/09/07/madad-news-agency-presents-a-new-newsletter -from-anṣar-al-shariah-in-yemen-news-report-issue-24″/.

173.   Al-Qaeda in the Arabian Peninsula, "News Report Issue #12," Jihadology, March 7, 2012, https://jihadology.net/wp-content/uploads/_pda/2012/03/ane1b9a3c481r-al-sharc4ab _ah-in-yemen-e2809cnews-report-issue-12e2808b3.pdf.

174.   Amnesty International, *Conflict in Yemen*, 24.

175.   Author interview, AQ03, April 2023.

176.   Author interview, AQ04, June 2023.

177.   Al-'Abab, "Gains and Benefits."

178.   Al-'Abab.

179.   Al-Qaeda in the Arabian Peninsula, "Eyes on the Event #1," Jihadology, November 2, 2011, https://jihadology.net/2011/11/02/madad-news-agency-presents-a-new-video -message-from-anṣar-al-shariah-in-yemen-eye-on-the-event-1/; Al-Qaeda in the Arabian Peninsula, "Eyes on the Event #3."

180.   Al-Qaeda in the Arabian Peninsula, "Eyes on the Event #1."

181.   International Crisis Group, "Yemen's al-Qaeda," 11.

182.   France 24, "Report from an al Qaeda-Controlled City."

183.   Hakim Almasmari, "Al Qaeda Militants Take Control of Another Yemen Province," *National*, March 12, 2012, https://www.thenational.ae/uae/al-qaeda-militants-take -control-of-another-yemen-province-1.602233.

184.   Almasmari, "Al Qaeda militants"; Amnesty International, *Conflict in Yemen*, 22; "Tribes in Yemen: An Introduction to the Tribal System," ACAPS Thematic Report (ACAPS,

August 2020), 6, https://www.acaps.org/sites/acaps/files/products/files/20200813_acaps _thematic_report_tribes_in_yemen_0.pdf.

185. William McCants, *ISIS Apocalypse*, 58; Raghavan, "In Yemen."

186. Al-Haidari, "Relief in Yemen's Mukalla."

187. Al-Haidari.

188. Amnesty International, *Conflict in Yemen*, 4, 13, 22–24.

189. Abdul-Ahad, "Al Qaeda in Yemen."

190. Amnesty International, *Conflict in Yemen*, 20.

191. Phillips, "What Comes Next in Yemen?," 77.

192. Al-Qaeda in the Arabian Peninsula, "Online Questions and Answers."

193. Al-Qaeda in the Arabian Peninsula, "News Report Issue #24."

194. Al-Qaeda in the Arabian Peninsula, "News Report Issue #12."

195. Al-Ganad et al., *387 Days of Power*, 9.

196. Al-Ganad et al., 18.

197. Brandt, "The Global and the Local," 124.

198. Kendall, "AQAP Post-Arab Spring," 47; Brandt, "The Global and the Local," 124; Kendall, "Al-Qaeda and Islamic State," 95.

199. Al-Batati, "Al Qaeda Stormed My City"; International Crisis Group, "Yemen's al-Qaeda," 11.

200. France 24, "Report from an al Qaeda-Controlled City."

201. Al-Wuhayshi, "Letters to Droukdel."

CONCLUSION

1. Daniel Green, "Tribal Boots on the Ground in Iraq," Washington Institute for Near East Policy, October 13, 2014, https://www.washingtoninstitute.org/policy-analysis/tribal -boots-ground-iraq.

2. Bert Suykens, "Comparing Rebel Rule Through Revolution and Naturalization: Ideologies of Governance in Naxalite and Naga India," in *Rebel Governance in Civil War*, ed. Ana Arjona (Cambridge University Press, 2015), 145–147. An interesting exception in this regard is the case of the Lashkar-e-Taiba in Pakistan, mentioned in this book.

3. Megan A. Stewart, "Civil War as State-Making: Strategic Governance in Civil War," *International Organization* 72, no. 1 (2018): 206, https://www.jstor.org/stable/26569466.

4. Jeremy Weinstein, *Inside Rebellion: The Politics of Insurgent Violence* (Cambridge University Press 2007), 171–172; Radha Sarkar and Amar Sarkar, "The Rebels' Resource Curse: A Theory of Insurgent-Civilian Dynamics," *Studies in Conflict & Terrorism* 40, no. 10 (December 2016): 872–874, https://doi.org/10.1080/1057610X.2016.1239992.

5. Marta Furlan, *The Exploitation of Natural Resources in the Financing of Terrorism: The Case of Syria and Iraq* (Konrad Adenauer Stiftung, March 2019), 9–13, https://www .researchgate.net/publication/319153234_The_Exploitation_of_Natural_Resources_in _the_Financing_of_Terrorism#fullTextFileContent; Patrick Blannin, "Islamic State's Financing: Sources, Methods and Utilisation," *Counter Terrorist Trends and Analyses* 9,

no. 5 (May 2017): 15–21, https://www.jstor.org/stable/26351519; Alaa Nassar and Jodi Brignola, " 'From the Gutter to the Rain': Inside HTS's Takeover of Northwestern Syria," *Syria Direct*, February 25, 2019, https://syriadirect.org/news/from-the-gutter -to-the-rain-inside-hts-takeover-of-northwestern-syria/; Charles Lister, "Profiling Jabhat al-Nusra," Analysis Paper No. 245 (Brookings Institution July 2016), 25, https://www.brookings.edu/wp-content/uploads/2016/07/iwr_20160728_profiling _nusra.pdf; International Crisis Group, "Yemen's al-Qaeda: Expanding the Base," Middle East Report No. 174 (International Crisis Group, February 2017), 17, https:// www.crisisgroup.org/middle-east-north-africa/gulf-and-arabian-peninsula/yemen /174-yemen-s-al-qaeda-expanding-base; Faisal Edroos and Saleh al-Batati, "After al-Qaeda: No Signs of Recovery in Yemen's Mukalla," *Al Jazeera*, January 11, 2018, https://www.aljazeera.com/features/2018/1/11/after-al-qaeda-no-signs-of-recovery -in-yemens-mukalla; Christopher Swift, "Arc of Convergence: AQAP, Ansar al-Shari'a and the Struggle for Yemen," *CTC Sentinel* 5, no. 6 (June 2012): 3, https://ctc .westpoint.edu/arc-of-convergence-aqap-ansar-al-sharia-and-the-struggle-for -yemen.

6. Mara Revkin, "What Explains Taxation by Resource-Rich Rebels? Evidence from the Islamic State in Syria," *Journal of Politics* 82, no. 2 (January 2019): 762, https://doi.org /10.1086/706597; Samer Bakkour and Gareth Stansfield, "The Significance of ISIS's State Building in Syria," *Middle East Policy* 30, no. 2 (May 2023): 132–135, https://doi.org/10 .1111/mepo.12681; Sarah Almukhtar, "ISIS Finances Are Strong," *New York Times*, May 19, 2015, https://www.nytimes.com/interactive/2015/05/19/world/middleeast/isis -finances.html?mtrref=www.google.com.

7. Weinstein, *Inside Rebellion*, 171–172; Sarkar and Sarkar, "The Rebels' Resource Curse," 872–874.

8. Stathis Kalyvas, "Rebel Governance During the Greek Civil War," in Arjona et al., *Rebel Governance in Civil War*, 132–134.

9. Carla Del Ponte et al., "Rule of Terror," *Cairo Review of Global Affairs*, no. 19 (Fall 2015): 55–62, https://www.thecairoreview.com/essays/rule-of-terror/.

10. Pauline Moore, "When Do Ties Bind? Foreign Fighters, Social Embeddedness, and Violence Against Civilians," *Journal of Peace Research* 56, no. 2 (March 2019): 286–291, https://www.jstor.org/stable/48595943.

11. Zachariah Mampilly, *Rebel Rulers* (Cornell University Press, 2011), 192.

12. Nate Rosenblatt and David Kilcullen, "How Raqqa Became the Capital of ISIS," *New America*, July 25, 2019, https://www.newamerica.org/future-security/reports/how-raqqa -became-capital-isis/raqqa-isis-capital/.

13. Charles Caris and Samuel Reynolds, "ISIS Governance in Syria," Middle East Security Report No. 22 (Institute for the Study of War, July 2014), 25, https://www.understandingwar .org/report/isis-governance-syria; Mona Mahmood, "Life in Mosul One Year On: 'Isis with All Its Brutality Is More Honest than the Shia Government,' " *Guardian*, June 10, 2015, https://www.theguardian.com/world/2015/jun/10/mosul-residents-one-year-on-isis -brutality.

14. Dareen Khalifa, "Idlib and the Hayat Tahrir al-Sham Conundrum in Syria," in *The Rule Is for None but Allah: Islamist Approaches to Governance*, ed. Joana Cook and Shiraz Maher (Hurst & Co., 2023), 258.

15. Sebastian Van Baalen and Niels Terpstra, "Behind Enemy Lines: State-Insurgent Cooperation on Rebel Governance in Cote d'Ivoire and Sri Lanka," *Small Wars & Insurgencies* 34, no. 1 (August 2022): 226–227, https://doi.org/10.1080/09592318.2022.2104297; Till Förster, "Dialogue Direct: Rebel Governance and Civil Order in Northern Cote d'Ivoire," in Arjona et al., *Rebel Governance in Civil War*, 204; Shane Joshua Barter, "The Rebel State in Society: Governance and Accommodation in Aceh, Indonesia," in Arjona et al., *Rebel Governance in Civil War*, 231–241.

16. Mampilly, *Rebel Rulers*, 192; Suykens, "Comparing Rebel Rule," 152–154; Kalyvas, "Rebel Governance During the Greek Civil War," 126; Vidar B. Skretting, "Tribal Engagement Strategies in the Islamic Emirate of Azawad," *Third World Thematics* 6, nos. 1–3 (September 2022): 21, https://doi.org/10.1080/23802014.2022.2111461.

17. Van Baalen and Terpstra, "Behind Enemy Lines," 221.

18. Van Baalen and Terpstra, 226–227; Förster, "Dialogue Direct," 204; Barter, "Rebel State in Society," 231–241; Schievels and Colley, "Explaining Rebel-State Collaboration," 1334–1336, 1341–1348.

19. Matthew Levitt, "The Assad Regime's Business Model for Supporting the Islamic State," *Lawfare*, September 26, 2021, https://www.lawfaremedia.org/article/assad-regimes-business-model-supporting-islamic-state; Erika Solomon and Guy Chazan, "ISIS Inc.: How Oil Fuels the Jihadi Terrorists," *Financial Times*, October 14, 2015, https://www.ft.com/content/b8234932-719b-11e5-ad6d-f4ed76f0900a; Michael Becker, "When Terrorists and Target Governments Cooperate: The Case of Syria," *Perspectives on Terrorism* 9, no. 1 (February 2015): 95–103, https://www.jstor.org/stable/pdf/26297329.pdf?refreqid=fastly-default%3Acf568fd854f9f67bb4d3748bf9d458f3&ab_segments=&origin=&initiator=&acceptTC.

20. Stathis N. Kalyvas, *The Logic of Violence in Civil War* (Cambridge University Press, 2006), 101–104; Sukanya Podder, "Understanding the Legitimacy of Armed Groups: A Relational Perspective," *Small Wars and Insurgencies* 28, nos. 4–5 (July 2017): 687–691, https://doi.org/10.1080/09592318.2017.1322333.

21. Weinstein, *Inside Rebellion*, 171–172; Sarkar and Sarkar, "The Rebels' Resource Curse," 872–874.

22. Charles Lister, "The Fight for Supremacy in Northwest Syria and the Implications for global Jihad," *CTC Sentinel* 14, no. 7 (September 2021): 49–50, https://ctc.westpoint.edu/twenty-years-after-9-11-the-fight-for-supremacy-in-northwest-syria-and-the-implications-for-global-jihad/; Jerome Drevon and Patrick Haenni, "How Global Jihad Relocalises and Where It Leads: The Case of HTS, the Former AQ Franchise in Syria," RSC Working Paper 2021/08 (European University Institute, August 2021), 7, https://hdl.handle.net/1814/69795; "Jihadist HTS, Former al-Qaeda Affiliate, Seeks 'Moderate Rebrand' to Secure Seat in Syria's Political Process," *New Arab*, June 4, 2020, https://www.newarab.com/news/hts-seeks-moderate-rebrand-secure-seat-negotiations;

Nagwan Soliman, "The New Jihadists and the Taliban Model," Carnegie Endowment for International Peace, December 20, 2021, https://carnegieendowment.org/sada /86049.

23. Abu Mohammad al-Julani, interview by Martin Smith, *Frontline*, PBS, February 2021, https://www.pbs.org/wgbh/frontline/interview/abu-mohammad-al-jolani/.

24. Lister, "Fight for Supremacy," 49.

25. "Open Letter to Dr. Ibrahim Awwad al-Badri, Alias 'Abu Bakr al-Baghdadi,' and to the Fighters and Followers of the Self-Declared 'Islamic State,' " Royal Islamic Strategic Studies Centre, September 19, 2014, https://rissc.jo/wp-content/uploads/2019/04/Letter _to_Baghdadi-EN.pdf.

26. Alexandra Phelan, "Engaging Insurgency: The Impact of the 2016 Colombian Peace Agreement on FARC's Political Participation," *Studies in Conflict & Terrorism* 42, no. 9 (February 2918): 836–838, https://doi.org/10.1080/1057610X.2018.1432027.

27. Phelan, 837.

28. Devorah Margolin and Aaron Y. Zelin, "Introduction," in *Jihadist Governance and Statecraft*, ed. Devorah Margolin and Aaron Y. Zelin (Washington Institute for Near East Policy, 2024), 2.

29. Reyko Huang, "Rebel Diplomacy in Civil War," *International Security* 40, no. 4 (Spring 2016): 90, https://www.jstor.org/stable/43828315.

30. Bridget L. Coggins, "Rebel Diplomacy: Theorizing Violent Non-State Actors' Strategic Use of Talk," in Arjona et al., *Rebel Governance in Civil War*, 99.

31. Zachariah Mampilly and Megan Stewart, "A Typology of Rebel Political Institutional Arrangements," *Journal of Conflict Resolution* 65, no. 1 (January 2021): 17–21, https:// doi.org/10.1177/0022002720935642.

32. Matthew Bamber-Zyrd, "Cyclical Jihadist Governance: The Islamic State Governance Cycle in Iraq and Syria," *Small Wars & Insurgencies* 33, no. 8 (September 2022): 1323, https://doi.org/10.1080/09592318.2022.2116182; Marta Furlan, "Rebel Governance Between Ideology and Pragmatism: Al-Qa'ida in Yemen in 2011–2012 and 2015–2016," in *Rebel Governance in the Middle East*, ed. Ibrahim Fraihat and Abdilhadi Alijla (Palgrave Macmillan, 2023).

33. Isak Svensson et al., *Confronting the Caliphate: Civil Resistance in Jihadi Proto-States* (Oxford University Press, 2022); Matthew Bember and Isak Svensson, "Resisting Radical rebels: Variations in Islamist Rebel Governance and the Occurrence of Civil Resistance," *Terrorism & Political Violence* 35, no. 5 (February 2022): 1133–1139, https://doi .org/10.1080/09546553.2021.2019023.

BIBLIOGRAPHY

PRIMARY SOURCES

PRIMARY SOURCES OF AL-QAEDA IN THE ARABIAN PENINSULA

Al-Qaeda in the Arabian Peninsula. "Al-Malahim Media's lecture 'Loyalty to the Believers' Abu Zubayr Adil bin Abdullah al-Abab." Jihadology, August 17, 2010. https://jihadology.net/2010/08/17/the-global-islamic-media-front-presents-a-translation-of-al-malaḥim-medias-lecture-loyalty-to-the-believers-by-abu-zubayr-adil-bin-abdullah-al-abab/.

Al-Qaeda in the Arabian Peninsula. al-Masra, no. 7 (March 14, 2016). https://jihadology.net/wp-content/uploads/_pda/2016/03/al-masracc84-newspaper-7.pdf.

Al-Qaeda in the Arabian Peninsula. al-Masra, no. 8 (March 26, 2016). https://jihadology.net/wp-content/uploads/_pda/2016/03/al-masracc84-newspaper-8.pdf.

Al-Qaeda in the Arabian Peninsula. al-Masra, no. 10 (April 15, 2016). https://jihadology.net/wp-content/uploads/_pda/2016/04/al-masracc84-newspaper-10.pdf.

Al-Qaeda in the Arabian Peninsula. "The Collapse of the Shia Imamate." Jihadology, April 17, 2015. https://jihadology.net/wp-content/uploads/_pda/2015/04/shaykh-hc481rith-al-naeiba93c481rc4ab-22the-collapse-of-the-shc4abah-imamate22.pdf.

Al-Qaeda in the Arabian Peninsula. "Denying a Relationship with the Bombings of the Huthi Mosques in Sana'a." Jihadology, March 20, 2015. https://jihadology.net/2015/03/20/al-malaḥim-media-presents-a-new-statement-from-al-qaidah-in-the-arabian-peninsula-denying-a-relationship-with-the-bombings-of-the-ḥuthi-mosques-in-ṣanaa/.

Al-Qaeda in the Arabian Peninsula. "Do They Then Seek the Judgement of the Days of Ignorance?" Jihadology, April 13, 2013. https://jihadology.net/wp-content/uploads/_pda/2013/04/shaykh-ibrc481hc4abm-bin-sulaymc481n-al-rubaysh-22do-they-then-seek-the-judgement-of-the-days-of-ignorance22-en.pdf.

Al-Qaeda in the Arabian Peninsula. "The English Translation of Statement of Qaedat al-Jihad Organization in the Arabian Peninsula Statement of denying the news of forming a political party." Jihadology, January 2013. https://jihadology.net/wp-content/uploads/_pda/2013/01/al-qc481_idah-in-the-arabian-peninsula-denying-rumors-of-forming-a-political-party-en.pdf.

Al-Qaeda in the Arabian Peninsula. "Eyes on the Event #1." Jihadology, November 2, 2011. https://jihadology.net/2011/11/02/madad-news-agency-presents-a-new-video-message-from-an%e1%b9%a3ar-al-shariah-in-yemen-eye-on-the-event-1/.

Al-Qaeda in the Arabian Peninsula. "Eyes on the Event #3." Jihadology, February 3, 2012. https://jihadology.net/2012/02/03/madad-news-agency-presents-a-new-video-message-from-anṣar-al-shariah-in-yemen-eyes-on-the-event-3"/.

Al-Qaeda in the Arabian Peninsula. "Eyes on the Event #5." Jihadology, March 3, 2012. https://jihadology.net/2012/03/03/madad-news-agency-presents-a-new-video-message-from-anṣar-al-shariah-in-yemen-eyes-on-the-event-5"/.

Al-Qaeda in the Arabian Peninsula. "Eyes on the Event# 10." Jihadology, April 22, 2012. https://jihadology.net/2012/04/22/madad-news-agency-presents-a-new-video-message-from-anṣar-al-shariah-in-yemen-eyes-on-the-event-10"/.

Al-Qaeda in the Arabian Peninsula. "Fatwa on Fighting the Shia Houthis in the Southern Arabian Peninsula." Jihadology, January 2012. https://jihadology.net/wp-content/uploads/_pda/2012/01/al-qc481_idah-in-the-arabian-peninsula-22on-fighting-the-shc4abah-e1b8a5c5abthc4abs-in-the-southern-arabian-peninsula22.pdf.

Al-Qaeda in the Arabian Peninsula. "From the Shariah Court in the State of Abyan of the Imarah of Waqar on the Establishment of the Hadd Punishment of God on a Group of Spies." Jihadology, February 13, 2012. https://jihadology.net/2012/02/13/madad-news-agency-presents-a-new-statement-from-anṣar-al-shariah-in-yemen-from-the-shariah-court-in-the-state-of-abyan-of-the-imarah-of-waqar-on-the-establishment-of-the-ḥadd-pu/.

Al-Qaeda in the Arabian Peninsula. Inspire, no. 4 (January 2010). https://jihadology.net/wp-content/uploads/_pda/2011/01/inspire-magazine-4.pdf.

Al-Qaeda in the Arabian Peninsula. "Message from Shaykh Muhammad al-Haniq Following His Visit to the Emirate of Waqar in the State of Abyan." Jihadology, March 22, 2012. https://jihadology.net/2012/03/22/madad-news-agency-presents-a-new-video-message-from-shaykh-muḥammad-al-ḥaniq-message-following-his-visit-to-the-emirate-of-waqar-in-the-state-of-abyan/.

Al-Qaeda in the Arabian Peninsula. "News Report Issue #1." Jihadology, October 25, 2011. https://jihadology.net/2011/10/25/madad-news-agency-presents-a-new-newsletter-from-anṣar-al-shariah-in-yemen-news-report-issue-1/.

Al-Qaeda in the Arabian Peninsula. "News Report Issue #4." Jihadology, January 19, 2012. https://jihadology.net/2012/01/19/madad-news-agency-presents-a-new-newsletter-from-anṣar-al-shariah-in-yemen-news-report-issue-4"/.

Al-Qaeda in the Arabian Peninsula. "News Report Issue #7." Jihadology, January 26, 2012. https://jihadology.net/2012/01/26/madad-news-agency-presents-a-new-newsletter-from-anṣar-al-shariah-in-yemen-news-report-issue-7"/.

Al-Qaeda in the Arabian Peninsula. "News Report Issue #9." Jihadology, February 20, 2012. https://jihadology.net/2012/02/20/madad-news-agency-presents-a-new-newsletter-from -anṣar-al-shariah-in-yemen-news-report-issue-9/.

Al-Qaeda in the Arabian Peninsula. "News Report Issue #10." March 2, 2012. https://jihadology .net/2012/03/02/madad-news-agency-presents-a-new-newsletter-from-anṣar-al-shariah-i n-yemen-news-report-issue-10″/.

Al-Qaeda in the Arabian Peninsula. "News Report Issue #11." Jihadology, March 5, 2012. https:// jihadology.net/2012/03/05/madad-news-agency-presents-a-new-newsletter-from-anṣar-a l-shariah-in-yemen-news-report-issue-11″/.

Al-Qaeda in the Arabian Peninsula. "News Report Issue #12." Jihadology, March 7, 2012. https://jihadology.net/wp-content/uploads/_pda/2012/03/ane1b9a3c481r-al-sharc4ab_ah -in-yemen-e2809cnews-report-issue-12e280b3.pdf.

Al-Qaeda in the Arabian Peninsula. "News Report Issue #14." Jihadology, March 19, 2012. https://jihadology.net/2012/03/19/madad-news-agency-presents-a-new-newsletter-from-a nṣar-al-shariah-in-yemen-news-report-issue-14″/.

Al-Qaeda in the Arabian Peninsula. "News Report Issue #15." Jihadology, April 9, 2012. https:// jihadology.net/2012/04/09/madad-news-agency-presents-a-new-newsletter-from-anṣar-a l-shariah-in-yemen-news-report-issue-15″/.

Al-Qaeda in the Arabian Peninsula. "News Report Issue #16." Jihadology, May 8, 2012. https:// jihadology.net/2012/05/08/madad-news-agency-presents-a-new-newsletter-from-anṣar-a l-shariah-in-yemen-news-report-issue-16-17″/.

Al-Qaeda in the Arabian Peninsula. "News Report Issue #17." Jihadology, May 8, 2012. https:// jihadology.net/2012/05/08/madad-news-agency-presents-a-new-newsletter-from anṣar-a l-shariah-in-yemen-news-report-issue-16-17″/.

Al-Qaeda in the Arabian Peninsula. "News Report Issue #21." Jihadology, June 1, 2012 https:// jihadology.net/2012/06/01/madad-news-agency-presents-a-new-newsletter-from-anṣar-a l-shariah-in-yemen-news-report-issue-21″/.

Al-Qaeda in the Arabian Peninsula. "News Report Issue #22." Jihadology, June 4, 2012. https:// jihadology.net/2012/06/04/madad-news-agency-presents-a-new-newsletter-from-anṣar-a l-shariah-in-yemen-news-report-issue-22″/.

Al-Qaeda in the Arabian Peninsula. "News Report Issue #24." Jihadology, September 7, 2012. https://jihadology.net/2012/09/07/madad-news-agency-presents-a-new-newsletter-from -anṣar-al-shariah-in-yemen-news-report-issue-24″/.

Al-Qaeda in the Arabian Peninsula. "Online Questions and Answers Session." Translated by International Centre for the Study of Radicalisation and Political Violence. Jihadology, April 18, 2011. https://jihadology.net/wp-content/uploads/_pda/2011/04/ghorfah-minbar-al -ane1b9a3c481r-presents-a-new-audio-message-from-al-qc481_idah-in-the-arabian -peninsulas-shaykh-abc5ab-zc5abbayr-adc4abl-bc4abn-abdullah-al-abc481b-en.pdf.

PRIMARY SOURCES OF HAY'AT TAHRIR AL-SHAM

Hay'at Tahrir al-Sham. "Aspects of the Work of the Zakat Committee in the City of al-Dana: Collecting Zakat from Shops in the City." Jihadology, May 30, 2019. https://jihadology.net

/2019/05/30/new-video-message-from-hayat-ta%e1%b8%a5rir-al-sham-aspects-of-the
-work-of-the-zakat-committee-in-the-city-of-al-dana-collecting-zakat-from-shops-in
-the-city/.

Hay'at Tahrir al-Sham. "Collecting Zakat from Crops and Fruits from the Agricultural and Orchard Owners." Jihadology, June 20, 2019. https://jihadology.net/2019/06/20/new-video -message-from-hayat-ta%e1%b8%a5rir-al-sham-collecting-zakat-from-crops-and-fruits -from-the-agricultural-and-orchard-owners/.

Hay'at Tahrir al-Sham. "Coverage of the Opening of an Exhibition to Better Understand the Holy Prophet." Jihadology, December 1, 2020. https://jihadology.net/2020/12/01/new-video -message-from-hayat-taḥrir-al-sham-coverage-of-the-opening-of-an-exhibition-to-bett er-understand-the-holy-prophet/.

Hay'at Tahrir al-Sham. "Distribution of Zakat Shares to the Beneficiaries in the Town of Ati-mah." Jihadology, July 12, 2019. https://jihadology.net/2019/07/12/new-video-message-from -hayat-ta%E1%B8%A5rir-al-sham-distribution-of-zakat-shares-to-the-beneficiaries-in -the-town-of-a%E1%B9%ADimah/.

Hay'at Tahrir al-Sham. "Distribution of Zakat Shares to the Beneficiaries in the Town of Muhambal in the Western Idlib Countryside." Jihadology, November 13, 2019. https:// jihadology.net/2019/11/13/new-video-message-from-hayat-ta%E1%B8%A5rir-al-sham -distribution-of-zakat-shares-to-the-beneficiaries-in-the-town-mu%E1%B8%A5ambal-in -the-western-idlib-countryside/.

Hay'at Tahrir al-Sham. "Distribution of Zakat Shares to the Beneficiaries in the Town of Silwa with the Participation of the Town's Elders." Jihadology, June 21, 2019. https://jihadology .net/2019/06/21/new-video-message-from-hayat-ta%e1%b8%a5rir-al-sham-distribution -of-zakat-shares-to-the-beneficiaries-in-the-town-of-%e1%b9%a3ilwa-with-the -participation-of-the-towns-elders/.

Hay'at Tahrir al-Sham. "Distribution of Zakat Shares to the Beneficiaries in the Village of Bar-isha in the Western Idlib Countryside." Jihadology, February 7, 2020. https://jihadology .net/2020/02/07/new-video-message-hayat-taḥrir-al-sham-distribution-of-zakat-shares-t o-the-beneficiaries-in-the-village-of-barisha-in-the-western-idlib-cou/.

Hay'at Tahrir al-Sham. "Distribution of Zakat Shares in Salqin City in Western Idlib." Jihad-ology, November 10, 2019. https://jihadology.net/2019/11/10/new-video-message-from -hayat-ta%E1%B8%A5rir-al-sham-distribution-of-zakat-shares-to-the-beneficiaries-in -salqin-city-in-western-idlib-countryside/?utm_source=rss&utm_medium=rss&utm _campaign=new-video-message-from-hayat-ta%25e1%25b8%25a5rir-al-sham -distribution-of-zakat-shares-to-the-beneficiaries-in-salqin-city-in-western-idlib -countryside.

Hay'at Tahrir al-Sham. "Emergency Response of the General Authority of Zakat: Assistance for Our People from Ma'arat al-Nu'man and Its Countryside." Jihadology, December 22, 2019. https://jihadology.net/2019/12/22/new-video-message-from-hayat-taḥrir-al-sham-em ergency-response-of-the-general-authority-of-zakat-assistance-for-our-people-from- maarat-al-numan-and-its-countryside/.

Hay'at Tahrir al-Sham. "Notice from Salvation Government Ministry of Health." Aymmenjawad .org. Archive of Jabhat al-Nusra/Hay'at Tahrir al-Sham Service Documents. Specimen Z,

October 22, 2019. https://www.aymennjawad.org/2015/08/archive-of-jabhat-al-nusra-service
-documents.

Hay'at Tahrir al-Sham. "Notice to Local Councils." Aymmenjawad.org. Archive of Jabhat al-
Nusra/Hay'at Tahrir al-Sham Service Documents. Specimen H, August 20, 2017. http://
www.aymennjawad.org/2015/08/archive-of-jabhat-al-nusra-service-documents.

Hay'at Tahrir al-Sham. "The Process of Collecting Zakat in the City of Idlib." Jihadology,
June 14, 2019. https://jihadology.net/2019/06/14/new-video-message-from-hayat-ta%e1%b8
%a5rir-al-sham-the-process-of-collecting-zakat-in-the-city-of-idlib/.

Hay'at Tahrir al-Sham. "Setting Up an Independent Higher Education Council." Aymmen-
jawad.org. Archive of Jabhat al-Nusra/Hay'at Tahrir al-Sham Service Documents. Specimen L, July 26, 2017. https://www.aymennjawad.org/2015/08/archive-of-jabhat-al-nusra
-service-documents.

Hay'at Tahrir al-Sham. "Warning to Detain and Refer to Judiciary Anyone Openly Breaking
Fast During Ramadan Dar al-Qada in Salqin." Aymmenjawad.org. Archive of Jabhat al-
Nusra/Hay'at Tahrir al-Sham Service Documents. Specimen 1K, 2017. http://www.aymenn
jawad.org/2015/03/archive-of-jabhat-al-nusra-dar-al-qaa-documents.

PRIMARY SOURCES OF THE ISLAMIC STATE

Islamic State. *al-Naba*,' no. 23 (March 2016). https://jihadology.net/wp-content/uploads/_pda
/2016/03/the-islamic-state-e2809cal-nabacc84_-newsletter-2322.pdf.

Islamic State. "Amni Card, Mosul Area." Aymmenjawad.org. Archive of Islamic State Administrative Documents. Specimen 32C, June 25, 2014. http://www.aymennjawad.org/2016/09
/archive-of-islamic-state-administrative-documents-2.

Islamic State. "Announcement of Beginning of School Term with List of Schools." Aymmen-
jawad.org. Archive of Islamic State Administrative Documents. Specimen H, undated.
http://www.aymennjawad.org/2015/01/archive-of-islamic-state-administrative-documents.

Islamic State. "Application Form to Obtain Licensing for an Internet hall, Mosul." Aymmenjawad
.org. Archive of Islamic State Administrative Documents. Specimen 22L, January 11, 2016.
http://www.aymennjawad.org/2016/01/archive-of-islamic-state-administrative-documents-1.

Islamic State. "Ban on Importing Iranian Food and Medical Goods." Aymmenjawad.org.
Archive of Islamic State Administrative Documents. Specimen 4X, May 28, 2015. http://
www.aymennjawad.org/2015/01/archive-of-islamic-state-administrative-documents.

Islamic State. "Call for Shops to Close During Prayer Time, Raqqa Province, Northern Region."
Aymmenjawad.org. Archive of Islamic State Administrative Documents. Specimen 38M,
April 30, 2014. http://www.aymennjawad.org/2016/09/archive-of-islamic-state-administrative
-documents-2.

Islamic State. "Call for Staff of Raqqa National Hospital to Return to Work." Aymmenjawad
.org. Archive of Islamic State Administrative Documents. Specimen 10Q, undated. http://
www.aymennjawad.org/2015/01/archive-of-islamic-state-administrative-documents.

Islamic State. "Call for Submission of Complaints: Aleppo Province." Aymmenjawad.org.
Archive of Islamic State Administrative Documents. Specimen R, December 2014. http://
www.aymennjawad.org/2015/01/archive-of-islamic-state-administrative-documents.

Islamic State. "Certificate for Passing Shari'i Course, Ninawa." Aymmenjawad.org. Archive of Islamic State Administrative Documents. Specimen 41F, August 28, 2017. https://www .aymennjawad.org/2017/08/archive-of-islamic-state-administrative-documents-3.

Islamic State. "Childbirth Operations in Deir ez-Zor Province." Aymmenjawad.org. Archive of Islamic State Administrative Documents. Specimen A, October 26, 2014. http://www .aymennjawad.org/2015/01/archive-of-islamic-state-administrative-documents.

Islamic State. "City Cleaning Receipt, Mosul." Aymmenjawad.org. Archive of Islamic State Administrative Documents. Specimen 6M, July 19, 2015. http://www.aymennjawad.org/2015 /01/archive-of-islamic-state-administrative-documents.

Islamic State. "Competitions and Prizes Urum Al-Kubra (Aleppo Province)." Aymmenjawad.org. Archive of Islamic State Administrative Documents. Specimen 13U, December 2013. http://www.aymennjawad.org/2016/01/archive-of-islamic-state-administrative -documents-1.

Islamic State. "Conditions for Travel Outside of Mosul." Aymmenjawad.org. Archive of Islamic State Administrative Documents. Specimen 6G, undated. http://www.aymennjawad.org /2015/01/archive-of-islamic-state-administrative-documents.

Islamic State. "Confiscation of a Person's Property in Deir ez-Zor Province for Not Paying Zakat." Jihadology. Specimen I, dubious date. https://jihadology.net/2015/08/24/the -archivist-26-unseen-islamic-state-administrative-documents-overview-translation -analysis/.

Islamic State. "Confiscation Slip, Diwan al-Hisba, Qayyara Office." Aymmenjawad.org. Archive of Islamic State Administrative Documents. Specimen 24T, June 5, 2016. http:// www.aymennjawad.org/2016/09/archive-of-islamic-state-administrative-documents-2.

Islamic State. "Court Judgement of Death Penalty for Blasphemy." Aymmenjawad.org. Archive of Islamic State Administrative Documents. Specimen 14D, August 29, 2015. http://www .aymennjawad.org/2016/01/archive-of-islamic-state-administrative-documents-1.

Islamic State. *Dabiq*, no. 1 (July 2014). https://jihadology.net/2014/07/05/al-%e1%b8%a5ayat -media-center-presents-a-new-issue-of-the-islamic-states-magazine-dabiq-1/.

Islamic State. *Dabiq*, no. 2 (July 2014). https://jihadology.net/wp-content/uploads/_pda/2014 /07/islamic-state-e2809cdc481biq-magazine-2e2809b3.pdf.

Islamic State. *Dabiq*, no. 4 (July 2014). https://jihadology.net/2014/07/27/al-%e1%b8%a5ayat -media-center-presents-a-new-issue-of-the-islamic-states-magazine-dabiq-2/.

Islamic State. *Dabiq*, no. 5 (November 2014). https://jihadology.net/wp-content/uploads/_pda /2015/02/the-islamic-state-e2809cdc481biq-magazine-522.pdf.

Islamic State. *Dabiq*, no. 7 (February 2015). https://jihadology.net/wp-content/uploads/_pda /2015/02/the-islamic-state-e2809cdc481biq-magazine-722.pdf.

Islamic State. *Dabiq*, no. 9 (May 2015). https://jihadology.net/wp-content/uploads/_pda/2015 /05/the-islamic-state-e2809cdc481biq-magazine-9e2809b3.pdf.

Islamic State. *Dabiq*, no. 10 (July 2015). https://jihadology.net/wp-content/uploads/_pda/2015 /07/the-islamic-state-e2809cdc481biq-magazine-1022.pdf.

Islamic State. *Dabiq*, no. 13 (January 2016). https://jihadology.net/wp-content/uploads/_pda /2016/01/the-islamic-state-e2809cdacc84biq-magazine-13e2809b3.pdf.

Islamic State. "Denial of Expelling Kurds from Ninawa Province." Aymmenjawad.org. Archive of Islamic State Administrative Documents. Specimen 8Y, July 25, 2014. https://www.aymennjawad.org/2015/01/archive-of-islamic-state-administrative-documents.

Islamic State. "Document to Pass Through Hasakah Province Checkpoints." Aymmenjawad.org. Archive of Islamic State Administrative Documents. Specimen 14I, undated. http://www.aymennjawad.org/2016/01/archive-of-islamic-state-administrative-documents-1.

Islamic State. "Early Rulings Imposed in Mosul." Aymmenjawad.org. Archive of Islamic State Administrative Documents. Specimen 10M, June 18, 2014. http://www.aymennjawad.org/2015/01/archive-of-islamic-state-administrative-documents.

Islamic State. "Educational Plans of Diwan al-Ta'aleen in Raqqa Province." Aymmenjawad.org. Archive of Islamic State Administrative Documents. Specimen G, undated. https://www.aymennjawad.org/2015/01/archive-of-islamic-state-administrative-documents.

Islamic State. "Educational Regulations Notification Distributed in Aleppo Province." Aymmenjawad.org. Archive of Islamic State Administrative Documents. Specimen 3F, undated. http://www.aymennjawad.org/2015/01/archive-of-islamic-state-administrative-documents.

Islamic State. "Electricity Generator Operating Hours and Fees." Aymmenjawad.org. Archive of Islamic State Administrative Documents. Specimen 6C, July 6, 2015. http://www.aymennjawad.org/2015/01/archive-of-islamic-state-administrative-documents.

Islamic State. "Electricity Prices in Raqqa." Aymmenjawad.org. Archive of Islamic State Administrative Documents. Specimen 9K, July 11, 2015. http://www.aymennjawad.org/2015/01/archive-of-islamic-state-administrative-documents.

Islamic State. "Employment Opportunities with the Diwan al-Hisba, Raqqa Province." Aymmenjawad.org. Archive of Islamic State Administrative Documents. Specimen K, undated. http://www.aymennjawad.org/2015/01/archive-of-islamic-state-administrative-documents.

Islamic State. "Employment Opportunities with the Diwan al-Zakat in Raqqa Province." Aymmenjawad.org. Archive of Islamic State Administrative Documents. Specimen J, December 3, 2014. http://www.aymennjawad.org/2015/01/archive-of-islamic-state-administrative-documents.

Islamic State. "Establishment of the Islamic Court, Deir ez-Zor City." Specimen 5Q, October 2013. http://www.aymennjawad.org/2015/01/archive-of-islamic-state-administrative-documents.

Islamic State. "Excerpt on a Text on Creed and Jurisprudence for Primary School Children." Aymmenjawad.org. Archive of Islamic State Administrative Documents. Specimen 3M, undated. http://www.aymennjawad.org/2015/01/archive-of-islamic-state-administrative-documents.

Islamic State. "Fatwa on Selling Passports." Aymmenjawad.org. Archive of Islamic State Administrative Documents. Specimen 2B, December 20, 2014. https://www.aymennjawad.org/2015/01/archive-of-islamic-state-administrative-documents.

Islamic State. "Fatwa on Women's Travel: Al-Buhuth wa al-Eftaa Committee." Aymmenjawad.org. Archive of Islamic State Administrative Documents. Specimen 1Y,

February 25, 2014. http://www.aymennjawad.org/2015/01/archive-of-islamic-state-administrative-documents.

Islamic State. "Form for Reception of Newcomers, Ramadi Area." Aymmenjawad.org. Archive of Islamic State Administrative Documents. Specimen 13J, undated. http://www.aymennjawad.org/2016/01/archive-of-islamic-state-administrative-documents-1.

Islamic State. "Form to Record a Case, Islamic Court in Palmyra." Aymmenjawad.org. Archive of Islamic State Administrative Documents. Specimen 35C, undated. http://www.aymennjawad.org/2016/09/archive-of-islamic-state-administrative-documents-2.

Islamic State. "Friday Sermon for Ninawa Province Mosques." Aymmenjawad.org. Archive of Islamic State Administrative Documents. Specimen 1Q, February 2, 2015. http://www.aymennjawad.org/2015/01/archive-of-islamic-state-administrative-documents.

Islamic State. "Further Internet Restrictions in Mosul." Aymmenjawad.org. Archive of Islamic State Administrative Documents. Specimen 18V, July 19, 2016. http://www.aymennjawad.org/2016/01/archive-of-islamic-state-administrative-documents-1.

Islamic State. "Hisba Regulations Against Smoking, Hit, Anbar Province." Aymmenjawad.org. Archive of Islamic State Administrative Documents. Specimen Q, November 2, 2014. https://jihadology.net/2015/08/24/the-archivist-26-unseen-islamic-state-administrative-documents-overview-translation-analysis/.

Islamic State. " 'I Am Muslim'—Primary School Textbook for Reading." Aymmenjawad.org. Archive of Islamic State Administrative Documents. Specimen 6X, undated. http://www.aymennjawad.org/2015/01/archive-of-islamic-state-administrative-documents.

Islamic State. "Imposition of the Niqab in Raqqa." Aymmenjawad.org. Archive of Islamic State Administrative Documents. Specimen 12V, January 2014. http://www.aymennjawad.org/2016/01/archive-of-islamic-state-administrative-documents-1.

Islamic State. "Increasing Penalty for Smoking, Aleppo Province." Aymmenjawad.org. Archive of Islamic State Administrative Documents. Specimen 14K, March 2016. http://www.aymennjawad.org/2016/01/archive-of-islamic-state-administrative-documents-1.

Islamic State. "Islamic State Diwan al-Ta'aleem Primary School Level One Textbook (Grades 1–3) on Creed and Jurisprudence." Aymmenjawad.org. Archive of Islamic State Administrative Documents. Specimen 2O, undated. http://www.aymennjawad.org/2015/01/archive-of-islamic-state-administrative-documents.

Islamic State. "Jizya payment receipt in Raqqa." Aymmenjawad.org. Archive of Islamic State Administrative Documents. Specimen 2X, January, 27 2015. http://www.aymennjawad.org/2015/01/archive-of-islamic-state-administrative-documents.

Islamic State. "Leave Permit, Aleppo Province." Aymmenjawad.org. Archive of Islamic State Administrative Documents. Specimen 12O, undated. http://www.aymennjawad.org/2016/01/archive-of-islamic-state-administrative-documents-1.

Islamic State. "List of Hudud Punishments (Aleppo Province)." Aymmenjawad.org. Archive of Islamic State Administrative Documents. Specimen 1C, undated. http://www.aymennjawad.org/2015/01/archive-of-islamic-state-administrative-documents.

Islamic State. "Mathematics & Arabic Language Text Books Issued by Diwan al-Ta'aleem for First Grade, Primary School, Year 1436 AH." Aymmenjawad.org. Archive of Islamic State

Administrative Documents. Specimen 1X, January 27, 2015. http://www.aymennjawad.org /2015/01/archive-of-islamic-state-administrative-documents.

Islamic State. "Medical Leave Permit." Aymmenjawad.org. Archive of Islamic State Administrative Documents. Specimen 40V, October 29, 2016. https://www.aymennjawad.org/2017 /08/archive-of-islamic-state-administrative-documents-3.

Islamic State. "Note for Providing Aid to Displaced Persons from Salah al-Din Province." Aymmenjawad.org. Archive of Islamic State Administrative Documents. Specimen 40L, undated. https://www.aymennjawad.org/2017/08/archive-of-islamic-state-administrative -documents-3.

Islamic State. "Note on Punishing Those Who Try to Flee to the Abode of Kufr." Aymmenjawad .org. Archive of Islamic State Administrative Documents. Specimen 34V, unclear date. http:// www.aymennjawad.org/2016/09/archive-of-islamic-state-administrative-documents-2.

Islamic State. "Notice on Buying Sex Slaves, Homs Province." Aymmenjawad.org. Archive of Islamic State Administrative Documents. Specimen 13Y, June 15, 2015. http://www .aymennjawad.org/2016/01/archive-of-islamic-state-administrative-documents-1.

Islamic State. "Notice to Internet Cafes, Raqqa Province." Aymmenjawad.org. Archive of Islamic State Administrative Documents. Specimen 6L, July 19, 2015. http://www .aymennjawad.org/2015/01/archive-of-islamic-state-administrative-documents.

Islamic State. "Notice to Members of Ramadi Teaching Hospital." Aymmenjawad.org. Archive of Islamic State Administrative Documents. Specimen 4B, May 18, 2015. http://www .aymennjawad.org/2015/01/archive-of-islamic-state-administrative-documents.

Islamic State. "Notice to the Employees of the Gasworks in Ramadi." Aymmenjawad.org. Archive of Islamic State Administrative Documents. Specimen 4Z, June 10, 2015. http:// www.aymennjawad.org/2015/01/archive-of-islamic-state-administrative-documents.

Islamic State. "Notification for Kurds to Leave Raqqa City." Aymmenjawad.org. Archive of Islamic State Administrative Documents. Specimen 5M, undated. https://www.aymennjawad .org/2015/01/archive-of-islamic-state-administrative-documents.

Islamic State. "Notification from the Diwan al-Siha in Aleppo Province." Specimen 13T, January 2015. http://www.aymennjawad.org/2016/01/archive-of-islamic-state-administrative -documents-1.

Islamic State. "Notification to Kurds Wishing to Reside in Raqqa Province." Aymmenjawad.org. Archive of Islamic State Administrative Documents. Specimen 37R, December 1, 2015. https:// www.aymennjawad.org/2016/09/archive-of-islamic-state-administrative-documents-2.

Islamic State. "On Movement of Women and the Garages: Raqqa Province." Aymmenjawad .org. Archive of Islamic State Administrative Documents. Specimen M, undated. http:// www.aymennjawad.org/2015/01/archive-of-islamic-state-administrative-documents.

Islamic State. "On Zakat al-Fitr, Aleppo Province." Aymmenjawad.org. Archive of Islamic State Administrative Documents. Specimen 2U, undated. http://www.aymennjawad.org/2015/01 /archive-of-islamic-state-administrative-documents.

Islamic State. "Opening of College for Sharia Sciences in Ninawa." Aymmenjawad.org. Archive of Islamic State Administrative Documents. Specimen 27V, unintelligible date. https://www .aymennjawad.org/2016/09/archive-of-islamic-state-administrative-documents-2.

Islamic State. "Opening of Kindergarten Center, Raqqa Province." Aymmenjawad.org. Archive of Islamic State Administrative Documents. Specimen 2W, April 4, 2015. http://www .aymennjawad.org/2015/01/archive-of-islamic-state-administrative-documents.

Islamic State. "Opening of Schools in Raqqa for Children of English-Speaking Foreign Fighters." Aymmenjawad.org. Archive of Islamic State Administrative Documents. Specimen 1W, undated. http://www.aymennjawad.org/2015/01/archive-of-islamic-state -administrative-documents.

Islamic State. "Opening of Sharia Institute for Men." Aymmenjawad.org. Archive of Islamic State Administrative Documents. Specimen D, undated. http://www.aymennjawad.org /15961/aspects-of-islamic-state-is-administration-in.

Islamic State. "Order to Close Shops During Prayer Time, Ramadi." Aymmenjawad.org. Archive of Islamic State Administrative Documents. Specimen 10G, May 29, 2015. http:// www.aymennjawad.org/2015/01/archive-of-islamic-state-administrative-documents.

Islamic State. "The Original Fatwa on Yezidis." Aymmenjawad.org. Archive of Islamic State Administrative Documents. Specimen 43T, August 9, 2014. https://www.aymennjawad.org /2017/08/archive-of-islamic-state-administrative-documents-3.

Islamic State. "Payment of 800 Syrian Pounds for Phone Subscription Service, Aleppo Province." Aymmenjawad.org. Archive of Islamic State Administrative Documents. Specimen 38N, undated. http://www.aymennjawad.org/2016/09/archive-of-islamic -state-administrative-documents-2.

Islamic State. "Permission Slip for Travel to Kuwait." Aymmenjawad.org. Archive of Islamic State Administrative Documents. Specimen 2J, October 25, 2014. http://www.aymennjawad .org/2015/01/archive-of-islamic-state-administrative-documents.

Islamic State. "Prohibition on Gender Mixing, Manbij, Aleppo Province." Aymmenjawad.org. Archive of Islamic State Administrative Documents. Specimen 7Y, February 28, 2014. http:// www.aymennjawad.org/2015/01/archive-of-islamic-state-administrative-documents.

Islamic State. "Prohibition on Shaving Beards." Aymmenjawad.org. Archive of Islamic State Administrative Documents. Specimen 6J, June 20, 2015. http://www.aymennjawad.org/2015 /01/archive-of-islamic-state-administrative-documents.

Islamic State. "Promise Not to Commit a Certain Offense Again." Aymmenjawad.org. Archive of Islamic State Administrative Documents. Specimen 18R, undated. https://www .aymennjawad.org/2016/01/archive-of-islamic-state-administrative-documents-1.

Islamic State. "Proof of Ownership of a Sex Slave, Mosul." Aymmenjawad.org. Archive of Islamic State Administrative Documents. Specimen 36L, August 16, 2016. http://www .aymennjawad.org/2016/09/archive-of-islamic-state-administrative-documents-2.

Islamic State. "Qur'an Memorization Competition (Raqqa Province)." Aymmenjawad.org. Archive of Islamic State Administrative Documents. Specimen I, September 2014. http:// www.aymennjawad.org/2015/01/archive-of-islamic-state-administrative-documents.

Islamic State. "Recruiting for the Diwan al-Ta'aleem, Ninawa Province." Aymmenjawad.org. Archive of Islamic State Administrative Documents. Specimen 17C, undated. http://www .aymennjawad.org/2016/01/archive-of-islamic-state-administrative-documents-1.

Islamic State. "Regulations on Internet Connections, 'Euphrates Province'—Albukamal." Aymmenjawad.org. Archive of Islamic State Administrative Documents. Specimen 7I, undated. http://www.aymennjawad.org/2015/01/archive-of-islamic-state-administrative -documents.

Islamic State. "Regulations on Sale of Child Sabaya with Prices, Wilayat al-Jazeera." Aymmen- jawad.org. Archive of Islamic State Administrative Documents. Specimen 44C, July 11, 2015. https://www.aymennjawad.org/2017/08/archive-of-islamic-state-administrative-docu ments-3.

Islamic State. "Repentance Cards, North Baghdad Province." Aymmenjawad.org. Archive of Islamic State Administrative Documents. Specimen 12L, August–September 2014. http:// www.aymennjawad.org/2016/01/archive-of-islamic-state-administrative-documents-1.

Islamic State. "Reprimand Penalties for Various Offences." Aymmenjawad.org. Archive of Islamic State Administrative Documents. Specimen 13S, 2014. http://www.aymennjawad .org/2016/01/archive-of-islamic-state-administrative-documents-1.

Islamic State. "Restrictions on Phone Use, Fallujah." Aymmenjawad.org. Archive of Islamic State Administrative Documents. Specimen 15J, May 31, 2016. http://www.aymennjawad .org/2016/01/archive-of-islamic-state-administrative-documents-1.

Islamic State. "Restrictions on Women's Clothing, Tel Abiyad, Raqqa Province." Aymmen- jawad.org. Archive of Islamic State Administrative Documents. Specimen 1I, Decem- ber 2013. http://www.aymennjawad.org/2015/01/archive-of-islamic-state-administrative -documents.

Islamic State. "Sharia Session for teachers, Raqqa province." Aymmenjawad.org. Archive of Islamic State Administrative Documents. Specimen L, undated. http://www.aymennjawad .org/2015/01/archive-of-islamic-state-administrative-documents.

Islamic State. "Shops and Cleaning Services, Manbij." Aymmenjawad.org. Archive of Islamic State Administrative Documents. Specimen 2S, September 2014. http://www.aymennjawad .org/2015/01/archive-of-islamic-state-administrative-documents.

Islamic State. "Statement on Punishment for Theft, Deir ez-Zor Province." Aymmenjawad.org. Archive of Islamic State Administrative Documents. Specimen 6F, undated. http://www .aymennjawad.org/2015/01/archive-of-islamic-state-administrative-documents.

Islamic State. "Summary of Various General Administrative Decisions from the Delegated Committee." Aymmenjawad.org. Archive of Islamic State Administrative Documents. Specimen 25J, August–September 2015. https://www.aymennjawad.org/2016/09/archive-of -islamic-state-administrative-documents-2.

Islamic State. "32 Islamic State Fatwas." Translated by Cole Bunzel. Jihadica, March 2, 2015. http://www.jihadica.com/32-islamic-state-fatwas/.

Islamic State. "Training Session for Teachers in Aleppo Province, May 2014." Aymmenjawad .org. Archive of Islamic State Administrative Documents. Specimen 3A, May 2014. http:// www.aymennjawad.org/2015/01/archive-of-islamic-state-administrative-documents.

Islamic State. "Transactions for Sabaya, Wilayat al-Jazeera." Aymmenjawad.org. Archive of Islamic State Administrative Documents. Specimen 44B, June 16, 2016. https://www .aymennjawad.org/2017/08/archive-of-islamic-state-administrative-documents-3.

Islamic State. "Travel Document, Deir az-Zor Province." Aymmenjawad.org. Archive of Islamic State Administrative Documents. Specimen 26K, undated. http://www.aymennjawad.org /2016/09/archive-of-islamic-state-administrative-documents-2.

Islamic State. "Travel Slip from 'Euphrates Province' to Damascus." Aymmenjawad.org. Archive of Islamic State Administrative Documents. Specimen 14N, undated. http://www .aymennjawad.org/2016/01/archive-of-islamic-state-administrative-documents-1.

Islamic State. "Ultimatum for Medical Professionals and Academics to Return to IS-Held Areas, Ninawa Province." Aymmenjawad.org. Archive of Islamic State Administrative Documents. Specimen 5I, May 18, 2015. http://www.aymennjawad.org/2015/01/archive-of -islamic-state-administrative-documents.

Islamic State. "Ultimatum for Owner of Medical Establishment to Return, Hasakah Province." Aymmenjawad.org. Archive of Islamic State Administrative Documents. Specimen 8O, August 26, 2015. http://www.aymennjawad.org/2015/01/archive-of-islamic-state -administrative-documents.

Islamic State. "Ultimatum for the Christians in Mosul." Aymmenjawad.org. Archive of Islamic State Administrative Documents. Specimen S, January 27, 2015. http://www.aymennjawad .org/2015/01/archive-of-islamic-state-administrative-documents.

Islamic State. "Ultimatum to Confiscate Property of Those Who Have Illegally Left Islamic State Territory." Aymmenjawad.org. Archive of Islamic State Administrative Documents. Specimen 25I, August 2016. http://www.aymennjawad.org/2016/09/archive-of-islamic-state -administrative-documents-2.

Islamic State. "Water and Municipality Services Tax Receipt, Euphrates Province." Aymmenjawad.org. Archive of Islamic State Administrative Documents. Specimen 29V, undated. http://www.aymennjawad.org/2016/09/archive-of-islamic-state-administrative -documents-2.

Islamic State. "Willingness to Address Grievances of People Against Personnel Tel Abiyad." Specimen 38K, March 8, 2014. http://www.aymennjawad.org/2016/09/archive-of-islamic -state-administrative-documents-2.

Islamic State. "Zakat Receipts, al-Ba'aj and Tel Abtah." Aymmenjawad.org. Archive of Islamic State Administrative Documents. Specimen 31J, undated. http://www.aymennjawad.org /2016/09/archive-of-islamic-state-administrative-documents-2.

PRIMARY SOURCES OF JABHAT AL-NUSRA

Jabhat al-Nusra. "Closing Down 'Free Police of Aleppo' Stations in North Aleppo Countryside." Aymmenjawad.org. Archive of Jabhat al-Nusra Dar al-Qaḍa Documents. Specimen C, January 7, 2015. http://www.aymennjawad.org/2015/03/archive-of-jabhat-al-nusra-dar-al -qaa-documents.

Jabhat al-Nusra. "Closing of Entertainment Stores with Billiards, Tabel Football & Computer Games—Houreitan, Aleppo Province." Aymmenjawad.org. Archive of Jabhat al-Nusra Dar al-Qaḍa Documents. Specimen B, December 28, 2014. http://www.aymennjawad.org/2015 /03/archive-of-jabhat-al-nusra-dar-al-qaa-documents.

Jabhat al-Nusra. "Closing Shops During Prayer Time: Kafr Hamra, Aleppo." Aymmenjawad .org. Archive of Jabhat al-Nusra Dar al-Qaḍa Documents. Specimen F, December 24, 2014. http://www.aymennjawad.org/2015/03/archive-of-jabhat-al-nusra-dar-al-qaa-documents.

Jabhat al-Nusra. "Educational Regulations Imposed in Darkush (Idlib, Sahel area)." Aymmenjawad.org. Archive of Jabhat al-Nusra Dar al-Qaḍa Documents. Specimen I, September 12, 2014. http://www.aymennjawad.org/2015/03/archive-of-jabhat-al-nusra-dar-al-qaa-documents.

Jabhat al-Nusra. "Executions for Homosexuality, Hureitan, Aleppo Province." Aymmenjawad.org. Archive of Jabhat al-Nusra Dar al-Qaḍa Documents. Specimen 1H, September 20, 2015. http://www.aymennjawad.org/2015/03/archive-of-jabhat-al-nusra-dar-al-qaa-documents.

Jabhat al-Nusra. "Implementation of Death Penalty: Qisas [Retaliation]: Hureitan, Aleppo Province." Aymmenjawad.org. Archive of Jabhat al-Nusra Dar al-Qaḍa Documents. May 5, 2015. http://www.aymennjawad.org/2015/03/archive-of-jabhat-al-nusra-dar-al-qaa-documents.

Jabhat al-Nusra. "Opening New Police Stations in North Aleppo Countryside." Aymmenjawad.org. Archive of Jabhat al-Nusra Dar al-Qaḍa Documents. Specimen D, January 10, 2015. http://www.aymennjawad.org/2015/03/archive-of-jabhat-al-nusra-dar-al-qaa-documents.

Jabhat al-Nusra. "Prohibition on Detention and Arrest by Military Factions: Salqin, Idlib Province." Aymmenjawad.org. Archive of Jabhat al-Nusra Dar al-Qaḍa Documents. Specimen O, April 1, 2015. http://www.aymennjawad.org/2015/03/archive-of-jabhat-al-nusra-dar-al-qaa-documents.

Jabhat al-Nusra. "Ruling for Execution of Two People for Fornication and Homosexuality, Hureitan, Aleppo Province." Aymmenjawad.org. Archive of Jabhat al-Nusra Dar al-Qaḍa Documents. Specimen 1G, August 1, 2015. http://www.aymennjawad.org/2015/03/archive-of-jabhat-al-nusra-dar-al-qaa-documents.

Jabhat al-Nusra. "Ruling of Execution for Alleged Regime Collaborators for Apostasy, Hureitan, Aleppo Province." Aymmenjawad.org. Archive of Jabhat al-Nusra Dar al-Qaḍa Documents. Specimen 1F, August 1, 2015. http://www.aymennjawad.org/2015/03/archive-of-jabhat-al-nusra-dar-al-qaa-documents.

Jabhat al-Nusra. "Shop Closed for Being Open During Prayer Time, Sarmada, Idlib." Aymmenjawad.org. Archive of Jabhat al-Nusra Dar al-Qaḍa Documents. Specimen K, undated. http://www.aymennjawad.org/2015/03/archive-of-jabhat-al-nusra-dar-al-qaa-documents.

Jabhat al-Nusra. "Stoning to Death for Fornication and Homosexuality, Huretian, Aleppo Province." Aymmenjawad.org. Archive of Jabhat al-Nusra Dar al-Qaḍa Documents. Specimen 1E, August 3, 2015. http://www.aymennjawad.org/2015/03/archive-of-jabhat-al-nusra-dar-al-qaa-documents.

Jabhat al-Nusra. "Vacancies at the Dar al-Qada: Salqin, Idlib Province." Aymmenjawad.org. Archive of Jabhat al-Nusra Dar al-Qaḍa Documents. Specimen T, April 11, 2015. http://www.aymennjawad.org/2015/03/archive-of-jabhat-al-nusra-dar-al-qaa-documents.

Jabhat al-Nusra. "Warning Against Eating in Public During Daytime in Ramadan, Hureitan, Aleppo Province." Aymmenjawad.org. Archive of Jabhat al-Nusra Dar al-Qaḍa Documents. Specimen 1A, June 15, 2015. http://www.aymennjawad.org/2015/03/archive-of-jabhat-al-nusra-dar-al-qaa-documents.

Jabhat al-Nusra. "On Water and Provision of Bread, Khan Sheikhoun." Aymmenjawad.org. Archive of Jabhat al-Nusra/Hayʾat Tahrir al-Sham Service Documents. Specimen B, June 2015. http://www.aymennjawad.org/2015/08/archive-of-jabhat-al-nusra-service-documents.

SECONDARY SOURCES

ʿAbab, Abu Zubair ʿAdil al-. "Gains and Benefits of Ansar al-Sharia Control of Parts of the Wilayas of Abyan and Shabwa." July 6, 2012. In Associated Press, "al-Qaeda Papers." Republished by *Long War Journal*. https://www.longwarjournal.org/images/al-qaida-papers -how-to-run-a-state.pdf.

Abbas, Yasir. "Another 'State' of Hate: Al-Nusra's Quest to Establish an Islamic Emirate in the Levant." Hudson Institute, April 29, 2016. https://www.hudson.org/research/12454-another -state-of-hate-al-nusra-s-quest-to-establish-an-islamic-emirate-in-the-levant.

Abdallah, Khaled, and Mohammed Mukhashaf. "Yemenis Aay al Qaeda Gave Town Security, at a Cost." Reuters, June 17, 2012. https://www.reuters.com/article/uk-yemen-jaar-idUKB RE85G0B120120617.

Abdul-Ahad, Gaith. "Al Qaeda in Yemen." *Frontline*. PBS, May 29, 2012. https://www.pbs.org /wgbh/frontline/film/al-qaeda-in-yemen/transcript/.

Abdul-Ahad, Gaith. "Al-Qaida's Wretched Utopia and the Battle for Hearts And Minds." *Guardian*, April 30, 2012. https://www.theguardian.com/world/2012/apr/30/alqaida-yemen -jihadis-sharia-law.

Abdul-Ahad, Gaith. "Syria's al-Nusra front—Ruthless, Organised and Taking Control." *Guardian*, July 10, 2013. https://www.theguardian.com/world/2013/jul/10/syria-al-nusra-front-jihadi.

Abedin, Syed Z., and Saleha M. Abedin. "Minorities." In *The Oxford Encyclopaedia of the Islamic World*, edited by John L. Esposito. Oxford University Press, 2009. https://www .oxfordreference.com/display/10.1093/acref/9780195305135.001.0001/acref-9780195305135-e -0536.

Abouzeid, Rania. "Interview with Official of Jabhat al-Nusra Syria's Islamist Militia Group." *Time*, December 25, 2012. http://world.time.com/2012/12/25/interview-with-a-newly -designated-syrias-jabhat-al-nusra/.

Abu al-Khair, Waleed. "Anger in Idlib over the Return of Tahrir al-Sham's al-Hesba." Diyaruna, May 4, 2020. https://diyaruna.com/en_GB/articles/cnmi_di/features/2020/05/14 /feature-02.

Adraoui, Mohamed-Ali. "Border and Sovereignty in Islamist and Jihadist Political Thought: Past and Present." *International Affairs* 93, no. 4 (July 2017): 917–935. https://doi.org/10.1093 /ia/iix123.

Adraoui, Mohamed-Ali. "The Case of Jabhat al-Nusra in the Syrian Conflict 2011–2016: Towards a Strategy of Nationalization?" *Mediterranean Politics* 24, no. 2 (October 2017): 260–267. https://doi.org/10.1080/13629395.2017.1392709.

Ahmad, Aisha. *Jihad & Co.: Black Markets and Islamist Power*. Oxford University Press, 2017.

Ahmad, Eqbal. "Revolutionary War and Counterinsurgency." *Journal of International Affairs* 25, no. 1 (1971): 1–47. https://www.jstor.org/stable/24356753.

Ahram, Ariel. "Sexual Violence, Competitive State Building, and Islamic State in Iraq and Syria." *Journal of Intervention and Statebuilding* 13, no. 2 (November 2018): 180–196. https:// doi.org/10.1080/17502977.2018.1541577.

Ajjoub, Orwa. "HTS Is not al-Qaeda, but It Is Still an Authoritarian Regime to Be Reckoned With." Middle East Institute, June 24, 2021. https://www.mei.edu/publications/hts-not-al -qaeda-it-still-authoritarian-regime-be-reckoned.

Akdedian, Harout. "On Violence and Radical Theology in the Syrian War: The Instrumentality of Spectacular Violence and Exclusionary Practices from Comparative and Local Standpoints." *Politics, Religion & Ideology* 20, no. 3 (August 2019): 361–380. https://doi.org /10.1080/21567689.2019.1656074.

Alami, Mona. "ISIS's Governance Crisis (Part II): Social Services." Atlantic Council, December 24, 2014. https://www.atlanticcouncil.org/blogs/menasource/isis-s-governance-crisis -part-ii-social-services/.

Al-Hal Net. "Civil Organizations in Idlib: Does Hayat Tahrir al-Sham Employ Civil and Relief Work for Its Own Benefit?" May 19, 2022. https://t.ly/O47W.

Al Jazeera. "Jaar's Experience of Living Under the Control of Ansar al-Sharia." June 22, 2012. https://www.youtube.com/watch?v=Q7b8M-_oejQ.

Al Jazeera. "Women Under ISIL: The Nurse." December 18, 2019. https://www.aljazeera.com /indepth/features/women-isil-nurse-191125091344781.html.

Al Jazeera. "Women Under ISIL: The Teacher." December 11, 2019. https://www.aljazeera.com /indepth/features/women-isil-teacher-191126053801151.html.

Al Jazeera. "Women Under ISIL: The Torturers." November 27, 2019. https://www.aljazeera .com/indepth/features/women-isil-torturers-191124095032690.html.

Al Jazeera. "Women Under ISIL: The Wives." December 4, 2019. https://www.aljazeera.com /features/2019/12/4/women-under-isil-the-wives.

Alkhouri, Laith, and Alex Kassirer. "Governing the Caliphate: The Islamic State Picture." *CTC Sentinel* 8, no. 8 (August 2015): 17–21. https://ctc.westpoint.edu/governing-the-caliphate-the -islamic-state-picture/.

Allsopp, Harriet. *The Kurds of Syria: Political Parties and Identity in the Middle East.* I. B. Tauris, 2014.

Almasmari, Hakim. "Al Qaeda Militants Take Control of Another Yemen Province." *National,* March 12, 2012. https://www.thenational.ae/uae/al-qaeda-militants-take-control-of -another-yemen-province-1.602233.

Almousa, Hamoud. "ISIS Curriculum and Educational System." Raqqa Is Being Slaughtered Silently, September 18, 2016. Site discontinued; accessed September 25, 2023. https://www .raqqa-sl.com/en/?p=1959.

Almousa, Hamoud. "Christians of Raqqa in a Succession of ISIS." Raqqa Is Being Slaughtered Silently, November 23, 2015. Site discontinued; accessed September 25, 2023. https://www .raqqa-sl.com/en/?p=1562.

Almousa, Hamoud. "Conversations: In Raqqa, Pharmacists Take an ISIS 'Re-Education Course.'" Raqqa Is Being Slaughtered Silently, January 18, 2015. Site discontinued; accessed September 25, 2023. https://www.raqqa-sl.com/en/?p=312.

Almousa, Hamoud. "Health Sector a New Victim of ISIS Economy in Tell Abiad." Raqqa Is Being Slaughtered Silently, March 13, 2015. Site discontinued; accessed September 25, 2023. https://www.raqqa-sl.com/en/?p=794.

Almousa, Hamoud. "Inside the Islamic State Capital: No End in Sight to Its Grim Rule." Raqqa Is Being Slaughtered Silently, February 22, 2015. Site discontinued; accessed September 25, 2023. https://www.raqqa-sl.com/en/?p=634.

Almousa, Hamoud. "ISIS Nurses Told They Must Speak ENGLISH Under Rules Stricter than NHS." Raqqa Is Being Slaughtered Silently, April 9, 2015. Site discontinued; accessed September 25, 2023. https://www.raqqa-sl.com/en/?p=941.

Almousa, Hamoud. "ISIS's Bureaus (Diwan), Between Structures of a State and Sources to Make Money." Raqqa Is Being Slaughtered Silently, March 31, 2016. Site discontinued; accessed September 25, 2023. https://www.raqqa-sl.com/en/?p=1755.

Almousa, Hamoud. "Raqqa: 'It Is a Very Sad Life Under ISIL.'" Raqqa Is Being Slaughtered Silently, January 9, 2015. Site discontinued; accessed September 25, 2023. https://www.raqqa-sl.com/en/?p=412.

Almousa, Hamoud. "Teachers Are the Victims of ISIS After the Educational Process." Raqqa Is Being Slaughtered Silently, March 2, 2015. Site discontinued; accessed September 25, 2023. https://www.raqqa-sl.com/en/?p=707.

Almousa, Hamoud. "The Truth of the Islamic State's Governance." Raqqa Is Being Slaughtered Silently, August 1, 2016. Site discontinued; accessed September 25, 2023. https://www.raqqa-sl.com/en/?p=1907.

Almukhtar, Sarah. "ISIS Finances Are Strong." New York Times, May 19, 2015. https://www.nytimes.com/interactive/2015/05/19/world/middleeast/isis-finances.html?mtrref=www.google.com.

Almukhtar, Sarah. "Life Under the Islamic State: Fines, Taxes and Punishments." New York Times, May 26, 2016. https://www.nytimes.com/interactive/2016/05/26/world/middleeast/isis-taxes-fines-revenue.html.

Alsayed, Gaith. "Vaccine Campaign Begins Amid Virus Surge in Rebel-Held Syria." Associated Press, May 2, 2021. https://apnews.com/article/syria-europe-middle-east-coronavirus-health-bd6b38e4608915e91c7b5f3406211825.

Alzoubi Zedoun, Khaled Iyad, Mamoun Othman, Houssam Alnahhas, and Omar Abdulaziz Hallaj. Reinventing State: Health Governance in Syrian Opposition-Held Areas. Friedrich Erbert Stiftung, November 2019. https://library.fes.de/pdf-files/bueros/beirut/15765.pdf.

Amnesty International. Conflict in Yemen: Abyan's Darkest Hour. Amnesty International, December 2012. https://www.amnesty.org/en/documents/mde31/010/2012/en/.

Amnesty International. "We Had Nowhere to Go": Forced Displacement and Demolitions in Northern Syria. Amnesty International, October 2015. https://www.amnesty.org/en/documents/mde24/2503/2015/en/.

Amos, Deborah. "Under ISIS, Life in Mosul Takes a Turn for the Bleak." National Public Radio, March 21, 2015. https://www.npr.org/sections/parallels/2015/03/21/394322708/under-isis-life-in-mosul-takes-a-turn-for-the-bleak.

Amr, Ayisha. "How al-Qaeda Rules in Yemen." Foreign Affairs, October 28, 2015. https://www.foreignaffairs.com/articles/yemen/2015-10-28/how-al-qaeda-rules-yemen.

Anzalone, Christopher. "The Multiple Faces of Jabhat al-Nusra/Jabhat Fath al-Sham in Syria's Civil War." Insight Turkey 18, no. 2 (2016): 41–50. https://www.insightturkey.com

/commentaries/the-multiple-faces-of-jabhat-al-nusrajabhat-fath-al-sham-in-syrias-civil
-war.

Anzalone, Christopher. "Organising Sharia Politics and Governing Violence: Al-Shabaab's Rebel Proto-State in Somalia." In Cook and Maher, *The Rule Is for None but Allah*, 101–124.

Aqeedi, Rasha al-. "Hisba in Mosul: Systematic Oppression in the Name of Virtue." Occasional Paper. Program on Extremism at George Washington University, February 2016. https://extremism.gwu.edu/sites/g/files/zaxdzs5746/files/downloads/Al%20Aqeedi.pdf.

Arango, Tim. "ISIS Fighters Seize Control of Government Headquarters in Ramadi, Iraq." *New York Times*, May 15, 2015. https://www.nytimes.com/2015/05/16/world/middleeast/isis -fighters-seize-government-headquarters-in-ramadi-iraq.html.

Arango, Tim. "ISIS Transforming Into Functioning State that Uses Terror as Tool." *New York Times*, July 21, 2015. https://www.nytimes.com/2015/07/22/world/middleeast/isis-trans forming-into-functioning-state-that-uses-terror-as-tool.html.

Arjona, Ana. "Civilian Cooperation and Non-Cooperation with Non-State Armed Groups: The Centrality of Obedience and Resistance." *Small Wars & Insurgencies* 28, nos. 4–5 (July 2017): 755–778. https://doi.org/10.1080/09592318.2017.1322328.

Arjona, Ana. "Civilian Resistance to Rebel Governance." In Arjona et al., *Rebel Governance in Civil War*, 180–202.

Arjona, Ana. "Institutions, Civilian Resistance, and Wartime Social Order: A Process-Driven Natural Experiment in the Colombian Civil War." *Latin America Politics and Society* 58, no. 3 (Fall 2016): 99–122. https://www.jstor.org/stable/24766058.

Arjona, Ana. *Rebelocracy: Social Order in the Colombian Civil War*. Cambridge University Press, 2016.

Arjona, Ana. "Wartime Institutions: A Research Agenda." *Journal of Conflict Resolution* 58, no. 8 (September 2014): 1360–1389. https://doi.org/10.1177/0022002714547904.

Arjona, Ana, Nelson Kasfir, and Zachariah Mampilly. "Introduction." In Arjona et al., *Rebel Governance in Civil War*, 1–20.

Arjona, Ana, Nelson Kasfir, and Zachariah Mampilly, eds. *Rebel Governance in Civil War*. Cambridge University Press, 2015.

Arvisais, Olivier, and Mathieu Guidère. "Education in Conflict: How Islamic State Established Its Curriculum." *Journal of Curriculum Studies* 52, no. 4 (May 2020): 498–515. https://doi .org/10.1080/00220272.2020.1759694.

Asal, Victor, Shawn Flanigan, and Ora Szekely. "Doing Good While Killing: Why Some Insurgent Groups Provide Community Services." *Terrorism & Political Violence* 34, no. 4 (May 2020): 835–855. https://doi.org/10.1080/09546553.2020.1745775.

Asal, Victor, Daniel Gustafson, and Peter Krause. "It Comes with the Territory: Why States Negotiate with Ethno-Political Organizations." *Studies in Conflict & Terrorism* 42, no. 4 (October 2017): 363–382. https://doi.org/10.1080/1057610X.2017.1373428.

Assil, Ibrahim al-. "Al-Qaeda Affiliate and Ahrar al-Sham Compete for Control in Idlib." Middle East Institute, June 29, 2017. https://www.mei.edu/publications/al-qaeda-affiliate-and -ahrar-al-sham-compete-control-idlib.

Assim, Ibrahim al-, and Randa Slim. "The Syrian Druze at Crossroads." Middle East Institute, July 13, 2015. https://www.mei.edu/publications/syrian-druze-crossroads.

Associated Press. Only Days After Fall of Mosul, Iraqis Return to Find Lower Prices, Restored Services and More." *Fox News*, December 5, 2014. https://www.foxnews.com/world/only -days-after-fall-of-mosul-iraqis-return-to-find-lower-prices-restored-services-and -more.

Aswad, Harun al-. "Syrian Free Police Disband Following HTS Militant Takeover in Idlib." *Middle East Eye*, January 16, 2019. https://www.middleeasteye.net/news/syrian-free-police -disband-following-hts-militant-takeover-idlib.

Ayboga, Ercan. "Consensus Is Key: New Justice System in Rojava." *New Compass*, October 13, 2014. http://new-compass.net/articles/consensus-key-new-justice-system-rojava.

Baalbaky, Rudayna al-, and Ahmad Mhidi. *Tribes and the Rule of the "Islamic State": The Case of the Syrian City of Deir Ez-Zor.* Issam Fares Institute for Public Policy and International Affairs; Konrad Adenauer Stiftung, December 2018. https://www.aub.edu.lb/ifi /Documents/publications/research_reports/2018-2019/20181221_tribes_and_islamic _state.pdf.

Baban, Salah Hassan. "Sold, Whipped and Raped: A Yazidi Woman Remembers ISIL Captivity." *Al Jazeera*, October 16, 2020. https://www.aljazeera.com/features/2020/10/16/separation -from-my-children-was-more-painful-than.

Baghdadi, Abu Bakr al-. "Audio Message to the Mujahidin and the Muslim Ummah in the Month of Ramadan." July 1, 2014. Site discontinued; accessed September 25, 2023. https:// kyleorton1991.wpcomstaging.com/2014/07/02/the-leader-of-the-islamic-state-explains -the-caliphates-vision/.

Baker, Aryn. "Why Bashar Assad Won't Fight ISIS." *Time*, February 26, 2015. https://time.com /3719129/assad-isis-asset/.

Bakkour, Samer, and Gareth Stansfield. "The Significance of ISIS's State Building in Syria." *Middle East Policy* 30, no. 2 (May 2023): 126–145. https://doi.org/10.1111/mepo .12681.

Bakulumpagi, Wamala, Amama Mbabazi, Kirunda Kivejinja, Zak Kaheru, Justin Sabiti, and James Tumusiime. *Mission to Freedom: Uganda Resistance News, 1981–1985.* Directorate of Information and Mass Mobilisation, NRM Secretariat, 1990.

Balanche, Fabrice. "Rojava's Sustainability and the PKK's Regional Strategy." Policy Watch 2680. Washington Institute for Near East Policy, August 24, 2016. https://www.washingtoninstitute .org/policy-analysis/view/rojavas-sustainability-and-the-pkks-regional-strategy.

Bamber, Matthew. " 'Without Us There Would Be No Islamic State': The Role of Civilian Employees in the Caliphate." *CTC Sentinel* 14, no. 9 (November 2021): 31–39. https://ctc .westpoint.edu/wp-content/uploads/2021/11/CTC-SENTINEL-092021.pdf.

Bamber, Matthew, and Isak Svensson. "Resisting Radical Rebels: Variations in Islamist Rebel Governance and the Occurrence of Civil Resistance." *Terrorism & Political Violence* 35, no. 5 (February 2022): 1126–1146. https://doi.org/10.1080/09546553.2021.2019023.

Bamber-Zyrd, Matthew. "Cyclical Jihadist Governance: The Islamic State Governance Cycle in Iraq and Syria." *Small Wars & Insurgencies* 33, no. 8 (September 2022): 1314–1344. https:// doi.org/10.1080/09592318.2022.2116182.

Bandula-Irwin, Tanya, Max Gallien, Ashley Jackson, Vanessa van den Boogaard, and Florian Weigand. "Beyond Greed: Why Armed Groups Tax." *Studies in Conflict & Terrorism* 47, no. 12 (February 2022): 1–24. https://doi.org/10.1080/1057610X.2022.2038409.

Barclay, Jack. "Tawhid al-Hakimiyah: A Jihadi Achilles Heel?" *Terrorism Monitor* 8, no. 29 (July 2010): 6–9. https://jamestown.org/program/tawhid-al-hakimiyah-a-jihadi-achilles -heel/.

Baron, Adam. "Yemen's Defense Minister Visits Zinjibar, Jaar—Freed from al Qaida-Linked Militants' Control." *Miami Herald*, June 13, 2012. https://www.miamiherald.com/latest -news/article1940567.html.

Barter, Shane Joshua. "The Rebel State in Society: Governance and Accommodation in Aceh, Indonesia." In Arjona et al., *Rebel Governance in Civil War*, 226–243.

Batati, Saleh al-. "When Al Qaeda Stormed My City: Reporter's Notebook." *New York Times*, April 10, 2015. https://www.nytimes.com/times-insider/2015/04/10/when-al-qaeda-stormed -my-city-reporters-notebook/.

Batati, Saleh al-. "Yemen: The Truth Behind al-Qaeda's Takeover of Mukalla." *Al Jazeera*, September 16, 2015. https://www.aljazeera.com/news/2015/09/16/yemen-the-truth-behind-al -qaedas-takeover-of-mukalla/.

Batati, Saleh al-, and Eric Schmitt. "Yemenis See Turning Point After Ousting Qaeda Militants in South." *New York Times*, October 7, 2017. https://www.nytimes.com/2017/10/07 /world/middleeast/yemen-al-qaeda.html.

BBC News. "Inside Mosul: What's Life Like Under Islamic State?" June 9, 2015. https://www .bbc.com/news/world-middle-east-32831854.

BBC News. "Mosul Diaries: Poisoned by Water." December 19, 2014. https://www.bbc.com/news /world-middle-east-29600573.

Becker, Michael. "When Terrorists and Target Governments Cooperate: The Case of Syria." *Perspectives on Terrorism* 9, no. 1 (February 2015): 95–103. https://www.jstor.org/stable/pdf /26297329.pdf?refreqid=fastly-default%3Acf568fd854f9f67bb4d3748bf9d458f3&ab _segments=&origin=&initiator=&acceptTC.

Becker Aarseth, Mathilde. *Mosul Under ISIS: Eyewitness Accounts of Life in the Caliphate.* I. B. Tauris, 2021.

Becker Aarseth, Mathilde. "Resistance in the Caliphate's Classrooms: Mosul Civilians vs IS." *Middle East Policy* 25, no. 1 (March 2018): 46–63. https://doi.org/10.1111/mepo.12324.

Beckett, Ian. *Modern Insurgencies and Counter-Insurgencies: Guerrillas and their Opponents Since 1750.* Routledge, 2011.

Begin, Menachem. *The Revolt.* Steimatzky, 1977.

Béjar, Héctor. *Peru 1965: Notes on a Guerrilla Experience.* Translated by William Rose. Monthly Review Press, 1970.

Belli, Onur Burcak, Andrea Böhm, Alexander Bühler et al. "The Business of the Caliph." *Zeit*, December 3, 2014. https://www.zeit.de/feature/islamic-state-is-caliphate.

Benraad, Myriam. "Iraq's Tribal 'Sahwa': Its Rise and Fall." *Middle East Policy* 18, no. 1 (March 2011): 121–131. https://doi.org/10.1111/j.1475-4967.2011.00477.x.

Berti, Benedetta. "From Cooperation to Competition: Localization, Militarization and Rebel Co-Governance Arrangements in Syria." *Studies in Conflict & Terrorism* 46, no. 2 (June 2020): 209–227. https://doi.org/10.1080/1057610X.2020.1776964.

Berti, Benedetta. "Non-State Actors as Providers of Governance: The Hamas Government in Gaza Between Effective Sovereignty, Centralized Authority and Resistance." *Middle East Journal* 69, no. 1 (2015): 9–31. https://www.jstor.org/stable/43698207.

Berti, Benedetta. "Violent and Criminal Non-State Actors." In *The Oxford Handbook of Governance and Limited Statehood*, edited by Thomas Risse, Tanja A. Börzel, and Anke Draude, 272–292. Oxford University Press, 2018.

Biberman, Yelena, and Megan Turnbull. "When Militias Provide Welfare: Lessons from Pakistan and Nigeria." *Political Science Quarterly* 133, no. 4 (December 2018): 697–727. https://doi.org/10.1002/polq.12832.

bin Laden, Usama. "Letter to Nasir al-Wuhayshi." Undated, presumably early 2011. Combating Terrorism Center at West Point. Accessed September 25, 2023. https://ctc.westpoint.edu/harmony-program/letter-to-nasir-al-wuhayshi-original-language-2/.

bin Laden, Usama. "Letter to Abu Mus'ab Abd Al-Wadud from Zamray." Undated, presumably, October 2010. Office of the Director of National Intelligence. Accessed September 25, 2023. https://www.dni.gov/files/documents/ubl2017/english/Letter%20to%20Abu-Musa%20b%20Abd-al-Wadud.pdf.

Birke, Sarah. "How ISIS Rules." *New York Review of Books*, December 9, 2014. https://www.nybooks.com/daily/2014/12/09/how-isis-rules/.

Blannin, Patrick. "Islamic State's Financing: Sources, Methods and Utilisation," *Counter Terrorist Trends and Analyses* 9, no. 5 (May 2017): 13–22. https://www.jstor.org/stable/26351519.

BLU Radio. "Relatos de pesadillas que vivieron niños reclutados por FARC. ELN y paramilitares." February 10, 2018. https://www.bluradio.com/nacion/relatos-de-pesadillas-que-vivieron-ninos-reclutados-por-farc-eln-y-paramilitares.

Bocanegra, Nelson, and Julia Symmes Cobb. "After Decades of War, Colombia's FARC Rebels Debut Political Party." Reuters, August 27, 2017. https://www.reuters.com/article/us-colombia-peace-politics/after-decades-of-war-colombias-farc-rebels-debut-political-party-idUSKCN1B705U/.

Boege, Volker, M. Anne Brown, and Kevin P. Clements. "Hybrid Political Orders, not Fragile States." *Peace Review* 21, no. 1 (February 2009): 13–21. https://doi.org/10.1080/10402650802689997.

Boone, Jeb, and Shatha al-Harazi. "As Yemen Unites, Will Al Qaeda Fall?" *MinnPost*, April 20, 2011. www.minnpost.com/global-post/2011/04/yemen-unites-will-al-qaeda-fall.

Bouhlel, Ferdaous, and Yvan Guichaoua. "Norms, Non-Combatants' Agency and Restraint in Jihadi Violence in Northern Mali." *International Interactions* 47, no. 5 (March 2021): 855–872. https://doi.org/10.1080/03050629.2021.1898954.

Boutz, Jennifer, Hannah Benninger, and Alia Lancaster. "Exploiting the Prophet's Authority: How Islamic State Propaganda Uses *Hadith* Quotation to Assert Legitimacy." *Studies in Conflict & Terrorism* 42, no. 11 (February 2018): 924–996. https://doi.org/10.1080/1057610X.2018.1431363.

Boyraz, Cemil. "Alternative Political Projects of Territoriality and Governance During the Syrian War: The Caliphate vs Democratic Confederalism," *Geopolitics* 26, no. 4 (December 2020): 1095–1120. https://doi.org/10.1080/14650045.2020.1855580.

Brandt, Marieke. "The Global and the Local: Al-Qaeda and Yemen's Tribes." In *Tribes and Global Jihadism*, edited by Virginie Collombier and Olivier Roy, 105–130. Oxford University Press, 2017.

Breslawski, Jori. "The Social Terrain of Rebel Held Territory." *Journal of Conflict Resolution* 65, nos. 2–3 (August 2020): 453–479. https://doi.org/10.1177/0022002720951857.

Breslawski, Jori, and Colin Tucker. "Ideological Motives and Taxation by Armed Groups." *Conflict Management & Peace Science* 39, no. 3 (August 2021): 333–350. https://doi.org/10.1177/07388942211033229.

Brüggeman, Ulf. "Al-Qaeda and the Islamic State: Objectives, Threat, Countermeasures." Security Policy Working Paper No. 9. Federal Academy for Security Policy, 2016. https://www.baks.bund.de/sites/baks010/files/working_paper_2016_09.pdf.

Bulos, Nabih. "Life Under Islamic State Was Strict and Brutal, but Some Moments Didn't Seem So Bad, Sunni Iraqis Say." *Los Angeles Times*, October 28, 2016. https://www.latimes.com/world/middleeast/la-fg-iraq-sunni-villages-20161027-story.html.

Bunker, Robert J. "Changing Forms of Insurgency: Pirates, Narco Gangs and Failed States." In *The Routledge Handbook of Insurgency and Counterinsurgency*, edited by Paul B. Rich and Isabelle Duyvesteyn, 45–53. Routledge, 2012.

Bunzel, Cole. "From Paper State to Caliphate: The Ideology of the Islamic State." Analysis Paper No. 19. Brookings Project on US Relations with the Islamic Word, March 2015. https://www.brookings.edu/research/from-paper-state-to-caliphate-the-ideology-of-the-islamic-state.

Byman, Daniel. "Fighting *Salafi-Jihadist* Insurgencies: How Much Does Religion Really Matter?" *Studies in Conflict & Terrorism* 36, no. 5 (April 2013): 353–371. https://doi.org/10.1080/1057610X.2013.775417.

Byman, Daniel. "ISIS Goes Global: Fight the Islamic State by Targeting Its Affiliates." *Foreign Affairs*, March–April 2016. https://www.foreignaffairs.com/articles/middle-east/isis-goes-global.

Cabral, Amilcar. *Resistance and Decolonization.* Rowman & Littlefield International, 2016.

Cafarella, Jennifer. "Jabhat al-Nusra in Syria: An Islamic Emirate for al-Qaeda." Middle East Security Report No. 25. Institute for the Study of War, December 2014. https://www.understandingwar.org/sites/default/files/JN%20Final.pdf

Callimachi, Rukmini. "For Women Under ISIS, a Tyranny of Dress Code and Punishment." *New York Times*, December 12, 2016. https://www.nytimes.com/2016/12/12/world/middleeast/islamic-state-mosul-women-dress-code-morality.html.

Callimachi, Rukmini. "ISIS Enshrines a Theology of Rape." *New York Times*, August 13, 2015. https://www.nytimes.com/2015/08/14/world/middleeast/isis-enshrines-a-theology-of-rape.html.

Cambanis, Thanassis, and Rebecca Collard. "How ISIS Runs a City." *Time*, February 26, 2015. https://time.com/3720063/isis-government-raqqa-mosul/.

Carenzi, Silvia. "A Downward Scale Shift? The Case of Hayat Tahrir al-Sham." *Perspectives on Terrorism* 14, no. 6 (December 2020): 91–105. https://www.jstor.org/stable/26964728.

Carenzi, Silvia. "How Do Non-State Actors Seek Legitimacy? The Case of Idlib." Italian Institute for International Political Studies, September 15, 2022. https://www.ispionline.it/en/publication/how-do-non-state-actors-seek-legitimacy-case-idlib-36156.

Caris, Charles, and Samuel Reynolds. "ISIS Governance in Syria." Middle East Security Report No. 22. Institute for the Study of War, July 2014. https://www.understandingwar.org/report/isis-governance-syria.

Center for International Security and Cooperation. "Hayat Tahrir al-Sham." CSIS Terrorism Backgrounder, October 4, 2018. https://www.csis.org/programs/transnational-threats -project/terrorism-backgrounders/hayat-tahrir-al-sham-hts.

Chacko, Rose. "Ghalia Rahhal: The Idlib-Based Women's Rights Defender Fighting for Female Empowerment." *New Arab*, June 17, 2022. https://www.newarab.com/features/mazaya -female-led-initiative-promotes-womens-empowerment.

Chaliand, Gérard. *Guerrilla Strategies: An Historical Anthology from the Long March to Afghanistan*. University of California Press, 1982.

Cheterian, Vicken. "ISIS Genocide Against the Yazidis and Mass Violence in the Middle East." *British Journal of Middle Eastern Studies* 48, no. 4 (October 2019): 629–641. https://doi.org /10.1080/13530194.2019.1683718.

Chick, Kristen. "Their Town Now Liberated, Iraqi Christians Talk of Life Under ISIS." *Christian Science Monitor*, November 28, 2016. https://www.csmonitor.com/World/Middle-East /2016/1128/Their-town-now-liberated-Iraqi-Christians-talk-of-life-under-ISIS.

Chilcote, Ronald. "The Political Thought of Amilcar Cabral." *Journal of Modern African Studies* 6, no. 3 (1968): 373–388. https://doi.org/10.1017/S0022278X0001747X.

Chitwood, Ken. "What Is a Caliph? The Islamic State Tries to Boost Its Legitimacy by Hijacking a Historic Institution." *Conversation*, November 14, 2019. https://theconversation.com /what-is-a-caliph-the-islamic-state-tries-to-boost-its-legitimacy-by-hijacking-a-historic -institution-126175.

Clancy, Timothy. "Theory of an Emerging-State Actor: The Islamic State of Iraq and Syria (ISIS) Case." *Systems* 6, no. 16 (May 2018): 1–24. https://doi.org/10.3390/systems6020016.

Clark, Justine, and Mohammad Abdulsattar Ibrahim. "The State of Rojava: A Month-Long Reporting Series from Syria Direct." *Syria Direct*, November 5, 2017. https://syriadirect.org /news/the-state-of-rojava-a-month-long-reporting-series-from-syria-direct/.

Clark, Victoria. *Yemen: Dancing on the Heads of Snakes*. Yale University Press.

Clausen, Maria-Louise. "Competing for Control over the State: The Case of Yemen." *Small Wars and Insurgencies* 29, no. 3 (May 2018): 560–578. https://www.tandfonline.com/doi /epdf/10.1080/09592318.2018.1455792?needAccess=true.

Clausen, Maria-Louise. "Islamic State in Yemen: A Rival to al-Qaeda?" *Connections* 16, no. 1 (2017): 50–62. https://www.jstor.org/stable/26326470.

Clements, Kevin P., Volker Boege, Anne Brown, Wendy Foley, and Anna Nolan. "State Building Reconsidered: The Role of Hybridity in the Formation of Political Order." *Political Science* 59, no. 1 (June 2007): 45–56. https://doi.org/10.1177/003231870705900106.

Cockburn, Patrick. "For This Iraqi Tribe Massacred by Isis Fear of the Group's Return Is a Constant Reality." *Independent*, July 4, 2018. https://www.independent.co.uk/news/world /middle-east/iraq-tribe-isis-massacre-war-hit-albu-nimr-baghdad-sunni-a8431466.html.

Cockburn, Andrew, and Alex Potter. "Before the War." *Harper's Magazine*, June 25, 2015. https://harpers.org/2015/06/before-the-war.

Coggins, Bridget. *Power Politics and State Formation in the Twentieth Century: Dynamics of Recognition*. Cambridge University Press, 2014.

Coggins, Bridget. "Rebel Diplomacy: Theorizing Violent Non-State Actors' Strategic Use of Talk." In Arjona et al., *Rebel Governance in Civil War*, 98–118.

Colasanti, Nathalie, Rocco Frondizi, Joyce Liddle, and Marco Meneguzzo. "Grassroots Democracy and Local Government in Northern Syria: The Case of Democratic Confederalism." *Local Government Studies* 44, no. 6 (July 2018): 807–825. https://doi.org/10.1080/03003930.2018.1501366.

Collard, Rebecca. "Life in Mosul Gets Back to Normal." *Time*, June 19, 2014. https://time.com/2901388/mosul-isis-iraq-syria/.

Cook, Joana. *"Their Fate Is Tied to Ours": Assessing AQAP Governance and Implications for Security in Yemen*. International Centre for the Study of Radicalization, October 2019. https://icsr.info/wp-content/uploads/2019/10/ICSR-Report-Their-Fate-is-Tied-to-Ours-Assessing-AQAP-Governance-and-Implications-for-Security-in-Yemen.pdf.

Cook, Joana, Haid Haid, and Inga Trauthig. "Jurisprudence Beyond the State: An Analysis of Jihadist 'Justice' in Yemen, Syria and Libya." *Studies in Conflict and Terrorism* 46, no. 5 (June 2020): 559–578. https://doi.org/10.1080/1057610X.2020.1776958.

Cook, Joana, Shiraz Maher, eds. *The Rule Is for None but Allah: Islamist Approaches to Governance*. Hurst & Co., 2023.

Cook, Thomas R. "The Financial Arm of the FARC: A Threat Finance Perspective." *Journal of Strategic Security* 4, no. 1 (Spring 2011): 19–36. http://dx.doi.org/10.5038/1944-0472.4.1.2.

Coombs, Casey L., and Hannah Poppy. "Is AQAP to Blame for the String of Assassinations in Yemen?" *CTC Sentinel* 7, no. 1 (January 2014): 18–20. https://ctc.westpoint.edu/is-aqap-to-blame-for-the-string-of-assassinations-in-yemen/.

Corera, Gordon. "Unraveling Zarqawi's al-Qaeda Connection." *Terrorism Monitor* 2, no. 24 (May 2005). https://jamestown.org/program/unraveling-zarqawis-al-qaeda-connection/.

Cronin, Audrey Kurth. "ISIS Is Not a Terrorist Group." *Foreign Affairs*, March–April 2015. https://www.foreignaffairs.com/articles/middle-east/2019-02-18/isis-not-terrorist-group.

Darwish, Ali. "Innocent Here; Convicted There: Two Separate Judiciaries in Northern Syria." *Enab Baladi*, February 13, 2021. https://english.enabbaladi.net/archives/2021/02/innocent-here-convict-there-two-separate-judiciaries-in-northern-syria/.

Dawod, Hosham. "Iraqi Tribes in the Land of Jihad." In *Tribes and Global Jihadism*, edited by Virginie Collombier and Olivier Roy, 15–32. Oxford University Press, 2017.

Daily Sabah. "Idlib Follows Suit in Adopting Turkish Lira to Shield Region from Plummeting Syrian Pound." June 16, 2020. https://www.dailysabah.com/business/economy/idlib-follows-suit-in-adopting-turkish-lira-to-shield-region-from-plummeting-syrian-pound.

Dassouky, Ayman al-. *The Role of Jihadi Movements in Syrian Local Governance*. Omran for Strategic Studies, July 2017. https://omranstudies.org/publications/papers/the-role-of-jihadi-movements-in-syrian-local-governance.html.

Dawsari, Nadwa al-. *Foe Not Friend: Yemeni Tribes and al-Qaeda in the Arabian Peninsula*. Project on Middle East Democracy, February 2018. https://mideastdc.org/wp-content/uploads/2018/02/Dawsari_FINAL_180201.pdf.

Daymon, Chelsea, and Devorah Margolin. *Women in American Violent Extremism: An Examination of Far-Right and Salafi-Jihadist Movements*. Program on Extremism at George Washington University, June 2022. https://extremism.gwu.edu/sites/g/files/zaxdzs5746/files/Women-in-American-Violent-Extremism_Daymon-and-Margolin_June-2022.pdf.

Debray, Régis. *Revolution in the Revolution?* Grove Press, 1967.

de Leede, Seran. "Women in Jihad: A Historical Perspective." ICCT Policy Brief. International Center on Counter Terrorism, September 2018. https://www.jstor.org/stable/resrep19608.

Del Ponte Carla, Karen Koning AbuZayd, Paulo Pinheiro, and Vitit Muntarbhorn. "Rule of Terror." *Cairo Review of Global Affairs* 19 (Fall 2015): 48–65. https://www.thecairoreview .com/essays/rule-of-terror/.

Dimashqi, Youmna al-. "Conversations: Life as a Paramedic During ISIS' Rule of Raqqa." *New Humanitarian*, December 7, 2017. https://deeply.thenewhumanitarian.org/syria/articles /2017/12/07/conversations-life-as-a-paramedic-during-isis-rule-of-raqqa.

Dinc, Pinar. "The Kurdish Movement and the Democratic Federation of Northern Syria: An Alternative to the (Nation-)State Model?" *Journal of Balkan and Near Eastern Studies* 22, no. 1 (January 2020): 47–67. https://doi.org/10.1080/19448953.2020.1715669.

Devron, Jerome, and Patrick Haenni. "The Consolidation of a (Post-Jihadi) Technocratic State-Let in Idlib." Project on Middle East Political Science, 2020. https://pomeps.org/the -consolidation-of-a-post-jihadi-technocratic-state-let-in-idlib.

Drevon, Jerome, and Patrick Haenni. "How Global Jihad Relocalises and Where It Leads: The Case of HTS, the Former AQ Franchise in Syria." RSC Working Paper 2021/08. European University Institute, August 2021. https://hdl.handle.net/1814/69795.

Droukdel, Abdelmalek. "Letter from Abu Mus'ab 'Abdel-Wudoud to His Brother Emirs and Members of the Shura Council of the Organization and Ansar ed-Din in the Great Desert." Undated, presumably July 2012. In Associated Press, "Al-Qaida Papers: Al-Qaida's Sahara Playbook." Accessed September 25, 2023. https://www.documentcloud.org/documents /838898-aqp-sahara-playbook.html.

Dukhan, Haian. "Critical Analysis of Attempts to Coopt the Tribes in Syria." London School of Economics, May 2, 2019. https://blogs.lse.ac.uk/crp/2019/05/02/critical-analysis-of -attempts-to-co-opt-the-tribes-in-syria/.

Dukhan, Haian, Amma Al-Hamad, and Karam Shaar. "The Kin Who Count: Mapping Raqqa's Tribal Typology." Middle East Institute, March 24, 2021. https://www.mei.edu/publications /kin-who-count-mapping-raqqas-tribal-topology.

Dukhan, Haian, and Sinan Hawat. "The Islamic State and the Arab Tribes in Eastern Syria." In *Caliphates and Islamic Global Politics*, edited by Timothy Poirson and Robert L. Oprisko, 49–56. E-International Relations, 2014.

Ebaa. "Idlib Is a Bright Example of Contemporary Revolutions." June 30, 2018. https://ebaa. news/visuals/report-vid/2018/06/4631/.

Edroos, Faisal, and Saleh al-Batati. "After al-Qaeda: No Signs of Recovery in Yemen's Mukalla." *Al Jazeera*, January 11, 2018. https://www.aljazeera.com/features/2018/1/11/after-al-qaeda-no -signs-of-recovery-in-yemens-mukalla.

Edwards, Madeline, and Mohammad Abdulsattar Ibrahim. "Widows in Syria's Idlib Told to Move In with Male Guardian." *Middle East Eye*, December 15, 2017. https://www .middleeasteye.net/news/widows-syrias-idlib-told-move-male-guardian.

El Tiempo. "Nace el Movimiento Bolivariano de las FARC." April 29, 2000. https://www .eltiempo.com/archivo/documento/MAM-1291569.

El-Badawi, Emman, Milo Comerford, and Peter Welby. *Inside the Jihadi Mind: Understanding Ideology and Propaganda*. Tony Blair Institute for Global Change, October 2015. https://institute.global/insights/geopolitics-and-security/inside-jihadi-mind-understanding-ideology-and-propaganda.

Enab Baladi. "Formation of the 'Salvation Government' in Northern Syria" [in Arabic]. November 2, 2017. https://www.enabbaladi.net/archives/181916.

Enab Baladi. "Security Deployment of 'Tahrir al-Sham' in Idlib . . . al-Julani in the Camps" [in Arabic]. May 16, 2020. https://www.enabbaladi.net/archives/384887/amp.

Enab Baladi. "Tahrir al-Sham Hands Over Its Services Institution to the Salvation Government" [in Arabic]. November 7, 2017. https://www.enabbaladi.net/archives/182737.

Enab Baladi. "Turkey Admits Telecommunication Towers into Idlib Governorate." July 7, 2018. https://english.enabbaladi.net/archives/2018/07/turkey-admits-telecommunication-towers-into-idlib-governorate/.

Erhaim, Zaina, and Jomana Qaddour. "Women in Idlib Challenge Islamic Extremists." Middle East Institute, July 26, 2017. https://www.mei.edu/publications/women-idlib-challenge-islamic-extremists.

Fadhil Ali, Rafid. "Al-Qaeda's in the Arabian Peninsula Growing War with North Yemen's Houthis Movement." *Terrorism Monitor* 9, no. 2 (January 2011). https://jamestown.org/program/al-qaeda-in-the-arabian-peninsulas-growing-war-with-north-yemens-houthist-movement/.

Favier, Agnès. "Local Governance Dynamics in Opposition-Controlled Areas in Syria." In *Inside Wars: Local Dynamics of Conflicts in Syria and Libya*, edited by Luigi Narbone, Agnès Favier, and Virginie Collombier, 6–15. European University Institute, 2016.

Fick, Carolyn E. "The Haitian Revolution and the Limits of Freedom: Defining Citizenship in the Revolutionary Era." *Social History* 32, no. 4 (May 2008): 394–414. https://doi.org/10.1080/03071020701616696.

Firestone, Reuven. "'Jihadism' as a New Religious Movement." In *Cambridge Companion to New Religious Movements*, edited by Olav Hammer and Mikael Rothstein, 263–285. Cambridge University Press, 2012.

Fishman, Brian. "After Zarqawi: The Dilemmas and Future of Al Qaeda in Iraq." *Washington Quarterly* 29, no. 4 (January 2010): 19–32. https://doi.org/10.1162/wash.2006.29.4.19.

Fishman, Brian. "Redefining the Islamic State: The Fall and Rise of Al-Qaeda in Iraq." National Security Studies Program Policy Paper. New America Foundation, August 2011. https://static.newamerica.org/attachments/4343-redefining-the-islamic-state/Fishman_Al_Qaeda_In_Iraq.023ac20877a64488b2b791cd7e313955.pdf.

Florea, Adrian. "Rebel Governance in De Facto States." *European Journal of International Relations* 24, no. 4 (May 2020): 1004–1031. https://doi.org/10.1177/1354066120919481.

Florea, Adrian, and Romain Malejacq. "The Supply and Demand of Rebel Governance." *International Studies Review* 26, no. 1 (March 2024): 1–27. https://doi.org/10.1093/isr/viae004.

Förster, Till. "Dialogue Direct: Rebel Governance and Civil Order in Northern Cote d'Ivoire." In Arjona et al., *Rebel Governance in Civil War*, 203–225.

Fox, Tessa. "Iraq Government Employees Face Prosecution for Working Under ISIL." *Al Jazeera*, July 9, 2019. https://www.aljazeera.com/news/2019/7/9/iraq-government-employees -face-prosecution-for-working-under-isil.

Fraihat, Ibrahim, and Abdilhadi Alijla. *Rebel Governance in the Middle East*. Palgrave Macmillan, 2023.

France 24. "A Report from an al Qaeda-Controlled City in Yemen." July 8, 2015. https://observers .france24.com/en/20150708-yemen-mukalla-al-qaeda-control.

France 24. "Syria's Idlib Enclave: How Does It Work?" June 28, 2019. https://www.france24.com /en/20190628-syrias-idlib-enclave-how-does-it-work.

Freeman, Jack. "The al Houthi Insurgency in the North of Yemen: An Analysis of the Shabaab al Moumineen." *Studies in Conflict & Terrorism* 32, no. 11 (October 2009): 1008–1019. https://doi.org/10.1080/10576100903262716.

Fukuyama, Francis. *State Building: Governance and World Order in the XXI Century*. Cornell University Press, 2004.

Furlan, Marta. *The Exploitation of Natural Resources in the Financing of Terrorism: The Case of Syria and Iraq*. Konrad Adenauer Stiftung, March 2019. https://www.kas.de/documents /266761/6686921/The+Exploitation+of+Natural+Resources+in+the+Financing+of +Terrorism+English.pdf/ef5616d5-4bb9-bafb-9c89-9895365d4ef6?version=1.2&t =1583487620551.

Furlan, Marta. "Rebel Governance at the Time of Covid-19: Emergencies as Opportunities for Rebel Rulers." *Studies in Conflict & Terrorism* 46, no. 8 (September 2020): 1440–1463. https://doi.org/10.1080/1057610X.2020.1816681.

Furlan, Marta. "Rebel Governance Between Ideology and Pragmatism: Al-Qa'ida in Yemen in 2011–2012 and 2015–2016." In *Rebel Governance in the Middle East*, edited by Ibrahim Fraihat and Abdilhadi Alijla, 217–248. Palgrave Macmillan, 2023.

Furlan, Marta. "State Weakness, al-Qaeda, and Rebel Governance." *Middle East Journal* 76, no. 1 (2022): 14–17. https://doi.org/10.3751/76.1.11.

Furlan, Marta. "Understanding Governance by Insurgent Non-State Actors: A Multi-Dimensional Typology." *Civil Wars* 22, no. 4 (June 2020): 478–511. https://doi.org/10.1080 /13698249.2020.1785725.

Galula, David. *Counterinsurgency Warfare: Theory and Practice*. Praeger Security International, 2006.

Ganad, Tawfeek al-, Muhammed al-Katheri, and Gregory D. Johnsen. *387 Days of Power: How al-Qaeda Seized, Held and Ultimately Lost a Yemeni City*. Sana'a Center for Strategic Studies, December 2020. https://sanaacenter.org/files/387_Days_of_Power_en.pdf.

Gartenstein-Ross, Daveed. "Druze Clues." Foundation for the Defense of Democracies, October 6, 2015. https://www.fdd.org/analysis/2015/10/06/druze-clues/.

Gartenstein-Ross, Daveed, and Tara Vassefi. "Perceptions of the 'Arab Spring' Within the Salafi-Jihadi Movement." *Studies in Conflict and Terrorism* 35, no. 2 (November 2012): 838–848. https://doi.org/10.1080/1057610X.2012.720241.

George, Alexander L., and Andrew Bennett. *Case Studies and Theory Development in the Social Sciences*. MIT Press 2005.

Gerges, Fawaz. *The Far Enemy: Why Jihad Went Global*. Cambridge University Press, 2005.

Gerges, Fawaz. *ISIS: A History*. Princeton University Press, 2016.

Gerges, Fawaz. "The Rise and Fall of Al-Qaeda: Debunking the Terrorist Narrative." *Huffington Post*, January 3, 2012. https://www.huffpost.com/entry/the-rise-and-fall-of-alqa_b_1182003?ref=tw.

Gerring, John. *Case Study Research: Principles and Practice*. Cambridge University Press, 2006.

Gerring, John. "Qualitative Methods." *Annual Review of Political Science* 20, no. 1 (2017): 15–36. https://doi.org/10.1146/annurev-polisci-092415-024158.

Gerring, John. "What Is a Case Study and What Is It Good for?" *American Political Science Review* 98, no. 2 (May 2004): 341–354. https://doi.org/10.1017/S0003055404001182.

Giap, Vo Nguyen. *People's War, People's Army*. University Press of the Pacific, 2001.

Giglio, Mike, and Munzer al-Awad. "This Is What It's Like to Be Christian and Live Under ISIS." *BuzzFeed News*, January 9, 2016. https://www.buzzfeednews.com/article/mikegiglio/this-is-what-its-like-to-be-christian-and-live-under-isis.

Giustozzi, Antonio. "Hearts, Minds and the Barrell of a Gun." *PRISM* 3, no. 2 (2012): 71–80. https://apps.dtic.mil/sti/pdfs/AD1042581.pdf.

Giustozzi, Antonio. *The Taliban at War: 2001–2018*. Oxford University Press, 2019.

Glawion, Tim, and Anne-Clémence Le Noan. "Rebel Governance or Governance in Rebel Territory? Extraction and Services in Ndele, Central African Republic." *Small Wars & Insurgencies* 34, no. 1 (November 2022): 24–51. https://doi.org/10.1080/09592318.2022.2137282.

Gott, Richard. *Rural Guerrillas in Latin America*. Penguin, 1973.

Green, Daniel. "Defeating al-Qaeda's Shadow Government in Yemen." Policy Focus No. 159. Washington Institute for Near East Policy, September 2019. https://www.washingtoninstitute.org/policy-analysis/defeating-al-qaedas-shadow-government-yemen-need-local-governance-reform.

Green, Daniel. "Tribal Boots on the Ground in Iraq." Washington Institute for Near East Policy, October 13, 2014. https://www.washingtoninstitute.org/policy-analysis/tribal-boots-ground-iraq.

Grynkewich, Alexus G. "Welfare as Warfare: How Violent Non-State Groups Use Social Services to Attack the State." *Studies in Conflict & Terrorism* 31, no. 4 (April 2008): 350–370. https://doi.org/10.1080/10576100801931321.

Guardian. "Shia Alliance Wins Iraq Elections." January 20, 2006. https://www.theguardian.com/world/2006/jan/20/iraq.

Guevara, Ernesto. *Guerrilla Warfare*. Ocean Press, 2006.

Gunes, Cengiz. *The Kurds in a New Middle East: The Changing Geopolitics of Regional Conflict*. Palgrave Macmillan, 2019.

Gunning, Jeroen. *Hamas in Politics: Democracy, Religion, Violence*. Hurst, 2008.

Gutiérrez Sanín, Francisco, and Elisabeth Jean Wood. "Ideology in Civil War: Instrumental Adoption and Beyond." *Journal of Peace Research* 51, no. 2 (March 2014): 213–226. https://doi.org/10.1177/0022343313514073.

Haas, Mark L., and David W. Lesch. *The Arab Spring: The Hope and Reality of the Uprisings*. Avalon Publishing, 2016.

Haid, Haid. "HTS Attempts State-Building as Survival Strategy in Idlib." *Arab News*, April 24, 2019. https://www.arabnews.com/node/1487521.

Haid, Haid. *HTS's Offline Propaganda: Infrastructure, Engagement and Monopoly.* International Centre for the Study of Radicalisation, September 2019. https://icsr.info/wp-content/uploads/2019/09/ICSR-Report-HTS's-Offline-Propaganda-Infrastructure-Engagement-and-Monopoly.pdf.

Haid, Haid. *Resisting Hayat Tahrir al-Sham: Syrian Civil Society on the Frontlines.* Adopt a Revolution, December 2017. https://adoptrevolution.org/wp-content/uploads/2017/12/2017_11_10_HTS_Studie-eng.pdf.

Haidari, Fawaz al-. "Relief in Yemen's Mukalla After al-Qaeda's Rule." Agence France-Press, May 4, 2016. https://sg.news.yahoo.com/relief-yemens-mukalla-qaeda-rule-115221471.html.

Halab Today Tv. " 'Legitimate, Modest Dress . . .' New Restrictions Imposed by the 'University of Idlib' on Its Students" [in Arabic]. March 6, 2019. https://halabtodaytv.net/archives/59735.

Hamdan, Hussam. "The Sharia Board in Aleppo . . . Multiple Roles." *Al Jazeera*, June 12, 2013. https://www.aljazeera.net/news/reportsandinterviews/2013/6/12/الهيئة-الشرعية-بحلب-أدوار-متعددة.

Hamou, Ammar, and Avery Edelman. "Property Seizures by Hardline Rebels Stoke Fears Among Idlib Province's Fading Christian Community." *Syria Direct*, December 13, 2018. https://syriadirect.org/property-seizures-by-hardline-rebels-stoke-fears-among-idlib-provinces-fading-christian-community/.

Hansen, Stig Jarle. *Al-Shabaab in Somalia: The History and Ideology of a Militant Islamist Group, 2005–2012.* Oxford University Press, 2013.

Hardan, Mohammed. "HTS Finesses Tribes in Syria's Idlib." *Al-Monitor*, May 6, 2021. https://www.al-monitor.com/originals/2021/05/hts-finesses-tribes-syrias-idlib.

Hardan, Mohammed. "HTS Leader Tours Idlib on Eid al-Fitr." *Al-Monitor*, May 11, 2022. https://www.al-monitor.com/originals/2022/05/hts-leader-tours-idlib-eid-al-fitr.

Hardan, Mohammed. "Syrian Jihadi Leader Courts Druze Community in Idlib." *Al-Monitor*, June 16, 2022. https://www.al-monitor.com/originals/2022/06/syrian-jihadi-leader-courts-druze-community-idlib.

Hardan, Mohammed. "Syrian Jihadist Group in Idlib Replaces Security Squad with 'Moral Police.'" *Al-Monitor*, September 13, 2021. https://www.al-monitor.com/originals/2021/09/syrian-jihadist-group-idlib-replaces-security-squad-moral-police.

Hardan, Mohammed. "Syrian Tribe Forms Shura Council in Idlib with Blessing from Jihadist Group." *Al-Monitor*, September 8, 2021. https://www.al-monitor.com/originals/2021/09/syrian-tribe-forms-shura-council-idlib-blessing-jihadist-group.

Hardan, Mohammed. "Turkey Offers to Supply Electricity to Idlib." *Al-Monitor*, May 7, 2021. https://www.al-monitor.com/originals/2021/05/turkey-offers-supply-electricity-idlib.

Hardy, Sam. "Landmark Sufi Shrine Destroyed by Islamists in Yemen." *Hyperallergic*, February 11, 2015. https://hyperallergic.com/181925/landmark-sufi-shrine-destroyed-by-islamists-in-yemen/.

Harik, Judith. *The Public and Social Services of the Lebanese Militias.* Centre for Lebanese Studies, 1994.

Hassan, Hassan. "Out of the Desert: ISIS's Strategy for a Long War." Policy Paper No. 8. Middle East Institute, September 2018. https://www.mei.edu/sites/default/files/2018-11/PP10_Hassan_ISISCT.pdf.

Hassan, Hassan. "The Sectarianism of the Islamic State: Ideological Roots and Political Context." Carnegie Endowment for International Peace, June 2016. https://carnegieendowment.org/research/2016/12/the-sectarianism-of-the-islamic-state-ideological-roots-and-political-context?lang=en.

Hassan, Hassan. "We Have Not Yet Seen the Full Impact of ISIS Sleeper Cells Coming Back to Life." *National*, April 18, 2018. https://www.thenational.ae/opinion/comment/we-have-not-yet-seen-the-full-impact-of-isis-sleeper-cells-coming-back-to-life-1.722796.

Hassan, Hassan. "What ISIS Did to My Village." *Atlantic*, April 27, 2019. https://www.theatlantic.com/ideas/archive/2019/04/isis-i-study-today-not-isis-my-past/588088/.

Hassan, Mona. *Longing for the Lost Caliphate: A Transregional History*. Princeton University Press, 2016.

Hawar News. "Final Statement of Autonomous Administration of North, East Syria." September 7, 2018. https://hawarnews.com/en/haber/final-statement-of-autonomous-administration-of-north-east-syria-h3608.html.

Hayek, Caroline. "Universities in Idlib Threatened by Hayat Tahrir al-Sham." *L'Orient-Le Jour*, February 5, 2019. https://www.lorientlejour.com/article/1155484/universities-in-idlib-threatened-by-hayat-tahrir-al-sham.html.

Haykel, Bernard. "On the Nature of Salafi Thought and Action." In Roel, *Global Salafism*, 34–57.

Heck, Paul L. "Taxation." In *Encyclopaedia of the Qur'an*, edited by Jane Dammen McAuliffe. Brill, 2006.

Hegghammer, Thomas. *Jihad in Saudi Arabia*. Cambridge University Press, 2010.

Heller, Sam. "Keeping the Lights on in Rebel Idlib." Century Foundation, November 29, 2016. https://tcf.org/content/report/keeping-lights-rebel-idlib/.

Heller, Sam. "Syrian Jihadists Jeopardize Humanitarian Relief." Century Foundation, June 1, 2017. https://tcf.org/content/report/syrian-jihadists-jeopardize-humanitarian-relief/.

Herber, Irénée, and Jerome Drevon. "Engaging Armed Groups at the International Committee of the Red Cross: Challenges, Opportunities and Covid-19." *International Review of the Red Cross*, no. 915 (January 2022): 1021–1031. https://international-review.icrc.org/articles/engaging-armed-groups-at-icrc-challenges-opportunities-covid-19-915.

Hinnebusch, Raymond, Omar Imady, and Tina Zintl. "Civil Resistance in the Syrian Uprising: From Peaceful Protest to Sectarian Civil War." In Roberts et al., *Civil Resistance in the Arab Spring*, 223–247.

Hisham, Marwan, and Molly Crabapple. *Brothers of the Gun: A Memoir of the Syrian War*. One World, 2018.

Hoffman, Bruce. *Inside Terrorism*. Columbia University Press, 2006.

Hoffmann, Kasper. "Myths Set in Motion: The Moral Economy of Mai Mai Governance." In Arjona et al., *Rebel Governance in Civil War*, 158–179.

Hoffmann, Kasper, and Judith Verweijen. "Rebel Rule: A Governmentality Perspective." *African Affairs* 118, no. 471 (April 2019): 352–374. https://doi.org/10.1093/afraf/ady039.

Holtz, Mackenzie. "Examining Extremism: Hayat Tahrir al-Sham." Center for Strategic and International Studies, August 3, 2023. https://www.csis.org/blogs/examining-extremism/examining-extremism-hayat-tahrir-al-sham-hts.

Horton, Michael. "Fighting the Long War: The Evolution of al-Qa'ida in the Arabian Peninsula." *CTC Sentinel* 10, no. 1 (January 2017): 17–23. https://ctc.westpoint.edu/fighting-the-long-war-the-evolution-of-al-qaida-in-the-arabian-peninsula/.

Horton, Michael. "The Hadramawt: AQAP and the Battle for Yemen's Wealthiest Governorate." *Terrorism Monitor* 13, no. 14 (July 2015). https://jamestown.org/program/the-hadramawt-aqap-and-the-battle-for-yemens-wealthiest-governorate/.

Huang, Reyko. "Rebel Diplomacy in Civil War." *International Security* 40, no. 4 (Spring 2016): 89–126. https://www.jstor.org/stable/43828315.

Huang, Reyko. *The Wartime Origins of Democratization: Civil War, Rebel Governance and Political Regimes.* Cambridge University Press, 2016.

Hubbard, Ben. "Al-Qaeda Tries New Tactic to Keep Power: Sharing It." *New York Times*, June 10, 2015. https://www.nytimes.com/2015/06/10/world/middleeast/qaeda-yemen-syria-houthis.html.

Hubbard, Ben. "Islamist Rebels Create Dilemma on Syria Policy." *New York Times*, April 27, 2013. https://www.nytimes.com/2013/04/28/world/middleeast/islamist-rebels-gains-in-syria-create-dilemma-for-us.html.

Hubbard, Ben. "Life in a Jihadist Capital: Order with a Darker Side." *New York Times*, July 23, 2014. https://www.nytimes.com/2014/07/24/world/middleeast/islamic-state-controls-raqqa-syria.html?_r=0.

Human Rights Watch. "Daily Life in the Caliphate." December 8, 2015. https://www.hrw.org/news/2015/12/08/daily-life-caliphate-0.

Human Rights Watch. "Iraq: ISIS Abducting, Killing, Expelling Minorities." July 19, 2014. https://www.hrw.org/news/2014/07/19/iraq-isis-abducting-killing-expelling-minorities.

Human Rights Watch. "Iraq: ISIS Ruel Marked by Executions, Cruelty." July 10, 2016. https://www.hrw.org/news/2016/07/10/iraq-isis-rule-marked-executions-cruelty.

Human Rights Watch. *Living in Fear: Child Soldiers and the Tamil Tigers in Sri Lanka.* Human Rights Watch, November 2004. https://www.hrw.org/sites/default/files/reports/srilanka1104.pdf.

Human Rights Watch. "Syria: Arrests, Torture by Armed Group." January 28, 2019. https://www.hrw.org/news/2019/01/28/syria-arrests-torture-armed-group.

Human Rights Watch. "Syria: Extremists Restricting Women's Rights." January 13, 2014. https://www.hrw.org/news/2014/01/13/syria-extremists-restricting-womens-rights.

Human Rights Watch. *Under Kurdish Rule: Abuses in PYD-Run Enclaves of Syria.* Human Rights Watch, June 2014. https://www.hrw.org/report/2014/06/19/under-kurdish-rule/abuses-pyd-run-enclaves-syria.

Human Rights Watch. "You Can Still See Their Blood." October 10, 2013. https://www.hrw.org/report/2013/10/10/you-can-still-see-their-blood/executions-indiscriminate-shootings-and-hostage.

Ibrahim, Mohammed Abdulssattar. "HTS Takes Over Opposition Police Stations in Northern Syria." *Al-Monitor*, February 3, 2019. https://www.al-monitor.com/pulse/iw/originals/2019/01/syria-aleppo-hayat-tahrir-al-sham-control-free-syrian-police.html.

Ibrahim, Mohammed Abdulssattar, Ammar Hamou, and Alice Al Maleh. "Free Syrian Police in Northwestern Syria to 'Dissolve' Amid HTS Takeover." *Syria Direct*, January 10, 2019.

https://syriadirect.org/free-syrian-police-in-northwestern-syria-to-dissolve-amid-hts
-takeover/.

Ibrahim, Raymond, ed. and trans. *The Al Qaeda Reader*. Doubleday, 2007.

Idler, Annette, and James J. F. Forest. "Behavioral Patterns Among (Violent) Non-State Actors: A Study of Complementary Governance." *Stability* 4, no. 1 (January 2015): 1–19. https://doi .org/10.5334/sta.er.

Ingram, Haroro J., Craig Whiteside, and Charlie Winter. *The ISIS Reader: Milestone Texts of the Islamic State Movement*. Oxford University Press, 2020.

International Crisis Group. "The Best of Bad Options for Syria's Idlib." Middle East Report No. 197. International Crisis Group, March 2019. https://www.crisisgroup.org/middle-east -north-africa/eastern-mediterranean/syria/197-best-bad-options-syrias-idlib.

International Crisis Group. "Exploiting Disorder: Al-Qaeda and the Islamic State." Special Report No. 1. International Crisis Group, March 2016. https://www.crisisgroup.org/global /exploiting-disorder-al-qaeda-and-islamic-state.

International Crisis Group. "Fighting ISIS: The Road to and Beyond Raqqa." Middle East Briefing No. 53. International Crisis Group, April 2017. https://www.crisisgroup.org/middle -east-north-africa/eastern-mediterranean/syria/b053-fighting-isis-road-and-beyond -raqqa.

International Crisis Group. "Flight of Icarus? The PYD's Precarious Rise in Syria." Middle East Report No. 151. International Crisis Group, May 2014. https://www.crisisgroup.org/middle -east-north-africa/eastern-mediterranean/syria/flight-icarus-pyd-s-precarious-rise -syria.

International Crisis Group. "The Huthis: From Saada to Sanaa." Middle East Report No. 154. International Crisis Group, June 2014. https://www.crisisgroup.org/middle-east-north -africa/gulf-and-arabian-peninsula/yemen/huthis-saada-sanaa.

International Crisis Group. "The PKK's Fateful Choice in Northern Syria." Middle East Report No. 176. International Crisis Group, May 2017. https://www.crisisgroup.org/middle-east -north-africa/eastern-mediterranean/syria/176-pkk-s-fateful-choice-northern-syria.

International Crisis Group. "Voices of Idlib." July 11, 2018. https://titwane.fr/voices-of-idlib -international-crisis-group.

International Crisis Group. "Yemen's al-Qaeda: Expanding the Base." Middle East Report No. 174 International Crisis Group, February 2017. https://www.crisisgroup.org/middle-east -north-africa/gulf-and-arabian-peninsula/yemen/174-yemen-s-al-qaeda-expanding -base.

Ishakhan, Benjamin, and Sofya Shahad. "The Islamic State's Destruction of Yezidi Heritage: Responses, Resilience, and Reconstruction After Genocide." *Journal of Social Archaeology* 20, no. 1 (November 2019): 3–25. http://dx.doi.org/10.1177/1469605319884137.

Issa, Jana al-, and Hassan Ibrahim. "Will Tahrir al-Sham Succeed Where Others Fail? Investment in Idlib Under the Mantle of Salvation Govt." *Enab Baladi*, September 19, 2022. https://english.enabbaladi.net/archives/2022/09/investment-in-idlib-under-the-mantle -of-salvation-govt/.

Jabouri, Najim Abed al-, and Sterling Jensen. "The Iraqi and AQI Roles in the Sunni Awakening." *PRISM* 2, no. 1 (December 2010): 3–18. https://www.jstor.org/stable/10.2307/26469091.

Jackson, Ashley. *Life Under the Taliban Shadow Government*. Overseas Development Institute, June 2018. https://odi.org/en/publications/life-under-the-taliban-shadow-government/.

Jackson, Roy. "Authority." In *Islamic Political Thought: An Introduction*, edited by Gerhard Bowering, 25–36. Princeton University Press, 2015.

Jaffal, Omar al-. "Iraqi Hospitals Under IS Suffer Lack of Medicine, Staff." *Al-Monitor*, January 15, 2015. https://www.al-monitor.com/originals/2015/01/iraq-anbar-mosul-hospitals-islamic-state.html.

Jansen, Bram, Vivian Salama, and Lee Keath. "Life Under the Islamic State." Associated Press, June 4, 2015. http://interactives.ap.org/2015/inside-islamic-state/.

Jha, Prashant. *Battles of the Republic: A Contemporary History of Nepal*. Hurst & Co., 2014.

Jihadology. "Coronavirus and the Salvation Government—Hayat Tahrir al-Sham." July 9, 2020. https://jihadology.net/coronavirus-and-the-salvation-government-hayat-tahir-al-sham/.

Joes, Anthony James. *Modern Guerrilla Insurgency*. Greenwood, 1992.

Johnsen, Gregory D. *The Last Refuge: Yemen, al-Qaeda, and America's War in Arabia*. W. W. Norton & Co., 2013.

Johnsen, Gregory. "The End of AQAP as a Global Threat." Sana'a Center for Strategic Studies, March 5, 2020. https://sanaacenter.org/publications/analysis/9164.

Johnsen, Gregory. "Waning Vigilance: Al-Qaeda Resurgence in Yemen." Policy Watch No. 1551. Washington Institute for Near East Policy, July 2009. https://www.washingtoninstitute.org/policy-analysis/waning-vigilance-al-qaedas-resurgence-yemen.

Johnson, Thomas H. "Taliban Adaptations and Innovations." *Small Wars & Insurgencies* 24, no. 1 (February 2013): 3–27. https://doi.org/10.1080/09592318.2013.740228.

Johnson, Thomas H. *Taliban Narratives: The Use and Power of Stories in the Afghanistan Conflict*. Oxford University Press, 2017.

Johnson, Thomas H., and Matthew C. DuPee. "Analysing the New Taliban Code of Conduct (Layeha): An Assessment of Changing Perspectives and Strategies of the Afghan Taliban." *Central Asian Survey* 31, no. 1 (March 2012): 77–91. https://core.ac.uk/download/pdf/45464654.pdf.

Jones, Seth G. *A Persistent Threat: The Evolution of al-Qa'ida and Other Salafi-Jihadists*. RAND, 2014.

Jones, Seth G., and Patrick B. Johnston. "The Future of Insurgency." *Studies in Conflict and Terrorism* 36, no. 1 (June 2012): 1–25. https://doi.org/10.1080/1057610X.2013.739077.

Jones, Seth G., Charles Vallee, Danika Newlee, Nicholas Harrington, Clayton Sharb, and Hannah Byrne. *The Evolution of the Salafi-Jihadist Threat*. Center for Strategic and International Studies, November 2018. https://csis-website-prod.s3.amazonaws.com/s3fs-public/publication/181221_EvolvingTerroristThreat.pdf.

Jongerden, Joost. "Governing Kurdistan: Self-Administration in the Kurdistan Regional Government in Iraq and the Democratic Federation of Northern Syria." *Ethnopolitics* 18, no. 1 (November 2018): 61–75. https://doi.org/10.1080/17449057.2018.1525166.

Joscelyn, Thomas. "An al Qaeda Commander Comes Out from Shadow." *Long War Journal*, December 16, 2015. https://www.longwarjournal.org/archives/2015/12/an-al-qaeda-commander-comes-out-from-the-shadows.php.

Joscelyn, Thomas. "AQAP Provides Social Services, Implements Sharia While Advancing in Southern Yemen." *Long War Journal*, February 3, 2016. https://www.longwarjournal.org /archives/2016/02/aqap-provides-social-services-implements-sharia-while-advancing-in -southern-yemen.php.

Joscelyn, Thomas. "Fifteen Years After the 9/11 Attacks, al Qaeda Fights On." *Long War Journal*, September 11, 2016. https://www.longwarjournal.org/archives/2016/09/fifteen-years -after-the-911-attacks-al-qaeda-fights-on.php.

Julani, Abu Mohammad al-. Interview by Martin Smith. *Frontline*. PBS, February 2021. https:// www.pbs.org/wgbh/frontline/interview/abu-mohammad-al-jolani/.

Julani, Abu Muhammad al-. "Oh People of al-Sham." 2012. Jihadology. Accessed September 25, 2023. https://azelin.files.wordpress.com/2012/12/abc5ab-mue1b8a5ammad-al-jawlc481n c4ab-al-golani-220h-people-of-ash-shc481m-we-sacrifice-our-souls-for-you22-en.pdf.

Jusoor for Studies. "Al-Julani's Frequent Appearances Between Propaganda and Targeted Messages" [in Arabic]. May 25, 2020. https://www.jusoor.co/public/details/ظهور-الجولاني-المتكرّر-بين -الدعاية-والرسائل-الموجّهة/693/ar.

Kadercan, Burak. "Territorial Logic of the Islamic state: An Interdisciplinary Approach." *Territory, Politics, Governance* 9, no. 1 (March 2019): 94–110. https://doi.org/10.1080/21622671 .2019.1589563.

Kalyvas, Stathis N. "Is ISIS a Revolutionary Group and If Yes, What Are the Implications?" *Perspectives on Terrorism* 9, no. 4 (August 2015): 42–47. https://www.jstor.org/stable /26297413.

Kalyvas, Stathis N. *The Logic of Violence in Civil War*. Cambridge University Press, 2006.

Kalyvas, Stathis N. "Rebel Governance During the Greek Civil War." In Arjona et al., *Rebel Governance in Civil War*, 119–137.

Kaneva, Nadia, and Andrea Stanton. "An Alternative Vision of Statehood: Islamic State's Ideological Challenge to the Nation State." *Studies in Conflict & Terrorism* 46, no. 5 (June 2020): 640–658. https://doi.org/10.1080/1057610X.2020.1780030.

Kanj, Sultan al-. "Hayat Tahrir al-Sham Leader Seeks More Support in Syria's Idlib." *Al-Monitor*, April 8, 2022. https://www.al-monitor.com/originals/2022/04/hayat-tahrir-al -sham-leader-seeks-more-popular-support-syrias-idlib.

Kanj, Sultan al-. "Syria's Idlib University Bans Mixed-Gender Online Groups." *Al-Monitor*, June 22, 2021. https://www.al-monitor.com/originals/2021/06/syrias-idlib-university-bans -mixed-gender-online-groups.

Kanj, Sultan al-. "Syrian Jihadi Leader Golani Meets with Idlib's Christians." *Al-Monitor*, July 27, 2022. https://www.al-monitor.com/originals/2022/07/syrian-jihadi-leader-golani -meets-idlibs-christians.

Karouny, Mariam. "In Northeastern Syria, Islamic State Builds a Government." Reuters, September 4, 2014. https://www.reuters.com/article/us-syria-crisis-raqqa-insight/in-northeast -syria-islamic-state-builds-a-government-idUSKBN0GZ0D120140904.

Kasfir, Nelson. "Guerrillas and Civilian Participation: The National Resistance Army in Uganda, 1981–6." *Journal of Modern African Studies* 43, no. 2 (June 2005): 271–296. https:// www.jstor.org/stable/3876207.

Kasfir, Nelson. "Rebel Governance—Constructing a Field of Inquiry: Definitions, Scope, Patterns, Order, Causes." In Arjona et al., *Rebel Governance in Civil War*, 21–46.

Kassim, Abdulbasit. "Defining and Understanding the Religious Philosophy of *Jihadi-Salafism* and the Ideology of Boko Haram." *Politics, Religion & Ideology* 16, nos. 2–3 (September 2015): 173–200. https://doi.org/10.1080/21567689.2015.1074896.

Kendall, Elisabeth. "Al-Qaeda and Islamic State in Yemen." In *Jihadism Transformed: Al-Qaeda and Islamic State's Global Battle of Ideas*, edited by Simon Staffell and Akil Awan, 89–110. Oxford University Press, 2016.

Kendall, Elisabeth. "Contemporary Jihadi Militancy in Yemen: How Is the Threat Evolving?" Policy Paper No. 7. Middle East Institute, July 2018. https://www.mei.edu/sites/default/files /publications/MEI%20Policy%20Paper_Kendall_7.pdf.

Kendall, Elisabeth. "How Can al-Qaeda in the Arabian Peninsula Be Defeated?" *Washington Post*, May 3, 2016. https://www.washingtonpost.com/news/monkey-cage/wp/2016/05/03 /how-can-al-qaeda-in-the-arabian-peninsula-be-defeated/?utm_term=.180b422c87e2.

Kepel, Gilles. *Jihad: The Trail of Political Islam*. Harvard University Press, 2002.

Khaddour, Kheder. "How Regional Security Concerns Uniquely Constrain Governance in Northeastern Syria." Carnegie Endowment for International Peace, March 23, 2017. https:// carnegie-mec.org/2017/03/23/how-regional-security-concerns-uniquely-constrain -governance-in-northeastern-syria-pub-68380.

Khaddour, Kheder, and Kevin Mazur. "Eastern Expectations: The Changing Dynamics in Syria's Tribal Regions." Carnegie Endowment for International Peace, February 28, 2017. https://carnegie-mec.org/2017/02/28/eastern-expectations-changing-dynamics-in-syria-s -tribal-regions-pub-68008.

Khalaf, Rana. *Governing Rojava: Layers of Legitimacy in Syria*. Chatham House, 2016.

Khalifa Barnard, Ines, and Charlie Winter. "Reframing Jihadism: Deciphering the Identity, Politics, Agenda of Hayat Tahrir al-Sham in Northwest Syria." In *The Handbook of Media and Culture in the Middle East*, edited by Joe F. Khalil, Gholam Khiabany, Tourya Guaaybess, and Bilge Yesil, 396–413. John Wiley & Sons, 2023.

Khalifa, Dareen. "Idlib and the Hayat Tahrir al-Sham Conundrum in Syria." In Cook and Maher, *The Rule Is for None but Allah*, 249–264.

Khalifa, Dareen. "The Jihadist Factor in Syria's Idlib: A Conversation with Abu Muhammad al-Julani." International Crisis Group, February 20, 2020. https://www.crisisgroup.org /middle-east-north-africa/east-mediterranean-mena/syria/jihadist-factor-syrias-idlib -conversation-abu-muhammad-al-jolani.

Khalifa, Ninar. "Idlib's Druze Complain of Persecution." Syrians for Truth & Justice, November 24, 2022. https://stj-sy.org/en/idlibs-druze-complain-of-persecution/.

Khan, Adnan R. "Life Under ISIS: Four Stories of Terror Endured." *Maclean's*, December 14, 2016. https://www.macleans.ca/news/world/life-under-isis-four-stories-of-terror-endured/.

Khatab, Sayed. *The Political Thought of Sayyid Qutb: The Theory of Jahiliyyah*. Routledge, 2006.

Khateb, Khaled al-. "Al-Qaeda-Linked Leader Again Descends on Idlib Streets to Polish His Image." *Al-Monitor*, February 2, 2021. https://www.al-monitor.com/originals/2021/02/syria -idlib-hts-leader-public-appearance-terrorist-list.html.

Khateb, Khaled al-. "Christians in Syria's Idlib hold major mass." *Al-Monitor*, September 4, 2022. https://www.al-monitor.com/originals/2022/09/christians-syrias-idlib-hold-major -mass.

Khateb, Khaled al-. "Hayat Tahrir al-Sham in Consultations on Planned Military and Civil Administrations in Idlib." Chatham House, February 21, 2019. https://kalam.chathamhouse .org/articles/hayat-tahrir-al-sham-in-consultations-on-planned-military-and-civil -administrations-in-idlib/.

Khateb, Khaled al-. "Idlib Residents Demand Release of Detainees in Jihadist Group's Prisons." *Al-Monitor*, January 26, 2022. https://www.al-monitor.com/originals/2022/01/idlib -residents-demand-release-detainees-jihadist-groups-prisons.

Khateb, Khaled al-. "Reshuffle of HTS-Linked Government Fails to Bring Hope in Idlib." *Al-Monitor*, December 29, 2019. https://www.al-monitor.com/pulse/originals/2019/12/syria -idlib-hayat-tahrir-al-sham-government-protests.html.

Khateb, Khaled al-. "Syrian Jihadist Group Opens Food Market in North of Idlib." *Al-Monitor*, December 26, 2021. https://www.al-monitor.com/originals/2021/12/syrian-jihadist-group -opens-food-market-north-idlib.

Khatib, Lina. "Is the Syrian Regime 'Winning' the War?" *Asharq al-Awsat*, March 13, 2018. https://aawsat.com/english/home/article/1203536/lina-khatib/syrian-regime-winning -war.

Khatib, Lina. *The Islamic State's Strategy.* Carnegie Endowment for International Peace, June 2015. https://carnegieendowment.org/research/2015/06/the-islamic-states-strategy -lasting-and-expanding?lang=en.

Kilcullen, David. "Countering Global Insurgency." *Journal of Strategic Studies* 28, no. 4 (January 2007): 597–617. https://doi.org/10.1080/01402390500300956

Kilcullen, David. *Counterinsurgency.* Oxford University Press, 2010.

Kilcullen, David. *Out of the Mountains: The Coming Age of the Urban Guerrilla.* Oxford University Press, 2013.

Koheler-Derrik, Gabriel. *A False Foundation? AQAP, Tribes and Ungoverned Spaces in Yemen.* Combating Terrorism Center at West Point, September 2011. https://www.files.ethz.ch/isn /133147/CTC_False_Foundation2.pdf.

Koontz, Kayla. "Borders Beyond Borders: The Many (Many) Kurdish Political Parties of Syria." Policy Paper 2019-21. Middle East Institute, October 2019. https://www.mei.edu /publications/borders-beyond-borders-many-many-kurdish-political-parties-syria.

Lackner, Helen. "The Change Squares of Yemen: Civil Resistance in an Unlikely Context." In Roberts et al., *Civil Resistance in the Arab Spring*, 141–168.

Ladbury, Sarah, Hamsatu Allamin, Chitra Nagarajan, Paul Francis, and Ukoha Okorafor Ukiwo. "Jihadi Groups and State-Building: The Case of Boko Haram in Nigeria." *Stability: International Journal of Security and Development* 5, no. 1 (2016): 1–19. https:// stabilityjournal.org/articles/10.5334/sta.427.

Lahoud, Nelly. "The Neglected Sex: The Jihadis' Exclusion of Women from Jihad." *Terrorism and Political Violence* 26, no. 5 (February 2014): 780–802. https://doi.org/10.1080/09546553 .2013.772511.

Lakomy, Miron. "Crouching *Shahid*, Hidden *Jihad*: Mapping the Online Propaganda Campaign of the Hayat Tahrir al-Sham-Affiliated Ebaa News Agency." *Behavioral Sciences of Terrorism and Political Aggression* 15, no. 3 (September 2021): 361–389. https://doi.org/10.1080/19434472.2021.1977372.

Laqueur, Walter. *Guerrilla Warfare: A Historical and Critical Study*. Routledge, 1976.

Lecomte-Tilouine, Marie. "Terror in a Maoist Model Village in Mid-Western Nepal." In *Windows into a Revolution: Ethnographies of Maoism in India and Nepal*, edited by Alpa Shah and Judith Pettigrew, 207–232. Routledge, 2017.

Ledwidge, Frank. *Rebel Law: Insurgents, Courts and Justice in Modern Conflict*. Hurst & Co., 2017.

Lee, Chris. "The FARC and the Colombian Left: Time for a Political Solution?" *Latin American Perspectives* 39, no. 1 (January 2012): 28–42. https://www.jstor.org/stable/23238966.

Leezenberg, Michiel. "The Ambiguities of Democratic Autonomy: The Kurdish Movement in Turkey and Rojava." *Southeast European and Black Sea Studies* 16, no. 4 (October 2016): 671–690. https://doi.org/10.1080/14683857.2016.1246529.

Lefler, Jenna. "Life Under ISIS in Mosul." Institute for the Study of War, July 28, 2014. http://www.iswresearch.org/2014/07/life-under-isis-in-mosul.html.

Levant 24. "Idlib Local Authorities Continue to Improve New Water-Pump Station." August 1, 2022. https://levant24.com/news/2022/08/idlib-local-authorities-continue-to-improve-new-water-pump-station/.

Levitt, Matthew. "The Assad Regime's Business Model for Supporting the Islamic State." *Lawfare*, September 26, 2021. https://www.lawfaremedia.org/article/assad-regimes-business-model-supporting-islamic-state.

Lewis, Jessica. "Al-Qaeda in Iraq Resurgent: The Breaking Walls Campaign, Part I." Middle East Security Report 14. Institute for the Study of War, September 2013. https://www.understandingwar.org/report/al-qaeda-iraq-resurgent.

Lewis, Jessica. "Al-Qaeda in Iraq Resurgent Part II." Middle East Security Report 15. Institute for the Study of War, October 2013. https://www.understandingwar.org/report/al-qaeda-iraq-resurgent-part-ii.

Lewis, Jessica. "The Islamic State: A Counter-Strategy for a Counter-State." Middle East Security Report 21. Institute for the Study of War, July 2014. https://www.understandingwar.org/sites/default/files/Lewis-Center%20of%20gravity.pdf.

Lia, Brynjar. *Architect of Global Jihad: The Life of Al Qaeda Strategist Abu Mus'ab Al-Suri*. Columbia University Press, 2008.

Lia, Brynjar. "The Islamic State's tribal policies in Syria and Iraq." *Third World Thematics* 6, nos. 1–3 (November 2022): 32–51. https://doi.org/10.1080/23802014.2022.2147990.

Lia, Brynjar. "The *Jihādī* Movement and Rebel Governance: A Reassertion of a Patriarchal Order?" *Die Welt des Islam* 57, nos. 3–4 (2017): 459–478. https://www.jstor.org/stable/26568534.

Lia, Brynjar. "Understanding Jihadi Proto-States." *Perspectives on Terrorism* 9, no. 4 (August 2015): 31–41. https://pt.icct.nl/article/understanding-jihadi-proto-states.

Lister, Charles. "The Fight for Supremacy in Northwest Syria and the Implications for Global Jihad." *CTC Sentinel* 14, no. 7 (September 2021): 44–62. https://ctc.westpoint.edu/twenty

-years-after-9-11-the-fight-for-supremacy-in-northwest-syria-and-the-implications-for
-global-jihad/.

Lister, Charles. "Hayat Tahrir al-Sham: To Unite or To Divide the Ranks?" In *How al-Qaeda Survived Drones, Uprisings, and the Islamic State,* edited by Aaron Zelin, 20–31. Washington Institute for Near East Policy, 2017.

Lister, Charles. "ISIS's Extortion and 'Taxation' Are Lucrative and Hard to Suppress." *New York Times,* November 20, 2015. https://www.nytimes.com/roomfordebate/2015/11/20/draining
-isis-coffers/isis-extortion-and-taxation-are-lucrative-and-hard-to-suppress.

Lister, Charles. "Jihadi Rivalry: The Islamic State Challenges al-Qaeda." Brookings Doha Center Analysis Paper No. 16. Brookings Institution, January 2016. https://www.brookings
.edu/articles/jihadi-rivalry-the-islamic-state-challenges-al-qaida/.

Lister, Charles. "Profiling the Islamic State." Brookings Doha Center Analysis Paper No. 13. Brookings Institution, November 2014. https://www.brookings.edu/wp-content/uploads
/2014/12/en_web_lister.pdf.

Lister, Charles. "Profiling Jabhat al-Nusra." Analysis Paper No. 245. Brookings Institution July 2016. https://www.brookings.edu/wp-content/uploads/2016/07/iwr_20160728_profiling
_nusra.pdf.

Lister, Charles. *The Syrian Jihad: Al-Qaeda, the Islamic State and the Evolution of an Insurgency.* Oxford University Press, 2015.

Loidolt, Bryce. "Managing the Global and Local: The Dual Agenda of Al Qaeda in the Arabian Peninsula." *Studies in Conflict & Terrorism* 34, no. 2 (January 2011): 102–123. https://
doi.org/10.1080/1057610X.2011.538831.

Lokmanoglu, Ayse, and Alexandra Phelan. "Monetary Economics, Illicit Economies, and Legitimation: The Case of Islamic State." In Cook and Maher, *The Rule Is for None but Allah,* 167–186.

Maher, Shiraz. *Salafi-Jihadism: The History of an Idea.* Oxford University Press, 2016.

Mahmood, Mona. "Life in Mosul One Year On: 'Isis with All Its Brutality Is More Honest than the Shia Government." *Guardian,* June 10, 2015. https://www.theguardian.com/world/2015
/jun/10/mosul-residents-one-year-on-isis-brutality.

Malejacq, Romain. "From Rebel to Quasi-State: Governance, Diplomacy and Legitimacy in the Midst of Afghanistan's Wars (1979–2001)." *Small Wars & Insurgencies* 28, nos. 4–5 (July 2017): 867–886. https://doi.org/10.1080/09592318.2017.1322332.

Maley, William. *The Afghanistan Wars.* Palgrave Macmillan, 2009.

Malkasian, Carter. *The American War in Afghanistan: A History.* Oxford University Press, 2021.

Mallat, Chibli, and Edward Mortimer. "The Background to Civil Resistance in the Middle East." In Roberts et al., *Civil Resistance in the Arab Spring,* 1–29.

Mampilly, Zachariah. "Performing the Nation-State: Rebel Governance and Symbolic Processes." In Arjona et al., *Rebel Governance in Civil War,* 74–97.

Mampilly, Zachariah. *Rebel Rulers: Insurgent Governance and Civilian Life During War.* Cornell University Press, 2011.

Mampilly, Zachariah. "Rebel Taxation: Between Moral and Market Economy." In *Rebel Economies: Warlords, Insurgents, Humanitarians,* edited by Nicola Di Cosmo, Didier, Fassin, Clémence Pinaud, 77–100. Rowman & Littlefield, 2021.

Mampilly, Zachariah, and Megan Stewart. "A Typology of Rebel Political Institutional Arrangements." *Journal of Conflict Resolution* 65, no. 1 (January 2021): 15–45. https://doi.org/10.1177/0022002720935642.

Mansour, Hadia. "Syria: Confusion Reigns in Kfar Nabel School System." Institute for War and Peace Reporting, June 19, 2015. https://iwpr.net/global-voices/syria-confusion-reigns-kfar-nabels-school.

Mapping Militants Project. "Revolutionary Armed Forces of Colombia—People's Army." Center for International Security and Cooperation, last modified July 1, 2019. https://mappingmilitants.org/profiles/revolutionary-armed-forces-of-colombia-peoples-army?highlight=farc.

March, Andrew, and Mara Revkin. "Caliphate of Law." *Foreign Affairs*, April 15, 2015. https://www.foreignaffairs.com/articles/syria/2015-04-15/caliphate-law.

Marchal, Roland. "The Rise of a Jihadist Movement in a Country at War. Harakat al-Shabaab al-Muajhidin in Somalia." Research Report. Sciences Po, 2011. https://sciencespo.hal.science/hal-03641269.

Margolin, Devorah, and Aaron Zelin. "Introduction." In *Jihadist Governance and Statecraft*, edited by Devorah Margolin and Aaron Y. Zelin, 1–7. Washington Institute for Near East Policy, 2024.

Marighella, Carlos. *Mini-Manual of the Urban Guerrilla*. Abraham Guillen Press, 2002.

Martin, Maxwell. "Al-Qaeda's Syrian Judiciary—Is It Really What al-Jolani Makes It Out to Be?" *Syria Comment*, November 9, 2014. https://www.joshualandis.com/blog/al-qaedas-syrian-judiciary-really-al-jolani-makes/.

Martínez, José Ciro, and Brent Eng. "Stifling Stateness: The Assad Regime's Campaign Against Rebel Governance." *Security Dialogue* 49, no. 4 (2018): 235–253.

Mason, Ann. "Colombia's Conflicts and the Theories of World Politics." *Items & Issues* 4, nos. 2–3 (2003): 7–11. https://issuu.com/ssrcitemsissues/docs/i_i_vol_4_no_2-3_2003.

Matraji, Nour, and Richard Hall. "The Other Islamic State: Al-Qaeda Is Still Fighting for an Emirate of Its Own." Public Radio International, May 2, 2016. https://www.pri.org/stories/2016-04-29/other-islamic-state-al-qaeda-still-fighting-emirate-its-own.

Mawardi, Abdul Hassan al-. *Al-Ahkam as-Sultaniyyah: The Laws of Islamic Governance*. Translated by Asadullah Yate. Ta-Ha publishers, 1996.

McCants, William. "Experts Weigh In (Part 6): Is ISIS Good at Governing?" Brookings, March 22, 2016. https://www.brookings.edu/blog/markaz/2016/03/22/experts-weigh-in-part-6-is-isis-good-at-governing/.

McCants, William. "How ISIS Got Its Flag." *Atlantic*, September 22, 2015. https://www.theatlantic.com/international/archive/2015/09/isis-flag-apocalypse/406498/.

McCants, William. *The ISIS Apocalypse: The History, Strategy, and Doomsday Vision of the Islamic State*. St. Martin's Press, 2015.

McLoughlin, Paul. "Syria Weekly: Idlib Civilians Demand No Assad, No Jolani." *New Arab*, November 8, 2019. https://english.alaraby.co.uk/english/indepth/2019/11/9/syria-weekly-idlib-civilians-demand-no-assad-no-jolani.

Meijer, Roel, ed. *Global Salafism: Islam's New Religious Movement*. Oxford University Press, 2013/

Meijer, Roel. "Introduction." In Roel, *Global Salafism*, 1–31.

Mendelsohn, Barak. "The Limits of Ideologically-Unlikely Partnerships: Syria's Support for Jihadi Terrorist Groups." *Studies in Conflict & Terrorism* 46, no. 9 (January 2021): 1653–1677. https://doi.org/10.1080/1057610X.2020.1868094.

Metz, Steven. *Rethinking Insurgency*. U.S. Army War College, 2007.

Michlig, Georgia J., Riyadh Lafta, Maha al-Nuaimi, and Gilbert Burnham. "Providing Healthcare Under ISIS: A Qualitative Analysis of Healthcare Worker Experiences in Mosul, Iraq Between June 2014 and June 2017." *Global Public Health* 14, no. 10 (April 2019): 1414–1427. https://doi.org/10.1080/17441692.2019.1609061.

Middle East Monitor. "Iraqi Court Sentences 24 to Death Over Speicher Massacre." July 9, 2015. https://www.middleeastmonitor.com/news/middle-east/19749-iraqi-court-sentences-24 -to-death-over-speicher-massacre.

Moaveni, Azadeh. "ISIS Women and Enforcers in Syria Recount Collaboration, Anguish and Escape." *New York Times*, November 21, 2015. https://www.nytimes.com/2015/11/22/world /middleeast/isis-wives-and-enforcers-in-syria-recount-collaboration-anguish-and -escape.html.

Molloy, Mark. "Islamic State textbooks Featuring Tanks and Guns Used to Teach Children Maths in School." *Telegraph*, February 16, 2017. https://www.telegraph.co.uk/news/2017/02 /16/isis-textbooks-featuring-guns-tanks-used-teach-children-maths/.

Moore, Pauline. "When Do Ties Bind? Foreign Fighters, Social Embeddedness, and Violence Against Civilians." *Journal of Peace Research* 56, no. 2 (March 2019): 279–294. https://www .jstor.org/stable/48595943.

Moughty, Sarah. "Gaith Abdul Ahad's Journey 'Into Al-Qaeda Heartland.'" *Frontline*. PBS, May 29, 2012. https://www.pbs.org/wgbh/frontline/article/ghaith-abdul-ahads-journey -into-al-qaeda-heartland/.

Muqrin, Abd al-Aziz al-. *A Practical Course for Guerrilla Warfare*. In *Al-Qaida's Doctrine for Insurgency: Abd Al-Aziz Al-Muqrin's* A Practical Course for Guerrilla Warfare. Translated and analyzed by Norman Cigar. Potomac Books, 2009.

Muslimi, Farea al-. "How Sunni-Shia Sectarianism Is Poisoning Yemen." Carnegie Endowment for International Peace, December 29, 2015. https://carnegieendowment.org/middle-east /diwan/2015/12/how-sunni-shia-sectarianism-is-poisoning-yemen?lang=en&center =middle-east.

Nadarajah, Suthaharan, and Luxshi Vimalarajah. "The Politics of Transformation: the LTTE and the 2002–2006 Peace Process in Sri Lanka." Transition Series No. 4. Berghof Foundation, April 2008. https://berghof-foundation.org/library/the-politics-of-transformation-the -ltte-and-the-2002-2006-peace-process-in-sri-lanka.

Nagi, Ahmed. "Yemen's Houthis Used Multiple Identities to Advance." Carnegie Endowment for International Peace Middle East Center, March 19, 2019. https://carnegie-mec.org/2019 /03/19/yemen-s-houthis-used-multipleidentities-to-advance-pub-78623.

Nagl, John A. "Foreword." In *Counterinsurgency Warfare: Theory and Practice*, by David Galula. Praeger Security international, 2006.

Nagl, John A. *Learning to Eat Soup with a Knife*. Chicago University Press, 2005.

Naji, Abu Bakr. *The Management of Savagery.* Translated by Will McCants. John M. Olin Institute for Strategic Studies at Harvard University, 2006.

Nasr, Seyyed Hossein. *The Study Quran.* Harper Collins, 2015.

Nassar, Alaa, and Alice al-Maleh. "Civil Society Activist Defies War and Islamist Intimidation in Her Efforts to Empower Women." *Syria Direct*, April 25, 2018. https://syriadirect .org/civil-society-activist-defies-war-and-islamist-intimidation-in-her-efforts-to -empower-women/#.WuMjbjJqbP8.twitter.

Nassar, Alaa, and Jodi Brignola. "'From the Gutter to the Rain': Inside HTS's Takeover of Northwestern Syria." *Syria Direct*, February 25, 2019. https://syriadirect.org/news/from-the -gutter-to-the-rain-inside-hts-takeover-of-northwestern-syria/.

National Public Radio. "Syrian Christians Face New Threat from Rebel Alliance." July 3, 2015. https://www.npr.org/2015/07/03/419824382/syrian-christians-face-new-threat-from-rebel -alliance.

Neuendorf, Henri. "Al-Qaeda Militants Destroy Sufi Shrine in Yemen." *Artnet*, February 16, 2015. https://news.artnet.com/art-world/al-qaeda-militants-destroy-sufi-shrine-in-yemen -255050.

New Arab. "Jihadist HTS, Former al-Qaeda Affiliate, Seeks 'Moderate Rebrand' to Secure Seat in Syria's Political Process." June 4, 2020. https://www.newarab.com/news/hts-seeks -moderate-rebrand-secure-seat-negotiations.

New Arab. "North-West Syria Receives Covid-19 Vaccines Amid Delta Variant Surge." September 7, 2021. https://english.alaraby.co.uk/news/northwest-syria-receives-covax-delivery -amid-delta-surge.

New Humanitarian. "Behind Militia Lines in Jaar." March 27, 2012. http://www .thenewhumanitarian.org/report/95176/yemen-behind-militia-lines-jaar.

Nofal, Walid al-, and Madeline Edwards. "'Blood for Blood': Murder, Retribution Killings Mire Syria's Eastern Desert as Tribes Avenge Islamic State-Era Abuses." *Syria Direct*, August 22, 2018. https://syriadirect.org/news/'blood-for-blood'-murder-retribution-killings-mire -syria's-eastern-desert-as-tribes-avenge-islamic-state-era-abuses/.

Nusse, Andrea. *Muslim Palestine: The Ideology of Hamas.* RoutledgeCurzon, 2003.

Obeid, Ahmad. "Inside HTS' Most Dangerous Prison." *Syria Untold*, October 9, 2020. https:// syriauntold.com/2020/10/09/inside-hts-most-dangerous-prison/.

O'Neill, Bard E. *Insurgency and Terrorism: From Revolution to Apocalypse.* Manas, 2006.

Orient Net. "Details of the Salvation Government's Confiscation of Christian Property in Idlib" [in Arabic]. November 22, 2018. https://orient-news.net/ar/news_show/156949/0 تفاصيل-مصادرة-حكومة-الإنقاذ-أملاك-المسيحيين-في-إدلب/.

Özçelik, Burcu. "Explaining the Kurdish Democratic Union Party's Self-Governance Practices in Northern Syria, 2012–18." *Government and Opposition* 55, no. 4 (October 2020): 690–710. https://doi.org/10.1017/gov.2019.1.

Page, Michael, Lara Challita, and Alistair Harris. "Al Qaeda in the Arabian Peninsula: Framing Narratives and Prescriptions." *Terrorism & Political Violence* 23, no. 2 (March 2011): 150–172. https://doi.org/10.1080/09546553.2010.526039.

Pankhurst, Reza. *The Inevitable Caliphate? A History of the Struggle for Global Islamic Union, 1942 to the Present.* Oxford University Press, 2013.

Payne, Kenneth. "Building the Base: Al Qaeda's Focoist Strategy." *Studies in Conflict & Terrorism* 34, no. 2 (2011): 124–143. https://doi.org/10.1080/1057610X.2011.538832.

Paz, Reuven. "Debates Within the Family." In Roel, *Global Salafism*, 268–280.

Péclard, Didier, and Delphine Mechoulan. "Rebel Governance and the Politics of Civil War." Working Paper 1/2015. Swisspeace, July 2015. https://www.swisspeace.ch/assets/publications /downloads/Working-Papers/3b4a3caa24/Rebel-Governance-and-the-Politics-of-Civil -War-Working-Paper-15-swisspeace-didier_peclard.pdf

Péclard, Didier, Martina Santschi, Jon Schubert, Gilson Lázaro, Leben Moro, and Ousmane Zina. "Civil Wars and State Formation: Violence and the Politics of Legitimacy in Angola, Cote d'Ivoire and South Sudan." Working Paper. Swiss Network of International Studies, July 2019. https://snis.ch/wp-content/uploads/2020/01/2016_Pe%CC%81clard_Working-Paper.pdf.

Perkins, Brian M. "Yemen: Between Revolution and Regression." *Studies in Conflict and Terrorism* 40, no. 4 (July 2016): 300–317. https://doi.org/10.1080/1057610X.2016.1205368.

Phelan, Alexandra. "Engaging Insurgency: The Impact of the 2016 Colombian Peace Agreement on FARC's Political Participation." *Studies in Conflict & Terrorism* 42, no. 9 (February 2918): 836–852. https://doi.org/10.1080/1057610X.2018.1432027.

Phillips, Sarah. "Al-Qaeda and the Struggle for Yemen." *Survival* 53, no. 1 (2011): 95–120. https://www.tandfonline.com/doi/epdf/10.1080/00396338.2011.555605?needAccess=true.

Phillips, Sarah. "Making al-Qa'ida Legible: Counter-Terrorism and the Reproduction of Terrorism." *European Journal of International Relations* 25, no. 4 (April 2019): 1132–1156. https://doi.org/10.1177/1354066119837335.

Phillips, Sarah. "What Comes Next in Yemen? Al-Qaeda, the Tribes and State-Building." In *Yemen on the Brink*, edited by Christopher Boucek and Marina Ottaway, 75–90. Carnegie Endowment for International Peace, 2010.

Phillips, Sarah, and Rodger Shanahan. "Al-Qa'ida, Tribes and Instability in Yemen." Analysis. Lowy Institute for International Policy, November 2009. https://www.jstor.org/stable /resrep10126.

Phillips Erb, Kelly. "Islamic State Warns Christians Convert, Pay Tax, Leave or Die." *Forbes*, July 19, 2014. https://www.forbes.com/sites/kellyphillipserb/2014/07/19/islamic-state-warns -christians-convert-pay-tax-leave-or-die/#1af0149e2c25.

Physicians for Human Rights. "Destruction, Obstruction and Inaction: The Makings of a Health Crisis in Northern Syria." December 15, 2021. https://phr.org/our-work/resources /syria-health-disparities/.

Pierret, Thomas, and Laila Alrefaai. "Religious Governance in Syria Amid Territorial Fragmentation." In *Return to Islamic Institutions in Arab States: Mapping the Dynamics of Control, Co-option and Contention*, edited by Frederic Wehrey, 1–33. Carnegie Endowment for International Peace, 2021.

Plebani, Andrea. "The Unfolding Legacy of al-Qaeda in Iraq: From al-Zarqawi to the New Islamic Caliphate." In *New (and Old) Patterns of Jihadism: Al-Qa'ida, the Islamic State and Beyond*, edited by Andrea Plebani, 1–25. ISPI, 2014.

Podder, Sukanya. "Understanding the Legitimacy of Armed Groups: A Relational Perspective." *Small Wars and Insurgencies* 28, nos. 4–5 (July 2017): 686–708. https://doi.org/10.1080 /09592318.2017.1322333.

Pool, David. *From Guerrillas to Government: The Eritrean People's Liberation Front.* University Press, 2001.

Potgieter, Jakkie. "Taking Aid from the Devil Himself: UNITA's Support Structures." In *Angola's War Economy: The Role of Oil and Diamonds*, edited by Jakkie Cilliers and Christian Dietrich, 255–274. Institute for Security Studies, 2000.

Provost, Renée. "FARC Justice: Rebel Rule of Law." *UC Irvine Law Review* 8, no. 2 (March 2018): 227–274. https://escholarship.org/uc/item/72q1w1h0.

Provost, René. *Rebel Courts: The Administration of Justice by Armed Insurgents.* Oxford University Press, 2021.

Qurashi, Abu Ubayd al-. "Revolutionary Wars." Translated by Michael W. S. Ryan. In *Decoding Al-Qaeda's Strategy: The Deep Battle Against America*, by Michael W. S. Ryan, 269–279. Columbia University Press, 2013.

Qutb, Sayyid. *Milestones.* Islamic Book Service, 2005.

Radio al-Kul. "The Saraqib Power Station Supplies Electricity to the Homes of the Village of Maardabsa" [in Arabic]. March 30, 2017. https://www.radioalkul.com/p103792/.

Radio al-Kul. "Al-Nusra Imposes Zakat on the Merchants of the Town of al-Dana in Idlib" [in Arabic]. June 29, 2015. https://www.radioalkul.com/%D8%A7%D9%84%D9%86%D8%B5%D8%B1%D8%A9-%D8%AA%D9%81%D8%B1%D8%B6-%D8%A7%D9%84%D8%B2%D9%83%D8%A7%D8%A9-%D8%B9%D9%84%D9%89-%D8%AA%D8%AC%D8%A7%D8%B1-%D8%A8%D9%84%D8%AF%D8%A9-%D8%A7%D9%84%D8%AF%D8%A7%D9%86%D9%86/.

Radman, Hussam. *Al-Qaeda's Strategic Retreat in Yemen.* Sana'a Center for Strategic Studies, April 2019. https://sanaacenter.org/publications/analysis/7306.

Rafaat, Lina, and Charles Lister. "From Goods and Services to Counterterrorism: Local Messaging in Hay'at Tahrir al-Sham Propaganda." Jihadica, September 12, 2018. http://www.jihadica.com/from-goods-and-services-to-counterterrorism/.

Raghavan, Sudarsan. "In Yemen, Tribal Militias in a Fierce Battle with al-Qaeda Wing." *Washington Post*, September 10, 2012. https://www.washingtonpost.com/world/middle_east/in-yemen-tribal-militias-in-a-fierce-battle-with-al-qaeda-wing/2012/09/10/0cce6f1e-f2b2-11e1-b74c-84ed55e0300b_story.html.

Rahhal, Ghalia. "I Have Huge Faith in Syrian Women." *Syria Campaign*, March 8, 2022. https://diary.thesyriacampaign.org/i-have-huge-faith-in-syrian-women/.

Rahman, Sadiq Abdul. "From the Events of Four Days in Saraqib" [in Arabic]. *al-Jumhuriya*, July 25, 2017. https://aljumhuriya.net/ar/2017/07/25/38504/.

Reno, William. "Predatory Rebellions and Governance: The National Patriotic Front of Liberia, 1989–1992." In Arjona et al., *Rebel Governance in Civil War*, 265–287.

Reuters. "First Batch of Covid-19 Vaccines Arrives in Northwest Syria." April 1, 2021. https://www.reuters.com/world/middle-east/first-batch-covid-19-vaccines-arrives-northwest-syria-2021-04-21/.

Revkin, Mara. "Competitive Governance and Displacement Decisions Under Rebel Rule: Evidence from the Islamic State in Iraq." *Journal of Conflict Resolution*, August 25, 2020. https://dx.doi.org/10.2139/ssrn.3365503.

Revkin, Mara. "Does the Islamic State Have a 'Social Contract?' Evidence from Iraq and Syria." Working Paper No. 9. Program on Governance and Local Development, 2016. https://papers.ssrn.com/sol3/papers.cfm?abstract_id=3732239.

Revkin, Mara. "ISIS's Social Contract." *Foreign Affairs*, January 10, 2016. https://www.foreignaffairs.com/articles/syria/2016-01-10/isis-social-contract.

Revkin, Mara. "The Legal Foundations of the Islamic State." Analysis Paper No. 23. Brookings Project on US Relations with the Islamic World, July 2016. https://www.brookings.edu/wp-content/uploads/2016/07/Brookings-Analysis-Paper_Mara-Revkin_Web.pdf.

Revkin, Mara. "What Explains Taxation by Resource-Rich Rebels? Evidence from the Islamic State in Syria." *Journal of Politics* 82, no. 2 (January 2019): 757–764. https://doi.org/10.1086/706597.

Revkin, Mara, and Ariel Ahram. "Perspectives on the Rebel Social Contract: Exit, Voice and Loyalty in the Islamic State in Iraq and Syria." *World Development*, no. 132 (August 2020): 1–9. https://doi.org/10.1016/j.worlddev.2020.104981.

Revkin, Mara, and William McCants. "Experts Weigh In: Is ISIS Good at Governing?" Brookings, November 20, 2015. https://www.brookings.edu/blog/markaz/2015/11/20/experts-weigh-in-is-isis-good-at-governing/.

Revkin, Mara, and Elisabeth Jean Wood. "The Islamic State's Patterns of Sexual Violence: Ideology and Institutions, Policies and Practices." *Journal of Global Security Studies* 6, no. 2 (July 2020): 1–20. https://doi.org/10.1093/jogss/ogaa038.

Richani, Nazih. *Systems of Violence: The Political Economy of War and Peace in Colombia.* State University of New York Press, 2002.

Richards, Joanne. "An Institutional History of the Liberation Tigers of Tamil Eelam (LTTE)." CCDP Working Paper No. 10. Center of Conflict Development and Peacebuilding, October 2014. https://repository.graduateinstitute.ch/record/292651?v=pdf.

Risse, Thomas. *Governance Without a State? Policies and Politics in Areas of Limited Statehood.* Columbia University Press, 2011.

Risse, Thomas. "Limited Statehood: A Critical Perspective." In *The Oxford Handbook of Transformations of the State*, edited by Stephan Leibfried, Evelyine Huber, Matthew Lange, Jonah D. Levi, Frank Nullmeier, and John D. Stephen, 152–168. Oxford University Press, 2015.

Roberts, Adam. "Civil Resistance and the Fate of the Arab Spring." In Roberts et al., *Civil Resistance in the Arab Spring*, 270–325.

Roberts, Adam. "The Fate of the Arab Spring: Ten Propositions." *Asian Journal of Middle Eastern and Islamic Studies* 12, no. 3 (January 2019): 273–289. https://doi.org/10.1080/25765949.2018.1546977.

Roberts, Adam, Michael J. Willis, Rory McCarty, and Timothy Garton Ash, eds. *Civil Resistance in the Arab Spring: Triumphs and Disasters.* Oxford University Press, 2016.

Robinson, Eric. "Cutting the Islamic State's Money Supply." *National Interest*, July 20, 2016. https://nationalinterest.org/blog/the-buzz/cutting-the-islamic-states-money-supply-17046.

Robinson, Eric, Daniel Egel, Patrick B. Johnston, Sean Mann, Alexander D. Rothenberg, and David Stebbins. *When the Islamic State Comes to Town.* RAND, 2017.

Rocchi, Daniele. "Syria: Idlib, Christians' Christmas Under al-Qaeda rule, with No Lights But with the Light." *Agensir*, December 23, 2019. https://archivio.agensir.it/2019/12/23/syria-idlib -christians-christmas-under-al-qaeda-rule-with-no-lights-but-with-the-light/.

Rodriguéz-Franco, Diana. "Internal Wars, Taxation and State Building." *American Sociological Review* 81, no. 1 (December 2015): 190–213. https://doi.org/10.1177/0003122415615903.

Roggio, Bill. "Al Qaeda Seizes More Territory in Southern Yemen." *Long War Journal*, February 11, 2016. https://www.longwarjournal.org/archives/2016/02/al-qaeda-seizes-more -territory-in-southern-yemen.php.

Roggio, Bill. "AQAP Destroys Tombs in Southern Yemen." *Long War Journal*, June 15, 2012. https://www.longwarjournal.org/archives/2012/06/aqap_destroys_shrine.php.

Rosenberg, Matthew, Nicholas Kulish, and Steven Lee Myers. "Predatory Islamic State Wrings Money from Those It Rules." *New York Times*, November 29, 2015. https://www.nytimes .com/2015/11/30/world/middleeast/predatory-islamic-state-wrings-money-from-those-it -rules.html.

Rosenberg, Matthew, Nicholas Kulish, and Steven Lee Myers. "A System of Extortion Mimicking a Real State with Revenue Raised in Taxes and Fines." *New York Times*, November 29, 2015. https://www.pulitzer.org/finalists/new-york-times-staff-1.

Rosenblatt, Nate, and David Kilcullen. "How Raqqa Became the Capital of ISIS." *New America*, July 25, 2019. https://www.newamerica.org/future-security/reports/how-raqqa-became -capital-isis/raqqa-isis-capital/.

Ross, Carne. "Power to the People: A Syrian Experiment in Democracy." *Financial Times*, October 23, 2015. https://www.ft.com/content/50102294-77fd-11e5-a95a-27d368e1ddf7.

Rossomando, John. "ISIS Inflicts Saudi-Style Religious Police on Syrians." Investigative Project on Terrorism, March 4, 2014. http://www.investigativeproject.org/4303/isis-inflicts -saudi-stylereligious-police-on.

Rotberg, Robert I. "The Failure and Collapse of Nation States: Breakdown, Prevention and Repair." In *When States Fail: Causes and Consequences*, edited by Robert I. Rotberg, 1–50. Princeton University Press, 2004.

Roy, Olivier. *Globalised Islam*. Hurst & Co., 2004.

Rozana Radio. "Idlib . . . Women Dress Code and the Suffocating Laws of Hayat Tahrir al-Sham." May 25, 2020. https://www.rozana.fm/english/article/96107-idlib%E2%80%A6 -women-dress-code-and-the-suffocating-laws-of-hay%E2%80%99at-tahrir-al-sham.

Rubin, Barnett R. "The Political Economy of War and Peace in Afghanistan." *World Development* 28, no. 10 (2000): 1787–1803. https://doi.org/10.1016/S0305-750X(00)00054-1.

Rujouleh, Ruwan. "Splitting Civil Society from the Jihadists in Idlib." Policy Watch No. 2858. Washington Institute for Near East Policy, September 2017. https://www.washingtoninstitute .org/policy-analysis/view/splitting-civil-society-from-the-jihadists-in-idlib.

Ruthven, Malise. *Islam in the World*. Penguin, 2000.

Ryan, Michael W. S. *Decoding Al-Qaeda's Strategy: The Deep Battle Against America*. Columbia University Press, 2013.

Sabates-Wheeler, Rachel, and Philip Verwimp. "Extortion with Protection: Understanding the Effect of Rebel Taxation on Civilian Welfare in Burundi." *Journal of Conflict Resolution* 58, no. 8 (September 2014): 1474–1499. https://doi.org/10.1177/0022002714547885.

Sadiki, Larbi, ed. *Routledge Handbook of the Arab Spring: Rethinking Democratization*. Routledge, 2015.

Salmoni, Barak A., Bryce Loidolt, and Madeline Wells. *Regime and Periphery in Northern Yemen: The Huthi Phenomenon*. RAND, 2010.

Samaha, Nour. "Trapped Between Assad, Israel, and al-Qaeda." *Foreign Policy*, June 22, 2015. https://foreignpolicy.com/2015/06/22/druze-syria-assad-israel-netanyahu/.

Sarkar, Radha, and Amar Sarkar. "The Rebels' Resource Curse: A Theory of Insurgent-Civilian Dynamics." *Studies in Conflict & Terrorism* 40, no. 10 (December 2016): 870–898. https://doi.org/10.1080/1057610X.2016.1239992.

Sarvananthan, Mattukrishan. *Economy of the Conflict Region in Sri Lanka: From Embargo to Repression*. East West Center, 2007. https://www.eastwestcenter.org/publications/economy-conflict-region-sri-lanka-embargo-repression.

Scahill, Jeremy. "Washington's War in Yemen Backfires." *Nation*, February 15, 2012. https://www.thenation.com/article/archive/washingtons-war-yemen-backfires/.

Schalk, Peter. "Historisation of the Martial Ideology of the Liberation Tigers of Tamil Eelam (LTTE)." *South Asia: Journal of South Asian Studies* 20, no. 2 (May 2997): 35–72. https://doi.org/10.1080/00856409708723295.

Scheuer, Michael. "Yemen's Role in al-Qaeda's Strategy." Jamestown Foundation, February 7, 2008. https://jamestown.org/program/yemens-role-in-al-qaedas-strategy/.

Schievels, Jelte Johannes, and Thomas Colley. "Explaining Rebel-State Collaboration in Insurgency: Keep Your Friends Close but Your Enemies Closer." *Small Wars & Insurgencies* 32, no. 8 (October 2020): 1332–1361. https://doi.org/10.1080/09592318.2020.1827847.

Schwab, Regine. "Governance of Jabhat Al-Nusra." Paper presented at the Islamist Rebel Governance Workshop. Graduate Institute of International and Development Studies. Geneva, Switzerland, October 8, 2020.

Schwab, Regine. "Insurgent Courts in Civil Wars: The Three Pathways of (Trans)Formation in Today's Syria (2012–17)." *Small Wars & Insurgencies* 29, no. 4 (August 2018): 801–826. https://doi.org/10.1080/09592318.2018.1497290.

Schwarze, Erika. *Public Opinion and Political Response in Palestine: Leadership, Campaigns and Elections Since Arafat*. I. B. Tauris, 2016.

Shaam Network. "Tahrir al-Sham Unleashes the Hand of the Goodwill Corps in Idlib . . . Smuggling Cigarettes, Islamic Dress and Mixing Are Its Main Goals . . .?!" [in Arabic]. April 10, 2017. http://www.shaam.org/news/syria-news/تحرير-الشام-تطلق-يد-سواعد-الخير-في-إدلب-وته ريب-الدخان-واللباس-الشرعي-والاختلاط-أبرز-أهدافها-؟.html.

Shaheen, Kareem. "IS Controls '50% of Syria' After Seizing Historic City of Palmyra." *Guardian*, May 21, 2015. https://www.theguardian.com/world/2015/may/21/isis-palmyra-syria-islamic-state.

Shami, Leila. "Women Are at the Forefront of Challenging Extremism in Idlib." Chatham House, July 3, 2018. https://kalam.chathamhouse.org/articles/women-are-at-the-forefront-of-challenging-extremism-in-idlib/.

Shavit, Uriya. "Is Shura a Muslim Form of Democracy? Roots and Systemization of a Polemic." *Middle Eastern Studies* 46, no. 3 (August 2010): 349–374. https://doi.org/10.1080/0026320 0902917085.

Sheikh, Futoun al-, Joseph Adams, Ammar Hamou, and Kristen Demilio. "Every Child Left Behind in the Islamic State's New Elementary School." *Syria Direct*, October 27, 2015. https://syriadirect.org/news/every-child-left-behind-in-the-islamic-state's-new-elementary-schools/.

Shinn, James. "'NATO Has the Watches, We Have the Time.'" *Wall Street Journal*, October 26, 2009. https://www.wsj.com/articles/SB10001424052748704335904574497120548934550.

Shuja Al-Deen, Maysaa. "Yemen's War-Torn Rivalries for Religious Education." In *Islamic Institutions in Arab States: Mapping the Dynamics of Control, Co-Option, Contention*. Edited by Frederic Wehrey. Carnegie Endowment for International Peace.

Simcox, Robin. "Ansar al-Sharia and Governance in Southern Yemen." Hudson Institute, December 27, 2012. https://www.hudson.org/research/9779-ansar-al-sharia-and-governance-in-southern-yemen.

Şimşek, Bahar, and Joost Jongerden. "Gender Revolution in Rojava: The Voices Beyond Tabloid Geopolitics." *Geopolitics* 26, no. 4 (October 2018): 1023–1045. https://doi.org/10.1080/14650045.2018.1531283.

Singh, Rashmi. "A Preliminary Typology Mapping Patterns of Learning and Innovation by Modern Jihadist Groups." *Studies in Conflict & Terrorism* 40, no. 7 (September 2016): 624–644. http://dx.doi.org/10.1080/1057610X.2016.1237228.

Sissons, Miranda and Abdulrazzaq al-Saiedi. *A Bitter Legacy: Lessons of De-Baathification in Iraq*. International Center for Transitional Justice, March 2013. https://www.ictj.org/sites/default/files/ICTJ-Report-Iraq-De-Baathification-2013-ENG.pdf.

Skjelderup, Michael Weddegjerde. "Jihadi Governance And Traditional Authority Structures: Al-Shabaab and Clan Elders in Southern Somalia, 2008–2012." *Small Wars & Insurgencies* 31, no. 6 (August 2020): 1174–1195. https://doi.org/10.1080/09592318.2020.1780686.

Skretting, Vidar B. "Pragmatism and Purism in Jihadist Governance: The Islamic Emirate of Azawad Revisited." *Studies in Conflict & Terrorism* 47, no. 7 (January 2022): 725–749. https://doi.org/10.1080/1057610X.2021.2007562.

Skretting, Vidar B. "Tribal Engagement Strategies in the Islamic Emirate of Azawad." *Third World Thematics* 6, nos. 1–3 (September 2022): 12–31. https://doi.org/10.1080/23802014.2022.2111461.

Sky News Arabia. "Jaar After the Withdrawal of Ansar al-Sharia" [in Arabic]. June 29, 2012. https://www.skynewsarabia.com/video/30677-الشريعة-أنصار-تنظيم-انسحاب-جعار.

Sly, Liz. "Islamic Law Comes to Rebel-Held Areas of Syria." *Washington Post*, March 19, 2013. https://www.washingtonpost.com/world/middle_east/islamic-law-comes-to-rebel-held-syria/2013/03/19/b310532e-90af-11e2-bdea-e32ad90da239_story.html.

Sly, Liz. "Syria Tribal Revolt Against Islamic State Ignored, Fueling Resentment." *Washington Post*, October 20, 2014. https://www.washingtonpost.com/world/syria-tribal-revolt-against-islamic-state-ignored-fueling-resentment/2014/10/20/25401beb-8de8-49f2-8e64-c1cfbee45232_story.html.

SMART News. "The Salvation Government Announces the Names of the New Ministers in Its Third Session" [in Arabic]. December 16, 2019. https://smartnews-agency.com/ar/wires/2019-12-16-الثالثة-دورتها-في-الجدد-الوزراء-أسماء-تعلن-الإنقاذ-حكومة.

Soguel, Dominique. "Heard at Syria's Border: Life in the Islamic State Is Orderly, but Brutal." *Christian Science Monitor,* September 21, 2014. https://www.csmonitor.com/World/Middle-East/2014/0921/Heard-at-Syria-s-border-Life-in-the-Islamic-State-is-orderly-but-brutal.

Soliman, Nagwan. "The New Jihadists and the Taliban Model." Carnegie Endowment for International Peace, December 20, 2021. https://carnegieendowment.org/sada/86049.

Solomon, Christopher. "HTS: Evolution of a Jihadi Group." Wilson Center, July 13, 2022. https://www.wilsoncenter.org/article/hts-evolution-jihadist-group.

Solomon, Erika. "Fines, Sell-Offs and Subsidy Cuts: Life Under Cash-Squeezed Isis." *Financial Times,* February 27, 2015. https://www.ft.com/content/15b493ca-bdbb-11e4-9d09-00144feab7de.

Solomon, Erika, and Guy Chazan. "ISIS Inc.: How Oil Fuels the Jihadi Terrorists." *Financial Times,* October 14, 2015. https://www.ft.com/content/b8234932-719b-11e5-ad6d-f4ed76f0900a.

Speckhard, Anne, and Ahmet S. Yayla. "The ISIS Emni: Origins and Inner Workings of ISIS's Intelligence Apparatus." *Perspectives on Terrorism* 11, no. 1 (February 2017): 2–16. https://www.jstor.org/stable/26297733.

Spencer, Richard. "Militant Islamist Group in Syria Orders Christians to Pay Protection Tax." *Telegraph,* February 27, 2014. https://www.telegraph.co.uk/news/worldnews/middleeast/syria/10666257/Militant-Islamist-group-in-Syria-orders-Christians-to-pay-protection-tax.html.

Spyer, Jonathan. "Facts on the Ground: The Growing Power of Hamas's Gaza Leadership." *Middle East Review of International Affairs* 16, no. 2 (June 2012): 44–51. https://ciaotest.cc.columbia.edu/journals/meria/v16i2/f_0029678_23996.pdf.

Staffell, Simon, and Akil N. Awan, "Introduction." In *Jihadism Transformed: Al-Qaeda and Islamic State's Battle of Ideas,* edited by Simon Staffell and Akil N. Awan, 1–20. Hurst & Co., 2016.

Stewart, Megan A. "Civil War as State-Making: Strategic Governance in Civil War." *International Organization* 72, no. 1 (Winter 2018): 205–226. https://www.jstor.org/stable/26569466.

Stokke, Kristian. "Building the Tamil Eelam State: Emerging State Institutions and Forms of Governance in LTTE-Controlled Areas in Sri Lanka." *Third World Quarterly* 27, no. 6 (2004): 1021–1040. https://www.jstor.org/stable/4017738.

Stout, Mark. "In Search of Salafi-Jihadist Strategic Thought: Mining the Words of the Terrorists." *Studies in Conflict & Terrorism* 32, no. 10 (September 2009): 876–892. https://doi.org/10.1080/10576100903185578.

"Striving for Hegemony: The HTS Crackdown on al-Qaida and Friends in Northwest Syria." Al-Muraqib, Jihadica, September 15, 2020. https://www.jihadica.com/striving-for-hegemony-the-hts-crackdown-on-al-qaida-and-friends-in-northwest-syria/.

Suleiman, Jalal. "Jihadi Group in Syria's Idlib Seeks Control of NGOs." *Al-Monitor,* June 8, 2022. https://www.al-monitor.com/originals/2022/06/jihadi-group-syrias-idlib-seeks-control-ngos.

Sullivan, Kevin, and Karla Adam. "Hoping to Create a New Society, the Islamic State Recruits Entire Families." *Washington Post,* December 24, 2014. https://www.washingtonpost.com/world/national-security/hoping-to-create-a-new-homeland-the-islamic-state-recruits

-entire-families/2014/12/24/dbffceec-8917-11e4-8ff4-fb93129c9c8b_story.html?utm_term
=.71bc49832e1b.

Suri, Abu Mus'ab al-. "The Muslims in Central Asia and the Upcoming Battle for Islam." Document AFGP-2002-002871. Harmony Database, Combating Terrorism Center at West Point. https://ctc.westpoint.edu/harmony-program/the-muslims-in-central-asia-and-the-upcoming-battle-of-islam-original-language-2/.

Suykens, Bert, "Comparing Rebel Rule Through Revolution and Naturalization: Ideologies of Governance in Naxalite and Naga India." In Arjona et al., *Rebel Governance in Civil War*, 138–157.

Svensson, Isak, and Daniel Finnbogason. "Confronting the Caliphate: Explaining Civil Resistance in Jihadist Proto-States." *European Journal of International Relations* 27, no. 2 (2021): 572–595. https://www.diva-portal.org/smash/get/diva2:1585191/FULLTEXT01.pdf.

Svensson, Isak, Daniel Finnbogason, Dino Krause, Luís Martínez Lorenzo, and Nanar Hawach. *Confronting the Caliphate: Civil Resistance in Jihadi Proto-States*. Oxford University Press, 2022.

Svoboda, Eva. "Aid and the Islamic State." IRIN/HPG Crisis Brief. Overseas Development Institute and IRIN News, December 2014. https://reliefweb.int/sites/reliefweb.int/files/resources/9390.pdf.

Swift, Christopher. "Arc of Convergence: AQAP, Ansar al-Shari'a and the Struggle for Yemen." *CTC Sentinel* 5, no. 6 (June 2012): 1–6. https://ctc.westpoint.edu/arc-of-convergence-aqap-ansar-al-sharia-and-the-struggle-for-yemen/.

Syria Direct. "Idlib Druze Agree to Forced Conversion, Destroyed Shrines Under Nusra Rule." March 17, 2015. https://syriadirect.org/news/idlib-druze-agree-to-forced-conversion-destroyed-shrines-under-nusra-rule/.

Syria Justice and Accountability Centre. *Judge, Jury and Executioner: The ISIS Bureau of Justice and Grievances*. Syria Justice and Accountability Centre, January 2020. https://syriaaccountability.org/judge-jury-and-executioner-the-isis-bureau-of-justice-and-grievances/.

Syria Report. "Will HTS Give Back Seized Druze Properties in Jabal al-Summaq?" June 14, 2022. https://hlp.syria-report.com/hlp/will-hts-give-back-seized-druze-properties-in-jabal-al-summaq/.

Syrian Network for Human Rights. "ISIL Torture and Detention Centers." April 25, 2016. https://sn4hr.org/blog/2016/04/25/21031/.

Syrian Network for Human Rights. "The Most Notable Hayat Tahrir al-Sham Violations Since the Establishment of Jabhat al-Nusra to Date." January 31, 2022. https://snhr.org/wp-content/pdf/english/The_Most_Notable_Hayat_Tahrir_al_Sham_Violations_Since_the_Establishment_of_Jabhat_al_Nusra_to_Date_1_en.pdf.

Syrian Observatory for Human Rights. "After al-Raqqa and 'al-Forat State' ISIS Closes the Internet Cafes in al-Mayadin Around Its Headquarters." August 8, 2015. http://www.syriahr.com/en/?p=28275.

Syrian Observatory for Human Rights. "80 Executions During the 22nd Month." April 29, 2016. https://www.syriahr.com/en/46213/.

Syrian Observatory for Human Rights. "Islamic State Imposes Taxes (Zakat) on the Rich." December 21, 2014. http://www.syriahr.com/en/?p=8268.

Syrian Observatory for Human Rights. "'Islamic State' Storms Internet Cafes in the City of al-Raqqa, While Closes Others in 'al-Furat State' and Asks Their Owners to Issue Licences." August 3, 2015. http://www.syriahr.com/en/?p=27749.

Syrian Observatory for Human Rights. "Islamic Terror Group Confiscating Christian-Owned Properties in Syria." May 5, 2020. https://www.syriahr.com/en/163224/.

Syrian Observatory for Human Rights. "IS Militants Collect 'al-Zakat Money' from the Owner of Stores in the Town of al-Bsiri." January 30, 2015. http://www.syriahr.com/en/?p=11120.

Syrian Observatory for Human Rights. "IS Organization Starts to Distribute Applications for 'Employing Teachers.'" February 26, 2015. https://www.syriahr.com/en/13576/.

Syrian Observatory for Human Rights. "With Support of the Salvation Government Turkey Private Company Accomplishes Last Stages of Providing Power Supply to Idlib." May 4, 2021. https://www.syriahr.com/en/215590/.

Syrian Observer. "Students in Idleb Protest Closure of Universities." March 7, 2019. https://syrianobserver.com/EN/news/49009/students-in-idleb-protest-closure-of-universities.html.

Syrians for Truth & Justice. "Hayat Tahrir al-Sham/HTS Impose Control Over Service and Civil Institutions in Saraqib City, Idlib Countryside." December 25, 2017. https://stj-sy.org/en/369/.

Syrians for Truth & Justice. "HTS Confiscates No Less Than 550 Homes and Businesses Belonging to Christians in Idlib." January 14, 2020. https://stj-sy.org/en/hts-confiscates-no-less-than-550-homes-and-businesses-belonging-to-christians-in-idlib/.

Szekely, Ora. "Doing Well by Doing Good: Understanding Hamas' Social Services as Political Advertising." *Studies in Conflict & Terrorism* 38, no. 4 (February 2015): 275–292. https://doi.org/10.1080/1057610X.2014.995565.

Taber, Robert. *The War of the Flea: The Classic Study of Guerrilla Warfare.* Brassey's, 2002.

Taim, Mouneb. "Syrian Jihadist Group HTS Accused of Blocking Married Women from Studying." *Al-Monitor,* September 3, 2022. https://www.al-monitor.com/originals/2022/08/syrian-jihadist-group-hts-accused-blocking-married-women-studying.

Talhami, Yvette. "The *Fatwas* and the Nusayri/Alawis of Syria." *Middle Eastern Studies* 46, no. 2 (April 2010): 175–194. https://doi.org/10.1080/00263200902940251.

TamilNet. "LTTE Opens First Thamileelam Court in Trincomalee District." December 2, 2002. https://www.tamilnet.com/art.html?catid=13&artid=7925.

TamilNet. "Thamil Eelam Judiciary Said a Basis for Rebuilding North-East." October 30, 2003. https://www.tamilnet.com/art.html?catid=79&artid=10277.

Tamimi, Aymenn J. al-. "Additional Notes on the Druze of Jabal al-Summaq." Aymennjawad.org, October 6, 2015. http://www.aymennjawad.org/2015/10/additional-notes-on-the-druze-of-jabal-al-summaq.

Tamimi, Aymenn J. al-. "A Caliphate Under Strain: The Documentary Evidence." *CTC Sentinel* 9, no. 4 (April 2016): 1–8. https://ctc.westpoint.edu/a-caliphate-under-strain-the-documentary-evidence/.

Tamimi, Aymenn J. al-. "Critical Analysis of the Islamic State's Health Department." Jihadology, August 27, 2015. https://jihadology.net/2015/08/27/the-archivist-critical-analysis-of-the-islamic-states-health-department/.

Tamimi, Aymenn J. al-. "Education in Jabal al-Summaq: Interview." Aymennjawad.org, April 27, 2021. https://aymennjawad.org/2021/04/education-in-jabal-al-summaq-interview.

Tamimi, Aymenn J. al-. "The Evolution in Islamic State Administration: The Documentary Evidence." *Perspectives on Terrorism* 9, no. 4 (August 2015): 117–129. https://pt.icct.nl/article/evolution-islamic-state-administration-documentary-evidence.

Tamimi, Aymenn J. al-. *From Jabhat al-Nusra to Hay'at Tahrir al-Sham: Evolution, Approach and Future.* Konrad Adenauer Stiftung, December 2017. https://www.kas.de/c/document_library/get_file?uuid=8cfa4cdb-e337-820d-d0bd-4cd998f38612&groupId=252038.

Tamimi, Aymenn J. al-. "The Harem Town Council: Interview." Aymennjawad.org, December 25, 2019. http://www.aymennjawad.org/2019/12/the-harem-town-council-interview.

Tamimi, Aymenn J. al-. "Hayat Tahrir al-Sham and Civil Society in Jabal al-Summaq." *Syria Comment*, March 4, 2017. https://www.joshualandis.com/blog/hayat-tahrir-al-sham-civil-society-jabal-al-summaq/.

Tamimi, Aymenn J. al-. "Hayat Tahrir al-Sham's Abu al-Fatah al-Farghali on Minority Sects." Aymmenjawad.org, June 17, 2021. https://www.aymennjawad.org/2021/06/hayat-tahrir-al-sham-abu-al-fatah-al-farghali-on.

Tamimi, Aymenn J. al-. "A Hay'at Tahrir al-Sham Perspective on Democracy." Aymennjawad.org, February 9, 2019. http://www.aymennjawad.org/2019/02/a-hayat-tahrir-al-sham-perspective-on-democracy.

Tamimi, Aymenn J. al-. "Idlib and Its Environs." Policy Notes No. 75. Washington Institute for Near East Policy, February 2020. https://www.washingtoninstitute.org/sites/default/files/pdf/PolicyNote75-Tamimi.pdf.

Tamimi, Aymenn J. al-. "The Internal Structure of the Islamic State's Hisba Apparatus." Middle East Center for Reporting and Analysis, June 1, 2018. https://www.mideastcenter.org/islamic-state-hisba-apparat.

Tamimi, Aymenn J. al-. *The Islamic State and Its Treatment of "Out Groups": A Comparative Analysis.* Center for Justice and Accountability, August 2023. https://cja.org/wp-content/uploads/2023/09/Al-Tamimi_theislamicstateandoutgroups.pdf.

Tamimi, Aymenn J. al-. "Jabhat al-Nusra and the Druze of Idlib Province." *Syria Comment*, January 24, 2015. https://www.joshualandis.com/blog/jabhat-al-nusra-druze-idlib-province/.

Tamimi, Aymenn J. al-. "The Local Council in Kukanaya: Interview." Aymennjawad.org, January 3, 2020. http://www.aymennjawad.org/2020/01/the-local-council-in-kukanaya-interview.

Tamimi, Aymenn J. al-. "The Massacre of Druze Villagers in Qalb Lawza, Idlib Province." *Syria Comment*, June 15, 2015. https://www.joshualandis.com/blog/the-massacre-of-druze-villagers-in-qalb-lawza-idlib-province/.

Tamimi, Aymenn J. al-. "'Principles in the Administration of the Islamic State'—Full Text and Translation." Aymennjawad.org, December 7, 2015. https://www.aymennjawad.org/18215/principles-in-the-administration-of-the-islamic.

Terpstra, Niels, and Georg Frerks. "Governance Practices and Symbolism: De Facto Sovereignty and Public Authority in 'Tigerland.'" *Modern Asian Studies* 52, no. 3 (May 2018): 1001–1042. https://doi.org/10.1017/S0026749X16000822.

Terpstra, Niels, and Georg Frerks. "Rebel Governance and Legitimacy: Understanding the Impact of Rebel Legitimation on Civilian Compliance with the LTTE Rule." *Civil Wars* 19, no. 3 (October 2017): 279–307. https://doi.org/10.1080/13698249.2017.1393265.

Thompson, Peter G. *Armed Groups: The 21st Century Threat*. Rowman & Littlefield, 2014.

Toguslu, Erkan. "Caliphate, *Hijra* and Martyrdom as Performative Narrative in ISIS *Dabiq* Magazine." *Politics, Religion & Ideology* 20, no. 1 (December 2018): 94–120. https://doi.org/10.1080/21567689.2018.1554480.

Tolan, Casey. "These Are the Textbooks Supposedly Used by the Islamic State." *Splinter*, October 28, 2015. https://splinternews.com/these-are-the-textbooks-supposedly-used-by-the-islamic-1793852375.

Tønnessen, Truls Hallberg. "The Group that Wanted to Be a 'State:' The Rebel Governance of the Islamic State." In *Islamists and the Politics of the Arab Uprisings: Governance, Pluralization and Contention*, edited by Hendrik Kraetzschmar and Paola Rivetti, 54–69. Edinburgh University Press, 2018.

Tony Blair Institute for Global Change. "The Druze: Solidarity and Allegiance in Syria." October 30, 2014. https://www.institute.global/insights/geopolitics-and-security/druze-solidarity-and-allegiance-syria.

Trew, Bel. "Mukalla: Life After al-Qaeda in Yemen." *Independent*, August 17, 2018. https://www.independent.co.uk/news/world/middle-east/mukalla-yemen-al-qaeda-civil-war-after-jihadi-terror-group-a8495636.html.

"Tribes in Yemen: An Introduction to the Tribal System." ACAPS Thematic Report. ACAPS, August 2020. https://www.acaps.org/sites/acaps/files/products/files/20200813_acaps_thematic_report_tribes_in_yemen_0.pdf.

Trinquier, Roger. *Modern Warfare: A French View of Counterinsurgency*. Praeger, 1964.

TRT World. "First Batch of Covid-19 Jabs Arrives in Northwest Syria." April 22, 2021. https://www.trtworld.com/magazine/first-batch-of-covid-19-jabs-arrive-in-northwestern-syria-46124.

Tse-Tung, Mao. *On Guerrilla Warfare*. Translated by Samuel B. Griffith III. University of Illinois Press, 2000.

Tsurkov, Elizabeth. "The Breaking of Syria's Rebellion." Forum for Regional Thinking, July 10, 2018. https://www.regthink.org/en/articles/the-breaking-of-syrias-rebellion.

Tsurkov, Elizabeth. "Hayat Tahrir al-Sham (Syria)." In *Guns and Governance: How Europe Should Talk with Non-State Armed Groups in the Middle East*. European Council on Foreign Relations, 2020. https://ecfr.eu/special/mena-armed-groups/hayat-tahrir-al-sham-syria/.

Turner, John A. *Religious Ideology and the Roots of the Global Jihad*. Palgrave Macmillan, 2014.

Ubaydi, Muhammad al-, Nelly Lahoud, Daniel Milton, and Bryan Price. *The Group that Calls Itself a State: Understanding the Evolution and Challenges of the Islamic State*. Combating Terrorism Center at West Point, December 2014. https://ctc.westpoint.edu/the-group-that-calls-itself-a-state-understanding-the-evolution-and-challenges-of-the-islamic-state/.

UN Habitat. *City Profile of Mosul, Iraq: Multi-Sector Assessment of a City Under Siege.* United Nations Human Settlements Programme in Iraq, 2016. https://unhabitat.org/city-profile -of-mosul-iraq-multi-sector-assessment-of-a-city-under-siege.

United Nations Human Rights Office of the High Commissioner. "UN Commission of Inquiry on Syria: IS Is Committing Genocide Against Yezidis." June 16, 2016. https://www.ohchr .org/en/press-releases/2016/06/un-commission-inquiry-syria-isis-committing-genocide -against-yazidis.

United Nations News. "In ISIL-Controlled Territory, 8 Million Civilians Living in 'State of Fear'—UN Expert." July 31, 2015. https://news.un.org/en/story/2015/07/505512-isil-controlled -territory-8-million-civilians-living-state-fear-un-expert.

United Nations Office for the Coordination of Humanitarian Affairs. "Improvements to Gaza Electricity Supply." July 16, 2019. https://www.ochaopt.org/content/improvements-gaza -electricity-supply.

Uyangoda, Jayadeva. "Ethnic Conflict, the State and the Tsunami Disaster in Sri Lanka." *Inter-Asia Cultural Studies* 6, no. 3 (December 2010): 341–352. https://doi.org/10.1080 /14649370500169979.

Vale, Gina. *Cubs in the Lions' Den: Indoctrination and Recruitment of Children Within Islamic State Territory.* International Centre for the Study of Radicalisation, July 2018. https://icsr. info/wp-content/uploads/2018/07/Cubs-in-the-Lions-Den-Indoctrination-and- Recruitment-of-Children-Within-Islamic-State-Territory.pdf.

Vale, Gina. "Liberated, Not Free: Yazidi Women After Islamic State Captivity." *Small Wars & Insurgencies* 31, no. 3 (April 2020): 511–539. https://doi.org/10.1080/09592318.2020.1726572.

Vale, Gina. "Piety Is in the Eye of the Bureaucrat: The Islamic State's Strategy of Civilian Control." *CTC Sentinel* 13, no. 1 (January 2020): 34–40. https://ctc.westpoint.edu/wp-content /uploads/2020/01/CTC-SENTINEL-012020.pdf.

Van Baalen, Sebastian, and Niels Terpstra. "Behind Enemy Lines: State-Insurgent Cooperation on Rebel Governance in Cote d'Ivoire and Sri Lanka." *Small Wars & Insurgencies* 34, no. 1 (August 2022): 221–246. https://doi.org/10.1080/09592318.2022.2104297.

Wagemakers, Joas. "Framing the 'Threat to Islam': *Al-Wala wa al-Bara*' in Salafi Discourse." *Arab Studies Quarterly* 30, no. 4 (Fall 2008): 1–22. https://www.jstor.org/stable/41858559.

Wagemakers, Joas. "A Purist Jihadi-Salafi: The Ideology of Abu Muhammad al-Maqdisi." *British Journal of Middle Eastern Studies* 36, no. 2 (August 2009): 281–297. https://www.jstor .org/stable/40593257.

Wagstaff, William A., and Danielle F. Jung. "Competing for Constituents: Trends in Terrorist Service Provision," *Terrorism & Political Violence* 32, no. 2 (September 2017): 293–324. https://doi.org/10.1080/09546553.2017.1368494.

Walmsley, Katie. " 'If Not Us, Then Who?' In the Bull's-Eye of ISIS." *CNN*, March 14, 2015. https://edition.cnn.com/2015/03/14/intl_world/iyw-aid-workers-in-danger/index.html.

Warrick, Joby. *Black Flags: The Rise of ISIS.* Doubleday, 2016.

Waters, Gregory. "The Promise of Local Councils: A Future for Syrians, by Syrians." *International Review,* November 21, 2017. https://international-review.org/promise-local-councils -future-syrians-syrians/.

Weigand, Florian. "Afghanistan's Taliban: Legitimate Jihadists or Coercive Extremists?" *Journal of Intervention & Statebuilding* 11, no. 3 (August 2017): 359–381. https://doi.org/10.1080/17502977.2017.1353755.

Weinstein, Jeremy. *Inside Rebellion: The Politics of Insurgent Violence*. Cambridge University Press, 2007.

Weiss, Michael, and Hassan Hassan. *ISIS: Inside the Army of Terror*. Regan Arts, 2015.

White, Jeffrey. "The Death of Zarqawi: Organizational and Operational Implications for the Insurgency." Washington Institute for Near East Policy, June 8, 2006. https://www.washingtoninstitute.org/policy-analysis/death-zarqawi-organizational-and-operational-implications-insurgency.

Whiteside, Craig, and Anas Elallame. "Accidental Ethnographers: The Islamic State's Tribal Engagement Experiment." *Small Wars & Insurgencies* 31, no. 2 (February 2020): 219–240. https://doi.org/10.1080/09592318.2020.1713529.

Wickham-Crowley, Timothy. "Del Gobierno de Abajo al Gobierno de Arriba . . . and Back: Transitions to and From Rebel Governance in Latin America: 1956–1999." In Arjona et al., *Rebel Governance in Civil War*, 47–73.

Wickham-Crowley, Timothy. *Guerrillas and Revolutions in Latin America: A Comparative Study of Insurgents and Regime Since 1956*. Princeton University Press, 1992.

Wickham-Crowley, Timothy. "The Rise (and Sometimes Fall) of Guerrilla Governments in Latin America." *Sociological Forum* 2, no. 3 (June 1987): 473–499. https://doi.org/10.1007/BF01106622.

Wicktorowicz, Quintan. "Anatomy of the Salafi Movement." *Studies in Conflict & Terrorism* 29, no. 3 (April 2005): 207–239. https://web.archive.org/web/20190712124836id_/http://www.clagsborough.uk:80/anatomy_of_the_salafi_movement.pdf.

Wood, Graeme. "What ISIS Really Wants." *Atlantic*, March 2015. https://www.theatlantic.com/magazine/archive/2015/03/what-isis-really-wants/384980/.

World Health Organization. "Updates on Covid-19 Vaccination in Syria, August 2021." August 11, 2021. http://www.emro.who.int/syria/news/updates-on-covid-19-vaccination-in-syria-august-2021.html?format=html.

Wuhayshi, Nasir al-. "First Letter from Abu Basir to the Emir of al-Qaida in the Islamic Maghreb." May 21, 2012. In Associated Press, "al-Qaida Papers." Republished by *Long War Journal*. https://www.longwarjournal.org/images/al-qaida-papers-how-to-run-a-state.pdf.

Wuhayshi, Nasir al-. "Letter to the Brother in Command (i.e., Usama Bin Ladin)." Undated, presumably early 2011. Office of the Director of National Intelligence. https://www.dni.gov/files/documents/ubl2016/english/Letter%20from%20Basir%20to%20the%20Brother%20in%20Command.pdf.

Yemen: Confronting al-Qaeda, Preventing State Failure: Hearing Before the Committee on Foreign Relations, United States Senate. 111th Cong., 2nd Sess. January 20, 2010. https://www.govinfo.gov/content/pkg/CHRG-111shrg62357/html/CHRG-111shrg62357.htm.

Yin, Robert. *Case Study Research: Design and Methods*. Sage Publications, 2003.

Yin, Robert. *Qualitative Research from Start to Finish*. Guilford Press, 2011.

Yosufi, Abdul Basir. "The Rise and Consolidation of Islamic State: External Intervention and Sectarian Conflict." *Connections* 15, no. 4 (Fall 2016): 91–110. https://www.jstor.org/stable /26326461.

Young, John. *Peasant Revolution in Ethiopia: The Tigray People's Liberation Front, 1975–1991.* Cambridge University Press, 1997.

Zaraee, Nisreen al-, and Kareem Shaar. "The Economics of Hayat Tahrir al-Sham." Middle East Institute, June 21, 2021. https://www.mei.edu/publications/economics-hayat-tahrir-al-sham.

Zawahiri, Aymann al-. *General Guidelines for Jihad.* As-Sahab Media, 2013.

Zawahiri, Aymann al-. Knights Under the Prophet's Banner. In His Own Words: A Translation of the Writings of Dr Aymann al-Zawahiri, translated by Laura Mansfield. Lulu Press, 2006.

Zawahiri, Aymann al-. "Letter to Abu Musʿab al-Zarqawi." July 9, 2005, Combating Terrorism Center at West Point. Accessed September 25, 2023. https://ctc.westpoint.edu/harmony -program/zawahiris-letter-to-zarqawi-original-language-2/.

Zelin, Aaron Y. "Al-Qaeda in Syria: A Closer Look at ISIS (Part I)." Policy Watch 2137. Washington Institute for Near East Policy, September 10, 2013. https://www.washingtoninstitute .org/policy-analysis/al-qaeda-syria-closer-look-isis-part-i.

Zelin, Aaron Y. "English Translation of 'Umar al-Jawfi's 'The Huthis and the Coming Project' from Issue #15 of al-Qa'idah in the Arabian Peninsula's Sada al-Malahim Magazine." Jihadology, January 13, 2011. https://jihadology.net/2011/01/13/english-translation-of-umar -al-jawfis-the-ḥuthis-and-the-coming-project-from-issue-15-of-al-qaidah-in-the-arabian -peninsulas-ṣada-al-malaḥim-magazine/.

Zelin, Aaron Y. "46 Scenes from the Islamic State in Syria." *BuzzFeed*, October 12, 2013. https:// www.buzzfeed.com/aaronyzelin/46-scenes-from-the-islamic-state-in-syria-dski.

Zelin, Aaron Y. "Hanging On in Idlib: Hayat Tahrir al-Sham's Expanding Tribal Engagement." Washington Institute for Near East Policy, June 11, 2021. https://www.washingtoninstitute .org/policy-analysis/hanging-idlib-hayat-tahrir-al-shams-expanding-tribal-engagement.

Zelin, Aaron Y. "Introducing the Islamic State Select Worldwide Activity Map." Washington Institute for Near East Policy, March 21, 2023. https://www.washingtoninstitute.org/policy -analysis/introducing-islamic-state-select-worldwide-activity-map.

Zelin, Aaron Y. "The Islamic State's Territorial Methodology." Research Notes No. 29. Washington Institute for Near East Policy, January 2016. https://www.washingtoninstitute.org /sites/default/files/pdf/ResearchNote29-Zelin.pdf.

Zelin, Aaron Y. "Jawlani's 'State of the Union.'" Jihadica, August 29, 2022. https://www.jihadica .com/jawlanis-state-of-the-union/.

Zelin, Aaron Y. "Jihadi Counterterrorism: Hayat Tahrir al-Sham Versus the Islamic State." *CTC Sentinel* 16, no. 2 (February 2023): 14–25.

Zelin, Aaron Y. "Living Long Enough to See Yourself Become the Villain: The Case of Abu Muhammad al-Maqdisi." Jihadica, September 9, 2020. https://www.jihadica.com/living -long-enough/.

Zelin, Aaron Y. "A Timeline of Abu Muhammad al-Jawlani's Appearances." Jihadology, May 27, 2020. https://jihadology.net/2020/05/27/a-timeline-of-abu-muhammad-al-jawlanis -appearances/.

Zelin, Aaron Y. "The War Between IS and al-Qaeda for Supremacy of the Global Jihadist Movement." Research Notes No. 20. Washington Institute for Near East Policy, June 2014. https://www.washingtoninstitute.org/sites/default/files/pdf/ResearchNote_20_Zelin .pdf.

Zimmerman, Katherine. "Al Qaeda in Yemen: Countering the Threat from the Arabian Peninsula." Critical Threats Project. American Enterprise Institute, October 2012. https://www .criticalthreats.org/analysis/al-qaeda-in-yemen-countering-the-threat-from-the-arabian -peninsula.

Zimmerman, Katherine. "AQAP: A Resurgent Threat." *CTC Sentinel* 8, no. 9 (September 2015): 19–23. https://ctc.westpoint.edu/aqap-a-resurgent-threat/.

Zimmerman, Katherine. "AQAP Post-Arab Spring and the Islamic State." In *How al-Qaeda Survived Drones, Uprisings, and the Islamic State*, edited by Aaron Zelin, 44–55. Washington Institute for Near East Policy, 2017.

INDEX

Page numbers in *italics* indicate figures.

GPSR Authorized Representative: Easy Access System Europe, Mustamäe tee
50, 10621 Tallinn, Estonia, gpsr.requests@easproject.com